"Not just an enlightening book but a game-changing one . . . *Rule Makers, Rule Breakers* suddenly makes sense of the puzzling behavior we see all around us—in colleagues, family, and even ourselves."
—Carol S. Dweck, author of *Mindset: The New Psychology of Success*

"Brightly written . . . Gelfand offers many intriguing observations. . . . A useful and engaging take on human behavior."
—*Kirkus Reviews*

"Visionary and wildly entertaining . . . This brilliant book will sharpen your vision and broaden your horizons."
—Joshua Greene, author of *Moral Tribes: Emotion, Reason, and the Gap Between Us and Them*

"A fascinating book that offers a fresh way of making sense of cultural differences."
—CNBC

"To read this book is to see both yourself and your neighbor for the first time—guided by rules of which you've both been unaware."
—Susan Cain, author of *Quiet: The Power of Introverts in a World That Can't Stop Talking*

"A delightful, insightful, and fascinating look at the remarkable diversity of human customs—where they come from and how they shape our lives."
—Daniel Gilbert, author of *Stumbling on Happiness*

"Offers a powerful new way of seeing the world . . . A new tool kit for change."
—Anne-Marie Slaughter, author of *Unfinished Business: Women, Men, Work, Family*

"Gelfand has exposed a universal fault line running beneath nations, states, organizations, and even families. . . . This idea, at once so simple and so powerful, will forever change how you see the world."
—Daniel H. Pink, author of *Drive: The Surprising Truth About What Motivates Us*

"Brilliant . . . full of well-documented insights that will change the way you look at yourself and at the world around you."
—Barry Schwartz, author of *The Paradox of Choice*, *Practical Wisdom* (with Kenneth Sharpe), and *Why We Work*

"Reveals how political divides, happiness and suicide rates, and the coexistence of crime and creativity can all be traced to a fundamental but neglected dimension of social norms. You'll never look at a workplace, a country, or a family the same way again."
—Adam Grant, *New York Times* bestselling author of *Originals* and *Give and Take*

"Gelfand has done much to unravel the mysteries of human motivation."
—Robert Cialdini, author of *Influence* and *Pre-Suasion*

"Fascinating and illuminating . . . We all build order into our days, but as Gelfand shows, some of us like hewing to a line, and others enjoy crossing it."
—Jonah Berger, author of *Contagious* and *Invisible Influence*

"Smart, provocative, and very entertaining . . . Gelfand argues that the tendency to devise and abide by rules or, alternatively, push behavioral limits is the fundamental distinction between human societies."
—Paul Bloom, author of *Against Empathy: The Case for Rational Compassion*

"A valuable lens for decoding the nature of our cultural conflicts and an intriguing new tool for solving them."
—Colin Woodard, author of *American Nations: A History of the Eleven Rival Regional Cultures of North America*

"Fascinating and profound . . . It's quite possibly this year's best book on culture."
—Roy F. Baumeister, coauthor of *Willpower* and author of *The Cultural Animal*

"A fascinating cross-cultural adventure . . . Tightness-looseness explains everything from how you cross the street to how you cross over from the living."
—Susan T. Fiske, coauthor of *The Human Brand: How We Relate to People, Products, and Companies*

"If you're going to read one book this year to better understand the world's problems and what can be done to solve them, Gelfand's masterpiece should be it."
—Alon Tal, author of *The Land Is Full*

"A thought-provoking look at the contours of modern tribalism—one that uses a deceptively simple dividing line: the split between 'tight' and 'loose' cultures and personalities."
—Dante Chinni, coauthor of *Our Patchwork Nation:
The Surprising Truth About the "Real" America*

"A particularly timely analysis for our current Age of Anxiety and uncertainty, where people and nations no longer feel confident in what the next generation and near future will bring."
—Scott Atran, cofounder of the Centre for the Resolution of
Intractable Conflict at Oxford University

"Fantastic . . . Its beauty derives from the breadth of its insight as Gelfand focuses in to illuminate, in succession, countries, states, corporations, groups, and individuals."
—Michael L. Tushman, coauthor of *Winning through
Innovation* and *Lead and Disrupt*

"Extremely important . . . Gelfand has identified and explored a hugely significant aspect of culture that accounts for why and when we fall into step with a group or, alternatively, set off on our own path."
—Richard E. Nisbett, author of *The Geography of Thought:
How Asians and Westerners Think Differently . . . and Why*

"Brilliant . . . Gelfand's findings, which are backed by massive empirical evidence, go far to explain why the people of different countries have different worldviews."
—Ronald F. Inglehart, director of the World Values Survey
and author of *Cultural Evolution*

"A must-read book that will fundamentally change the way you look at the world, particularly at our bewildering cultural moment."
—Todd Kliman, author of *The Wild Vine: A Forgotten
Grape and the Untold Story of American Wine*

"Dazzling . . . When people don't abide by socially expected rules, families, businesses, and whole societies splinter apart. But is there a downside to following the rules too closely? Read *Rule Makers, Rule Breakers* to find out."

—Peter Turchin, author of *Ultrasociety: How 10,000 Years of War Made Humans the Greatest Cooperators on Earth*

"Everyone should read this book!"

—Timothy D. Wilson, author of *Redirect: Changing the Stories We Live By*

RULE MAKERS, RULE BREAKERS

Tight and Loose Cultures and
the Secret Signals That Direct Our Lives

MICHELE GELFAND

SCRIBNER
New York   London   Toronto   Sydney   New Delhi

*Dedicated to Martin J. Gelfand, my father, who encouraged
me to explore the world, and Harry C. Triandis, my mentor,
who gave me the scientific tools to understand it*

Scribner
An Imprint of Simon & Schuster, Inc.
1230 Avenue of the Americas
New York, NY 10020

First Scribner trade paperback edition August 2019

SCRIBNER and design are registered trademarks of The Gale Group, Inc.,
used under license by Simon & Schuster, Inc., the publisher of this work.

For information about special discounts for bulk purchases,
please contact Simon & Schuster Special Sales at
1-866-506-1949 or business@simonandschuster.com.

The Simon & Schuster Speakers Bureau can bring authors to your live event.
For more information or to book an event, contact the Simon & Schuster Speakers
Bureau at 1-866-248-3049 or visit our website at www.simonspeakers.com.

Manufactured in the United States of America

10 9 8 7 6 5 4 3 2

Library of Congress Control Number: 2018026903

ISBN 978-1-5011-5293-1
ISBN 978-1-5011-5294-8 (pbk)
ISBN 978-1-5011-5295-5 (ebook)

Contents

Contents

Introduction

It's 11:00 p.m. in Berlin. Not a single car is in sight, yet a pedestrian waits patiently at the crosswalk until the light turns green. Meanwhile, four thousand miles away in Boston, at rush hour, commuters flout the "Do Not Cross" sign as they dart in front of cabs. To the south, where it's 8:00 p.m. in São Paulo, locals are frolicking in string bikinis in public parks. Up in Silicon Valley, it's midafternoon and T-shirted employees at Google are playing a game of Ping-Pong. And in Zurich, at the Swiss bank UBS, which for years mandated a forty-four-page dress code, executives burning the midnight oil have barely loosened their ties.

We may tease Germans for being excessively orderly or Brazilians for showing too much skin, but we rarely consider how these differences came about. Far beyond dress codes and pedestrian patterns, people's social differences run deep and broad—from politics to parenting, management to worship, and vocations to vacations. In the past several thousand years humanity has evolved to the point where there now exist 195 countries, and more than seven thousand languages and many thousands of religions. Even within a single nation, such as the United States, there are countless differences in fashion, dialect, morals, and political orientation—sometimes among those who live in close proximity. The diversity of human behavior is astonishing, especially since 96 percent of the human genome is identical to that of chimpanzees, whose lifestyles, unlike humans, are far more similar across communities.

We rightly celebrate diversity and condemn division, yet we're shockingly ignorant of what underlies both of these things: *culture.* Culture is a stubborn mystery of our experience and one of the last uncharted frontiers. We've used our big brains to accomplish unbelievable technical feats. We've discovered the laws of gravity, split the atom, wired the Earth, eradicated fatal diseases, mapped the human genome, invented the iPhone, and even trained dogs to ride skateboards. But somehow, despite all of our technical prowess, we've made surprisingly little progress in understanding something equally important: our own cultural differences.

Why are we so divided, despite the fact that we're more technologically connected than ever? Culture is at the heart of our divisions, and we need to know more about it. For years, policy experts and laypeople alike have struggled to find a deep underlying factor to explain our sprawling, complex cultural traits and distinctions. Many times we focus on superficial characteristics that are the "symptoms of culture." We try to explain our cultural divides in terms of geography, thinking that people behave the way they do because they live in blue states or red states, in rural or urban areas, in Western or Eastern nations, in the developing or developed world. We wonder if culture can be explained by differences in religion or our different "civilizations." These distinctions have typically left us with more questions than answers because they miss the deeper basis of our differences—they don't get at the underlying *primal template of culture.*

A more compelling answer has been hiding in plain sight. Just as simple principles can explain a whole lot in fields such as physics, biology, and mathematics, many cultural differences and divides can be explained through a simple shift in perspective.

Behavior, it turns out, largely depends on whether we live in a *tight* or *loose* culture. The side of the divide that a culture exists on reflects the strength of its social norms and the strictness with which it enforces them. All cultures have social norms—rules for acceptable behavior— that we regularly take for granted. As children, we learn hundreds of social norms—for example, to not grab things out of other people's hands; to walk on the right side of the sidewalk (or the left, depending on where you live); to put on clothes each day. We continue to absorb new social norms throughout our lives: what to wear to a funeral; how to behave at a rock concert versus a symphony; and the proper way to perform rituals—from weddings to worship. Social norms are the glue that holds groups together; they give us our identity, and they help us coordinate in unprecedented ways. Yet cultures vary in the *strength* of their social glue, with profound consequences for our worldviews, our environments, and our brains.

Tight cultures have strong social norms and little tolerance for deviance, while loose cultures have weak social norms and are highly permissive. The former are *rule makers*; the latter, *rule breakers*. In the United States, a relatively loose culture, a person can't get far down their street without witnessing a slew of casual norm violations, from littering to jaywalking to dog waste. By contrast, in Singapore, where norm violations are rare, pavements are pristine, and jaywalkers are nowhere to be found. Or consider Brazil, a loose culture, where clocks on city streets all read a different time, and arriving late for business meetings is more the rule than the exception. In fact, if you want to be very sure someone will arrive on time in Brazil, you say "*com pontuali-dade britânica*," which means "with British punctuality." Meanwhile, in Japan, a tight country, there's a huge emphasis on punctuality—trains almost *never* arrive late. On the rare days that delays do occur, some train companies will hand out cards to passengers that they can submit to their bosses to excuse a tardy arrival at work.

For centuries, people assumed there were as many explanations for these cultural permutations and rifts as there were examples of them. But what I'll show in this book is that there is a deep structure that underlies cultural variation. A pivotal discovery is that the strength of a culture's norms isn't random or accidental. It has a hidden logic that makes perfectly good sense.

Intriguingly, the same tight-loose logic that explains differences across nations also explains differences across states, organizations, social classes, and households. Tight-loose differences emerge in boardrooms, classrooms, and bedrooms, around negotiating tables and dinner tables. Seemingly idiosyncratic features of our everyday lives—including how we behave on public transit and at the gym, and the kinds of conflicts we have with our friends, partners, and children—all fundamentally reflect tight-loose differences. Are you a rule maker or a rule breaker? I'll show you some of the reasons why you might lean in either direction.

Beyond our immediate community, tight-loose differences can explain global patterns of conflict, revolution, terrorism, and populism. Around the world, tight-loose operates as a universal fault line, causing cultural cohesion to buckle and rifts to open up. The rifts aren't just blared in headlines; they surface in daily interactions.

Tight-loose not only explains the world around us, but actually can predict the conflicts that will erupt—and suggests ways to avoid them. Tight-loose is the key to anticipating our divides—mild clashes, in the case of a construction worker rolling his eyes at a gold-cuff-linked Wall Streeter, or more lethal ones, such as when those who live by the tenets of a sacred text come in contact with those who dismiss guiding texts altogether. For many, to enter this book will be to enter "The Matrix" and see the world in a completely different way.

4

PART I

Foundations:
The Power of a Primal Social Force

1

A Cure for Chaos

Imagine a world where people are always late. Trains, buses, and airplanes don't abide by any fixed schedule. In conversations, people interrupt each other frequently, get handsy with new acquaintances, and never make eye contact. People wake up whenever they want and leave their houses with or without putting on clothes. At restaurants—which are open *whenever*—people demand food that isn't on the menu, chew with their mouths open, belch frequently, and, without asking, eat off of strangers' plates. Board a crowded elevator, and you'll find people singing, shaking their wet umbrellas on each other, and facing the wrong direction. In schools, students talk on their phones throughout lectures, pull pranks on the teachers, and cheat openly on exams. On city streets, no one pays attention to stoplights, and people drive on both sides of the road. Pedestrians litter heedlessly, steal strangers' bicycles off racks, and curse loudly. Sex isn't reserved for private settings like bedrooms; it happens on public transportation, on park benches, and in movie theaters.

This is a world without social norms—a world where people don't have any socially agreed-upon standards of behavior.

Luckily, humans—much more than any other species—have an

uncanny ability to develop, maintain, and enforce social norms to avoid the above scenarios. In fact, we're a super-normative species: Without even realizing it, we spend a huge amount of our lives following social rules and conventions—even if the rules don't make any sense.

Consider a few examples: In New York City on the last day of every year, millions of people stand in the freezing cold and cheer wildly at a ball dropping from a pole. There are the equally bizarre New Year's practices of eating twelve grapes at midnight with great passion in Spain, eating a spoonful of lentils for good luck in Chile, and filling barbed wire with flammable material and swinging it around one's head in Scotland. And every year, thousands of people excitedly crowd into stadiums to cheer, holler, and even scream as they watch other people tackle each other, play music, or tell jokes.

These routines are mostly carried out in large groups, but many of our behaviors that are less crowd-encouraged are just as odd. Why do women wear a colorless white dress on one of the happiest days of their lives? Why do people cut down perfectly good trees in December, decorate them, and then let them die in their living rooms? In the United States, why do we forbid our children from talking to strangers but, on October 31, encourage them to put on costumes and roam the streets begging adults for candy? Around the world we observe equally puzzling behaviors. For example, why on certain days in India do millions of people joyfully gather to wade in a frigid, polluted river in celebration of Kumbh Mela?

From the outside, our social norms often seem bizarre, but from the inside, we take them for granted. Some social norms are codified into regulations and laws (obey stop signs; don't steal someone's bicycle); others are unspoken (don't stare at people on the train; cover your mouth when you sneeze). They can manifest in daily, mundane behaviors, such as putting clothes on or saying hello when you answer the phone and goodbye when you hang up. Or they can take the form of the ritualistic, learned behaviors we perform at out-of-the-ordinary, special occasions, such as the Kumbh Mela or Halloween.

Social norms are all around us—we follow them constantly. For our species, conforming to social norms is as natural as swimming upstream is for a salmon. Yet, ironically, while social norms are omnipresent, they're largely *invisible*. Many of us rarely notice how much of our behavior is driven by them—or, more important, how much they're needed.

This is a great human puzzle. How have we spent our entire lives under the influence of such powerful forces and not understood or even noticed their impact?

BORN TO RUN . . . OR FOLLOW

At what age would you guess children start picking up on social norms? At age three, when many enter preschool, or at age five, when they go to kindergarten? It turns out that our normative instincts manifest much earlier: Studies show that babies follow norms and are willing to punish norm violators even before they have formal language.

In a groundbreaking study, researchers demonstrated that infants will indicate a clear preference for animal hand puppets that engage in socially normative behavior (those that help other puppets open a box with a rattle inside and those that return a toy ball that another puppet has dropped) relative to puppets that engage in antisocial behavior (those that prevent other puppets from opening a box and who take toy balls away from them).

In fact, by the time we're three years old, we're actively berating norm violators. In one study, two-year-olds and three-year-olds drew pictures or made clay sculptures next to two puppets who also made their own crafts. When one of the puppets left, the other puppet began to destroy the picture or the sculpture that the puppet had made. Two-year-olds seemed almost entirely unperturbed at seeing this, but approximately one-quarter of the three-year-olds spoke up, saying to the rude puppet things like "No, you're not supposed to do that!" Young children will declare their disapproval in situations that are not ethically charged as well. After being taught a certain arbitrary behavior and then witnessing a puppet incorrectly imitating it, three-year-olds vigorously protested. Quite clearly, children learn not only to interpret social norms from their environment, but also to actively shape and enforce them.

Humans have evolved to have a very sophisticated normative psychology that develops as soon as we leave the womb. In fact, it makes us unique among species. To their credit, many species do engage in highly sophisticated social learning. The nine-spined stickleback fish, for instance, will prioritize feeding spots where other fish are feeding over relatively empty locations. Norway rats will eat food that they see a demonstrator rat eating. And birds are also keenly attuned to their flock's didactic songs when making foraging decisions. But there's no evidence so far that animals copy others for social reasons such as simply fitting in and belonging.

Researchers in Germany conducted a very creative experiment that illustrated just this point. They designed a puzzle box with three compartments, each with a small hole at the top. At the experiment's beginning, subjects—both young children and chimpanzees—learned that dropping balls into one of the box's compartments would get rewarded with a tasty snack. Next, they were shown another child or chimpanzee interacting with the box, and they saw that he could get food after dropping pellets into a completely different compartment. When the subjects took their turn at the puzzle box, an experimenter took note of where they dropped the balls. Children often changed compartments to match the behavior of other children, especially when those children were watching them. This suggests that children don't just change strategies because they think their peer's strategy is better; they also do it for *social* reasons— as a sign of affiliation and conformity. By comparison, few chimps switched strategies to match the behavior of their fellow chimps. Chimpanzees, like many nonhuman animals, might have the ability to learn from each other, but they don't generally apply that social learning absent a material benefit. Only humans appear to follow social norms to be part of the group.

THE POWER OF SOCIAL NORMS

Imagine you've signed up to participate in a psychological study. After arriving at a laboratory, you're asked to sit in a room with about eight other participants. The researcher comes in and gives each person a piece of paper showing one line on the left side of the page and multiple lines of differing lengths on the right side of the page labeled Line A, Line B, and Line C, as seen in Figure 1.1. He asks you all to determine independently which line on the right side of the page is the same length as the line on the left. It's completely obvious to you that Line A is the correct answer. He then calls on participants one by one to give their responses. The other participants all answer Line B; no one says Line A. You're the second-to-last person to state your answer. Will you stick with A or switch to B?

If you'd taken part in this experiment, it's likely you would have questioned your judgment and agreed with the group at some point. That's what social psychologist Solomon Asch found when he ran this now classic study in 1956. In Asch's study, each participant, unbe-

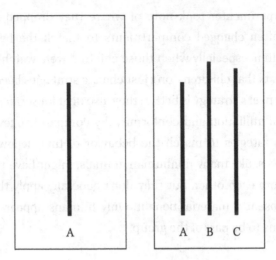

Figure I.I. Solomon Asch's line-judgment task.

knownst to them, was in a group made up of pretend research subjects, who were told to give a clearly incorrect answer on a number of trials. Asch's results showed that out of the 123 participants across groups, three-quarters sided with the group on at least one occasion. That is, the majority changed their answers to match the wrong but popular choice.

The results of this quirky little experiment speak to a broader truth. Without even realizing it, we're all prone to following group norms that can override our sense of right and wrong.

Outside of the laboratory, we follow many norms that arguably seem irrelevant. Take, for example, the handshake, arguably the most common mode of greeting people in the world. Scholars speculate that the handshake may have originated in ancient Greece in the ninth century BC as a gesture designed to show a new acquaintance that you weren't concealing any weapons. Today, few of us walk around with axes or swords hidden under our sleeves, but the handshake contin-

Figure I.2. Handshake between King Shalmaneser III of Assyria
and a Babylonian ruler found on a ninth-century BC relief.

ues to serve as a physical accompaniment to how we greet others. Its original purpose disappeared, but the handshake remained.

Perhaps even more puzzling is that we sometimes follow social norms that are downright dangerous. Take the festival of Thaipusam, a Hindu celebration engaged in by Tamil communities around the world. As part of Thaipusam, participants take part in the "Kavadi Attam," which means "Burden Dance" in English, and for good reason. A testament of commitment to Lord Murugan, the Hindu god of war, the Kavadi requires people to choose their "burden," or method of self-inflicted pain. It's fairly common, for example, to pierce one's skin, tongue, cheeks, or all three with "vel" skewers—holy spears or hooks. Others elect to wear a portable shrine, which is decorated and attached to the body with up to 108 vels piercing the skin. On the island of Mauritius, which serves as a major site for the Thaipusam festival, participants must climb a mountain to reach the Temple of Murugan. The trip is over four hours, during which participants must carry their burden while walking barefoot on uneven surfaces. To make things more difficult, some choose to conduct the entire walk while strapped to planks of nails.

Although few rituals can stack up to the torturous Kavadi Attam, many others are similarly arduous. For example, in San Pedro Manrique, Spain, June 23 marks the beginning of a summer solstice ritual. Each year, around three thousand spectators pack into the tiny village of six hundred residents to watch volunteers walk across twenty-three feet of burning coals as part of a long-standing local tradition. Some people walk in fulfillment of a community vow, while others simply get caught up in the excitement. Volunteers often carry relatives on their backs as they cross the white-hot walkway, which can reach temperatures as high as twelve hundred degrees Fahrenheit. After the ritual is over, people rejoice and celebrate for the rest of the night.

The question is, why do they do it?

THE TIES THAT BIND

Whether it's something simple like the handshake or a complex ritual like the Kumbh Mela, social norms are far from random. Rather, they evolve for a highly functional reason: They've shaped us into one of the most cooperative species on the planet. Countless studies have shown that social norms are critical for uniting communities into cooperative, well-coordinated groups that can accomplish great feats.

Social norms are, in effect, the ties that bind us together, and scientists have collected evidence to prove it. For example, a team of anthropologists had a rare opportunity to study the actual physiology of the fire-walking ritual's attendees in San Pedro Manrique. They strapped transmitter belts to fire-walkers and attendees to measure their heart rates during the ritual. The results showed a remarkable synchronization in the heart rates of ritual participants, as well as their friends and family in the audience. Specifically, when participants' hearts began to beat faster, their friends' and families' hearts also sped up. Quite literally, the fire-walking ritual resulted in many hearts beating as one, suggesting that rituals can increase community cohesion.

Some of the same anthropologists who studied heart rates during fire-walking also conducted research on performers in the Kavadi Attam. In these investigations, an experimenter approached participants immediately after their march and asked them how much they'd be willing to anonymously donate to their temple. The result was a powerful testament to the social glue of ritual: Those who performed in the Kavadi Attam donated significantly more than did people who'd been praying in the temple three days earlier—about 130 rupees as compared with 80 rupees, a difference equivalent to half a day's salary for an unskilled worker.

We needn't travel to faraway places to see how following social norms, like participating in rituals, can increase group cohesion and cooperation. In a series of experiments, psychologists put people into groups and then had them endure an unpleasant experience together. They couldn't ask their participants to walk across hot coals or put skewers through their chests (that would be a bit much for the ethics board!), but they did ask them to stick their hands in ice water, do painful squats, or eat chili peppers together. As compared with groups that didn't experience any collective painful experience, the groups that endured pain reported a remarkably higher sense of bonding. They also cooperated much more in subsequent economic games where each person in the group had opportunities to be selfish and take money for themselves.

Research also suggests that merely following the same exact routine with others is sufficient to increase cooperation. In a study at New Zealand's University of Otago, groups that marched around a stadium together in sync later put more effort into a group task (picking up coins scattered on the stadium floor) as compared with those who walked at their own pace. Being in sync with others actually enables us to coordinate to perform complex tasks. In one study, pairs of participants who moved synchronously were later better able to work together to maneuver a ball through a challenging maze as compared to those who didn't. These results tell us how extraordinarily important it is for human groups to follow social norms, especially if they want to succeed at collective activities that require good coordination, such as hunting, foraging, or warfare.

The fact is, human groups often follow social norms even when they don't appear to fulfill their original function. Let's revisit the handshake. Researchers from Harvard Business School have found that negotiators who shake hands are friendlier toward their negotiation partners and routinely generate better outcomes than those who don't. By facilitating cooperation, handshakes, it seems, took on a vital social function even as their original purpose became obsolete.

COORDINATION, SUPERSIZED

In the past, norms helped bind us to others in very small groups. But today they're critical for helping us coordinate on an extremely large scale—with thousands, if not millions, of people globally. Every day, we're collectively engaged in a colossal exercise in norm coordination. We do it so effortlessly that we may take it for granted—call it "normative autopilot." For instance, you stop when the light is red, and go when it turns green. You get in the back of lines instead of cutting to the front. When you enter a library, movie theater, elevator, or airplane, you quiet down, as do those around you. This is coordination on a large scale, and social norms are the mechanism that enables us to do it.

Social norms are the building blocks of social order; without them, society would crumble. If people didn't abide by socially expected rules, their behavior would be unbearably unpredictable. We wouldn't be able to coordinate our actions to do most anything—from getting place to place to having meaningful conversations to running a large organization. Schools wouldn't function. Police, if there were any, would be ineffective, given the lack of rules and shared standards for adhering to laws and respecting their authority. Government services would cease to operate, resulting in the inability to provide the public with highways, sanitation services, clean water, or national defense. Unable to control their employees' behaviors, companies would quickly go out of business. Without these shared standards of behavior, families would splinter apart.

Clearly, it's in our interest to adhere to social norms. Indeed, according to anthropologist Joseph Henrich, our survival as a species has depended on it. Let's face it: Physically, humans are quite weak compared with many other species. We're not very fast, don't have good camouflage abilities, have poor climbing skills, and don't hear or see particularly well, Henrich argues in *The Secret of Our Success: How Culture Is Driving Human Evolution, Domesticating Our Species, and Making Us Smarter*. We'd soon perish if we were stranded on an island with little food or protection from predators. Then how did we end up eating other animals rather than being eaten?

Henrich makes an important point: We can't just credit our high IQs. If we were stranded alone on that island, our advanced ability to reason wouldn't save us. Rather, when people have thrived in the face of adversity, they've done so because of other people and the social norms they've created together. Social norms have helped us cooperate for millennia. Groups that have cooperated have been able to not only survive the toughest environmental conditions, but also thrive and spread across the entire planet in ways that no other nonhuman species has. Indeed, we learned that if we don't follow our group's cultural norms, we end up in deep trouble. Ignoring social norms not only can damage our reputations, but also may result in ostracism, even death. From an evolutionary perspective, people who developed keen abilities to follow social norms may have been more likely to survive and thrive. This powerful fact has made us a remarkably cooperative species—but only so long as the interactions are between people who share the same basic norms. When groups with fundamentally *different* cultural mind-sets meet, conflict abounds.

Thus the paradox: While norms have been the secret to our success, they're also the source of massive conflict all around the world.

Past vs. Present: The More Things Change, the More They Stay the Same

In 1994, a teenager from Dayton, Ohio, found himself at the center of a major international controversy. Michael Fay, then eighteen, was living with his mother and stepfather in Singapore and attending an international school when he was accused of theft and vandalism. Along with other foreign students, Fay pleaded guilty to participating in a ten-day spree of spray-painting and throwing eggs at eighteen cars. For the crimes, Fay was sentenced to a punishment that was routine in Singapore: four months in jail, a fine of 3,500 Singapore dollars, and six strokes of a cane to be delivered full-force by a prison officer.

Over in the United States, articles in the *New York Times*, the *Washington Post*, and the *Los Angeles Times* expressed moral outrage and condemned what they saw as a barbaric punishment, which involved strapping the convicted into a bent-over position and striking the buttocks with a cane moving at over a hundred miles per hour. Meting out caning strokes for violent crimes can result in copious amounts of shed blood and flesh, fainting, and long-lasting physical and psychological scars. President Clinton and numerous U.S. senators stepped in, pressuring the Singaporean government to grant Fay clemency. But Singapore is proud of its low crime rate and orderliness, and its officials pushed back. They insisted that caning keeps crime rates down as compared with the disorder and chaos that plagued New York City, where "even police cars are not spared the acts of vandals." Ultimately, the Singaporean government reduced Fay's caning sentence from six lashes to four. But the incident caused a major intercultural rift and created lasting tensions between two countries that had long been allies.

The Michael Fay incident broadcasted a fundamental cultural clash that pitted a nation with strict norms and punishments against one that is more lax and tolerant of deviant behavior. This contrasting attitude toward setting rules and following them is one of the most important ways that human groups have varied from prehistory to the modern era.

FROM THE FINE COUNTRY TO THE FLIGHTLESS BIRDS

A tiny nation of about 5.6 million people, Singapore boasts exceptional discipline and order. In fact, it's known as the "fine city" for its hefty fines, which are doled out for even seemingly minor offenses. If you spit on the street, you could be fined up to a thousand dollars. If you are caught importing gum into the country, you may face a fine of up to a hundred thousand dollars and/or jail time of up to two years. Drinking alcohol in public is banned from 10:30 p.m. to 7:00 a.m. and is outlawed altogether on weekends in many "Liquor Control Zones." Anyone caught smuggling illicit drugs can receive the death penalty. Making too much noise in public, singing obscene songs, or distributing offensive photos can lead to either imprisonment, fines, or both. Even urination is subject to scrutiny. If you forget to flush a toilet in a public bathroom stall, you face a fine of up to a thousand dollars. And if one drunken night, you're tempted to pee in an elevator, you should know that some elevators in Singapore are equipped with urine detection devices that, if activated, lock the doors until the authorities arrive to identify the shameless urinator.

Government rules extend into people's personal lives. Expect a fine if you're spotted wandering around your house naked with the curtains open. Homosexual acts can get you imprisoned for two years. Online dissent, particularly against the government, can lead to incarceration, as it did for Amos Yee, a former actor who, at age sixteen, was sentenced to four weeks in prison after releasing a video in which he referred to the prime minister as "power-hungry and malicious." The state might even try to play matchmaker. In 1984, the Singaporean government established the "Social Development Unit," which arranges dates between citizens and educates them on what constitutes a good marriage.

Singapore's tight culture isn't a deterrence to its citizens' love of country. While not always agreeing with its policies, over 80 percent of the nation's residents express support for the government.

Now let's take a plane ride over to New Zealand, a highly permissive culture that couldn't be more different. In New Zealand, people can drive with open bottles of alcohol in their cars as long as they remain within the legal blood alcohol limit. New Zealand is also one of the most sexually open-minded societies in the world. Same-sex marriage is legal, and discrimination against gays and lesbians has been outlawed since 1994. Women have the highest number of sexual partners in the world—an average of 20.4 during their lifetime (the global average is 7.3). Prostitution has long been decriminalized; according to the unique "New Zealand Model," anyone over age eighteen can engage in it, complete with workplace protections and health-care benefits. Pornography is legal and thriving. New Zealanders are frequent users of the website Pornhub, ranking in their per capita viewership behind only residents of the United States, the United Kingdom, Canada, and

Ireland in 2015. Deviant behavior is showcased in the media: Over one-third of popular music videos portray at least one incident of violence, whether it be fighting, gunshots, battles, suicides, murders, or bomb explosions, and at least one-fifth include examples of antisocial behavior, from vandalism to littering—a stark contrast to Singapore, which places huge restrictions on these very behaviors.

"Kiwis," as New Zealanders playfully call themselves (after the flightless bird), tend to become acquainted very quickly, and they eschew formal titles. People are known to walk barefoot on city streets, in grocery stores, and in banks. Public dissent and protests are frequent. Even couch burnings have been a common sight in New Zealand's universities. And in the 1970s, when a man dressed as a wizard and began traveling from city to city, engaging in various shenanigans—from raindancing at rugby games to building a large nest on the roof of a library and even hatching himself from a human-sized egg at an art gallery—he wasn't shunned as a social deviant. Instead, in 1990, New Zealand's prime minister, Mike Moore, proclaimed him to be the nation's official wizard, with the duty "to protect the Government, to bless new enterprises . . . cheer up the population, [and] attract tourists."

MAPPING THE TIGHT-LOOSE SPECTRUM

In any culture, social norms are the glue that binds groups together. Singapore and New Zealand, however, make it clear that the strength of this glue varies greatly. Singapore, with its many rules and strict punishments, is *tight*. New Zealand, with its lax rules and greater permissiveness, is *loose*.

In my travels around the world, I've observed these differences firsthand—from the hushed and virtually sterile train cars in Tokyo, in which you can hear a pin drop, to the very loud and disorderly trains in Manhattan in which people shout words that might make you cringe.

But these are just personal observations. To gain a more objective view, I worked with colleagues from a wide range of countries—from Australia to Hong Kong, the Netherlands to South Korea, Mexico to Norway, Ukraine to Venezuela, and more—to implement one of the largest studies of cultural norms. I wanted to develop measures that could directly compare the strength of social norms across cultures, explore their evolutionary roots, and identify the pros and cons of norms being relatively strong or weak. While we initially focused on national differences, eventually we examined differences in tightness and looseness far and wide—across states, social classes, organizations, and communities.

Our sample of approximately seven thousand people, hailing from over thirty countries and five continents, spanned a wide array of occupations, genders, ages, religions, sects, and social classes. The survey was translated into over twenty languages—from Arabic to Estonian, Mandarin to Spanish, and Norwegian to Urdu. People were asked about their attitudes and worldviews, as well as how much freedom or constraint they had in many different social situations. Most important, they were asked to directly rate the overall strength of their country's norms and punishments. Here are some of the questions we asked:

▶ Are there many social norms that people are supposed to abide by in this country?

▶ Are there very clear expectations for how people should act in most situations?

▶ If someone acts in an inappropriate way, will others strongly disapprove in this country?

▶ Do people in this country have the freedom to choose how they want to act in most situations?

▶ Do people in this country almost always comply with social norms?

The results, published in the journal *Science* in 2011 and covered by media outlets all over the globe, showed that people's answers to our questions revealed an underlying pattern. In some countries, people agreed that social norms in their country were clear and pervasive, and often entailed strong punishments for people who didn't follow them. That is, their countries were tight. People in other countries agreed that the norms in their country were less clear and fewer in number, and that people followed norms less often and were punished less for deviance. Their countries were loose.

The results of this survey gave us a direct way of organizing many cultures on the basis of their strength of norms. With the responses we received, we gave each of the thirty-three nations a tightness-looseness score (see Figure 2.1). According to our findings, some of the tightest nations in our sample were Pakistan, Malaysia, India, Singapore, South Korea, Norway, Turkey, Japan, China, Portugal, and Germany (formerly East). The loosest nations were Spain, the United States, Australia, New Zealand, Greece, Venezuela, Brazil, the Netherlands, Israel, Hungary, Estonia, and the Ukraine. Tightness-looseness is a *continuum*, with extreme cases at either end and varying degrees in between.

We also examined the data to see what it revealed about cultural regions. Tightness is highest in South and East Asian nations, followed by Middle Eastern nations and European countries of Nordic and Germanic origin. By contrast, Latin-European, English-speaking, and Latin American cultures are much less tight, with Eastern European and former Communist nations the loosest.

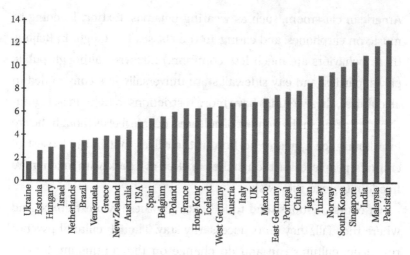

Figure 2.1. Scores on tightness-looseness around the world (2011).

The data also provided insight into how much constraint or latitude people experience in over a dozen everyday social settings, including public parks, restaurants, libraries, banks, elevators, buses, movie theaters, classrooms, and parties. For each setting, respondents told us how much freedom they had to choose what to do, whether they had clear rules for appropriate behavior, and whether they were required to monitor their own behavior and "watch what they do." They also told us how appropriate or inappropriate it would be to engage in various behaviors in these settings, such as arguing, cursing, singing, laughing, crying, listening to music, and eating.

The data clearly indicated that there are far fewer acceptable behaviors in tight cultures. Intriguingly, even though some situations—such as being in a job interview, a library, or a classroom—have a restricted range of behavior in *all* cultures (how often have you seen someone sing in the library or dance at a job interview?), in loose cultures there's still a wider range of behaviors allowed in these situations. (As a professor, I can attest to the types of crazy behaviors you might see in an

American classroom, such as wearing pajamas, texting, listening to music on earphones, and eating; in the classes I've taught in Beijing, these behaviors are much less common.) Likewise, although public parks, parties, and city sidewalks are universally less constrained in all cultures, these settings have more restrictions in tight ones. Figuratively speaking, in the tightest of cultures, people feel as though they're in a library for a greater portion of their lives. But in the loosest of cultures, people feel as though they're often at a park, with much more freedom to do as they wish.

Of course, nations tend to fall between these two extremes. And where they fall, they don't necessarily stay. Though cultural psyches run deep, cultures can and do change on the continuum. Several forces—including the Machiavellian kind—can tip a nation's tight-loose equilibrium quite dramatically. Moreover, just as a person might be generally extroverted most of the time but sometimes have introverted moments, most, if not all, nations have pockets that allow for the release of tightness or the tightening of looseness.

For example, even tight nations have select domains where anything goes—where citizens can let off normative steam. The looseness of these contexts tends to be carefully designated. Take Takeshita Street in Tokyo. Within the confines of this narrow pedestrian shopping street, Japan's cultural demands for uniformity and order are completely suspended. On Takeshita Street, people stroll and preen in zany costumes, ranging from anime characters to sexy maids to punk musicians. Japanese youth and major celebrities from across the globe (including Lady Gaga, Rihanna, Nicki Minaj, and K-pop superstar G-Dragon) flock here to take part in these eccentricities and purchase the unique clothing, accessories, and souvenirs that are for sale. Japanese culture also encourages its straitlaced businessmen to take a designated break from the intense pressures of their jobs to drink, sometimes to excess. Even in the tightest of societies, there are underground spaces for looseness. Amid heavy censorship, Iran's capital, Tehran, has developed a vibrant artistic culture. Finding ways around the country's strict rules regarding political, religious, and sexual material in plays, songs, novels, and films has developed into a creative art form itself. Theater and musical groups put on shows for large crowds, whether in isolated fields, tunnels, or caves. And the Facebook page "My Stealthy Freedom" garnered more than one million likes for its photos of Iranian women removing their hijabs in public and enjoying other forbidden moments of independence.

Likewise, loose societies have designated domains of tightness. While they may seem random at first, they reflect values that are deeply important to citizens and therefore evolve to be regulated to ensure they don't fade away. Take, for example, the American value of privacy, which is tightly regulated. We punish people who violate this norm, looking down on people who invade our personal space, take up too much of our time, and show up at our house unannounced. And in Israel, where people generally loathe regulations that constrain behavior and celebrate nonconformists, strong norms have developed around couples having large families, and serving in the army for Israelis remains a tight commitment among all who can serve. Even in Australia, with their overall lax behavioral rules, people tightly guard their strong egalitarian values. So much so that they have a special put-down for anyone who shows off their wealth or status: "tall poppies."

Despite the fact that all countries have domains that are tight and domains that are loose, countries differ in the *overall* degree to which they emphasize tightness or looseness.

The tightness-looseness lens is a new way of viewing cultures on the global map. For example, there is no linear relationship between nations' scores on tightness-looseness and their economic development. Singapore and Germany, both tight, enjoy significant economic success, but Pakistan and India, also tight, still struggle. The United States and Australia, both loose, are wealthy, but the Ukraine and Brazil, also loose, have comparatively lower gross domestic products. Tightness-looseness is also distinct from previous ways that scholars have compared cultures, such as whether they're collectivist or individualist (collectivist cultures emphasize family ties; individualist cultures stress self-reliance). There are plenty of nations in each of the four quadrants: collectivist and tight (Japan and Singapore), collectivist and loose (Brazil and Spain), individualist and loose (the United States and New Zealand), and individualist and tight (Austria and Germany).

AN ANCIENT PATTERN

Our cross-cultural survey illustrated that tightness-looseness is a key way that modern nations vary. But groups have varied for thousands of years in the relative strength of their social norms. While the content of those social norms has changed over the centuries as human civilization has evolved, the underlying cultural template of tight and loose hasn't. Some early societies resembled the rule-bound and orderly nation of modern Singapore, while others mimicked the Kiwis of New Zealand, with their lax rules.

Imagine yourself in Sparta, a strict, militarized culture in ancient Greece that existed in the late fifth century BC, well over two thousand years before Singapore was founded as a nation. What would you see?

From cradle to grave, the lives of Spartan citizens—their education, career, and marriage; their clothing style and personal beliefs—were all governed by rigid, nonnegotiable requirements. Take, for example, the life of a young Spartan boy. At age seven, he'd be sent off to a fifteen-year, state-run boot camp to be groomed into a courageous warrior. If he showed signs of fear on the battlefield, he'd be forced to shave off half his beard as a shameful emblem of his timidity. If he was an actual coward in battle, he would lose his Spartan citizenship altogether. Off the battlefield, public floggings tested his tolerance of pain.

The daily life of Spartans likewise resembled life in a military camp. In addition to following highly regulated diets, men and women were expected to frequently exercise to maintain a fit physique. The Spartans found obesity grotesque, so those who were overweight were banished from the city-state. Men and women who failed to pass physical exams (along with those who engaged in illegal activity or didn't marry) were shunned, lost their citizenship, or had to wear special clothing as signs of societal disgrace. Sparta's cutthroat physical standards even applied to newborn babies: If an infant was deemed weak or deformed, it was left at the foot of a mountain to die.

Spartans abided by clear-cut mannerisms taught in childhood. They were trained to wear solemn expressions and speak concisely. Children were disciplined to never cry, speak in public, or express fear. Spartans appreciated laughter and humor, but had to adhere to strict rules on what was acceptable and unacceptable: Jokes were to be refined and witty, never slapstick. It was also important for Spartan citizens, who considered themselves a superior race of warriors, to remain unpolluted by non-Spartan culture. Total uniformity in dress, hairstyle, and behavior was demanded. Foreigners and foreign influence were prohibited, and Spartan citizens were forbidden to travel abroad.

While the tight lifestyle might sound rather austere, Sparta was a proud culture, and its practices paid off: The radical discipline of Sparta's citizens enabled it to achieve military predominance across Greece. Famous ancient Greeks and Romans, ranging from Plato to Augustus Caesar, were enthralled by Sparta's legendary soldiers and their total devotion to the state.

Now let's travel about 150 miles away to Sparta's military rival and cultural nemesis: Athens. In contrast to Sparta's strict lifestyle, Athens had permissive norms, with frequent gorging and drinking. Strolling the streets of Athens, you would have noticed a wide range of fashion styles, accessorized with jewelry pieces from the bustling Athenian marketplace, the *agora*. There you'd witness unbridled self-expression by artists, pastry chefs, actors, writers, and public intellectuals from different schools of thought. You might run into famous figures, like Socrates, who urged Athenian youths to reconsider all their conventions and preconceived notions about the world. Or you might meet Diogenes of Sinope, a philosopher who lived out of an abandoned tub in the streets of the *agora*, challenging the need for stultifying etiquette, which he believed prevented people from being their authentic selves. He was known to approach random Athenians and hold a lit candle to their faces in search of more genuine souls.

Perhaps due to their proximity to the Aegean Sea, which supported robust foreign trade, Athenians, unlike the more geographically isolated Spartans, experienced a lot of cultural mixing. With new ideas and artistic techniques coming in from outside cultures, the Athenians innovated the arts of theater, pottery, and sculpture. Every ten days, thousands of Athenians from all walks of life engaged in lively political debate, full of opposing viewpoints about current events, much like modern-day New Zealand. If you were a model citizen, you'd have the ability to express your ideas fluently and passionately in a public forum. Accordingly, schools in Athens cultivated students' intellectual and creative prowess, with an emphasis on literature, music, and rhetoric—not just their combat skills. Radical new ideas transformed politics, ultimately paving the way for the establishment of the first democracy in Western civilization.

This was Athens: a loose place where new ideas clashed, dissolved, and altered, and where dissent was celebrated. The Spartans—prizing order and discipline—would have found Athens to be a pestilent scene of abject eccentricity.

The tight-loose distinction recurs throughout the history of human societies. Consider how tightness manifested among the Nahua culture of central Mexico in the early to mid-1900s. An ancient culture derived from the great Aztec Empire, the Nahua valued restraint and discipline. Ethnographers living among them documented their many rules and strict punishments, which share some remarkable similarities with Sparta and Singapore. Guarded and reserved in their interactions, the Nahua believed mannerisms should reflect self-control, a trait that helped them fulfill their society's intense agricultural duties.

From early childhood, the Nahua taught their sons and daughters to be obedient and abide by norms. By age six, children completed many of the family's daily tasks, such as taking care of siblings, helping in the fields and around the house, and going to the market. By age fifteen, girls did all the housework of grown women, while boys drove plows, planted and harvested crops, and raised cattle. The Nahua placed a great emphasis on "good" behavior in children. Sexuality was discouraged from childhood on, and curiosity about bodily functions was forbidden. Parents in Nahua strongly believed that children lacking self-discipline would grow up to become poor workers and bring great shame to their families. To ward off this fate, children who fell short of their parents' expectations were severely punished—whipped, beaten, kicked, ridiculed, or denied food or sleep for offenses such as losing things or grumbling.

Later, marriageability depended on one's willingness to follow the rules. If a young man's mother learned that his intended was known for being lazy or disobedient, she would object to the union. In public, women and girls were expected to be demure and unassuming at all times, lest their behavior be labeled shamelessly flirtatious. Since women were expected to remain virgins before marriage, any appearance of a sexual drive could damage their reputations and was severely punished by their parents. Once married, wives were expected to be compliant and faithful. To ensure nothing could destabilize the new family structure, they were discouraged from keeping female friends, who might act as a go-between for a wife and her prospective lover. Men also discontinued their friendships with other men, lest intimacy develop between these men and their wives. Divorce was highly frowned upon. Community members reported on the wrongdoings of others, and appropriate conduct was maintained through unrelenting gossip, accusations of sorcery, and, in severe cases, expulsion from the community.

Now contrast the Nahua with the Copper Inuit, who've lived in the central Arctic region in Canada as hunter-gatherers for over three millennia. They, too, were observed by ethnographers in the mid-twentieth century. Their looseness might make modern Kiwis blush.

Growing up, Copper Inuit children enjoyed an unstructured and informal lifestyle. The parenting style was laissez-faire to say the least. Diamond Jenness, a pioneer of Canadian anthropology, described children growing up like "wild plants" until puberty, roaming about on their own, roughhousing with peers, and not hesitating to interrupt or correct their parents. Children had total autonomy over their schedules, including whether to attend school. Parents rarely used any form of physical punishment with their kids; they mostly ignored misbehavior or briefly teased children who acted out of line.

Unlike the Nahua, the Copper Inuit were known to be easygoing about sexual matters. Intercourse was fairly common among adolescents, who had sex even in their parents' house. If and when couples eventually did get married, the process was rather informal: They established a separate home, but returned to their respective families' homes if things didn't work out. Open marriages were tolerated, including wife-swapping in some cases, which promoted alliances with members of unrelated families. Men and women had their own roles within the home, but these roles were flexible: women sometimes went hunting, and men learned how to cook and sew. Within the broader community, only "rudimentary law" existed, according to the legal anthropologist E. Adamson Hoebel; there was no centralized power to resolve conflicts between community members. The fact that individuals were left to manage conflict on their own undoubtedly contributed to the high rates of homicide and blood feuds among the Copper Inuit.

Despite their differences in time, place, and customs, groups from Sparta and Athens to the Nahua and Inuit varied in the same way that modern societies do: Some of these groups were loose; others were tight.

In the twentieth century, anthropologists started to notice these distinctions in many other cultural groups. In the 1930s, American anthropologist Ruth Benedict contrasted cultures as either "Apollonian" or "Dionysian" after the sons of Zeus. Like Apollo, the god of reason and rationality, tight "Apollonian" cultures, such as the Native American Zunis, valued restraint and order. And like Dionysus, the god of wine, who emphasized abandon, letting go, and excess, loose "Dionysian" cultures, such as the Plains Indians tribes, were prone to wildness and a lack of inhibition. Later, in the 1960s, Pertti Pelto, a Finnish American anthropologist, officially used the terms *tight* and *loose* to differentiate traditional societies.

Our own analysis of data from the anthropological record offers historical evidence of this ancient cultural template. The Standard Cross-Cultural Sample (SCCS) provides information on 186 preindustrial societies from around the world. The societies in the data set are highly diverse, from contemporary hunter-gatherers (the !Kung Bushmen) to early historic states (Aztecs). In their fieldwork, anthropologists meticulously rated the societies on various characteristics over the years—for example, the degree to which children were expected to have high levels of self-restraint and obedience, whether the community tried to control children's behavior, and whether children in these societies were severely punished for not obeying rules. We found that these hundreds of societies were scattered along the tightness-looseness spectrum. Cultures like the Inca in South America, the Goajiro in South America, and the Azande in Central Africa all scored high on tightness. The Tehuelche in South America, !Kung Bushmen in Southwest Africa, and the Copper Inuit from Canada were loose.

Just as our contemporary research on modern nations mapped divides between tight and loose cultures, it's clear that this template dates back to ancient history. Norms may change across the centuries, but their deep structure—tight or loose—is timeless.

3

The Yin and Yang of Tight and Loose

In 2013, I asked some of my research assistants to do something a little out of the ordinary. At my request, each donned a temporary tattoo, a (fake) skin piercing, a purple hair extension, or synthetic facial warts. I then sent them out to fourteen countries to ask strangers on city streets for help with directions or clerks in stores for help with a purchase. The results were clear: My students wearing the stigmas were more likely to receive help from strangers in loose cultures than in tight ones.

I'm not the only psychologist who has messed with environments to root out cultural differences. In 2008, researchers at the University of Groningen in the Netherlands did so quite literally: In one condition of their study, they temporarily added graffiti to an alley near a shopping area—in essence, making it an impromptu "loose" environment. In the other condition, they kept the alley clean, making it a spotless, tight environment. Then they hung useless leaflets that read "We wish everybody happy holidays" on the handlebars of parked bicycles in both conditions. It was an ingenious test. The bike owners would need to remove the leaflets from their handlebars to ride their bikes, yet there were no trash cans around. Would the riders take the leaflets with them or throw them on the ground? About 70 percent in the loose, graffiti-ridden alley littered; only about 30 percent in the tight, clean alley did.

As these studies show, tightness and looseness both have their pros and cons depending on your vantage point. Broadly speaking, loose cultures tend to be open, but they're also much more disorderly. On the flip side, tight cultures have a comforting order and predictability, but they're less tolerant. This is the *tight-loose trade-off*: advantages in one realm coexist with drawbacks in another.

LIVING THE TIGHT LIFE

In a 2017 episode of *Wait Wait . . . Don't Tell Me!*, the weekly U.S. National Public Radio comedy show, host Peter Sagal asked his panelists the following question: "Just like the United States, Japan has problems with its police force. In Japan, many police officers are in desperate need of what?" The answer to his question wasn't what you'd expect: new uniforms, faster cars, higher pay, or more time off. Quite the contrary, Sagal explained. "They need crime . . . Crime rates in Japan have fallen so low in the last thirteen years that police officers are literally looking for things to occupy their time." According to the *Economist*, as of 2014, Japan had one of the lowest murder rates in the world, just 0.3 per 100,000 people. The streets of Japan are so safe that some police officers have resorted to prodding individuals to steal: Policemen in the southern city of Kagoshima started leaving cases of beer in unlocked cars just to see if passersby would grab them. But even this sting was underwhelming; it took a week before they could revel in the opportunity to punish a hapless offender.

Beyond this one comical example, my statistical analyses of George Thomas Kurian's *Illustrated Book of World Rankings* show crime rates per hundred thousand people are all significantly lower in tight countries. Like Japan, China is known for its low level of crime, as are India and Turkey. In looser countries, like New Zealand, the Netherlands, and the United States, crime is much more common. And while violence has been falling for decades, as shown by renowned psychologist Steven Pinker in *The Better Angels of Our Nature*, murder rates still vary widely around the world in a predictable pattern: Looser nations have higher rates than tight ones.

How do tight cultures maintain social order and keep their crime rates low? First, through threat of serious punishments. Retention of the death penalty, as reported by Amnesty International, is highly correlated with tightness ratings. For example, possessing drugs can get you the death penalty in Singapore—as compared with the Netherlands, where marijuana is sold legally in coffee shops (and increasingly in some U.S. states). At least sixteen crimes can result in a death sentence in Saudi Arabia, including drug possession, burglary, rape, adultery, and gay sex. Get caught drinking alcohol, and you may face jail time and even a public flogging. And whether you agree or disagree with Singapore's caning practices, such deterrence appears to have helped make the country relatively crime free.

No doubt, extensive monitoring systems also keep a lid on crime. I've found that tight cultures tend to have more police per capita and employ more security personnel to check for inappropriate behavior in public spaces. Surveillance cameras are rampant in tight countries, reminding the public to behave themselves. In Saudi Arabia, high-tech cameras called *saher*, which translates to "one who remains awake," dot highways, exit roads, and intersections. They capture images of drivers talking on the phone, texting, not wearing seat belts, and driving over the speed limit, as well as tailgating and changing lanes excessively. Similarly, Japan has millions of surveillance cameras on streets, buildings, store entrances, taxis, and train stations.

Psychologists at Newcastle University in the United Kingdom tested the effectiveness of this "eyes are upon you" practice in fostering norm-compliant behavior. In their university coffee room, the researchers hung a banner with an image of a large pair of eyes above the coffee maker. Next to the machine, there was an "honesty box" as a collection receptacle for people's payments for coffee, tea, or milk. During weeks when the banner with eyes hung above the coffee machine (as compared with weeks when there was simply a picture of flowers), people put almost three times more money into the honesty box, on average. In another study, researchers found that hanging up a poster of eyes around a university cafeteria reduced student littering by half.

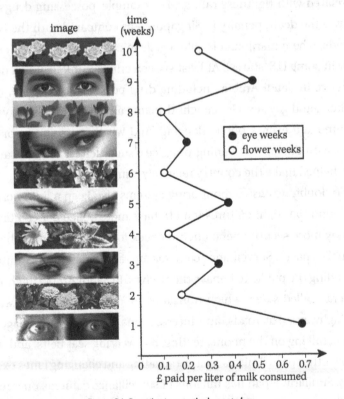

Figure 3.1. Contributions to the honesty box.

In another experiment, people who were prompted to think about religious concepts, such as preacher, prophet, saint, and church (a habit of mind that is more likely to occur in tight cultures, which rank higher on religiosity), were less likely to cheat. So whether the eyes belong to our neighbors, the government, or God, monitoring leads us to conform to prevailing norms. "Watched people are nice people," cultural psychologist Ara Norenzayan has aptly stated.

In addition to having less crime, tight nations tend to be more organized and cleaner. Here again, stronger norms and monitoring work hand in hand to bring this about.

In 2014, I asked my research assistants in other countries to examine signs of cleanliness in public settings. Even after factoring in national wealth, they found that tighter countries tend to have more cleaning personnel on city streets. They not only keep things tidy but also serve as a reminder to citizens about the value of doing so.

Many tight countries have a long tradition of keeping their cities clean. Germany and neighboring Austria, for example, are famous for their tidiness. On city streets in Vienna, "waste watchers" dole out hefty fines to litterbugs. In southern Germany, residents of apartment buildings strictly abide by a cleaning system called "*Kehrwoche*," or sweeping week, where each person is responsible for cleaning up the building's steps and sidewalks. In Oslo, Norway, whose spotless thoroughfares are perhaps rivaled only by the impeccably manicured streets of Singapore, an anti-littering mascot reminds people not to litter and organizes cleanup days that involve over two hundred thousand volunteers. Japan's obsession with cleanliness made international headlines after the nation's defeat in the 2014 World Cup, when Japanese fans swarmed over Brazil's Arena Pernambuco stadium with bright blue trash bags, gathering up litter to discard—a postgame tradition in their home country that they'd taken on the road.

By contrast, in an extreme show of loose behavior, when the Vancouver Canucks lost the Stanley Cup in 2011, the city transformed into a "drunken vomity hellhole" that cost around $4 million to repair, blogger Isha Aran reported. Slovenly behavior like this is generally more widespread in loose cultures. Seventy-five percent of Americans report littering in the last five years, a habit that entails over $11 billion annually in cleanup efforts. The government in Brazil spends hundreds of millions of dollars per year in the city of Rio alone to collect trash on streets and beaches. And in Greece, residents compound their country's financial crisis by tossing their garbage in makeshift landfills, causing fires and posing serious health and safety risks.

Interestingly, when we're exposed to untidy environments, it creates a powerful feedback loop that facilitates *more* norm violations and disorder. Imagine witnessing someone littering, not returning his shopping cart, or scrawling graffiti on the side of a building. If you saw this, would you be more likely to break a *different* norm or rule? Research suggests you would. People have been found to litter more when they witness illegal fireworks going off nearby or when they observe others not returning their shopping carts. This kind of "norm-breaking contagion" is much less likely to occur in tight cultures where fewer norm violations occur in the first place.

In addition to generally being cleaner, tight cultures tend to have less noise pollution. Germany has mandated quiet hours on Sundays and holiday evenings. During these quiet hours, you're forbidden to mow your lawn, play loud music, or run washing machines. The German courts take these restrictions very seriously. After one Cologne resident complained about a yapping dog, a judge allowed the dog to bark for only thirty minutes a day in ten-minute intervals. Likewise, in Japan, noise is tightly regulated. Commuters are expected to refrain from talking on the phone and to listen to music through headphones. By contrast, Dutch commuters often chat loudly while riding the train, even in cars that are designated "silent zones" (*stilte* in Dutch). In Israel, a transportation department video implored Israelis to be "more like the British" and stop yelling on the metro in 2016. Meanwhile, the *New York Times* labeled its namesake city "The City That Never Shuts Up." In 2016, more than 420,000 noise complaints were made in New York, double the number made in 2011, and reports show that the city suffers from dangerous decibel levels. Even libraries, which are supposed to be the quintessential haven for quiet, are rated as being much noisier in looser cultures, my research shows.

THE CLOCKS ON CITY STREETS

Another contributing factor to the greater order seen in tight cultures is their superior synchronization. Synchrony can be found in many human activities: swimming, marching bands, army drills, and more. It's also a feature of many nonhuman species. Fireflies have mastered synchrony with their well-timed flashing, as have crickets, whose chirping is so precise that we can use it to predict the temperature. Synchrony is all around us. In humans, cardiac pacemakers, firing neurons, intestinal activity, and applauding audiences all reflect synchronization. All nations need to be synchronized to some degree, or they'd collapse. Yet nations vary widely in their ability to synchronize actions, with tight cultures faring better at it than loose ones.

Take something as simple as clocks in city streets. You might assume all countries ensure their major clocks are perfectly synced to the right time, but a clever study led by psychologist Robert Levine suggests some countries are more successful at this than others. He had research assistants measure the time displayed on fifteen different clocks across the capitals of thirty-plus countries. In some countries, including Austria, Singapore, and Japan—all tight nations—

city-center clocks were highly in sync, deviating from each other by less than thirty seconds. But in loose countries like Brazil and Greece, clocks were off from one another by almost two minutes. My analysis of Levine's data shows that, generally speaking, synchronous clocks are likely to be found in tight nations, as seen in the figure below.

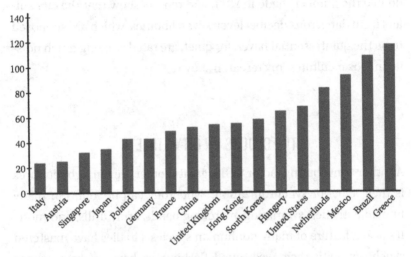

Figure 3.2. Clock deviation (in seconds) by country.

Transportation tends to be more coordinated in tight cultures. If you live in a tighter culture, you're more likely to be able to depend on the preset schedules of public transport, whereas if you're in a loose culture, you should expect delays. Japan's Shinkansen "bullet trains," which travel up to two hundred miles per hour, had an average delay of only fifty-four seconds in 2013. Likewise, the trains of the Swiss, renowned for their timeliness, boasted a 97 percent punctuality rate. In 2014, Singapore's main rail system had only fourteen delays lasting over thirty minutes. Rail operators can be fined up to one million Singapore dollars a year for delayed performance. When delays *do* happen in tighter countries, apologies and explanations flood in. When a power surge led to a two-hour delay on Singaporean trains, the national transport minister personally issued a public apology. And when German trains are late, passengers can expect a detailed explanation from the conductor. By contrast, train riders in loose countries are both more likely to face delays and less likely to receive apologies or explanations. The heavily trafficked New Jersey Transit line between the Big Apple and New Jersey prompted the endearingly titled website njtranshit.com, which tracks the almost-predictable daily delays and cancellations suffered by customers. On American railway Amtrak, an estimated 20 to 30 percent of trains run late on some of the busiest lines.

It's not just the clocks in tight cultures that are synchronized. People are more likely to dress the same, buy the same things, and generally downplay their uniqueness. Why? Because if everybody acts like everybody else, order and coordination become much easier. Take something as seemingly benign as which hand you use for writing. One of my studies found that there are far fewer "lefties" in tight cultures. For example, while about 12 percent of Americans write with their left hands, only about 3 percent of people in Turkey do. And the tighter a country is, the more likely it is to require school uniforms. This uniformity even extends to the cars people drive. I had my team of research assistants also venture into parking lots around the world. We found less variation in the make and color of cars in tight cultures as compared with loose ones.

Synchronization practices abound in tight cultures. The practice of "precision walking," also called *Shuudan Koudou*, which translates to "collective action," has been perfected by Japanese students walking together in amazingly complex routines that echo marching bands and the military. In China, radio calisthenics—exercises set to music and broadcast on the radio—are mandatory at state-owned companies and are part of the curriculum in many primary and secondary schools, and older women frequently gather in public squares at night to dance in synchrony in forms modeled after Tai Chi. In other cultures, religious practices are used to synchronize people. In the Middle East, the *adhan*, or Islamic call to prayer, resonates through the streets five times a day, synchronizing individuals throughout the region. Whether derived from clocks, clothes, cars, or calls to prayer, synchronization leads to the same predictable psychological consequence: enhanced cohesion and cooperation, as I discussed in Chapter 1.

Synchronization is also found in the most unexpected of places: the stock market. Analysts had long assumed that behavior on the stock market was primarily related to economic or political variables, like a country's wealth or information transparency. But a group of U.S. professors had a hunch that culture might play a role. In a paper published in the *Journal of Financial Economics*, Cheol Eun and his colleagues found that investors in tight cultures are more likely to make similar buying and selling decisions—what they call stock price synchronicity. In their study of stock price movements across forty-seven countries from 1990 to 2010, tighter countries, such as China, Turkey, and Singapore, featured greater synchronicity than loose nations such as the United States, New Zealand, and Brazil. Investors from tight areas evidently have more common experiences and perspectives, and are generally more sensitive to peer influence (or "herd behavior"), which leads them to make similar trading decisions.

TIGHTENING OUR BELTS

Due to their cultures' greater social regulation, it seemed plausible that people in tight cultures might have greater *self-regulation* than people in loose cultures. German sociologist Norbert Elias was the first to make the connection between social constraint and self-constraint in his book *The Civilizing Process*, published in 1939. The more people have to attune their conduct to others', he argued, the stronger their ability to regulate their impulses. My research supports this argument: People in tight cultures do indeed show higher self-control. For example, people in the United States, New Zealand, Greece, and Venezuela weigh much more than people in tight countries like India, Japan, Pakistan, and Singapore, even taking into account a country's wealth and people's average height. (As an aside, in the United States, over 50 percent of dogs and cats are overweight or obese, including my own dog, Pepper.) Some of the highest scores for alcohol consumption in liters per capita also came from loose countries such as Spain, Estonia, and New Zealand. Residents of tight nations such as Singapore, India, and China score low on alcohol consumption rates.

Spending habits also differ widely between tight and loose cultures. Residents of loose countries such as the United States, Hungary, and Estonia are more likely to gamble than residents of tight countries such as South Korea and Singapore. Loose nations also have lower gross national savings—a country's gross national income minus public and private consumption—even when taking into account wealth and income distribution, suggesting that economies in loose cultures are spending more income than they produce.

These differences aren't just found in scientific studies—they show up in international headlines. When the 2008 financial crisis hit the world markets, years of sloppy bookkeeping caught up with Greece, a loose culture, which plunged €300 billion into debt. Banks in tight Germany ended up shouldering a lot of Greece's debt, and much like a no-nonsense parent, the German government called on Greece to implement greater fiscal austerity. "You just have to ask the Swabian [a wealthy southwestern region of Germany] housewife," scolded Chancellor Angela Merkel. "She would have given us some worldly wisdom. You cannot live permanently beyond your means." Tellingly, the German word for debt and guilt is the same (*Schuld*). Greeks, in turn, hit the street and vehemently protested such strict measures. Tensions came to a head in July 2015, when Germany proposed that Greece leave the eurozone. In the end, another bailout was arranged, but the tight-loose fault line persisted.

LIVING THE LOOSE LIFE

Tight cultures generally have low crime, high synchrony, and a high degree of self-control. Loose cultures, on the flip side, can be highly disorganized and suffer from a host of self-regulation failures. Yet loose cultures have a significant edge when it comes to being open—to new ideas, different people, and change—qualities that tight cultures sorely lack. This is the tight-loose trade-off in action.

The human capacity to innovate sets us apart from other species, and has produced countless achievements—from the wheel to the lightbulb to the Internet. Creativity requires out-of-the-box thinking and acceptance of ideas that might violate preestablished norms, which gives loose cultures a clear innovation advantage.

In one study, management professors Roy Chua, Yanning Roth, and Jean-François Lemoine analyzed eleven thousand responses to ninety-nine creativity contests on a crowdsourcing platform where large monetary prizes were given to the best ideas. Creativity challenges posted included designing a new shopping mall in Spain, creating a TV commercial tailored to Egyptian culture, rebranding instant coffee for Australians, and designing a water bottle that was quintessentially "French." People from tight countries weren't only less likely to win these competitions, but also less likely to enter. Even more telling, judges in tight cultures gave fewer awards to foreign participants' ideas, presumably because these ideas were more radical than those the judges were accustomed to.

This study points to an interesting aspect of the tight-loose trade-off. Loose cultures may be less orderly than tight ones, but a certain level of disorderliness actually proves beneficial to thinking outside of the box. Imagine yourself in a psychology experiment in a well-organized room with a spotless desk, as shown in Figure 3.3. Then imagine yourself in a chaotic space with papers, open books, pens, and pencils strewn across the desk and the floor (this is how my office looks). How would these environments affect your creativity in the experiment?

Psychologist Kathleen Vohs and her collaborators found that people who spent time in a messy room performed better on a brainstorming task—specifically, listing more innovative uses for Ping-Pong balls. In another study, people in a messy room indicated that they'd rather order a menu option that was labeled "new" (the creative option) ver-

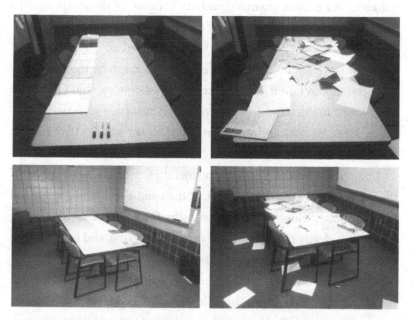

Figure 3.3. Orderly and disorderly rooms used in Vohs and colleagues' study.

sus one labeled "classic." Tight rooms—and tight cultures—enhance the status quo; by contrast, loose, messy environments may seem chaotic, but they encourage unconventional thinking.

Relatedly, while synchrony has its benefits for cooperation in tight cultures, there are benefits to being *unsynchronized* that loose cultures gain. In one study, my collaborators Joshua Jackson, Nava Caluori, Morgan Taylor, and I asked groups of people to perform a creativity task after they walked around campus either at the exact same pace or at their own pace. Groups that walked in sync were less creative than those that marched to their own beat.

In another study where groups chanted either the same or different words together at the same time, groups that chanted the same words were less likely to have individuals who voiced dissent in a later group-decision task that actually benefited from having different opinions.

From the ancient Athenians to the modern-day Dutch, loose cultures also exhibit greater creativity because of their exposure to multiple cultures. Research shows that people who have greater multicultural experience—meaning they've traveled or interacted with people from different cultures extensively—tend to be more creative than those who haven't. For example, in laboratory studies, people with more multicultural experiences brainstorm more unconventional ideas for gifts and are more likely to solve tasks that require novel solutions.

Imagine you're given a book of matches, a candle, and a box of thumbtacks and are asked to mount the candle to a wall so that the wax from the candle won't drip onto the table. Figure 3.4 shows the solution. It clearly requires a lot of creative thinking, and having more exposure to cultural diversity bolsters this ability.

Economists call this ability to cross boundaries and break out of the norm "fluidity." They argue that it's a key skill if you want to succeed as an entrepreneur. As Harvard psychologist Howard Gardner puts it,

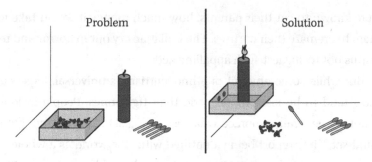

Figure 3.4. The Duncker Candle Problem.

"a lack of fit, an unusual pattern, or an irregularity"—quintessentially loose qualities—has the power to stimulate creativity. Indeed, our analyses of the 2015 Global Entrepreneurship Monitor, which examined attitudes in more than 120 countries, show that people in loose cultures, such as Brazil and Greece, are more likely to believe that entrepreneurship is a good career choice and that they have the capabilities to start their own business, as compared with those in tight cultures, such as Korea and Germany.

Loose cultures are not only more open to different ideas—they're open to different people. Centuries ago, Herodotus, known by his admirers as the father of history, observed in his travels circa 450 BC that all cultures are ethnocentric—that is, they believe their own way of doing things is far superior to that of others: "If one were to order all mankind to choose the best set of rules in the world, each group would, after due consideration, choose its own customs; each group regards its own as being by far the best."

Herodotus illustrates his point with a story in which King Darius, the ruler of Persia, asks a group of Greeks who were cremating their dead fathers how much money it would take for them to eat their fathers' corpses. The Greeks, shocked, reply that they'd never agree to do such a thing. The king then asks the Callatiae, an Indian tribe, who

49

were known to eat their parents, how much money it would take for them to cremate their corpses. The Callatiae cry out in horror and tell Darius not to suggest such appalling acts.

But while some amount of ethnocentrism is universal, loose cultures tend to be less ethnocentric than tight ones. People in loose countries generally embrace what psychologists call a cosmopolitan mind-set. They report being identified with "the world as a whole" to a greater extent than do people in tight cultures. This cosmopolitan mind-set also makes them more receptive to foreigners. When people from all over the world were asked if they would tolerate immigrants as their neighbors, it was the loose cultures, including Brazil, Australia, New Zealand, and the Netherlands, that were the most welcoming, whereas the tightest cultures—such as Malaysia, South Korea, and Turkey—were not. Loose nations back up those attitudes, too: They are literally home to a higher percentage of immigrants.

Generally, people in tight cultures are more likely to believe their culture is superior and needs to be protected from foreign influences. China, for example, ranks in the 90th percentile of countries with the most negative attitudes toward foreigners. And in Japan, where foreigners make up only 2 percent of the population, many landlords have a "no foreigners" policy, and certain bathhouses, shops, restaurants, and hotels deny entry to foreign customers. In 2016, the *Guardian* reported that a train conductor on an Osaka railway announced, "There are many foreign passengers on board today . . . this has caused serious congestion and is causing inconvenience to Japanese passengers." In Austria, another tight culture with little ethnic diversity, surveys show that almost thirty percent of Austrian citizens hold anti-Semitic attitudes. And Austria remains one of the most politically exclusive countries for non-EU immigrants, who reportedly have no voting rights and face very restrictive naturalization requirements.

People in loose cultures are also more tolerant of people with a range of commonly stigmatized identities. In surveys conducted with more than 33,000 people across nineteen countries, we found that people from loose cultures were much more willing to live next to a wider range of people, including homosexuals, individuals from a different race or religion, foreign workers, unmarried couples, and those who have AIDS.

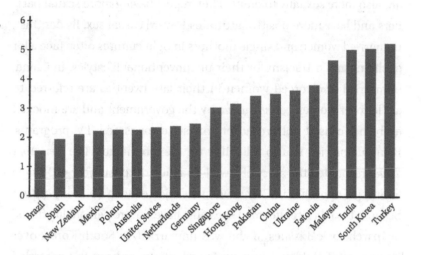

Figure 3.5. Unwillingness to live next to stigmatized groups increases as tightness increases.

International surveys by Gallup also show tight countries—such as South Korea, Pakistan, Malaysia, Turkey, and China—to be some of the worst places to live for gays and lesbians, while loose countries—such as Australia, New Zealand, and the Netherlands—are more accepting. San Francisco, Barcelona, Amsterdam, São Paulo, and Tel Aviv were rated as some of the most gay-friendly travel destinations in 2015. Meanwhile, bullying and discrimination of gay students is prevalent in Portugal and Turkey, and in Iran and Afghanistan being gay can be fatal: Same-sex intercourse is punishable by death for breaking Sharia law.

Take another stigma that might not be as obvious: marital status.

Are you single, married, or divorced? In loose cultures, such distinctions are comparably unimportant. There are multiple ways for people to cohabitate without being formally married in the Netherlands, such as through registered partnerships and cohabitation agreements. About half of all Dutch children are born to unmarried parents. Similarly high rates occur in New Zealand and Spain. Loose cultures are also more sexually tolerant. They report having more sexual partners and have more positive attitudes toward casual sex. By contrast, unmarried women and single mothers in tight cultures often face a lot of shame and ostracism for their unconventional lifestyles. In China, unmarried or divorced women in their late twenties are referred to as "leftover women," or *sheng nu*, by the government and are mocked as being "a used cotton jacket" on state-sponsored TV programs. Being unmarried is also a liability on the job market. The *New York Times* recounted the story of a well-qualified thirty-six-year-old single female job applicant in China who was rejected for an editor position because the recruiter deemed she must have "severe personality flaws" or "psychological issues" if she was unmarried. In South Korea, over 90 percent of children given up for adoption are born to unmarried mothers—mainly due to the stigma the mothers would face if they kept their children.

THE CULTURAL ROOTS OF INERTIA

Heraclitus, the ancient Greek philosopher (circa 500 BC), is credited for the notion that the only constant is change. Many centuries later, in 1992, the comedian Bill Hicks, more a truth-teller than a philosopher, made a similar declaration in one of his most acclaimed stand-up routines: "The world is like a ride in an amusement park . . . The ride goes up and down, around and around, it has thrills and chills . . . And we can change it anytime we want." Yet change is not evenly distributed around the world. Loose cultures, with their openness and permissiveness, embrace change and are more adaptable to new and potentially better ideas that come along. By contrast, with their greater social control and synchronization, tight cultures cling to stability and the status quo, taking much longer to adapt to new circumstances.

For example, when people in loose cultures were asked whether they'd ever engaged in or planned to engage in any kind of collective political action—from signing a petition to demonstrating—they overwhelmingly said yes, whereas people in tight cultures said no more often. Not only do loose cultures boast a highly open media that enables uncensored dissent, but people even support the expression of ideas they find repugnant. In 2007, at a rally against Iranian president Mahmoud Ahmadinejad, who was visiting Columbia University, one protester proudly held a sign that read "Free speech for all. Even douchebags" and commented, "To deny free speech to anybody, you deny it to everybody."

By contrast, tight countries place many restrictions on what people can say in public. Tight nations are more likely to have autocratic governments that don't hesitate to forcefully crack down on any dissent or censor the media. Not surprisingly, countries' looseness ratings correlate highly with the organization Freedom House's ratings of a nation's openness to the media and to journalists. Countries like New Zealand, Belgium, and Australia have a very open media environment, affording a wide range of ideas that go uncontested. Countries like China, Malaysia, and Singapore, by contrast, put a lid on what people can say, on- and off-line. Twitter's analytics division reported that Turkey's government and other officials made more requests to remove content from its citizens' accounts than any other country in 2017, even beating out Russia and its notoriously tight monitoring of irreverent Twitter content. China tasks its "web police" of two million people with conducting digital surveillance and eliminating rebellious ideas. To give citizens further incentive to stay in line, the government is reportedly working on a "social credit" system that would compile data about each individual citizen's behavior—such as their debt repayment, driving history, and even their treatment of their parents—into a single score, similar to a credit score, with points taken away and sanctions imposed on those causing "disturbances."

People in loose cultures might think these restrictions are excessive, and that the state should never interfere with the media. But many people in tight cultures actually embrace these restrictions. A 2008 Pew Research Center survey showed that over 80 percent of respondents in China think the Internet *should* be managed or controlled by the government. This reflects a broader trend: People in tight cultures believe that the most important responsibility of government is to maintain order, and they support strong leaders who do so, even if it means sacrificing some personal freedom.

With a huge marketplace of ideas and encouragement to challenge the status quo, cultural change can happen much more quickly in loose cultures than tight cultures. In fact, it's something artificial intelligence experts Dana Nau and Soham De and I have shown with computer simulations. When we introduced new norms that would give a population more benefits—analogous to better economic or social conditions— tight groups resisted the changes for much longer than loose groups.

Beyond the confines of artificial laboratory simulations, tight cultures react to change with great resistance. I visit Jordan frequently to do research on terrorism (I'll speak more about the connection between tightness-looseness and terrorism in Chapter 10). In 2016, Jordan's Ministry of Education rolled out a new school curriculum in an effort to promote tolerance and reduce radicalization among the country's youth. The changes were designed to foster a sense of acceptance toward non-Muslims: Pictures of women without the hijab, men without facial hair, and men vacuuming were added to textbooks, which retained a dominant Islamic point of view. The hope was these tweaks would immunize Jordanians against extremist ideologies, said Mohammed Momani, a government spokesperson for the project. But the effort completely backfired. Many viewed the changes as an attack on Islamic values. The teachers' union told educators to disregard the changes, and in the city of Amman, some educators burned the new textbooks, chanting, "We will teach them what we want." In this tight culture, the modifications were too threatening to the existing social order.

Tight societies have cornered the market on social order, synchrony, and self-regulation. Loose societies have made their own gains in achieving tolerance, creativity, and openness to change. Both invariably have potential assets and liabilities, as shown in Figure 3.6.

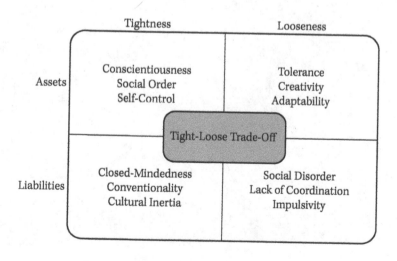

Figure 3.6. Tight-loose trade-off.

Of course, exploring the various trade-offs of tight and loose mindsets is not to suggest that all cultures have these respective characteristics. Take height and weight. To a very large degree, taller people weigh more. Yet each of us knows a tall person who is thin and a short person who is heavy. Tight-loose dynamics work the same way. Not all tight and loose cultures exhibit all of these trade-offs, but many do.

But why do these deep differences exist in the first place? Tight and loose countries aren't united by obvious qualities. They're not similar in terms of their location: The tight countries of Japan, Germany, Norway, Singapore, and Pakistan are all scattered around the planet, as are the loose countries of Netherlands, Brazil, Greece, and New Zealand. Groups of tight or loose countries don't speak the same language. They don't share any common religion or tradition. Tight countries aren't all the same age, nor are loose ones. Some, like Sparta and Singapore, or New Zealand and Athens, are separated by over two thousand years. What, then, *do* they have in common?

4

Disaster, Disease, and Diversity

The strength of a culture's norms and punishments isn't random. It has a secret logic that has been hiding in plain sight.

Though they were separated by miles and, in some cases, decades or centuries, the tight cultures of Sparta, the Nahua, and Singapore faced a common fate: Each had (or has) to deal with a high degree of threat, whether from Mother Nature and her constant fury of disasters, diseases, and food scarcity, or from human nature and the chaos caused by invasions and internal conflicts. And when we look at the loose cultures of New Zealand, Athens, and the Copper Inuit, we see the opposite pattern: These groups had (or have) the luxury of facing far fewer threats. They generally had the safety to explore new ideas, accept newcomers, and tolerate a wide range of behavior.

Herein lies the hidden rationale behind tight and loose cultures: Whether they dwelled in the ancient past or exist in the modern era, groups that deal with many ecological and historical threats need to do everything they can to create order in the face of chaos. Take, for example, societies like the Nahua, which are highly dependent on agriculture for their survival. When crops are bountiful, life is good. When there's a lasting drought, life is unpredictable and harsh; people suffer and die. It stands to reason that groups that are disciplined and that punish people who don't follow norms are better able to coordinate to cultivate crops and increase their chances of survival. By contrast, hunter-gatherers like the Inuit are highly self-reliant, with each family being responsible for foraging food; consequently, they don't have to coordinate their efforts. Strong rules and punishments, in effect, aren't as necessary. Beyond the Nahua and Inuit, many other groups show this same cultural logic. The Temne people of Sierra Leone, for example, rely on agricultural output for survival and thus require strict conformity to their rules, whereas the Eskimo of Baffin Island, a hunting society, allow members considerably more latitude.

Food, of course, is just one of many basic resources that human groups depend on for survival. Groups must protect themselves from many other threats besides starvation, including natural disasters, territorial threats, overpopulation, scarce natural resources, and pathogens. In fact, considering the innumerable wars that have taken place, the frequency of Mother Nature's fury, and the number of communicable diseases that have existed, it's a wonder that humans have been able to survive. How did they do it?

The emergence of social norms—a particularly human invention—is the key to this evolutionary puzzle. Strong norms are needed to cultivate the societal order that is necessary for surviving the most difficult circumstances. In contexts where there are fewer threats and thus less of a need for coordination, strong norms don't materialize.

SQUEEZED IN

Think about a time when you were packed into a crowded elevator. How did you feel and act? You were probably monitoring your behavior, trying not to fidget too much, or suppressing a laugh at something funny you were thinking about. Maybe you were irritated by fellow passengers doing weird things, like singing with their headphones on, taking up too much room, or divulging personal details to a friend on the phone.

Some countries are a lot like that crowded elevator. People live in small spaces in close proximity to their neighbors, contending with packed streets and cheek-to-jowl buses and trains. Compare Singapore, with its astonishing population density of over twenty thousand people per square mile as of 2016, with Iceland, which has only eight people per square mile. Or imagine being in Japan, with over eight hundred people per square mile, as compared with New Zealand, where there are more sheep than people (about six sheep per person, to be precise) and about forty-five people per square mile.

Population density varies dramatically around the globe. In many countries, it's dictated by topography or other geographical features. India is a case in point. The country has an impressively high population density of over a thousand people per square mile. The Himalayas, which comprise about 16 percent of India's territorial area, are far too cold for humans to survive. Because flatter areas have better access to water, which is ideal for human settlement, they've ended up with the most inhabitants. Similarly, given that around 70 percent of Japan is covered in uninhabitable mountains, and less than 15 percent of it is suitable for agriculture, residents cope with very little space. Switzerland, one of the most mountainous areas in Europe—and home to the Alps, which cover three-fifths of the country—copes with a high population density of over five hundred people per square mile.

High population density is a basic human threat. In societies where personal space is hard to come by, there's great potential for chaos and conflict. Even lab rats have been found to get stressed out when forced

Figure 4.I. Crowded street in Calcutta, India.

to live in close quarters: Female rats have more trouble carrying pregnancies to term, and male rats show symptoms ranging from sexual deviance to cannibalism.

Fortunately, humans, unlike rats, evolved to create strong social norms to minimize conflict and organize chaos when they're packed in tight, so they don't have to resort to cannibalism or other antisocial behaviors. Meanwhile, societies with low population density (such as Australia, Brazil, Venezuela, and New Zealand) can afford to be much looser. I've found that nations evolve this way: Areas that were populous in 1500, such as Pakistan and India, are tighter today, while Australia and Brazil, the least populous areas studied in 1500, are currently two of the loosest countries. Present-day population density, as well as predicted future population pressures, are also linked to countries' tightness scores. In short, the more packed in you are as a country, the stronger your rules.

The effects of population density trickle down and affect seemingly arbitrary aspects of society. Let's revisit Singapore's ban on selling gum. It seems preposterous to most outsiders, but the country's high population density suggests why this ban makes sense. During the 1980s, city workers struggled to keep up with cleaning chewing gum waste, which became a public crisis. The sticky wads gummed up mailboxes and elevator buttons, and even jammed apartment keyholes and the sensors on commuter train doors, causing frequent malfunctions. In a place with so many mouths per square mile, the solution was simple: Get rid of the temptation. By 1992, the sale of gum was prohibited in Singapore, and people caught selling the chewy treat faced hefty fines. The ban led to some frustration at first, but today it's widely upheld. And if you lived among more than twenty thousand people per square mile, chances are that you'd support it, too.

BARBARIANS AT THE GATE

When you look at a map of the world, there are some striking differences between nations that have and have not experienced chronic threats of invasion. In his book *The Revenge of Geography*, Robert Kaplan reminds us that the United States—with its safe separation from other continents by two large oceans—has felt few threats from outsiders throughout its history. The same is also true of New Zealand and Australia. Of course, these nations have had their share of traumatic conflict, but, overall, they haven't faced chronic threats from external forces trying to bust down their doors.

But other modern nations have had conflict on their soil for centuries. Take Germany. The Thirty Years' War in the early seventeenth century killed off 20 percent of Germany's (then Prussian) population; the Franco-Prussian War left tens of thousands of German soldiers dead; and the Soviet occupation of East Germany resulted in almost eleven million Germans displaced by 1950, more than six hundred thousand killed, and over two million who remain unaccounted for.

Conflict has been particularly prevalent in Asia. China has experienced massive conflict throughout its history, with an exceedingly long list of battles beginning in 206 BC during the Han Dynasty, extending into the Yuan and Ming Dynasties, and later into the Qing Dynasty (1644–1912). Thereafter, during the Second Sino-Japanese War (1937–1945), China suffered millions of deaths, widespread starvation, and devastation to its infrastructure. Today, China's location makes territorial threat a constant source of anxiety. It borders fourteen countries, and has had disputes with each of them.

Korea also has been repeatedly clobbered by its neighbors. The famous Korean proverb "When whales fight, the shrimp's back is broken" describes South Korea's predicament of being collateral damage over the course of many centuries while its neighboring countries have fought one another. Korea was invaded by Japan in the late 1500s and the Manchus in the early 1600s, and was the fighting ground for the beginning of the First Sino-Japanese War in the 1890s. In more recent history, Korea suffered under Japanese rule from 1910 to 1945, and later, more than a million South Korean civilians and military personnel died in the Korean War, which lasted from 1950 to 1953.

Countries in the Middle East have repeatedly faced invasions and colonization from foreign powers. Since the decline of its pharaohs many centuries ago, Egypt has endured the wrath of the Turks, Persians, Romans, Arabs, Greeks, French, and English. Both Pakistan and India have histories rife with conflicts on their own soil. India has had significant violent conflicts with Pakistan and China regarding contested territories, and Pakistan has had numerous border disputes with Afghanistan.

How could inhabitants of these countries best survive such hostile conditions? Nations with a history of external conflict, I speculated, would by necessity evolve to be tighter.

When nations face the possibility of invasion, they must strengthen internal order to ensure a united, coordinated front against the enemy. Tight social norms are essential to this defense. Presumably, in the past, groups that didn't have strong norms or punish norm violators would be at risk of buckling under these chronic high-pressure situations. "The exigencies of war with outsiders are what make peace inside, lest internal discord should weaken the we-group for war," remarked the American social scientist William Graham Sumner in 1906. Darwin himself also speculated that war with outsiders would create evolutionary pressures for cooperation and unity.

I set out to see if, indeed, there was a connection between a country's level of tightness and its history of territorial threat. Using the International Crisis Behavior database, I found data on territorial conflicts between nations between 1918 and 2001. My hypothesis was very specific: I speculated that the threat of conflict on a nation's *own* territory—not the overall amount of conflict the nation is involved with *abroad*—would, over the last century, correlate with strength of social norms.

Even when taking into account nations' wealth, I found that nations with a higher number of territorial threats over the last hundred years indeed were tighter than those with fewer territorial threats. India, China, and Pakistan had high levels of territorial threat and were some of the tightest among the nations surveyed. Meanwhile, New Zealand and the United States were low in territorial threat and high in looseness. Notably, even though the United States scores high on involvement in international conflicts abroad, this tendency to be the "world's policeman" does not correlate at all with tightness.

MOTHER NATURE'S FURY

Groups don't only have to deal with *human* threats of internal and external conflict. They also have to face *natural* threats: droughts, floods, landslides, tsunamis, typhoons, cyclones, volcanic eruptions, and earthquakes. China, for example, has lost nearly 450,000 lives in the past fifty years to natural disasters (twenty-five times more than the United States), in part due to the typhoons that torment its long coastline. India loses about $10 billion each year due to disasters, including droughts, landslides, flash floods, and cyclones. Indonesia's seventeen thousand islands are located between the world's two most seismically active areas, the Pacific Ring of Fire and the Alpide Belt, making them vulnerable to some of the world's worst natural disasters, including earthquakes.

Japan has also been one of Mother Nature's favorite targets. Throughout its history, Japan has experienced an onslaught of natural disasters. A combination of cold weather and volcanic activity led to the Kangi Famine from 1229 to 1232. During the Edo Period (1603–1868), more than 150 famines hit Japan, leaving at least hundreds of thousands dead. In the modern era, Japan has suffered from several devastating earthquakes, including the 2011 magnitude-nine Tohoku earthquake and tsunami, which killed thousands of people and cost Japan over $200 billion. Millions of survivors were forced to cope without water, heat, or food for days.

Nations like Japan need stronger norms to provide the order and coordination required to recover from chronic natural disasters. Without strong norms, people would be tempted to go rogue in such dire circumstances—looking out only for themselves or their immediate family, for example, by engaging in looting—causing total chaos. But with strong norms and punishments for deviance, such nations are in a much better position to cope and survive.

As a case in point, after the 1995 Kobe earthquake, over one million people stepped up to help those in need. After the 2011 Tohoku earthquake, volunteer administrators were so overwhelmed by offers of aid from ordinary citizens that they had to turn some away. Even the Japanese mafia—the yakuza—helped with relief efforts, sending in supply trucks and offering refuge to stranded victims. This impressive solidarity in response to natural disasters isn't unique to Japan. Other countries, including Malaysia—another tight nation prone to floods, tsunamis, landslides, forest fires, and cyclones—have had to come together as a well-coordinated nation in the face of disasters. Strong norms and punishments help in this quest.

By contrast, cultures that don't face chronic disasters don't necessarily *need* to have such a well-coordinated cultural machine, and thus can afford to be loose. Data I've analyzed support this hypothesis: Vulnerability to natural disasters, as measured by the Environmental Sustainability Index, correlates strongly with tightness, even accounting for national wealth. Japan, South Korea, and Pakistan—some of the most disaster-plagued nations—are also among the tightest. By contrast, nations like Ukraine, Hungary, and Greece, which have remained relatively unscathed by natural disasters, have looser norms.

SCARCITY

Frequent disasters have other devastating consequences. They often deplete natural resources, including arable land and drinking water supplies. Our data suggest that cultures that lack such resources are tighter than cultures that have them in abundance. The reason is simple: When cultures have few natural resources, managing them in a controlled, coordinated way is a matter of survival.

Here again, Singapore, a tight culture, is a case in point. "We faced tremendous odds with an improbable chance of survival. Singapore was not a natural country, but man-made," writes Lee Kuan Yew, the founding father of modern Singapore, in his autobiography. Commenting on the lack of natural resources, Lee further noted that forging a "tightly knit" society was crucial: "We had one simple guiding principle for our survival, that Singapore had to be more rugged, better organized, and more efficient than others in the region."

Lee was not a cross-cultural psychologist, but he had the right intuition. With data from the United Nations and other sources on arable land, food production, food supply, protein and fat supply, food deprivation, air quality, and water quality, we can see whether tight cultures have a lack of natural resources. The results show that countries cursed with fewer natural resources—from farmland to food supply to water—are much tighter than those blessed with abundance. Of the nations I surveyed, Pakistan, India, and China, all tight, had the fewest natural resources within their territories, with high levels of food deprivation and low access to safe water. Similarly, Norway, Hong Kong, and Singapore had the smallest amounts of farmland, while Hungary, loose in our data, had abundant farmland. Israel is barely bigger than New Jersey, but it ranks as the lowest for food deprivation. Societies reasonably react to a lack of natural resources by tightening social norms, which provides more order where there could be chaos.

DISEASE

Anyone who has seen the movie *Contagion* immediately cringes at the thought of little microbes spreading to decimate large populations, and with good reason: The plot wasn't just dreamed up by Hollywood screenwriters. Infectious diseases have menaced humans for as long as we've been on the planet. For thousands of years, large percentages of populations were regularly wiped out by diseases. The plague known as the "Black Death" killed at least seventy-five million people during the fourteenth century. Typhus claimed over ten million lives in the 1600s. Yellow fever killed tens of thousands during Napoleon's reign. A smallpox outbreak led hundreds of thousands of people to perish at the end of the eighteenth century, and the Spanish flu caused as many as fifty million deaths in the early twentieth century. Indeed, throughout history, pathogens that were brought by groups to new territories often wiped out entire populations who lacked immunity to them, as discussed in Jared Diamond's critically acclaimed book *Guns, Germs, and Steel.*

Today, advances in modern medicine have dramatically reduced the risk of death from pathogens, but societies still aren't invincible to viral diseases. An estimated thirty-five million people have been killed by AIDS, and more than thirty million people globally have died from tuberculosis-related illnesses since it was declared a global emergency by the World Health Organization in 1993. And to this day, millions of people contract malaria. With more than 200 million cases in 2016 alone, malaria remains a menace worldwide.

From an evolutionary perspective, humans needed to find ways to survive these threats. Our bodies did so by perfecting sophisticated physiological immune responses. In modern societies, we have likewise developed cutting-edge technologies to try to contain pathogens, including antibiotics, water treatments, infectious disease modeling, genomics, and electronic surveillance systems. Even food customs have also evolved in countries where infectious diseases have been rampant, such as dousing food with spices that can act as powerful antibiotics that kill off nasty bacteria.

Strong social norms turn out to be another shield for stopping germs. For example, when people feel more vulnerable to diseases, they tend to have a higher sense of cultural superiority and have more negative views toward other ethnic groups, presumably to avoid the transmission of diseases. And research shows that in times of high levels of disease threat and infant mortality, parents teach their children to be compliant and obedient. By restricting the range of permissible behavior, strong social norms help thwart the spread of disease and help people mount a coordinated response if and when outbreaks strike. By contrast, loose norms, which allow for permissiveness and exploration, can promote risky behaviors that expose people to deadly pathogens and thwart an effective response.

Singapore's response to the 2003 SARS outbreak is a case in point. Soon after SARS hit, the Singaporean government quickly implemented strict rules and restrictions on people's movement and somewhat intrusive early-detection measures, such as monitoring people's temperature at schools, work, and households (thermometers were distributed to over a million people). Webcams were even installed in the homes of quarantined citizens, who were phoned at random points during the day and required to present themselves in front of the camera to ensure they didn't leave home. Similarly, following the 2009 influenza outbreak in Japan, officials quickly set up medical counseling and outpatient centers to detect and prevent the spread of the virus. They also enacted temporary school closures, border screening at airports, and influenza surveillance systems throughout cities.

While this level of monitoring and restrictions may seem excessive to outsiders, they help countries with a history of pathogen outbreaks to avoid contamination. Across 230 geopolitical regions dating back to the 1940s, I've found that tighter countries, including Pakistan, India, Turkey, and Malaysia, have indeed been more burdened by infectious diseases, from malaria to typhus to tuberculosis, than loose countries such as Australia, Greece, Hungary, and Poland.

In all, the data show that many ecological and human threats—

from conflict to Mother Nature's fury—are related to tightness-looseness. Indeed, the link between threat and tightness isn't just found in modern nations—we've found it in our studies of traditional societies as well. Of course, physical threats are not the only ones that might drive tightness. In other cases, the "threat" that impels social order may be spiritual in nature. Nearly all religious traditions include extensive and detailed prohibitions to keep believers from engaging in behaviors that might threaten their purity and even afterlife. Religion tends to breed tightness, both today and in ancient history, according to our data. Beyond the codification of right and wrong, the belief in the Almighty inculcates the same tight accountability that security cameras bring to public spaces.

TEMPORARILY TIGHTENING UP

Societies evolve to be tighter when they face chronic threats over the course of many years, but I've shown they also tighten up when they face a sudden collective threat—even if it's short-lived. In 2013, right after the Boston Marathon bombing, which left three dead and more than a hundred wounded, Bostonians showed incredible unity, with many residents rushing to the site of the attack to help those lost or injured. Some marathon participants kept running past the finish line to the closest hospital to donate blood. After this tragedy, the phrase "Boston Strong" took hold as a symbol of the city's cohesion, strength, and pride.

I set up a field study in Boston to test whether the city's cultural norms had tightened in response to the event. People who reported being the most affected by the bombings were indeed more likely to report that the United States needed to have stronger social norms. They also reported that the American way of life needs to be protected against foreign influence, there should be more restrictions over people entering the country, and the United States is superior to other countries. These are all attitudes we see in nations that face chronic invasions.

Even the fear of a threat induced in the lab is sufficient for people to tighten up. In one study, I randomly assigned people to read one of two versions of a fictitious news article. Some read that their university was implementing a new terror alert system due to its proximity to the nation's capital, which could be attacked. Others in the study read that a foreign university was implementing a new terror alert system but that their university had rejected this proposal, given strong evidence *against* the school's becoming a target of terror. Compared with the students who read that their campus was safe, those who read that a terrorist attack was possible became significantly more biased against people who were seen as "deviant" and more likely to rate their culture as superior to others.

The fear of threat can even cause people's *brains* to sync up to help them coordinate. In a study we conducted in China, my research team and I designed three fictitious articles, which our participants thought were real. Some of our Chinese participants read an article about how Japan posed a severe threat to China in the coming decade, while others read an article about a conflict between two other countries (Ethiopia and Eritrea) or an article about China, but without any mention of external threat. Then, participants in each group were given a task that required them to coordinate quickly—namely, they had to count out loud at the exact same pace together, over many trials. During this task, we used a state-of-the-art neuroscience technique called "hyperscanning" to simultaneously record the brain waves of the interacting partners. When we analyzed our data, we found that Chinese who'd read about a threat from Japan showed higher *neural synchrony*—

specifically in their gamma waves, which signify fear—and this helped them coordinate faster on the task. People's neurons, it seems, begin to march in sync under external threat.

Even people who are made to feel like there's high population density in their immediate environment—like in Singapore—become tighter, at least temporarily. In another experiment, students at the University of Maryland were given one of two versions of a fictitious article purported to be from the school newspaper. Both articles gave a detailed ranking of population density of ten different U.S. universities from the most to the least dense, but with one small twist. In one condition, students read that UMD had the highest population density of all campuses listed, with a whopping 1,500 people per square mile. In another condition, they read that UMD had one of the lowest population densities—a mere 440 people per square mile. Next, we asked the students to evaluate a variety of norm violations on campus, such as littering in public places, fighting at a sports game, talking loudly at the library, or driving under the influence of alcohol. Across the board, those who thought they were going to school on a crowded campus had more negative reactions to people breaking norms. Just by suggesting their environment had very high density, we induced these Americans to become tighter like Singaporeans, at least temporarily.

In 2011, I took this "threat priming" paradigm into the field. When the previously mentioned pathogen-scare movie *Contagion* hit the movie theaters, I planted research assistants outside movie theaters all around Washington, D.C., to study people's reactions. *Contagion* wasn't just a big box-office hit; it was commended by scientists for its realism. It actually made viewers feel that they were part of a pandemic. I decided to take advantage of this feeling by surveying people who'd either just seen the film, or were about to see it. Sure enough, people who'd just seen the film and virtually experienced a pandemic showed more hostility toward social deviants than people who hadn't yet entered the theater.

These studies show that activating a threat can temporarily tighten the mind, in much the same manner that chronic threats cause tight cultures. It's only when a threat subsides that our need for strong norms subsides. Indeed, our computer simulations of how groups respond to threat show exactly this: A temporary increase in threat can cause a dramatic rise in tightness, but groups will revert to looseness unless the threat recurs.

Importantly, this research highlights that tightness-looseness is dynamic—it can change over time. As threats crop up, groups tighten. As threats subside, groups loosen. Threats don't even need to be real. As long as people perceive a threat, the perception can be as powerful as objective reality. In fact, long before Donald Trump, Marine Le Pen, or Viktor Orbán, politicians have been hyping up threats to tighten groups for centuries.

LEVERS OF LOOSENESS

Threat might be one of the biggest drivers of cultural tightness. But other factors can pull cultures in the opposite direction.

As a general rule, diversity exposes people to multiple perspectives and ultimately makes us more tolerant of a wider range of behaviors. Take Israel, for example. Crammed into just over eight thousand square miles are nearly 8.6 million people—that's about a thousand people per square mile. When Israel was founded, its settlers faced rampant malaria, typhus, and cholera. The country has fought numerous wars, mostly due to territorial issues and the long-held animosity between Arabs and Israelis, which continues to this day. Yet Israel is relatively loose, with its high levels of informality and chronic attempts to circumvent rules. Why?

There are multiple possibilities, but one stands out as especially compelling: Israel is highly diverse. Seventy-five percent of the nation is Jewish, 20 percent is Arab, and the remaining 5 percent are a mix of non-Arab Christian and Baha'i, among other groups. The country has high levels of ethnic diversity, with significant percentages of the citizenry hailing from Eastern Europe, Africa, and the Middle East. With so many different groups with different coexisting norms, it is hard to agree on any one standard for behavior. This general principle also applies to the traditional societies we encountered in Chapter 2. Ancient Athens, a bastion of looseness, also had encounters with many foreign countries thanks to its extensive trading.

Does diversity correlate with a country's looseness? Our data suggest that it does, at least up to a point. Nations that are heterogeneous on multiple markers, such as ethnicity and language, are much looser than those that are homogeneous, we've found, but an important caveat is in order. When diversity gets to be extreme, as it is in Pakistan, which has at least six major ethnic groups and over twenty spoken languages, and India, with its twenty-two official languages and hundreds of dialects, diversity can cause conflict, which, as we know, requires strict norms to manage. When diversity gets to be very high, tightness begins to increase markedly.

Another possible explanation for Israel's relative looseness is its fierce tradition of debate. As the joke goes, a Jew was asked by a non-Jew why Jews always answer a question with another question. "Why not?" he replied. Debate and dissent, which mandate the exploration of multiple perspectives, promote looseness and the rejection of dogma. (To quote another popular adage: Ask two Jews, get three

73

opinions.) In addition, Israel is a young, exploratory "start-up nation" made up of settlers who had the chutzpah to dive into something new, risky, and unknown.

Like Israel, the Netherlands also evolved to be quite loose, in part due to its history of high levels of mobility and exposure to multiculturalism. Its coastal location has promoted extensive travel among its citizens and a high dependency on international trade, giving the Dutch centuries of rich experiences with other cultures. The Dutch traded with France, Portugal, and countries around the Baltic Sea and the Mediterranean. Trade with Spain likewise flourished, and the Dutch controlled much of the trade with the English colonies in North America. With its tremendous mobility around the world and exposure to many different cultures, the Netherlands evolved to be tolerant. When the sale of books was restricted throughout Europe during the seventeenth century, booksellers flocked to the Netherlands, where censorship laws were far less strict. It's also perhaps no surprise that the world's first multinational corporation, the Dutch East India Company (VOC), which commercially linked the East and West through the seventeenth and eighteenth centuries, was also founded in the Netherlands.

Thanks in large part to its location and trading activity, the Netherlands has become home to an eclectic mix of ethnic, racial, and religious groups, which may have contributed to its looseness. For centuries, the Netherlands welcomed refugees from all over Europe, including French Protestants, Portuguese and German Jews, and English separatists, among many others. Today, over 20 percent of the population comes from abroad, including from other European countries, Indonesia, Turkey, Suriname, Morocco, and the Caribbean. The Netherlands is a veritable melting pot.

Tightness and looseness can evolve in different ways, but the outcome isn't random. Ecological and historical threats—real or perceived—push groups to be tighter, while diversity, mobility, and multicultural contact with outsiders foster looseness. Of course, these relationships aren't deterministic—they're only statistically probabilistic—and they needn't be the only factors that affect norm strength. But they help detect important patterns that have long remained hidden.

PART II

Analysis: Tight-Loose Here, There, and Everywhere

5

The War Between America's States

In November 2016, the U.S. presidential election shocked the world. Billionaire real-estate developer, businessman, and former reality TV star Donald Trump defeated Hillary Clinton, an attorney and former secretary of state, senator, and first lady, in a caustic race that virtually every poll had projected Clinton to win. The contest took America's state of polarization—already severe—to DEFCON 1. Exit poll data on Election Day showed tremendous divisions across class, race, gender, age, education, income, and religion on issues such as foreign policy and immigration. Pew Research found that half of Democrats and Republicans said they were literally "afraid" of the members of the other party. While millions of Americans couldn't fathom the idea of a Trump presidency, millions of others were horrified by the notion of a Clinton presidency. Trump supporters regularly chanted, "Lock her up!" at rallies; Clinton backers swore they'd move abroad if Trump were elected. Both candidates ultimately engendered unprecedented levels of dislike that shattered the illusion of a "united" fifty states.

Why are Americans so divided? For decades, political analysts, pundits, and academics have grappled with understanding America's schisms. Back in 1992, during his presidential campaign, conservative firebrand Pat Buchanan likened America's irreconcilable disunity to a "culture war" between conservatives and progressives. Others have nominated a number of possible root causes of America's fissures: urban versus rural, red versus blue, believers versus nonbelievers, universalists versus multiculturalists, populists versus elites, and so on. While all provide valuable insight and partial explanations, none gives the full picture or describes exactly *why* these divides exist in the first place.

Tight-loose is a key substructure for many of these tensions. This simple principle allows us to grasp the immense complexity of America's deep cultural divisions. Moreover, it shows us where these differences come from—tracing them back to the founding conditions and ecology of the fifty states that persist to this day. Tightness-looseness can also explain a swath of differences between American states that previously seemed unconnected. The tight-loose divide reveals, for example:

- ▶ Why alcohol abuse and debt are more common in New Hampshire and Connecticut than in Indiana and Tennessee, but discrimination rates are much higher in the latter two states.
- ▶ Why Oregon and Vermont show high levels of creativity but also high levels of divorce and mobility, whereas Kentucky and North Dakota show the opposite pattern.
- ▶ Why people in Colorado and New York score high on trait openness but low on trait conscientiousness, while people in Kansas and Alabama show the reverse personality profile.
- ▶ Why Arizona is more anti-immigration than New York, even though both states have roughly the same population of illegal immigrants.

► Why the startling outcome of the 2016 presidential election has more to do with cultural forces than a mesmerizing personality.

A DIFFERENT KIND OF MAP

As a nation of immigrants, the United States was predisposed to be a relatively loose nation. The very definition of a melting pot, America was formed by a motley collection of immigrants, united only by their sense of adventure, independent spirit, and thirst for freedom. Separated from other continents by two oceans, the country has faced little threat of invasion throughout its history and is blessed with abundant natural resources. Consequently, the United States has generally enjoyed the luxury of permissive rules and relaxed punishments.

Yet within the context of this general looseness, forces of tightness have surfaced throughout American history. To quantify levels of tight-loose across the fifty states, Jesse Harrington and I scoured research institutes and the Smithsonian archives for data on each state going back to the early 1800s, including records on punishment methods, state restrictions, cultural practices, and ecological and historical events. The patterns we discovered (which were published in the *Proceedings of the National Academy of Sciences*) were illuminating.

Take, for example, differences in the harshness of punishments across states. Compared with Alaska and Maine, Indiana and Texas spank far more students, execute more criminals, and punish marijuana possession more harshly. In 2011 alone, over twenty-eight thousand students were paddled or spanked in Texas schools. Meanwhile, in some public schools in Indiana, students must obey strict dress codes—no T-shirts, denim pants, or untucked shirts—or risk facing suspension.

Other states follow this "rule making" pattern: Sex toys have been criminalized in Alabama since 1998, tattoos were banned in Oklahoma in 1963 (and only legalized in 2006), and in Mississippi, you can be fined up to a hundred dollars for swearing in public. Kentucky and Utah have many more dry counties and more marriage restrictions relative to California and Hawaii. And just as some nations exhibit very little diversity within their borders, the same is true of some of the fifty states. Going as far back as 1860, states such as Montana, North Dakota, and West Virginia have had a much lower foreign population relative to places like Nevada, New Jersey, and California.

These differences aren't isolated trends. In fact, our research shows that these indicators all hang together. In states where children are more likely to be hit in school, there are higher rates of executions, more restrictions on alcohol, sterner views of marriage, fewer foreigners, and so on. These states are stricter—they're tight, *rule makers*. Meanwhile, states with more lenient punishments also have fewer restrictions on alcohol and marriage and have more foreigners. These states have more latitude—they're loose, *rule breakers*.

Figure 5.1 shows the tight-loose map of the United States. Some of the tightest states in the country include Mississippi, Alabama, Arkansas, Oklahoma, Tennessee, and Texas. At the looser end of the spectrum are California, Oregon, Washington, Nevada, Maine, and Massachusetts. Delaware, Iowa, Idaho, Nebraska, Florida, and Minnesota fall in the middle. From these rankings, regional patterns emerge: The South is tightest, the West and Northeast are loosest, and the Midwest is in the middle. You can see each state's tight-loose score in Table 5.1.

As with the global map, tightness-looseness provides a new way of understanding the culture within the United States. Levels of tightness-looseness in the fifty states are distinct from whether states are collectivist (emphasize family ties) or individualist (emphasize self-reliance).

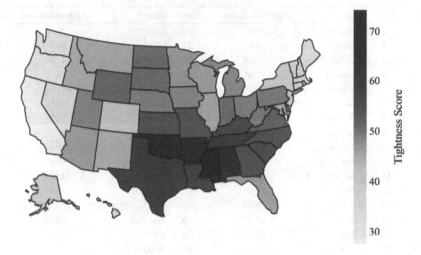

Figure 5.I. Tight-loose map of the United States.

In fact, states fall into each of the four quadrants—collectivist and tight (Texas), collectivist and loose (Hawaii), individualist and loose (Vermont), and individualist and tight (Kansas). Likewise, while there are connections between tightness and conservatism, on the one hand, and looseness and liberalism, on the other, the concepts are distinct. Conservatism reflects individuals' emphasis on traditional values and often manifests as resistance to change, whereas tightness is a state of *culture* that reflects the strength of social norms in one's environment. While tight states and countries have more conservatives and loose states and countries have more liberals, there are plenty of conservatives in loose regions and plenty of liberals in tight ones.

In fact, we've gotten so accustomed to referring to U.S. states as "red" and "blue" that we've forgotten how superficial this label is to a state's identity. Take three states that voted for Hillary Clinton in the 2016 presidential election: Hawaii, Illinois, and Virginia. Hawaii is loose, Illinois is fairly balanced, and Virginia is tight. Now take three

Rank	State	Tightness Score	Rank	State	Tightness Score
1	Mississippi	78.86	26	Iowa	49.02
2	Alabama	75.45	27	Michigan	48.93
3	Arkansas	75.03	28	Minnesota	47.84
4	Oklahoma	75.03	29	Arizona	47.56
5	Tennessee	68.81	30	Wisconsin	46.91
6	Texas	67.54	31	Montana	46.11
7	Louisiana	65.88	32	Illinois	45.95
8	Kentucky	63.91	33	Idaho	45.50
9	South Carolina	61.39	34	Maryland	45.50
10	North Carolina	60.67	35	New Mexico	45.43
11	Kansas	60.36	36	Rhode Island	43.23
12	Georgia	60.26	37	Colorado	42.92
13	Missouri	59.60	38	New Jersey	39.48
14	Virginia	57.37	39	New York	39.42
15	Indiana	54.57	40	Alaska	38.43
16	Pennsylvania	52.75	41	Vermont	37.23
17	West Virginia	52.48	42	New Hampshire	36.97
18	Ohio	52.30	43	Hawaii	36.49
19	Wyoming	51.94	44	Connecticut	36.37
20	North Dakota	51.44	45	Massachusetts	35.12
21	South Dakota	51.14	46	Maine	34.00
22	Delaware	51.02	47	Nevada	33.61
23	Utah	49.69	48	Washington	31.06
24	Nebraska	49.65	49	Oregon	30.07
25	Florida	49.28	50	California	27.37

Table 5.I. Tight-loose state-level rankings.

states that voted for Donald Trump: Alaska, Wisconsin, and South Carolina. Alaska is loose, Wisconsin is fairly balanced, and South Carolina is tight. As we'll see, the cultural differences between these voting allies are massive; sorting them by partisan leaning can badly distort their deeper identities. When we color America's map with shades of tight and loose instead of Republican red and Democratic blue, we start to see the hidden cultural logic behind—and the trade-offs involved with—the fifty states' distinctions and idiosyncrasies.

POLITE AND IN GOOD ORDER

I'm a native New Yorker, but I've lived in Washington, D.C., for twenty years. When I visit my hometown of New York, I'm immediately in sync with the chaotic pace, the public cursing and displays of affection, and the way people dash across red lights—even with kids in tow. But this state of mind can get me into trouble when I visit other states. In Kansas, if I venture into the street before the light turns, I hear grumbling behind me. When I take my kids skiing in tidy Park City, Utah, I'm hard pressed to find anyone cursing or losing their temper, and if I order a glass of wine in a restaurant, I'll also have to order food, according to Utah liquor laws. And in the South, where the politeness and friendliness I encounter blow me away, I have to control my natural "*You talkin' to me?*" New York response. It sometimes seems like people in some states are from Mars and others are from Venus.

I often assumed that people in different states have different personalities, but is that true? It wasn't just my intuition: Analyzing data from over a half million citizens, I found that the same personality profiles found in tight and loose nations are also detectable in tight and loose states. People in tight states are more likely to have a personality trait that psychologists call "conscientiousness," which entails self-discipline, rule following, and the desire for structure. These people report being more organized, careful, and dependable, and agree with statements such as "I see myself as someone who is a reliable worker," as someone who "makes plans and follows through with them," and as someone who "does things efficiently." By contrast, people in loose states report having less conscientiousness. More disorderly and less reliable (and honest enough to be self-critical!), they're more likely to agree that they can be "somewhat careless," "disorganized," and "easily distracted." It's true: If you spend time in states like North Carolina, Georgia, Utah, and Kansas, you'll generally find people who are more cautious, thorough, and orderly relative to people in loose states like Alaska, Maine, Hawaii, and Rhode Island, as shown below (New Mexico, a generally loose state, is an exception).

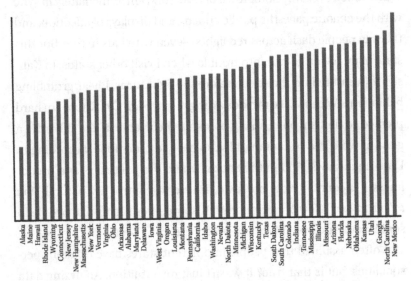

Figure 5.2. Personality conscientiousness increases as state tightness increases.

Beyond the individual discipline that shows up in tight state personality profiles, there is, in fact, also greater *social order* in these states. In the South, home to the tightest U.S. states, strong rules about etiquette, hospitality, formality, and, above all, respect prevail. Children learn to say "yes, ma'am" and "yes, sir" to adults and not to interrupt them. According to the *Encyclopedia of Southern Culture* (yes, such a text exists, in over twenty volumes), Southern lore warns children of the misfortunes that will afflict them if they forget their manners. For example, a young man who takes the last piece of food at the dinner table is told that he will never find a wife, and children who sing while they eat are warned that they will suffer from bad luck. For kids and grown-ups alike, proper behavior is an unstated requirement. Cursing is frowned upon. It's "ladies first" when it comes to entering buildings, receiving food or drinks, and getting on and off elevators. Modesty is the norm. If you seem a little too proud of yourself, the average Southerner might think you're "too big for your britches." Proper attire is also mandatory. Even at football games, it's not unusual to see Southern women in pearls and fancy dresses, or men in khakis and blazers.

To a Southerner, rude behavior can be a violation of honor—and one that demands strong punishment. In fact, psychologist Dov Cohen at the University of Illinois showed with hormonal measures that insults literally get under the skin of Southerners. In his experiments, research assistants were trained to insult Northern and Southern men in the laboratory (by calling them names like "you *asshole*"). Southerners reacted with a higher rise in cortisol, a hormone that indexes stress, as well as testosterone, a hormone that primes aggression in response to threat. It's no small wonder that people in the South try to avoid this kind of rude behavior in the first place.

As a New Yorker, I learned the hard way about the risks of insulting others in the tight South. In the mid-1990s, I was driving with my then boyfriend, now husband, on Interstate 95 in South Carolina. A car with a local license plate turned into our lane and slowed down right in front of us. Todd slammed the brakes, then passed the driver on the left, casually making an obscene gesture with the middle finger of his right hand. The driver proceeded to chase us down the highway for several miles, until Todd, noticing a rest stop, quickly crossed the grass median to escape. Much to our dismay, the driver followed us off the highway. At the rest stop, he pulled up to us, got out of his car, swore at us, and demanded an apology. At my urging, Todd eventually ceded to this demand, and we left the scene with a huge sigh of relief.

How could one minor gesture escalate into such a dangerous situation? To New Yorkers like me, showing that middle digit may be rude (okay, it *is* rude), but it isn't unusual. In fact, the *Village Voice* noted that New Yorkers are known for their "flamboyant, bird-flipping spirit." Everyday rudeness is not unusual, either. We New Yorkers take it in stride when people cut in line, bump into one another without apology, and shout on the street. New Yorkers speak so loudly that Amtrak now has quiet cars on most of its Northeast trains. Nevertheless, enforcement remains daunting: "The boorishness of noise polluters on these trains with their cellphones and their beeping musical computers is astonishing," commuter Alan M. Lieberman complained in the *New York Times*. New Yorkers' impudent behavior may well be exacerbated by the fact that rudeness is contagious. Psychologist Trevor Foulk and his collaborators from the University of Florida showed that if someone is rude to you, or even if you merely observe others being rude, you're more likely to behave rudely as well.

Rude behavior may be the normal M.O. in New York, but in our defense, we're not the only ones. The website TheTopTens polled thousands of site visitors on which U.S. states were the rudest. Their results were telling: Across the board, loose states ranked much ruder than tight states. New York was listed first as the "Most Rude," followed by Massachusetts and New Jersey. The least rude states leaned tight, such as North Carolina, Arkansas, and Wyoming.

Individuals' self-discipline in tight states extends far beyond how aggressively we act toward others. Like tight nations, residents of tight states are much better at regulating their behavior. For example, credit data I analyzed from TransUnion shows that residents of loose states are saddled with more debt than tight states, whether they have difficulty paying back their vehicle or education loans, managing their credit card debt, or paying their medical and utility bills in a timely manner. Drug use and binge drinking per capita are also lower in tight states like West Virginia, Mississippi, and Utah relative to loose states such as Rhode Island, Colorado, and New Hampshire (with the recent exception of opioids). By contrast, loose states have some of the most permissive attitudes around alcohol and psycho- active substances. Recreational marijuana use is now legal in nine states, all of them loose: Alaska, California, Colorado, Maine, Massa- chusetts, Oregon, Washington, Vermont, and Nevada. California has been nicknamed "America's cannabis bucket"; many marijuana entre- preneurs grow the plant large-scale on open farmlands. And in Wash- ington, Colorado, and Idaho, "419.99" mile markers on roads had to replace ones that read "420" because the signs kept getting stolen by pranksters on National Weed Day (April 20)!

THE NEIGHBORHOOD WATCH

At the national level, social norms are strongly enforced through a high degree of monitoring—whether from neighbors, police, or even reminders of the Almighty, all of which make people feel accountable for their behavior.

The same is true at the state level. States such as Mississippi, South Dakota, and Alabama have a higher percentage of rural areas and lower rates of mobility, compared to loose states such as Califor- nia, New Jersey, and Nevada. More rurality and less mobility produce an interesting cultural cocktail: You can bet that outside your home, neighbors and acquaintances know what you're doing, and they may have strong opinions about it. In these small, tight-knit communities, the neighborhood watch is on full alert. According to *Southern Liv- ing*, people in small towns often know whom every teenager is dating, which neighbors just made a large purchase, and even when the town mechanic has hired a new guy. The gossip mill, it turns out, has important social functions. For millennia, it has promoted cultural learning: Through gossip, we learn "how to behave—what to do and what not to do," according to psychologist Eric Foster. Gossip also serves as an informal policing mechanism. In towns where negative reputations can spread overnight, the fear of being bad-mouthed can help to deter bad behavior and promote cooperation.

Back-fence chatter is not the only social force patrolling tight communities. We've found that tight states tend to have more police and law enforcement officials, and citizens generally agree that the police should use strict punishment—including force—to keep the social order. Tight states also incarcerate a greater percentage of their populations. By contrast, in the urban and highly mobile areas common to loose states, you might pass thousands of strangers on your daily commute and find yourself living in relative anonymity, with little neighborly supervision. Other indicators of social disorder—such as higher divorce, single-parent households, and even homelessness— are higher in loose states.

In addition to cops or neighbors keeping community members in check, the supernatural has an undeniable and massive influence on tight states. Among Americans in tight states there is a remarkably high percentage of religious believers—80 percent in Kansas, for example. In Mississippi and South Carolina, among the most religious states in America, 83 percent and 78 percent of adults, respectively, are Christian. "Megachurches" with huge congregations of over two thousand people are found throughout the South (Lakewood Church in Houston tops them all, with more than fifty thousand attendees coming to worship each week), and Christian doctrine often leaks into public schools as well. In Texas, public school students can enroll in elective courses that teach morality lessons directly from the Bible. And since 1995, South Carolina has directed all public schools to provide a mandatory minute of silence every morning during which children pray.

Similarly, in Utah, over 60 percent of the population are Mormon, and strict regulations abound in their daily lives. Tea and coffee are banned at all times. Premarital sex is forbidden, as are pornography, masturbation, and homosexual acts. Sabbath Sunday is reserved for worship; working, shopping, eating out, playing sports, or other activities that may involve worldly temptations are not permitted. Bishops privately interview every adult Mormon to assess how well they've been adhering to the Mormon way of life and whether they're worthy of entering the temple. Much like an intelligence-gathering agency, the Mormon Church's Strengthening Church Members Committee (SCMC) keeps tabs on local Mormons to identify those who may be publicly criticizing the faith or its leadership. When it does, the SCMC promptly notifies the dissenter's bishop, who may charge the member with apostasy—the abandonment of religious faith.

It follows that tight states also uphold specific moral beliefs that reinforce their commitment to cultivating a norm-abiding culture. In his seminal book *The Righteous Mind*, social psychologist Jonathan Haidt discovered five foundational moral beliefs: harm to others, fairness, in-group loyalty, authority, and purity. Culture is a prime driver of differences in these moral foundations. Tight states defer to authorities more and have greater in-group loyalty than loose states. They are also more likely to aspire to a noble and pure lifestyle—or "a morality of purity." Purity means treating your body as a temple to be guarded from indecency—for example, by refraining from drug use and premarital sex (which—fun fact—is still illegal in Georgia, at least on the books). In contrast, in ultra-loose San Francisco, cars have been known to sport bumper stickers that read "Your Body's a Temple | Mine's an Amusement Park." People in tight states also report that they take a black-and-white view of what is right and wrong, while those in loose states see more shades of gray.

HOTBEDS OF INNOVATION AND TOLERANCE

Despite their relative lack of order and self-regulation problems, loose states, like loose nations, bring their own suite of advantages: openness, creativity, and adaptability. Using survey data we accessed from personality profiles of over half a million U.S. citizens, we found that people in loose states are more likely to view themselves as original, curious, deep thinkers, and imaginative—all indications of what is called "trait openness," as seen below.

No wonder, then, that the loose states are hotbeds of innovation. For starters, they generate far more patents for new inventions per capita, as seen in Figure 5.4. The first laser was built in California; the first portable

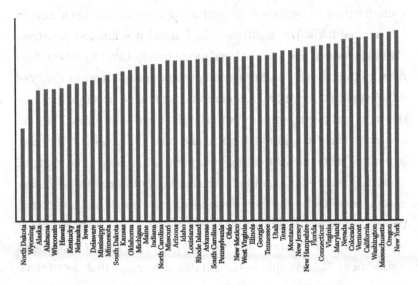

Figure 5.3. Personality openness increases as state looseness increases.

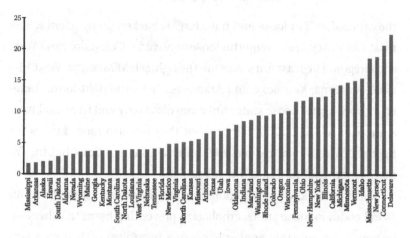

Figure 5.4. Patents per capita (1963–2011) by state.

fax machine and microwave oven were invented in Massachusetts; the first email was sent by a New Yorker; and the first washing machine was patented in New Hampshire—all loose states. Even the beloved game of Frisbee is a loose-state invention: The inspiration for the game came when Yale students started throwing around pie tins manufactured by Bridgeport, Connecticut's Frisbie Pie Company in 1871.

You'll also find that more creative types—including artists, painters, writers, and illustrators—per capita live in loose states. And people in loose states also seek out more creative experiences: They're far more likely to attend cultural events, read poetry and fiction, and watch or listen to arts programming at home. Their wider exposure to creative ideas surely promotes even greater openness and curiosity.

Along these lines, have you ever wondered which states are the most fun? Data analysts at WalletHub, a website that provides personal financing assistance, were determined to find out. They scored each of the fifty states on the strength of their recreational options (including amusement parks, movie theaters, beaches, and national parks) and nightlife (bars, music festivals, casinos, etc.). It turns out the expression "Let loose and have fun!" is backed up by science. The most fun states are among the loosest: Nevada, Colorado, New York, and Oregon. The least fun states are the tightest: Mississippi, West Virginia, Alabama, Kentucky, and Arkansas. Here's the tight-loose trade-off at work again: Loose states are more disorderly and rude, and have a litany of self-regulation failures, but they are also more fun; as for tight states, they may feature fewer entertainment options, but they're more orderly, polite, and self-regulated.

Not only are loose states more fun, but they're also more tolerant. Moral codes in loose states emphasize preventing harm to others—a universalistic code that applies to anyone, regardless of their race, language, religion, or creed. Indeed, the *Daily Beast* website created a tolerance score for each of the fifty states using a wide array of indicators, from hate crime incidents to level of religious tolerance. The scores were strongly related to our rankings of looseness. Using survey data from more than two thousand Americans across thirty-eight states, we also found that people in loose states were more likely to support interracial marriages between a white person and a minority, whether African American, Asian, or Hispanic, and they had more positive attitudes toward homosexuals.

Because these findings were based on surveys that directly asked people for their opinions, some may have hidden their overt prejudices. However, we found similar results when we evaluated people's hidden biases on a psychometric evaluation called the Implicit Association Task (IAT), where hiding one's true reactions is much more difficult. The IAT measures people's implicit prejudices based on their immediate responses to various stimuli. For instance, test-takers are instructed to categorize, as quickly as possible, a set of images as either "Good" or "Bad," and the images may be a mixture of words (such as *joy* or *awful*) as well as pictures depicting either "Gay People" (e.g., a same-sex couple holding hands) or "Straight People" (e.g., an opposite-sex couple holding hands). Categorizing images of a stigmatized group more quickly as "Bad" would suggest an implicit bias against, or stronger negative associations with, this group. We analyzed over three million Americans' implicit biases toward African Americans, the elderly, homosexuals, and the disabled, and found that people living in looser states possessed much lower implicit negative attitudes toward these groups than those in tighter states. Whether or not they're aware of it on a conscious level, people in tighter states are more likely to hold prejudices against members of stigmatized groups.

These overt and implicit attitudes toward difference translate into more equality in loose states, including higher percentages of minority-owned and female-owned firms, greater representation of women and minorities in public office, and stronger legal protections for traditionally stigmatized groups. One obvious inference to take from this is that if you have an identity that tends to be marginalized, you're better off living in a loose state. People with mental illness, for example, experience far better mental health care in loose states, as reflected in access to treatment, special education, jobs, and quality and cost of insurance. Tighter states, on the other hand, show greater discrimination across the board. The Equal Employment Opportunity Commission (EEOC) records far more employment discrimination cases per capita in tight states than loose states, as seen in Figure 5.5. In 2017 alone, 470 cases of discrimination were found in Massachusetts (.07 per capita), as compared with 2,144 in Missouri (.35 per capita), though the two states have similar population sizes and demographics.

Loose states, like loose nations, are also more open to immigrants. In the relatively tight state of Arizona, with some exceptions, undocumented residents cannot obtain their driver's licenses or receive the same in-state tuition rates at public colleges as legal residents. Meanwhile, in neighboring loose California, another state with a large population of immigrants from Mexico, immigrants have these benefits,

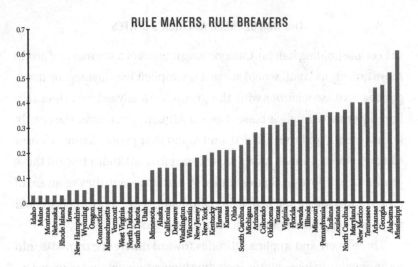

Figure 5.5. Equal Employment Opportunity Commission
discrimination charges per capita by state (2017).

and Governor Jerry Brown declared that all are welcome, regardless of their legal status. These different official stances reflect diverging views toward outsiders. In fact, residents of tight states are more likely to report that their states aren't good places for immigrants to live in. This negativity toward outsiders carries over to higher tight-state support for measures to "Buy American" or restrict imported products.

Adaptability is another asset of loose states, which have been the engines for social change in the United States. Historically, the Northeast has been a hotbed of progressive and unconventional movements, from transcendentalism to Unitarianism to women's suffrage. New York's Greenwich Village has served as "a magnet for cultural revolutionaries of all sorts: anarchist philosophers, free-verse poets, Cubist painters, feminists, gays, Freudian thinkers, hard-drinking writers, free-love playwrights, and idiosyncratic musicians," according to renowned historian Colin Woodard. Out west, loose California has consistently spearheaded social change. America's most populous state was the cofounder (along with New York and neighboring states on each coast) of the cultural revolution of the 1960s and the gay rights movement. On the flip side, tight states often resist social movements. In the late 1970s, tight states accounted for nearly 75 percent of the opposition *against* ratifying the Equal Rights Amendment, which would have banned discrimination based on gender.

THE FORCE OF THE FOUNDERS

Why did our differences develop in the first place? It might not be obvious, but differences in tightness-looseness across the fifty states were set in motion by the cultural characteristics of those who settled in different parts of the New World, and they've been evolving for centuries.

Let's go back in time to the 1700s, when large waves of migrants from northern Ireland and lowland Scotland began arriving in America. These migrants established an early presence around Pennsylvania and then moved southward, settling in states like West Virginia, the Carolinas, Georgia, Tennessee, Oklahoma, and Texas. There these pioneers unpacked their cultural suitcases, which were filled with the social norms and values of their motherlands. As descendants of Celtic herdsmen, they were known for their tight normative codes, which emphasized courage, strength, and a suspicion of outsiders—a combination of characteristics psychologists call a "culture of honor."

These cultural traits proved useful in the treacherous Southern environment they explored, where the threat of losing their livestock in raids from neighboring groups was constant. Given this danger, coupled with a lack of formal law enforcement, the settlers developed tight social norms to enforce cooperation and prevent pilfering. Norms for generosity and respect—which promoted group cohesion—were paramount. Settlers frequently entertained guests to showcase this generosity and to gain honor in the eyes of the community. These roots of "Southern hospitality" have persisted into the twenty-first century.

Yet despite their generosity and cooperation, these early settlers were ready to inflict quick and violent retribution on wrongdoers. Such demonstrations of valor helped them maintain a reputation for strength that could deter further attacks. Even teasing was considered a major norm violation in the South and could lead to an eruption of violence, particularly if one was insulted in public. The parents of Andrew Jackson, the seventh U.S. president, were Scotch-Irish immigrants to the Carolinas, where Jackson was born in 1767. His mother is known to have told him to always "sustain your manhood . . . the law affords no remedy for such outrages that can satisfy the feelings of a true man." Taking this advice to heart, Jackson was involved in more than a hundred documented disputes, including many duels, one where he killed a man. Above all, maintaining one's reputation for strength, honor, and willingness to punish others for violating norms helped to maintain order in the potentially chaotic and lawless herding economy of the South.

Eventually, these honor cultures spread into the Deep South— areas now known as the states of Louisiana, Mississippi, Alabama, and Georgia—and by 1790, Scotch-Irish settlers constituted the majority of the population of many Southern states. Today, these states are among America's tightest; they're where the culture of honor lives on.

Authoritarian tendencies that were at the foundation of the Southern slave economy also contributed to the region's tightness. As early as 1670, settlers from the colony of Barbados planted a hierarchical society in the American South. Strict norms were designed to control slaves, who outnumbered their masters. Those who tried to run away were to be whipped after a first attempt; after subsequent attempts their punishments escalated to anything from having an ear chopped off, to castration, to having an Achilles tendon severed, to execution. Fines were doled out to masters who didn't comply with these rules. Those who helped runaways were also fined, if not whipped or killed.

Meanwhile, the settlers in the northern and western United States couldn't have been more different. From the outset, the first settlers in these regions were known for religious pluralism and multicultural cohabitation, which we know pushes groups to be loose. Toward the beginning of the seventeenth century, a few decades before the Barbadians arrived in the Deep South, the Dutch (inhabitants of one of the loosest nations today) founded New York as a global trading hub that later attracted immigrants from Poland, Finland, Sweden, Ireland, and Portugal. The New York region attracted people who practiced many different faiths, including Catholics, Anglicans, Puritans, Quakers, and Jews.

Farther north in New England, the Massachusetts Bay Colony was settled by an English group of "separatist" Protestants known as the Puritans. Their practices were no doubt austere, and the colony was highly intolerant of other religious groups. But over the course of the seventeenth and eighteenth centuries, a singular Puritan authority was gradually overshadowed and diminished by a vast religious outgrowth of other Protestant sects, including Baptists, Methodists, Unitarians, and Quakers. By the mid-eighteenth century, new norms of tolerance had evolved in Massachusetts and throughout New England, with the populace rejecting the hierarchical and authoritarian practices taking hold in the South. Soon enough, Massachusetts was known as the "Cradle of Liberty" and as a haven for religious diversity.

This loose mentality was later reinforced with the rise of industrialization during the nineteenth century, which made the North more urban and diverse. In the 1870s, Massachusetts—currently the sixth-loosest state in the country—became the first state to have more people living in cities than rural areas. These city dwellers were less familiar with one another than those in rural towns and were therefore less monitored and more anonymous. Meanwhile, the South continued as a predominantly agrarian region marked by close-knit tight communities. According to historian Bertram Wyatt-Brown, who authored *Southern Honor: Ethics and Behavior in the Old South,* medicine, law, the clergy, and the military were the only tolerated non-agriculture professions in the South.

Out west, starting in the mid-eighteenth century, the state of California was a melting pot of Native Americans, Mexicans, Russians, and Europeans. In 1848, the discovery of gold at Sutter's Mill began luring more than three hundred thousand fortune-seeking newcomers from around the world, adding immigrants from Chile, Australia, Ireland, Italy, and China to an already diverse mix of settlers. A forerunner of sorts to the "start-up nation" of Israel, California became a "start-up state," luring risk-takers who were willing to make a treacherous journey for a better future on the West Coast. "Here were to be seen people of every nation in all varieties of costume, and speaking 50 different languages, and yet all mixing together amicably and socially," Canadian merchant William Perkins wrote about the mining town of Sonora in 1849. California, of course, has its own dark history of racism and exclusion, which is not completely eradicated even today. But early on, the seeds for cultural looseness were sown, and California has evolved to be one of the most tolerant states in the union.

By contrast, as shown by census data, diversity in tight states has been lacking since 1860. In fact, University of Pennsylvania data scientist Randy Olson has shown that some of the least diverse places in the country today can be found in tight states. Even now, there are counties in America that are nearly 100 percent white, including Tucker County, West Virginia; Robertson County, Kentucky; and Hooker

County, Nebraska. Tight states have less diversity—particularly ethnic diversity—our own analyses show.

Of course, loose communities exist within tight states, and vice versa, and tight-loose theory can predict where they'll take hold. Communities with a history of diversity tend to exhibit present-day looseness. In the tight state of Louisiana lies New Orleans, the historically diverse and cosmopolitan port city that is one of the most permissive in the country, as any witness of Mardi Gras and the jazz scene would attest. Dating back to French settlement of the city in 1718, New Orleans has been home to a diverse array of cultures—French, American Indian, Spanish, Cajun, Creole, Southern, and Caribbean—and today it's far looser than the rest of the U.S. South. In 2015, the New Orleans mayor, Mitch Landrieu, proclaimed, "New Orleans is an accepting, inviting city that thrives on its diversity and welcomes people from all walks of life with open arms." Likewise, there are tight communities in loose states, and they often display very low diversity. For example, the city of Colorado Springs, nestled in the loose state of Colorado, is almost 80 percent white, and Wyoming County in loose New York is 92 percent white.

TOUGH ECOLOGY, TIGHT NORMS

The roots of tightness and looseness date back to the norms and values that the early settlers brought with them hundreds of years ago, but that's not the only explanation. As with nations, the type of ecology the settlers contended with when they got here also played a strong role.

As we've seen, a group of people sharing a common territory will often mobilize to strategically tackle ecological threats by implementing strong norms. These threats can include the lack of a steady supply of natural resources, pathogens and outbreaks, and attacks by enemy invaders. The greater the threat, the tighter the community. By contrast, when groups don't have to worry about food, water, disease, or invasions, they don't need as many strict rules to coordinate, and they evolve into more permissive societies.

This principle clearly applies to nations, and it plays out in states, too. Mother Nature played a key part in perpetuating tight-loose differences across the U.S. states, and she continues to selectively cast her destructive spell over certain regions.

Many of the states that rank high in tightness, for example, were marked by difficult ecological conditions early on. In the nineteenth century, the Dakotas, Nebraska, Kansas, Oklahoma, and several areas westward were inhospitable territories that experienced very little rain—just twenty inches annually. In these states, "there were few places where agriculture could survive without the help of extensive irrigation projects," noted Colin Woodard. "The altitude was so high— even the plains and mountain valleys stood above the tallest summits of the Appalachians—that many familiar crops wouldn't grow at all."

Likewise, historically, the South also suffered more than its share of Mother Nature's wrath. In South Carolina, a series of wildfires swept through the state in the late nineteenth century, burning almost three million acres of forest land. In Galveston, Texas, a deadly hurricane killed approximately eight thousand people in 1900, and the state later suffered a 40 percent decrease in rainfall between 1949 and 1951 during one of the worst droughts in U.S. history. In nearby Oklahoma, now the fourth-tightest state in the country, recurrent droughts beginning in the 1910s culminated in the legendary "Dust Bowl days" of the 1930s. With the Great Depression also hitting Oklahoma, over four hundred thousand people ultimately abandoned the state during this time, many moving west to California and Arizona.

Tight states remain the most ecologically vulnerable even today. Data from 1950 to 1995 from the Disaster Center show that tight states have much higher tornado risk than loose states. For example, the tight states of Texas and Kansas have been recently plagued by tornadoes—147 and 92, respectively, on average per year—while tornadoes rarely touch down in the loose states of New Hampshire, Connecticut, and Washington. Data from 1979 to 2004 also show that tight states record higher death rates from heat, lightning, storms, and floods.

We also tracked where hurricanes hit with available data from 1851 to 2004. It's clear that a disproportionate number of tight states have gotten clobbered. In the list of over fifty of the deadliest hurricanes that have occurred in U.S. history, around 85 percent have done their worst damage in the ten tightest states. Mother Nature has recently been particularly cruel to tight states, deploying hurricanes Katrina, Harvey, and Irma.

Historically, tight states also had to cope with more disease. Examining Centers for Disease Control data from 1993 to 2007, we found that vulnerability to common diseases (e.g., malaria, measles, tuberculosis, rubella, typhoid) predicted states' tightness levels. While tight states such as Louisiana, Mississippi, and South Carolina scored high on pathogens, loose states such as Maine, New Hampshire, and Vermont scored low. Tight states exhibit higher rates of food insecurity, with fewer households having adequate access to food, and they also have less access to clean air. Tight Indiana, for example, has the poorest air quality in the country, followed by Ohio and Kentucky. By comparison, Oregon, Maine, and New Mexico—all loose states—are among the states with the clearest air. Summing up: Where there's threat, there's tightness.

There are exceptions, of course, to challenging ecological conditions leading to more tightness, just as we saw on the global map. Throughout American history, the state of California has been rocked by natural disasters ranging from earthquakes to wildfires to mudslides to heat waves. Yet California is a loose state, for reasons similar to an exception we noted when looking at individual nations—Israel. Thanks to the adventurous immigrants it's drawn from all around the world, the state boasts tremendous diversity, which has promoted loose subcultures from Hollywood to Venice Beach to Silicon Valley. One in ten jobs in California are held in creative industries, and Silicon Valley, famous for its concentration of start-ups and technology companies such as Apple, Facebook, and Google, is a mecca of innovation. As is the case in Israel, California's immense diversity and innovation cause the tight-loose pendulum to swing toward looseness.

Environmental threats and disease have played a crucial, but often hidden, role in shaping culture within the fifty states. In 2014, real-estate search website Estately mapped out Americans' most commonly experienced fears, including tornadoes, hurricanes, volcanoes, lightning, and even bears, spiders, snakes, and shark attacks. They then identified the "scariest places" to live in the United States by looking at which states harbored more of these fear-inducing threats. Remarkably, the resulting map coincides closely with our tightness-looseness map. Tight states like Florida, Georgia, and Texas were far scarier than loose states like Vermont, Alaska, and Nevada.

A NATION AT WAR WITH ITSELF

Mother Nature's fury isn't the only threat that tightens groups. As we've seen, nations tend to tighten up in response to external threats, most notably foreign invasion.

Of course, the United States has experienced tragic events throughout its history. From the time the earliest colonists arrived in the sixteenth century, there were brutal conflicts between Native Americans and white settlers, which ultimately led to the decimation of America's indigenous people. Americans have also dealt with attacks on their own soil, including the Revolutionary War, Pearl Harbor, 9/11, and the Boston Marathon bombing. However, after America won its independence from the British, the country hasn't faced any prolonged invasion or foreign occupation on its own soil since the War of 1812. But while its name might suggest otherwise, internal disputes and animosity have been a constant throughout the over two-hundred-year history of the "United" States.

The prime example is the Civil War. In the nineteenth century, the American South increasingly felt as though it was being "occupied" by "foreign" troops from the North, which had diametrically opposed views on how the nation should be governed. In 1861, the South and North entered into the bloodiest conflict in the nation's history with an outcome that only reinforced the South's tight culture. Southerners saw a need to defend their region's "peculiar institution," a euphemism for slavery, as indispensable to their agrarian-based economy. Northern efforts to curtail slavery's spread, they felt, threatened their lifestyle, and their survival.

Clearly, the Southern states that relied the most on slavery had the most to lose from a Union victory. According to this logic, today they should be tighter than Southern states that were less dependent on slave labor. And they are. There is a strong correlation between the percentage rankings of slave-owning families from the 1860 census and state-level tightness today. The tightest Southern states, such as Mississippi, South Carolina, and Georgia, had much higher levels of slave-owning families than did loose states, such as Delaware and Maryland.

By the war's end, the threat that Southern states perceived from the North had been fully realized. Left without slave labor, the Southern states faced economic ruin. Additionally, Southern lands had been devastated, since much of the war had been fought on Southern soil.

Even after the war, violent clashes persisted for years, with almost twenty thousand Northern soldiers remaining in the South to monitor and suppress sporadic raids from rebelling Southerners.

The South, with its already ecologically unstable territory now severely damaged by the war, also faced the unraveling of its well-defined social hierarchy in the postbellum period. The end of slavery and, later, the federal push toward nationwide desegregation disrupted the South's long-established social order. To prevent daily hostility between groups, people abided by implicit rules for social interaction, which served to signal their place in the social structure. The South's strong focus on etiquette helped ease daily social tensions, but kept obvious class divisions brewing underneath the surface. "Southerners ironically viewed manners and decorum as so vital to the maintenance of social order that defense of such codes warranted violence," explains Charles Reagan Wilson, professor of Southern studies at the University of Mississippi. To this day, rules pertaining to friendliness, writing thank-you cards, and saying "sir" or "ma'am" aren't frivolous habits in the South; they're a bulwark of social order and stability.

Centuries later, the memory of the Civil War defeat haunts the South, as seen in its ritualized battle reenactments and laws to protect confederate monuments in states like Alabama, North Carolina, Georgia, and Tennessee. While other American regions often have to be reminded of their pasts, "the ghosts of southern memory have remained strong into the 21st century," writes Thomas L. McHaney, emeritus professor of Southern literature at Georgia State University. "Defeat in the American Civil War led many white southerners to imagine and reimagine what southern life had been before the war came, a process that did much to shape a particular construction of southern identity." In the South, remembrance of the North as a sinister adversary revivifies perceptions of a persistent threat and reinforces a tight culture. These cultural "scars" linger on.

TIGHT-LOOSE SHIFTS AND SURGES

The fifty states have always been less united than the country's name implies. Cultural divides run deep in the American national soul: History, ecology, and demography have in concert led some states to be strict and others permissive, resulting in the tight-loose trade-offs and conflicts we see today.

Variation in strictness and permissiveness between states has developed slowly over time, but rapid cultural shifts also can occur—and tight-loose theory can predict them. When there's threat, even if it's temporary, merely imagined, or even manipulated, it can engender widespread fear and disorder, leading to people craving stronger norms and a tighter culture. In the twentieth and early twenty-first centuries, for example, threats from overseas enemies and acts of both foreign and homegrown terror have rocked Americans' sense of safety. In these frightening times, norms shifted to emphasize unity, austerity, and animus toward outsiders; the U.S. became tighter. But once these sources of fear were pacified, the United States as a whole reverted to its relatively loose culture.

The anti-Communist Red Scares, for instance, were reactions to both global and local threats. Americans feared the Communist overthrow of the Russian Empire in 1917 would be repeated in the United States. The first Red Scare was ignited shortly afterward in 1919 by a series of bombs detonated across the country by a few anarchists. These events amped up public fear and paranoia of politically radical groups, and then fear of immigrants and minorities. Laws were passed to deport immigrants, limit free speech, and infringe on the civil rights of suspected communities.

A few decades later, during the Cold War between the United States and an expanding Soviet Union, another era of tightness ensued. After the USSR tested its first nuclear weapon in 1949, Americans feared a nuclear war was imminent and that Soviet spies had infiltrated the U.S. government. A witch hunt against Communists ensued, as even established members of the left-leaning Hollywood community were targeted and stigmatized as Communists. Adding fuel to the country's anti-Communist hysteria, American troops entered the Korean War to combat Soviet-backed North Korea. Arrests, deportations, and investigations of potential Communist activities flared up across the country throughout the 1950s.

But when such threats aren't chronic, a country's system of norms loosens again. All the restrictions, monitoring, and punishments of the 1950s, for example, gradually gave way to the extreme looseness of the 1960s. During this "decade of change," the nation witnessed groundbreaking movements that sought to end discrimination toward traditionally marginalized groups—including women, African Americans, and gay Americans—and dismantle many of the country's long-held social norms and values. As more households acquired television sets, more Americans were exposed to new ideas and places. The following decades ushered in unbridled permissiveness, including greater recreational drug use and sexual promiscuity. "Whatever turns you on" and "Sex, drugs, and rock 'n' roll" were popular phrases of the day. Men tossed aside their hats, women raised their hemlines, and bold patterns became the norm. It was a legendary time for looseness.

Fast-forward to September 11, 2001, which unleashed another temporary wave of tightness. The surprise attack on the World Trade Center by members of the terrorist group al-Qaeda led to the loss of nearly three thousand lives, and a new era of fear dominated American politics, this time toward radical Islamic terrorist groups. Immediately following the 9/11 attacks, Congress introduced 130 new pieces of legislation, created over 260 new government organizations to secure the nation, and spent over $600 billion on homeland security from 2001 to 2011. The Patriot Act, hurriedly drafted and signed a month after the attacks by ninety-eight out of a hundred senators, ushered in unprecedented monitoring of Americans. Law enforcement officers were given permission to search homes and businesses without owners' or occupants' consent or knowledge. The Transportation Security Administration launched invasive security requirements and pre-screening processes at airports. Immigrant deportation rates rose by over 100 percent between 2001 and 2011.

Threats like 9/11 produced temporary shifts in tightness, but in the years following these national tragedies, remarkable loose accelerants spread across the country: Individual states and then the U.S. Supreme Court ushered in gay marriage, the first U.S. black president (one with a foreign heritage, no less) was elected, drug laws were loosened nationwide, and so on. Another turn to tightness, however, proved to be right around the corner.

HOW TRUMP PLAYED THE TIGHTNESS CARD

Tightness-looseness theory sheds light on one of the most seismic events in American history: the seemingly against-all-odds election of businessman and reality TV star Donald Trump as president in 2016.

While Trump isn't a cultural psychologist, he possessed an intuitive grasp of how threat tightens citizens' minds and leads them to yearn for strong leaders who'll combat these threats. He masterfully created a climate of threat: At campaign rallies throughout 2015 and 2016, Trump warned his ever-growing crowds that the United States was a nation on the brink of disaster. He cited mounting threats from Mexicans bringing violence across the border, global trade agreements and immigrants taking away jobs, radicalized Muslims plotting terror on American soil, and China "raping" the country. Throughout his campaign, he sent a clear message—that he was capable of restoring social order. "I alone can fix it," he declared to the American public. Trump used the psychology of tightness to pave a path all the way to the White House.

In the months prior to the 2016 election, Joshua Jackson, Jesse Harrington, and I conducted a nationwide survey aimed at peering into the minds of Trump supporters. Over 550 Americans from across the country and across demographic lines (gender, region, political affiliation, and race/ethnicity) answered questions about how fearful they felt about various external threats to the United States, such as ISIS and North Korea. They also responded to statements aimed at gauging their desire for cultural tightness, such as whether they felt the United States was too permissive or restrictive and whether American norms were being enforced either too strictly or not enough. Finally, they were asked about their attitudes toward policy issues such as surveillance and mass deportation and their support for different political candidates, including Trump.

The results were telling: People who felt the country was facing greater threats desired greater tightness. This desire, in turn, correctly predicted their support for Trump. In fact, desired tightness predicted support for Trump far better than other measures. For example, a desire for tightness predicted a vote for Trump with forty-four times more accuracy than other popular measures of authoritarianism. Concern about external threats also predicted support for many of the issues that Trump has championed, such as monitoring mosques, creating a registry of Muslim Americans, and deporting all undocumented immigrants. Perhaps unsurprisingly, Trump had the most support in tight states—where citizens felt the most threatened.

Clearly, even in an age where we like to fancy ourselves rational voters, the 2016 election turned largely on primal cultural reflexes—ones that had been conditioned not only by cultural forces, but by a candidate who was able to exploit them.

The meteoric rise of Trump, of course, is more than an American phenomenon. It's a reflection of a far broader principle that has echoed across human history and culture: Threats lead to desire for stronger rules, obedience to autocratic leaders, and—at worst—intolerance. Tightness-looseness can help account for the astounding political upheavals happening around the globe in the twenty-first century, including British citizens' 2016 vote to leave the European Union and the success of the Law and Justice Party in Poland's parliamentary election. Hungary has tightened considerably in recent years due to a different kind of "threat"—primarily Muslim refugees, whom Hungarian prime minister and strongman Viktor Orbán calls "invaders."

These cultural shocks show a common pattern: Perceived threat—often about terrorism, immigration, and globalization—tightens cultures and catapults autocratic leaders onto the national stage.

Threat, of course, isn't always an objective phenomenon. "Real threats have declined over human history, due to our growing ability to counter them, while manufactured or imaginary threats have increased dramatically," Israeli historian Yuval Noah Harari, the author of *Sapiens: A Brief History of Humankind*, told me. "Leaders and cultures could deliberately manufacture artificial threats or honestly see a major threat where none exists." The tight Nazi regime in Germany, Harari noted, rose in response to largely imagined rather than real threats.

Notably, both in the United States and abroad, autocratic leaders often garner sizable support from working-class and rural voters. In fact, just as the tight-loose axis differentiates countries and states, it also turns out to pit members of different socioeconomic groups against one another, with dramatic consequences.

6

Working Class vs. Upper Class: The Hidden Cultural Fault Line

In the fall of 2011, over a thousand demonstrators staged a massive protest in New York City's Financial District that they hailed as "Occupy Wall Street." The protesters were infuriated with the growing socioeconomic inequality in the United States and around the world. Within a few days, their numbers had grown into a movement of tens of thousands. But the fervor didn't stop in New York City. Major protests burst forth in hundreds of other U.S. cities; a month later, the campaign had swept the globe, with protests springing up in Europe, Asia, South America, and Africa.

"We are the 99 percent!" became the movement's trademark slogan, alluding to the rapidly widening income gap between society's wealthiest class, the "1 percent," and everyone else. Median household income growth from 1967 to 2015, according to U.S. Census Bureau data, showed a 101 percent rise in earnings for the nation's top 5 percent of earners while the lowest-income earners gained a dismal 25 percent. Such statistics pointed to a vast wealth gap as the rich grew significantly richer and the poor stagnated. While the Occupy campaign eventually disbanded into offshoot causes, such as raising the minimum wage and reforming Wall Street, its collective rallying cry can still be heard around the world.

Class divides have become a front-burner political issue. A 2017 Pew Research survey found that almost 60 percent of Americans believe there are "very strong" or "strong" conflicts between the rich and poor, up 12 percent from 2009. Respondents ranked class conflicts ahead of those between the young and the old and city and rural dwellers. This chasm between the haves and have-nots exists around the world. In 2016 in South Africa, the bottom 50 percent of earners took in only 10 percent of the country's net income, while the highest-earning 10 percent amassed 60 percent of it. In 2015, the "1 percenters" in China owned more than 33 percent of the country's wealth. Latin America, according to the World Economic Forum, has one of the biggest wealth gaps in the world, with its richest 10 percent holding 71 percent of the region's total wealth in 2014. Such inequality, social commentators contend, helped drive populist waves that crashed ashore in the 2016 U.S. election, the UK's Brexit decision, and nationalist movements in Europe. What's more, we increasingly live in our own echo chambers, with little contact across class lines. Our misconceptions about other social classes grow by the day, often leading us to inaccurate, unfair, and even dangerous conclusions.

These class divisions are as old as civilization itself. In one of the world's earliest urbanized societies, the region of Sumer in ancient Mesopotamia (circa 4500 BC), social order consisted of an elite class of kings and priests, an upper class of merchants, scribes, military men, and other officials, a lower class of farmers and craftsmen, and, at the lowest level, the slaves. Much like today, people's status and identity hinged upon their positions in their society's pecking order. Later, around the second millennium BC, a four-part caste system sprang up in India, while in China, a hierarchical social class structure was developed in 1000 BC during the Zhou Dynasty. Class divisions aren't even limited to the human species. Capuchin monkeys, baboons, pigeons, goby fish, mice, and even burying beetles have been known to demarcate themselves into clear social hierarchies.

Class divisions have been a perennial focus of philosophers, novelists, and filmmakers. From Plato, Marx, and Tolstoy to Shakespeare, Dickens, and Steinbeck, we see the ways in which the rules, expectations, and complications of class shape the destiny of humankind. The viral popularity of TV series like *The Crown* and *Downton Abbey* also reflects our deep-rooted fascination with the tastes, values, and attitudes of the wealthy. In popular films such as *City Lights*, *My Fair Lady*, *Slumdog Millionaire*, *Working Girl*, *Billy Elliot*, and *Pretty in Pink*, lead characters struggle to meet the expectations of their own social class while trying to win acceptance by another.

Yet despite the centrality of social class to the human experience, our understanding of it has generally been limited by categorical depictions: rich versus poor, blue collar versus white collar, urban versus rural, proletariat versus bourgeoisie. These categories are insufficient because they're derivative. Underlying them are deeper cultural codes. Just as a DNA test tells us more than a blood pressure reading, we need to uncover the cultural programming that defines these communities in a way that goes beyond differences in their bank accounts.

A MILE AWAY, WORLDS APART

It's 8:00 a.m. on Monday morning and James and David are each heading off to their respective workplaces. David, a thirty-two-year-old college graduate with a four-year degree from a private liberal arts school, heads off to his job at an accounting firm in Chicago. After arriving at work sometime between 8:30 and 9:00, he begins setting deadlines and priorities for the day. He decides on his schedule and gets down to work, pausing occasionally to check his Facebook feed and respond to incoming emails. At 10:30, he takes a quick coffee break and chats about the weekend with some coworkers. At 1:00 p.m., he heads off to a local restaurant for lunch, then remembers a brief errand he forgot to do over the weekend. He takes an extra half hour to get it done, since he's in the area anyway. Back at the office, he works off and on for another three hours and heads out the door by 5:30. That evening, he returns to his safe, upper-class neighborhood, where he and his wife own a nice house. He earns enough to sock away a significant amount of savings each year for vacations and college tuition for his kids.

A mile away the same morning, James, a thirty-two-year-old high school graduate, heads to his job as a machinist at a factory that makes industrial-grade bolts and screws. When he arrives at work at 7:00 a.m. sharp, his boss tells him his schedule and the tasks that must be completed by day's end. He heads for his machine on the factory floor after ensuring that any loose clothing is tucked away. He reminds himself to remain focused on the task at hand—getting anything caught in a machine or making a mistake while operating one could be a deadly affair. As he works, the foreman keeps tabs on his progress. At 10:45, an alarm signals a fifteen-minute coffee break. By 11:00, James is back at his machine. Similar bells signal lunch around noon and an additional afternoon break. By 5:30, James's shift is complete, and he's headed home to a working-class neighborhood. A warm, close-knit community, it's nonetheless a lower-income area with a higher crime rate than James would prefer for his family. He earns just enough money from his job to help support his family, so there's very little left over for savings.

THE ECOLOGY OF SOCIAL CLASS

Both David and James are hardworking people who have loving families to support. They live in the same city, just a mile away from each other, yet their lives and experiences are radically different. James is part of the lower class, also referred to as the working class, which includes people who haven't received a college degree, are employed in blue-collar, low-prestige jobs, and earn low incomes, but are above the poverty line. David is part of the upper class. He isn't among the top 1 percent—the elite who were the wrath of the Occupy Wall Street movement—but he represents many on the social class ladder who have a college education, occupy professional and prestigious jobs, and enjoy material wealth. While James and David live in the same city, speak the same language, and ride the same subways, they inhabit completely different cultures.

It's easy to identify the financial situations and educational credentials that distinguish the lower and upper classes. But beneath these statistics lies a distinction that is often invisible to the naked eye: the difference in the levels of threat they experience.

To point to one: The chance of falling into destitution is a constant threat among members of the lower class like James. In her article "The Class Culture Gap," legal scholar Joan Williams notes that "American working-class families feel themselves on a tightrope where one misstep could lead to a fall into poverty and disorder." Losing one's job and any semblance of security is a constant threat for the working class, who often live paycheck to paycheck. Author Joseph Howell similarly notes that slipping into *hard living*—a term he uses to describe the dregs of poverty—is a relentless preoccupation among the working class that motivates them to vigilantly guard their precarious status. Whereas upper-class individuals experience the world as safe and welcoming, lower-class individuals tend to view it as fraught with extreme danger. And because money can buy second chances, those who have it have a different attitude toward novelty and risk. Upper-class families know that they have a safety net if they run into problems and so they encourage their children to explore and take chances. Because lower-class families lack a safety net to offset the negative effects of careless mistakes and lapses in judgment, they tend to actively discourage this kind of experimentation. The fear of slipping into poverty "anchors working-class culture to stability rather than novelty, to self-discipline rather than self-actualization," Williams explains.

The threat of hard living isn't just theory; it resonates with people's everyday realities. Nicole Bethel, a thirty-one-year-old registered nurse in Dayton, Ohio, told the *Huffington Post* that she sometimes only has pennies to her name while waiting to be paid. "It's all you think about," she said. "It's constant. You can't relax or ever really have a day off." The fragile nature of work and health is a constant concern, according to Karen Wall, a teacher and part-time bartender in Texas. "If I got in a car accident, I'd be homeless," she said. "If I get laid off from any of my jobs, my kids will end up going hungry." Slipping into poverty is also a concern for Erlinda Delacruz, a high school graduate interviewed by CNN who had a full-time manufacturing job until the factory closed in 2009. Delacruz, who lives in rural Texas, was working three part-time jobs—clocking in sixty hours a week. "There's no such thing as a Friday," says Delacruz. "I live paycheck to paycheck."

In addition to facing economic uncertainty, the lower class is saddled with serious safety and health threats. Their jobs have much higher odds of injury, dismemberment, and death. Since 1992, the Bureau of Labor Statistics has conducted an annual Census of Fatal Occupational Injuries across jobs in the United States. Individuals working in lower-class occupations—such as construction, manufacturing, and agricultural work—always top this list for fatal and nonfatal work injuries. It is the awareness of the risks intrinsic to these jobs that spawns extensive workplace protocols and safety procedures, and makes for far less employee discretion. Since people like David experience far less threat on the job, they enjoy greater latitude and comparatively little oversight from supervisors.

Physical threats also abound in lower-class neighborhoods. According to the U.S. Bureau of Justice Statistics, poorer communities in the United States face more than double the rate of violent crime relative to higher-income communities. The Bureau of Justice Statistics reports that people living in lower-income areas are far more likely to be victims of gun violence, robbery, aggravated and simple assault, and sexual assault and rape. The lower class also experiences greater health vulnerabilities throughout their lives relative to their upper-class counterparts, showing higher rates of illnesses such as coronary heart disease, stroke, chronic bronchitis, diabetes, and ulcers. In fact, there's a staggering ten- to fifteen-year difference in the life expectancy rate between the top and bottom 1 percent in the United States.

Beyond threat, there are other important ways that social classes vary. The lower class tends to have less exposure to diversity. For example, we've found that lower-class neighborhoods have a much lower percentage of immigrants than upper-class neighborhoods. The lower class also has far fewer opportunities for mobility, making it harder for them to climb the social ladder.

THE TIGHTENING OF THE WORKING-CLASS MIND

The combination of high threat, low mobility, and low exposure to diversity is a perfect recipe for the evolution of tightness in the lower class. But are they actually tighter than the upper class?

To find out, Jesse Harrington and I surveyed hundreds of lower- and upper-class American adults in 2016. We measured the level of tightness these groups experienced in their childhood homes, workplaces, and life in general. In each setting, they were asked whether there were many rules they had to follow, whether there were strong punishments for violating them, how much they were monitored, and the extent to which they had choices in making decisions.

The results were telling. Lower-class adults were more likely to indicate that they faced stronger rules, harsher punishments, more monitoring, and fewer choices in their childhood home, current workplace, and lives more generally. They also reported that the situations they encounter on a daily basis are much tighter, with fewer behaviors that are deemed acceptable. What's more, the lower-class participants were more likely to *desire* a tighter society, as evidenced by their strong agreement with statements like "a functioning society requires strong punishments for wrongdoing." Put simply, they live in a tighter, circumscribed world, while the upper class experiences considerable looseness.

Just like citizens of tight nations and states, the lower class see the world through a prism of threat: They're more concerned with paying the rent or mortgage, losing their homes and jobs, obtaining proper medical care, and having enough food to eat. They also live in more dangerous places. We asked our participants to report their zip codes so we could assess the level of safety in their neighborhoods using data from the U.S. Census. Sure enough: Lower-class participants live in places with higher rates of unemployment and poverty, and thus greater vulnerability to economic and financial woes.

The data also revealed something very interesting: People from different social classes have completely different views about *rules*. The predominant upper-class view of rules is that they're made to be broken. Just look at popular books about success, like Marcus Buckingham and Curt Coffman's *First, Break All the Rules* and Angela Copeland's *Breaking the Rules & Getting the Job*. These books advise us that if we want to succeed, we'll need to cast aside established social norms and chart our own path. This advice overlooks the fact that for members of the lower class, rules are critical for survival. In communities where teens may be tempted to turn to drugs and gangs, strict rules laid down by authority figures are essential to keeping kids on track. And for people in low-wage, routinized jobs where creativity is discouraged, rule breaking can lead to getting fired. The upper class faces less threat and, as a result, can afford to break the rules. In fact, when we asked our survey respondents to free-associate from the word *rules*, upper-class respondents were more likely to write down negative words such as *bad, frustrating,* and *constricting,* while lower-class participants consistently wrote down positive words such as *good, safe,* and *structure.* Reactions to the phrase *following the rules* vary by class as well. Words like *listen* and *obey* were repeated answers from the lower class, whereas pejoratives like *goody-two-shoes* or *robotic* were more common among the upper class. For the lower class, rules are meant to be followed, as they provide moral order in a world of potential turmoil.

Overall, lower- and upper-class respondents showed the same differences in values and attitudes that we saw across tight and loose nations and states. Those in the lower classes were more likely to endorse survey items such as "I like order" and "I enjoy having a clear and structured mode of life" and to report that they "don't like change" and "prefer to stick with things that [they] know." They had lower openness to experience, and yearned for the "good old days." They had a strong distaste for morally ambiguous behaviors, such as euthanasia and drug and alcohol use, and were more likely to view homosexuality as immoral. Similarly, in studies on morality by psychologist Jonathan Haidt, members of the working class express moral condemnation when asked about actions that are disrespectful or disgusting yet objectively harmless, such as wiping a toilet with a flag, or eating an already dead dog for dinner. Their outrage reflects a tight mind-set. Meanwhile, people of higher socioeconomic status are more likely to take a loose, permissive stance, viewing such behaviors as matters of social convention or personal preference.

MAX, THE NORM-VIOLATING PUPPET

At what age do tight attitudes start to show up in lower-class children, and loose attitudes in upper-class kids? Since past research has found that children have a grip on social norms by age three, Jesse Harrington and I examined if toddlers vary in their responses to *norm violators*. We recruited three-year-old kids from the lower and upper classes in the Washington, D.C., area, asking their parents to bring them to our laboratory in exchange for a small payment. Of course, we couldn't ask three-year-olds to fill out a survey or answer questions about the degree to which violations of social norms make them uncomfortable. But fortunately for us, psychologists Hannes Rakoczy, Felix Warneken, and Michael Tomasello at the Max Planck Institute had previously devised an ingenious behavioral tool that could be used for this purpose: Max, the norm-violating puppet.

As in their study, we paired up each participating child with Max, a hand puppet, who was operated by a research assistant. After playing with the kids to make them feel comfortable, the experimenter then demonstrated to both the participating child and Max the proper and improper way to play each of four made-up games. For example, in the game "daxing," the experimenter demonstrated that the proper way to "dax" is to push a block off a Styrofoam board with a wooden stick. The improper way is to lift the board so the block slides off the end. Next, the child was given a turn to play the game; after that, it was Max's turn. At first, Max played the game according to the rules, but then

Figure 6.1. Jesse Harrington with participant and Max the puppet.

he did something unexpected: He exhibited improper behavior while exclaiming that he was doing it properly. "This is daxing!" he said while lifting the board and letting the blocks slide off. Within minutes, Max the puppet had become Max the norm violator.

Our study's results suggested that tight and loose attitudes were already deeply ingrained in these youngsters. Lower-class children were more likely to tell Max that he was doing the task wrong. "No! Not like that. Like this!" they might say, or, "That's not how daxing goes!" One child from a lower-socioeconomic-status family even accused Max of cheating. Children from this group were also quicker to protest Max's mistake. By contrast, upper-class children appeared to be more understanding and accepting of Max's norm violation, sometimes even laughing appreciatively. Even by age three, these more privileged kids thought there was nothing wrong with breaking the rules once in a while.

THE CULTURAL TRANSMISSION OF SOCIAL CLASS

Social class differences in tightness-looseness show up remarkably early in life, our results suggested. But why? It turns out that children in different social classes are exposed to radically different types of socialization. The working class has what psychologists call "strict" or "narrow" socialization, and the upper class has "lenient" or "broad" socialization.

The sociologist Melvin Kohn first documented this difference in his 1969 book *Class and Conformity*, in which he asked parents about the traits they thought were critical for their children to have. Lower-class parents stressed the importance of conformity, wanting their children to be obedient and neat. Upper-class parents wanted their kids to have self-direction—to be independent. Kohn also found striking contrasts in parental attitudes about punishment of wrongdoing. Lower-class parents punished their children for disobedience and for the negative consequences of their behavior, regardless of whether it was intentional or accidental. By contrast, not only were upper-class parents less likely to punish their children, but they also chose whether and how to punish based on the *intent* behind their child's behavior. Five decades later, and consistent with Kohn's work, our studies showed that lower-class parents more often say that there are firm rules their children have to follow, more often monitor their children's behavior, and more often mete out punishments to correct poor behavior. A recent Pew Research Center poll appears in line with this, reporting that parents with a high school education or lower are almost three times more likely to spank their children than parents who have an advanced degree.

Just as parents send their children to school with umbrellas after spotting stormy skies on the horizon, they also give their kids the psychological tools that they think they'll need to be successful adults.

Knowing that their children will likely have to navigate a world of social threat—and work at jobs where they have little discretion— lower-class parents emphasize the importance of conformity to try to help them succeed. After all, not following protocol at work can get one fired or badly hurt. "In the working class, people perform jobs in which they are closely supervised and are required to follow orders and instructions," Alfred Lubrano explains in his book *Limbo: Blue-Collar Roots, White-Collar Dreams*, so parents "bring their children up in a home in which conformity, obedience, and intolerance for back talk are the norm—the same characteristics that make for a good factory worker." In these contexts, self-direction is actually counterproductive, but it's a necessary trait for those navigating loose worlds and occupations, hence a trait that upper-class parents foster in *their* children.

It's not just parental attitudes that help prepare children for their respective tight and loose worlds. Three important factors—the ways households are organized, the unwritten codes that guide conversations, and children's experiences in the classroom—all reinforce differences in tightness-looseness among the lower and upper classes. In his 1970 book *Class, Codes, and Control*, British sociologist Basil Bernstein discusses how the structure and rigidity of lower-class life, as compared with the flexibility of upper-class life, can be readily discerned even from the layouts of the classes' respective households. Lower-class households, he argues, tend to have rooms that are strongly separated and strictly bounded by function—the kitchen is for cooking, the dining room is for eating family meals, and so on. Upper-class households, on the other hand, have more open and flexible floor plans with rooms that have multiple uses. Bernstein also notes that relationships between parents and children are structured and rigid in lower-class households (with parents as authority figures and children as subordinates), whereas in upper-class households authority lines are much more blurred.

Bernstein also found a fascinating connection between social class and the way that people use language. The working class uses what he calls a "restricted code" form of speech defined by simpler and more concrete grammatical constructions with fewer counterfactual statements (like *what if*). Meanwhile, the middle class has an "elaborated code" of speech that is more abstract and complex and more flexible. As Bernstein explains, language forms in part from how we see the world, so it's not surprising that the language used by working-class people reflects a social world that is lacking in flexibility and higher in structure. By contrast, the language of the middle class matches the complexity and comparatively unstructured experiences they encounter in their daily lives.

Children also encounter these structural differences in school. Metaphorically speaking, schools with a predominantly lower-class population are more likely to resemble the military, with their strong emphasis on rules and obedience, whereas schools with upper-class populations resemble universities, with their comparable freedom. In the latter, teachers cultivate a loose mind-set: They encourage students to ask questions, express their individuality, and move freely. In her comparison of schools in northern New Jersey, educator Jean Anyon noted that in suburban schools, which generally have upper-class populations, teachers encourage children to engage in creative writing every day and to use craft projects, murals, and graphs to represent what they learn.

By contrast, lower-class city-district schools prep children for a tight mind-set. They have comparatively less latitude and engage in more structured activities. In these schools, children are assigned rote tasks such as copying notes and completing standardized math problems—all geared toward assessing their knowledge of a subject, rather than their creative interpretation of school materials. Schools, in effect, reproduce the tight and loose norms of their corresponding social classes.

From a very young age, the lives of the children of the lower and upper classes begin to diverge—from the values their parents enforce, to the language they speak, to the structure of their households and schools, even to how they react to Max, the norm-violating puppet. These cultural differences have a profound impact on how these children behave as adults.

WHAT COLOR PEN WOULD YOU CHOOSE?

Imagine you're out walking and someone approaches you about taking a short survey. After completing it, you're presented with five pens to choose from as a thank-you gift. Four of the pens are green, and the fifth is orange. Which pen would you choose?

Choosing a pen based on its color may seem like a decision of little import, but it actually says quite a lot about you: namely, whether you prefer to conform or stand out. In a clever study where individuals were given a pen as compensation for participating, psychologists Nicole Stephens, Hazel Markus, and Sarah Townsend found that 72 percent of lower-class participants chose a pen that was in the majority color, whereas only 44 percent of upper-class participants did. When given the opportunity to conform or stand out, lower-class individuals, this study showed, prefer to blend in whereas upper-class individuals prefer to be unique.

Just as tight nations have stronger preferences for uniformity, members of the lower class prefer making choices that others like to make, too. In another study by these researchers, participants were asked to imagine that they bought a new car, only to learn that their friend bought the same car the next day. Members of the lower class were more likely to say things like "I'd feel good about it" or "I would be delighted," whereas those from the upper class tended to respond,

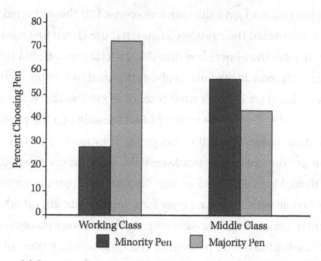

Figure 6.2. Percentage of participants who chose majority/minority pen by social class.

"I would feel slightly irritated" or "I'd probably be upset." From a tight-loose perspective, these differences make a whole lot of sense. When you experience a lot of threat in life, being in sync with others feels safe.

People who are lower on the social ladder are also more easily influenced by the opinions of others. In one study, some people were asked to recall a time when they felt someone else had control over them. Other people were asked to recall a time when they had control over someone else. The former situation is much more common in the lives of the lower class, who tend to feel less of a sense of personal control. They then completed a very tedious and boring sentence-formation task. Before people rated how much they enjoyed the task, the experimenters showed them glowing reviews of the task from prior participants. On a scale from one to eleven, most had answered between nine and eleven, meaning they enjoyed the task "very much." These were, of course, fake reviews. Those who'd been primed to feel a sense of greater control ignored the fact that other people supposedly had fun during the task and gave the task low scores. But those primed to feel less control shifted their ratings to match those they'd just read.

Members of the upper class may resist social pressure, but they also can be much more lackadaisical about the need to comply with social norms—a loose trait. That's what researchers at the University of California, Berkeley, found when they hid on the side of a busy California intersection and watched the cars go by. They noted the make of the car and its corresponding social class: the nicer the car, the higher the class (think Mercedes-Benz versus Toyota). Their results were astonishing: People with nicer cars were far more likely to cut off other cars in an intersection with four-way stop signs than were owners of more run-of-the-mill cars—30 percent of the time versus 8 percent of the time, to be exact. In fact, owners of nicer vehicles were also more likely to cut off *pedestrians* who were waiting to cross the street, an illegal act in California. Drivers of the cars that ranked lowest on luxury cut off people on foot 0 percent of the time, while drivers in the nicest cars cut people off a whopping 46 percent of the time. Clearly, people of higher social status are less concerned about yielding to pedestrians (and following the law!).

Beyond their more reckless driving behavior, people higher in social class take more liberty in violating conversational etiquette. In one study, researchers recruited participants and videotaped them interacting with a stranger for a five-minute time period. Some people made great eye contact and responded to their partners with laughs and nods, while other participants were ill-mannered conversationalists. They doodled on their notebooks, fidgeted with nearby objects, and were generally more disengaged. Can you guess how these behaviors broke down along class lines? That's right: The lower-class participants were more likely to follow conventional etiquette and norms during these short interactions; upper-class participants were more likely to dismiss them.

The loose behavior of upper-class individuals can even make them less ethical. Studies have shown that they're far more likely to say they'd engage in unethical actions ranging from cheating on a test, to stealing software, to keeping extra change from a cashier. In our surveys of hundreds of people, working-class individuals were less likely to endorse unscrupulous actions like stealing supplies at work or cheating on tests. Other research has found similar results: In one lab study, participants were told that a higher dice role would get them more money. When they had to report the results of their dice roles, those from a higher socioeconomic background were more likely to lie about the numbers rolled. In another study, people who felt they were in a higher social class were more likely to take candy that they knew was supposed to be for children participating in a lab study next door!

INSIDE OR OUTSIDE THE BOX?

Take sixty seconds to list as many uses as you can possibly think of for a paper clip. Now do the same for a brick. In one of our studies, Jesse Harrington and I had people from different social classes complete this classic creativity task. We found that upper-class participants provided far more creative responses for how these objects could be used. Some of their novel suggestions for a brick included cracking open walnuts, building an artistic sculpture, and making an ochre paint by grinding the brick up. Other uses they gave for a paper clip included using it to hang a Christmas ornament or replace a broken zipper.

We've seen that the lower class tends to be tighter—more conforming, norm-abiding, and cooperative—while the upper class is looser—more deviant, less cooperative, and even a bit more unethical. Yet being unleashed from constraints also has its upsides: Like the typical inhabitant of a loose nation or state, people from the upper class are much more innovative, as our results show. In other studies where people were primed to feel either powerful or powerless—conditions that mirror the power differential between the upper and lower classes—researchers found similar effects. When asked to plan a new menu for a restaurant or to generate three new names for types of pasta, radioactive elements, and pain-relief medicines, people who felt powerful were more creative than low-power participants.

Psychologist Murray Straus found discrepancies in creativity are inculcated early. He worked with families from different socioeconomic backgrounds and asked them to complete problem-solving tasks while an observer took detailed notes on their ideas. Among the sixty-four American families participating, those with higher socioeconomic status attempted many more creative solutions to the tasks than did families from lower-class backgrounds. The same results were found in India and Puerto Rico. In short, members of the lower class, while more likely to abide by rules and norms and even be more ethical, are less likely to think outside of the box.

This leads us to the final element of the tight-loose trade-off: openness to those who are different. In loose nations and states, there's a high degree of openness and tolerance of individuals who are different, including immigrants, while in tight nations and states, people react more negatively to those who threaten the social order. Remarkably, the same tight-loose signature applies to social class: Studies show that, in general, members of the lower class report more negative attitudes toward homeless people, homosexuals, Muslims, the disabled, and even people with tattoos. Across many countries, lower-class individuals also harbor more negative attitudes toward immigrants, believing they're detrimental to their nation.

In sum, class distinctions reflect deep cultural differences that have evolved to adapt to specific ecological and historical challenges. Of course, while the basic tight-loose contrast between classes is well established, there are also important exceptions. Just as there are loose cities in tight states, it's not difficult to find individuals in lower socioeconomic groups with loose mind-sets and vice versa. Outside the United States, class barriers can look quite different. Nevertheless, focusing on income differences misses the critical role culture plays in forming and sustaining class divides around the world.

The tight-loose distinction is also useful for understanding other group differences beyond socioeconomic status, including gender and race. The term *white privilege* has become a political hot potato, but a noncontroversial principle underlies the concept: Groups that have greater power—those that control important resources—have far more latitude to deviate from rules. In many societies, whites, males, and heterosexuals, regardless of class, tend to have greater power. They live in looser worlds. By contrast, women, minorities, and homosexuals have less power and less latitude, and are subjected to stronger punishments, even for the same norm violations. They, in short, live in much tighter worlds.

In one study demonstrating this, managers that I surveyed read about someone breaking workplace rules, including going against a boss's decision, stealing from a coworker, covering up mistakes, sabotaging company equipment or merchandise, or lying about hours worked. Crucially, we manipulated the gender and the race of the person who had broken the rules by using names pre-validated to signal race and gender: Participants read about either a white man (Greg), a white woman (Kristen), a black man (Jamal), or a black woman (Latoya). They were then asked to rate how serious the violation described was and to indicate whether the person should be punished. The results were telling. When women and minorities were said to engage in these behaviors, managers thought they were much more serious and warranted more punishment than when the *same* behaviors were done by majority males. Similarly, a study looking at the financial advisor industry found that although misconduct is more frequent among male employees, women are more likely to be punished, and more severely so.

When it comes to criminal justice, the results also show that some groups disproportionately receive harsher punishments for the same violations. For example, African American criminals are punished more harshly and sentenced to more time behind bars than white criminals with comparable histories. In the United States, African Americans are imprisoned at a rate that is five times the imprisonment rate of whites. African Americans are also far more likely to be targeted, brutalized, and killed by police, a phenomenon that prompted the Black Lives Matter movement in 2013. In Ferguson, Missouri, for example, one in two African Americans was pulled over for traffic stops that year, as compared to one in eight whites.

The pattern is clear: People with different levels of status and power—whether that status and power are based on income, race, gender, sexual orientation, or another individual characteristic—live in different cultural worlds.

SOCIAL CLASS CULTURE SHOCK

While you might expect an American moving to Japan or a German moving to New Zealand to experience culture shock, it may be less evident that someone moving between classes might have just as much trouble adapting. This is particularly the case for members of the working class, who are typically ill-prepared to cross into upper-class schools and workplaces that have been effectively designed to promote looseness. Though it's often not obvious, the working class is inadvertently put at a cultural disadvantage in these spaces.

We view college as a stepping stone to greater economic opportunity and mobility, but this stepping stone looms like a mountain to some. The loose norms and openness of many college campuses are comfortable for upper-class students, but they can be disorienting and alienating to students from working-class backgrounds. In 2012, psychologist Nicole Stephens and her collaborators surveyed over 260 high-level college administrators at the top fifty U.S. universities and the top twenty-five liberal arts colleges to determine the schools' prevailing cultural norms. They were given a list of traits, and asked to choose which traits were most important for their students. The vast majority said that their universities expected students to develop personal opinions rather than simply appreciating the opinions of others, to pave their own innovative pathways rather than following in others' footsteps, and to challenge rather than accept established rules.

In other words, the schools' norms were designed to reward nonconformity and independence. No small wonder, then, that upper-class children, who are more likely to have grown up in loose cultures where individuality and creativity are fostered, tend to flourish in university environments. Meanwhile, lower-class children, who have grown up in tight environments that emphasize conformity over independence, structure over creativity, and obedience over deviance, are more likely to struggle. For them, attending college, even one close to home, can feel like traveling to a foreign country.

A recent study of over 145,000 students at six large public universities found startling evidence of this cultural mismatch. Working-class students reported less of a sense of belonging, less satisfaction with their educational experiences, and more stress and depression than their upper-class peers. Financially strapped, they often had to juggle their coursework with other jobs, and they had less time for other collaborative and academic activities on campus.

I witnessed these realities firsthand on my own campus. Jesse Harrington and I surveyed first-year students throughout the 2016–2017 year. By the end of their first semester, lower-class students felt less academically prepared, less successful at making friends, and more stressed out. These students were overwhelmed by the complexity of college life, and yearned for clarity and simplicity. They also felt a greater rift with their loved ones back home. They found themselves straddling two cultures and feeling isolated from both.

Lower-class students' alienation on campus translates to a higher likelihood of dropping out. According to studies done by the National Center for Education Statistics, students from high-income families are more than twice as likely to earn their bachelor's degree within six years after starting college compared with those from low-income families. Our system of higher education, touted as a "great equalizer," is falling far short of this lofty goal.

Just as cross-cultural training programs help people to adjust when they travel abroad, educational institutions need to take steps to reduce the culture shock experienced by lower-class individuals who are transitioning from tight to loose cultures. Harvard, Brown, and Arizona State have developed programs in which fellow students mentor first-generation students to help them transition to university life. Other universities have created web pages featuring the stories of first-generation students to help them feel like they belong. These programs can make a big difference. An ingenious study led by Nicole Stephens found that lower-class students who attended panel sessions wherein students from diverse backgrounds discussed how their social class shaped their college experiences were subsequently much more likely to seek out resources on campus and attained higher GPAs.

Providing more structure in university settings also helps to bridge tight-loose gaps. Take, for example, an innovative intervention developed at the University of North Carolina at Chapel Hill by Sarah Eddy and Kelly Hogan. In some classrooms, students were given more preparatory homework each week, provided with guided-reading questions to structure their time, and assigned more in-class small-group activities to foster a collaborative working environment. Compared with a control group that had no structure changes, this intervention improved performance for all students, the researchers found—and students from the lower class improved the most.

Young people from tight lower-class backgrounds don't only need help adjusting to the looseness of college life. People who don't graduate from college, which in the United States constitutes about two-thirds of adults, according to a 2017 Census Bureau report, need help attaining the skills required to succeed in an increasingly globalized economy. The looseness of American culture may be keeping them from meeting this goal.

Take Germany, a generally tight culture, where the government provides the nation's youth with a wide range of career options that don't require a college degree. For example, Germany has many vocational programs where you can earn a nationally recognized certificate. The government works with employers, educators, and union representatives to develop these standardized occupational tracks, ensuring that apprentices are learning the skills they need to meet the qualifications of their future employers. As Tamar Jacoby in the *Atlantic* writes, "Every young machinist training anywhere in Germany learns the same skills in the same order on the same timetable as every other machinist. This is good for apprentices: It guarantees high-quality programs where trainees learn more than one company's methods, making it possible for those who wish to switch jobs later on." But in the United States, a generally loose culture, there are no such uniform standards, which means that the skills taught at one company may not be valuable or needed at other companies. This can make it difficult for people to change jobs, which places a large burden on the working class. Given rapid changes across many industries, as well as the increasing threat of globalization to lower-class jobs, looser economies like America's would benefit from developing practices that tight cultures have honed to give working-class laborers more structure as they launch their careers.

CULTURAL ECHO CHAMBERS

Class differences are deeply cultural, and the world urgently needs greater cultural empathy across class lines. Arguably, we need this now more than ever. People from different social classes are increasingly isolated from one another, as seen in the growing urban-rural divides around the globe. We tend to further compartmentalize ourselves on social media and follow different media outlets (e.g., Fox News versus MSNBC) as well. As a result, we are left with little understanding of each other's cultures, which can lead us to form negative stereotypes about one another.

Many of the differences between the lower and upper classes have an underlying logic. Lower-class occupations, including plumbers, butchers, factory workers, janitors, and prison guards, require sophisticated technical and physical skills. They also require the ability to be dependable and follow rules. A tight mind-set is critical for success in these contexts. Meanwhile, upper-class jobs, such as those in law, engineering, medicine, academia, and management, among other white-collar professions, are built on alternative strengths, such as creativity, vision, independence, and even breaking from tradition. These strengths necessitate a looser mind-set. Neither set of strengths should be viewed as superior. Cultivating mutual respect for our different strengths will go a long way toward bridging today's social class divisions and conflicts.

This is becoming more and more important in our rapidly globalizing world. As technological advances jeopardize the already dwindling availability of lower-class jobs, the threat of permanent poverty is a real fear within these communities. McKinsey & Company found that a whopping 78 percent of predictable physical work, such as packaging and assembly line welding, could be automated by rapidly spreading technology. By contrast, jobs that require managing others, using specialized knowledge to create products or services, or making executive decisions and plans—that is, upper-class jobs—are the least likely to be affected. The difference is stark: For those in the lower class, globalization is a looming threat; for those in the upper class, it's an opportunity.

It is no small wonder, then, that the tight-loose fault line plays such a key role in world affairs, especially in the realm of politics. As globalization increases, this fault line is dividing groups around the world, with relatively well-off loose cultures that embrace innovation, change, and diversity on one side, and lower-class tight cultures that are financially threatened and seek stability, tradition, and rules on the other. For American voters who couldn't find work after a layoff, the decision to vote for Trump in 2016 came down to a desire to avoid destitution. "I never anticipated being in this situation," Californian Anthony Miskulin, who lost a well-paying job in the 2008 Great Recession, told the *Los Angeles Times* soon after the 2016 election. "My vote for Donald Trump, it wasn't out of bigotry. It wasn't out of hatred. It was about survival." In England, the fear of immigrants taking working-class jobs became a driving force behind many people's votes to leave the European Union during the 2016 referendum.

Perceptions of threat have led some in the working class to prefer populist leaders who promise to dismantle the social structures that have left them behind and restore traditional order. These leaders run on promises of delivering more tightness. Trump vowed to "restore law and order" to the American political system, tighten borders, keep out immigrants, and crack down on crime. France's Marine Le

Pen promised to "restore order" in France in five years. And the Polish populist party, named Law and Justice, ran on a platform of returning to traditional Polish values. Such rhetoric can be highly appealing to the increasingly threatened working class.

By viewing the culture of each social class through a tight-loose lens, we can develop greater respect for people across class lines and prevent harmful misunderstandings. During the 2016 U.S. presidential election, many members of the working class craved the law and order promised by Donald Trump because they believed it would help them ward off the very real threat of poverty. Some Clinton supporters were economically comfortable enough not to fear this threat, nor the threat of immigrants taking away their jobs. The two worlds of the upper class and the lower class have separate norms and preoccupations that have evolved based on their own ecologies. While we may never agree with others' voting choices, once we know that they stem from our cultural codes, we can at least begin to understand them.

7

Is Your Organization Tight or Loose?
It Matters More than You Think

In 1998, two auto industry giants, Daimler-Benz and Chrysler Corporation, tied the knot under the joint title of DaimlerChrysler. It was a massive coup that left the industry swooning over a marriage seemingly made in heaven. German automaker Daimler could sell more affordable cars than its Mercedes sedans, some of which cost more than $100,000. Chrysler, an American brand that sells mass-market vehicles, would finally crack the European market. Soon after DaimlerChrysler's November 17, 1998, debut on the New York Stock Exchange, its share price peaked at $108 in January 1999. With this stamp of approval from investors, a prosperous future seemed guaranteed.

The honeymoon didn't last long. Both companies were deeply enmeshed in their own way of doing business, and their cultural incompatibility soon became apparent. In cultural integration workshops at the conjoined company's headquarters in Stuttgart, American employees were taught German formalities, such as keeping their hands out of their pockets during professional interactions. German members of Daimler's team felt uncomfortable when their American counterparts called them by their first names, rather than by their title and last name. And while the Germans wanted thick files of prep work and a strict agenda for their team meetings, Americans approached these gatherings as a time to brainstorm and have unstructured conversations. For long-term assignments overseas, Americans were reluctant to downsize from their large suburban homes in Detroit to apartments in Stuttgart.

Integrating organizational structures was also arduous and complex. Daimler had a top-down, heavily managed, hierarchical structure devoted to precision. As a result, the company's manufacturing operations were rigid and bureaucratic. Much like its country of origin, Daimler leaned tight. Chrysler, on the other hand, was a looser operation with a more relaxed, freewheeling, and egalitarian business culture. Chrysler also used a leaner production style, which minimized unnecessary personnel and red tape.

As these company cultures collided, Daimler faced a decision: compromise or cannibalize. It chose the latter. Daimler CEO Jürgen Schrempp had promised Chrysler CEO Robert Eaton a "merger of equals," but his actions showed this was an acquisition rather than a merger. (Schrempp won the battle to call the new firm Daimler-Chrysler rather than the alphabetical ChryslerDaimler.) Over time, Daimler dispatched a German to head Chrysler's U.S. operations, replaced American managers with German ones, and laid off thousands of Chrysler employees, moves that fomented talk of "German invaders." Chrysler's dispirited employees coined a joke: "How do you pronounce DaimlerChrysler? Daimler—the Chrysler is silent."

As the $36 billion merger began to look like an underhanded takeover, trust between these two foreign units became irreparable. Key Chrysler executives left, and after nine years of declines in stock price and employee morale, the transnational pair finally divorced in 2007.

THE PRICE OF TIGHT-LOOSE MERGERS

DaimlerChrysler failed in large part due to a colossal underestimation of the tight-loose divide. Why were decision-makers so unprepared to deal with their cultural differences?

While merging with a company from another country can seem financially appealing, leaders often fail to recognize that deep-seated differences in tightness-looseness can cause significant intercultural strife. DaimlerChrysler's disaster is all too common. When organizations considering a merger neglect to assess their cultural compatibility, they can face dire financial consequences.

Can we put an actual price tag on these failed mergers? My colleague Chengguang Li, a professor at the Ivey Business School at Western University, and I set out to test how much tight-loose rifts impact cross-border mergers and acquisitions (M&As). We collated information on over six thousand international M&A deals involving more than thirty different countries that occurred from 1980 to 2013. None of the mergers included in our dataset was trivial—all had a price tag above $10 million. We looked at the length of the negotiation process, the daily stock price following an M&A announcement, and the overall return on assets (ROA) over four years to determine the success of the merging companies. Finally, we determined the relative tightness or looseness of the companies' home countries, which allowed us to measure the cultural gap between the merging pairs.

Did mergers that featured higher cultural incongruity suffer worse performance?

Yes: A substantial tight-loose gap meant costly setbacks. These mergers took longer to negotiate and finalize, had lower stock prices following the deal, and yielded much lower returns for the buyer in the deal. In fact, when there was a pronounced cultural mismatch, the acquiring company lost $30 million on average within five days of the merger's announcement. Very large disparities caused losses of over $100 million. These effects were found even after we accounted for many other factors, including deal size, monetary stakes, industry, and geographic distance.

THE CULTURAL ICEBERG

Culture is like an iceberg. Firms like Daimler and Chrysler may see value in capitalizing on each firm's apparent strengths, but fail to realize that formidable cultural obstacles lurk beneath the surface. Because organizational norms aren't always visible, diagnosing a company's relative tightness or looseness requires a deep dive to understand its practices, its people, and above all, its leaders.

Consider, for example, Israel. Within the borders of this highly loose country lies the greatest concentration of tech start-ups in the world—with one start-up for nearly every two thousand Israelis. Wix, one of Israel's most successful tech start-ups that now operates globally, has eschewed a hierarchical organizational structure, allowing employees to practice self-management. Employees need not work at individual desks or cubicles; they can share large tables in an open studio. Pet dogs roam freely. Offices are filled with an assortment of skateboards, boxing gear, and My Little Pony dolls. With rules few and far between, the atmosphere at Wix has been described as collaborative and playful, if at times chaotic. In Wix's Vilnius office, one manager keeps a loudspeaker on hand whenever she needs to corral the attention of rowdy staff members.

Israeli companies like Wix are proof that "the people make the place." As a "start-up nation," Israel is full of people who are exceedingly informal and rebellious, and harbor a relentless risk-taking spirit. Jon Medved, a leading venture capitalist in Israel's tech scene, summarizes the kind of employees attracted to the start-up scene with one Yiddish word, *chutzpah*, which means having "gall" or "guts." Israelis are notably leery of being told what to do; they prefer challenging rules and guidelines over obeying them. "An outsider would see *chutzpah* everywhere in Israel," explain Dan Senor and Saul Singer, authors of *Start-Up Nation: The Story of Israel's Economic Miracle*, "in the way university students speak with their professors, employees challenge their bosses, sergeants question their generals, and clerks second-guess government ministers. To Israelis, however, this isn't *chutzpah*, it's the normal mode of being."

To level the playing field, Israelis often call people in positions of authority by a diminutive (former prime minister Ariel Sharon was called "Arik"), or even by cheeky nicknames: six-foot-six-inch Moshe Levi, a chief of staff to Israel's military, went by the nickname "Moshe VeHetzi," or "Moshe and a half." Israeli tech blogger and entrepreneur Hillel Fuld explains how this culture-wide disobedience fuels the country's immense growth in start-ups: "The unwillingness to merge, whether on the highway or in business, is the same character that drives the world of innovation." Moreover, many Israelis love to take risks. Wix president and COO Nir Zohar joined the start-up team in its early days because he was attracted to the uncertainty and adventure that came with the project. "It was very exciting to go and do something completely new, to start from scratch, to take that risk," Zohar told the podcast *Startup Camel*. In a positive feedback loop, Israel boasts citizens with loose mind-sets who like to create loose businesses, where they perpetuate loose practices.

Of course, Israel doesn't have the market cornered on loose workplaces. In the United States, the loose state of California proved to be the perfect breeding ground for start-ups like Apple, Facebook, Google, and thousands more, outcompeting each other to offer employees unprecedented freedom and unconventional comforts (including anything from video arcade rooms, minibars, massages, and free cooking classes). And in loose New Zealand, office life at game-designing studio RocketWerkz is rambunctious. Employees are given unlimited paid leave so they can freely manage their work around their personal lives—no questions asked. If a pet dies or a relationship ends, they can guiltlessly skip work and tend to their broken hearts. But unusual perks may also lure them to the office, such as visits from stress-reducing kittens.

Now imagine companies from Israel or New Zealand, with their unbridled practices and people, merging with those from Singapore, where great formality, precision, and discipline permeate organizations. In business interactions, people show respect for the organizational hierarchy. Workers dress modestly and business cards are expected to be received with both hands as a sign of respect. Criticism of one's boss is taboo. Business settings are particularly tight in Singapore because work is an integral component of national identity. To compete effectively in regional markets, Singapore grew to adopt an intense work-centric culture. Indeed, while Singapore has a knack for quickly scaling up its business ventures, Israel has struggled to do so. "What Israelis have not done so well is grow their companies into the big leagues," reporter John Reed writes for the *Financial Times*, due to "a restless, risk-friendly culture of serial entrepreneurship" that has "favored quick exits over organic growth."

In their comparison of the two countries, authors Dan Senor and Saul Singer explain how Singapore "differs dramatically" from Israel. Singapore's focus on order and insistence on obedience, reflected in the country's immaculately clean streets and well-manicured lawns, contrast with the litter and trash you're more likely to see in the public spaces and front yards of Tel Aviv. Singapore's society-wide emphasis on order certainly has its perks, but it can generally lead corporations "to sacrifice flexibility for discipline, initiative for organization, and innovation for predictability," according to the authors. Israeli organizations may lack Singapore's order and discipline, but they're more likely to be nimble and innovative. This is the tight-loose trade-off in action.

Japanese organizations are also generally known for their many rules, formality, and hierarchy. For years, Toyota has operated under a traditional pyramid structure with many standardized processes. Employees shun conflict, and conservative business suits and complex bowing protocols are de rigueur. As part of their intensive orientation, new employees at Toyota are taught company history and have to fully master the "Toyota Way." And at the Japanese electronics corporation Panasonic, the workday starts with group calisthenics, singing the official company song, and chanting the company's "Seven Commandments."

Over in Korea, Samsung's onboarding process has been compared to a military boot camp, with sleep-deprived trainees memorizing every detail of the firm's history and learning to conform to its demanding corporate culture. Koreans face collective pressure to cooperate with social customs and formalities—conveyed with the Korean word *nunchi*, which describes one's ability to pick up on norms. Those who lack *nunchi* may be harshly criticized. "You have to fall in line," one former Samsung employee told *Bloomberg Businessweek*. "If you don't, the peer pressure's unbearable. If you can't follow a specific directive, you can't stay at the firm."

The formalities and norms found in Japanese and Korean organizations mirror their national cultures' strong emphases on discipline and traditional structures, features that developed over centuries in response to threat. Modern-day Korean workplaces remain highly influenced by their country's 2,500-year adherence to Confucian teachings, which emphasize the importance of obedience and discipline for a well-functioning society. In both Japanese and Korean society, an emphasis on respecting convention and following rules has helped create organizations prized for their efficiency and precision.

Tight-loose organizational contrasts can be seen beyond East and West. After noticing a spike in recent years of businesses relocating from tight Norway to loose Brazil, Thomas Granli from the University of Oslo conducted in-depth interviews with Brazilian and Norwegian team members to assess differences in work styles. The *jeitinho Brasileiro*, or "Brazilian way," refers to the common habit of bypassing formal customs and laws to get things done. This "beat the system" mentality can play out as cutting lines, finding legal loopholes, interrupting others, and devising ingenious life hacks. Meanwhile, the Brazilian version of "don't worry"—*fique tranquilo*—is a commonly used phrase, and it carries over from work time to play time. In an effort to spur employee motivation, Brazilian portfolio management firm Semco Partners has embraced one rule, which is to radically abandon all rules. Semco employees get to pick their own schedules, wages, holidays, evaluators, and overarching work goals.

Not surprisingly, tight cultures like Norway that do business in Brazil can struggle. Interviewees in Granli's study agreed, for instance, that Norwegians stressed punctuality, while Brazilians didn't. "Time has a lower priority in Brazil," one Norwegian said. "[Here] the deadlines need to be pushed more than home; things are done at the last minute." But if they tended to be tardy, Brazilian employees were also described as more flexible. Norwegians are sticklers for standard operating procedures; Brazilians embrace fluidity. This led one Brazilian manager to comment, "On a day to day basis, Norwegians are more efficient, but when the time comes to act, Norwegians are slow."

LEADERS, TIGHT AND LOOSE

Tight and loose organizations can seem like different universes, and their leaders personify this divergence. In the Daimler-Chrysler merger, a large cultural rift sprang up due to the companies' contrasting leadership styles. At Daimler, which revered work formalities, all business decisions came from top executives. "Anyone who isn't sure about what is and isn't allowed can find out by asking his or her supervisor," Daimler chairman Dieter Zetsche told *360°* magazine in 2009, after the firms separated. "Every employee must make sure his or her behavior is correct. And I expect our managers to set a good example." By contrast, Chrysler's executives often granted mid-level managers the ability to oversee their own projects, unconstrained from above. These irreconcilable leadership styles became the final nail in the coffin.

Leaders aren't born fully formed; they're raised with certain cultural mandates. The same leadership style that is revered in one culture can be the source of disdain in another. In the largest study ever done on leadership, a team of researchers known as GLOBE (short for Global Leadership and Organizational Behavior Effectiveness) recruited over seventeen thousand managers spanning over nine hundred organizations across sixty countries to assess their beliefs about what makes a leader effective. Which qualities mattered most? Acting independently? Working collaboratively? Being a visionary? In my own analysis of its dataset, I wanted to see the types of leaders that people in tight and loose cultures perceived to be effective.

True to form, they were opposite. People in loose cultures prefer visionary leaders who are collaborative. They want leaders to advocate for change and empower their workers. Ricardo Semler, CEO of Brazil's Semco Partners, exemplifies this leadership style. He's worked hard to get out of the way so that others may step up and innovate.

"Our people have a lot of instruments at their disposal to change directions very quickly, to close things, and open new things," Semler has said. "If we said there's only one way to do things around here and tried to indoctrinate people, would we be growing this steadily? I don't think so." In fact, it's hard to pinpoint if any single employee is in charge at Semco. All workers are taught how to read balance sheets, so the whole group—from the most senior analysts to cleaning crew members—can make informed votes on all company-wide decisions. Semler described an occasion when his employees vetoed an acquisition that he wanted to pursue: "I'm still sure we should have bought [the company]. But they felt we weren't ready to digest it, and I lost the vote." Although disappointed, Semler reasoned, "Employee involvement must be real, even when it makes management uneasy."

Organizational leaders in many Israeli companies go even further, intentionally fostering a culture of disagreement. "The goal of a leader should be to maximize resistance—in the sense of encouraging disagreement and dissent," explains Dov Frohman, founder of Intel Israel. "If you aren't aware that the people in the organization disagree with you, then you are in trouble."

The types of leaders preferred in tight cultures are dramatically different. People in tight cultures view effective leaders as those who embody independence and great confidence—that is, as people who like to do things their own way and don't rely on others, my analyses of the GLOBE study showed. That leadership style can be found at the Chinese firm Foxconn, a major supplier of electronics to companies like Apple, Sony, and Dell. Founded in 1974 by Terry Gou, Foxconn is one of China's largest exporters and employs over 1.2 million people. Gou has described his leadership philosophy as "decisive," and he views good leadership as "a righteous dictatorship." Valuing discipline and obedience among his workers, Gou executes command-and-control management within a rigidly hierarchical company. At Foxconn, mid-level managers model Gou's style by being forceful and autocratic, maintaining a clear power distance between themselves and low-level employees.

These examples all attest to the fact that there are large cross-national differences in the people, practices, and leaders in organizations. Tight organizations boast great order, precision, and stability, but have less openness to change. Loose organizations have less discipline and reliability, but compensate with greater innovation and appetite for risk. With these differences evolving from such powerful forces, it's not difficult to see why merging organizations from tight and loose nations is risky business.

THE CULTURE OF INDUSTRY: FROM MCKINSEY TO MCDONALD'S

The U.S. Department of Labor's O*Net database provides a gold mine of descriptions of jobs in as many industries as you can imagine. From karate instructor to nuclear plant operator, from graphic designer to short order cook, this rich data source provides scores of details on thousands of jobs, including the tasks performed, types of personalities needed, and typical working conditions. But hidden beneath these thousands of descriptions is an underlying structure that explains how industries differ. It all has to do with the strength of social norms.

Just as countries have practical reasons for becoming collectively tighter or looser, so do industries. Tightness abounds in industries that face threat and need seamless coordination. Sectors such as nuclear power plants, hospitals, airlines, police departments, and construction evolve into tight cultures due to their life-or-death stakes.

Take the construction industry. Balfour Beatty, one of the largest construction contractors in the United States, runs a tight ship. Like many organizations in the construction industry, it's responsible for handling the logistics, hiring, and design details of complex building projects. This means its leaders must assure all their workers are safe while they perform some of the most dangerous jobs in the world. On construction sites, a single error can have grave consequences. Turning too swiftly while unloading metal pipes can critically injure nearby personnel. Machinery defects, tiny communication failures, or scaffolding that unexpectedly slips can kill workers. Due to the life-endangering risks involved in this line of work, dependability and predictability are critical, and Balfour Beatty takes this responsibility seriously. It's much the same at construction sites around the world, which typically are subject to hazard assessments and inspections, as well as strict rules on safety, work attire, and training. Construction's tight culture is critical for worker safety and productivity.

The military is the iconic example of tightness. In every country, armed services impose strong norms and tremendous levels of discipline on soldiers, who must be trained to brave the hardships of warfare. Cultivating well-coordinated units and absolute reverence for authority is the backbone of maintaining these strong norms. From day one, U.S. Marine recruits endure a punishing boot camp and indoctrination period that turn individual soldiers into one synchronous corps who, above all, respect their leaders. "The military is like a machine built out of hierarchy," American marine Steve Colley told me in an interview in 2017. "And if you break the hierarchy, you're breaking the machine." In the course of a single day, the typical soldier is repeatedly called on to respect this hierarchical system, from the insignia on her uniform to the salutes she gives her superiors. Forgetting rules can lead to severe punishments, from an aggressive tongue-lashing to having to do hundreds of push-ups in front of one's peers. "We have standards for things as seemingly insignificant as how we dress and as complicated as how to maintain the most advanced main battle tank in the world," described James D. Pendry, a retired command sergeant major with the U.S. Army. "Meeting seemingly insignificant standards is as important as meeting the most complicated ones—meeting one establishes the foundation for meeting the other."

Industries that face less threat, on the other hand, evolve to be loose. In these fields, there are benefits to changing gears quickly, instilling freedom, and thinking outside the box. Employees at the global design company Frog Design Inc., which was founded in 1969, are professionally compelled to question, provoke, self-express, and reinvent conventional tastes. Frog's employees typically enjoy pushing boundaries. "You need to be a rebel in your heart, which means that you like to challenge and question things," said Kerstin Feix, a former member of the company's executive team, in a 2014 interview posted on *Core77*. Frog's former director of marketing James Cortese agrees: "I'm trying to qualify what makes a frog. It's a combination of someone who has an original point of view, but they're also very democratic and open to new ideas."

American online shoe retailer Zappos has the same loose ethos. Now based in Las Vegas and a subsidiary of Amazon, the firm began as a start-up and emerged as the top web-based footwear retailer by 2009. Despite its massive growth, Zappos has clung to its start-up culture and remains proudly loose to this day. The company's bottom-up, egalitarian practices are best exemplified in its adoption of "holacracy," a system of self-management that abolishes the traditional business hierarchy. Employees can self-organize into democratically run "circles" to meet various organizational needs on their own terms. No single person is limited to one circle or role. Everyone's roles are fluid, and team leaders, or "lead links," are more like friendly guides, who don't have the authority to fire people.

Loose organizations like Frog and Zappos are characterized by highly informal, mobile, and diverse work groups. To remain successful, design companies, R&D groups, and start-ups need to always have their eye on innovating and evolving. Compared with workers in industries such as manufacturing or finance (let alone the military), employees are less restricted to their area of specialization, and the comparative lack of strong rules enables them to prosper.

Drilling down further, we see that even within the *same industry*, different ecological contexts can drive tight-loose differences. McKinsey and IDEO are both consulting firms, but the former work culture veers tight, while the latter leans loose. This makes sense when we consider their clients: McKinsey's work tends to include strategy and risk assessments for corporate finance industry and government organizations, while IDEO mainly works on more creative and artistic projects for companies such as Coca-Cola and Apple. McKinsey values a hard-nosed list of company-wide objectives. Unlike IDEO consultants, McKinsey-ites have far more standardized procedures to observe at work. New hires must absorb the infamous "McKinsey way" of doing business in a rigorous training program, learning rules about how to brainstorm as a team member, make client presentations, and follow specific problem-solving steps to break down a business issue. IDEO's loose company values, on the other hand, urge employees to "learn from failure" and "embrace ambiguity." At IDEO, self-governing teams aren't beholden to managers. The relaxed dress code is tied to a more laid-back interpretation of professionalism. "Just be yourself, wear whatever," IDEO's global head of talent, Duane Bray, has told job candidates.

Zooming in to any specific organization, we can see why certain units evolve to be tight versus loose even in the *same* organization. Some occupations are inherently more accountable to laws and regulations, even in the absence of physical threat—think lawyers, auditors, bankers, and government officials. These jobs are bound to high standards of professional accountability. As a result, their work unit cultures foster much stronger norms and compliance monitoring. For companies like the Big Four accounting firm Deloitte, which has a range of units with disparate work goals, the auditing unit's culture is highly distinct from the culture found among consultants. Consultants often hustle through an unpredictable suite of projects—traveling to new places—and need to quickly acclimate to new norms that change as they juggle diverse clientele.

More and more, we see this tight-loose mix within organizations. At Ball Corporation, there's a radically mixed work culture that combines tight manufacturing units with loose R&D divisions. Founded in the late 1800s, Ball supplies bottles and cans to some of the biggest-name brands, including Coca-Cola, Pepsi, Coors, and Budweiser. Ball is also a pioneer in aerospace technology, collaborating with NASA on spacecraft and satellites. The aerospace side includes R&D units of engineers and physicists. Due to its product development goals, this division has evolved into a loose work environment that inspires creativity with less structure and monitoring. By comparison, Ball's manufacturing division follows a highly regimented, routinized process to expediently package and ship out millions of cans every day.

The tight-loose framework helps us make sense of differences not only between nations, but also across and within industries and even among units in the same organizations. These groups all follow a very similar logic, as shown in Figure 7.1. Think about your own employer, profession, or industry. Where is it on the tight-loose spectrum? Can you see why it might have turned out that way?

Tight Organizational Cultures	Loose Organizational Cultures
People	
Conscientious	Open
Careful	Risk-Taker
Practices	
Standardized	Flexible
Efficient	Experimental
Formal	Informal
Strong socialization	Weak socialization
Leadership	
Autonomous	Collaborative
Confident	Visionary

Figure 7.I. Tight versus loose organizational cultures.

But tightness-looseness in organizations isn't static. In today's highly dynamic marketplace, organizations often have to adapt their cultures to fit new demands and negotiate their levels of tight and loose. This mandate can be a tall order, given deep differences in companies' cultural DNA and the clash of people, practices, and leaders.

NEGOTIATING TIGHT-LOOSE CONFLICT IN ORGANIZATIONS

In the spring of 2017, I interviewed a senior leader of a large manufacturing firm headquartered in the United States. The company clearly ran a tight operation. As a publicly traded company, detailed reports and strong oversight were integral parts of its business dealings. As is typical in the manufacturing sector, employees adhered to well-defined processes and frequent evaluations to maximize their overall efficiency. The business developed core strengths of tightness, including reliable delivery and operational efficiency.

Over the firm's eighty years, it had grown to thousands of employees worldwide. Now a multibillion-dollar operation, the company's next step in remaining competitive was to innovate its product offerings. This meant introducing more looseness to its product development side. Although the company historically had been quite risk-averse, its leaders acquired an R&D company, primarily for its cutting-edge technology. The firm's leaders hoped the R&D company's agile, innovative approach would have a dynamic impact on its own culture. But soon after the acquisition was finalized, tight-loose tensions flared. While the R&D group prioritized the creation of disruptive and inventive solutions, it fell behind on team deadlines and failed to get its product to market on time. No one seemed to own any decisions, and soon the division was losing money. From the R&D team's vantage point, the tight mother ship's expectations were unreasonable. The new division had always worked under flexible deadlines, had little supervision, and took a long-term view—they wanted to build the most creative product possible. It was a familiar pattern establishing itself: The very qualities that the acquiring company found so appealing initially in its acquisition were causing major culture clashes.

Other companies face the opposite predicament—they face major pushback when they try to tighten. Take Microsoft in the mid-1990s. The young company's sales were off the charts, but operations were lagging. "We had to close books at the end of the quarter to show investors and shareholders our numbers, but it always took way too long," former Microsoft chief operating officer Bob Herbold told me in an interview. This was due to the company's sloppy and unsystematic bookkeeping. Many of Microsoft's subsidiary offices across the globe had developed their own rogue systems. "There was no coordination at Microsoft," Herbold told me. "Even in marketing, nobody had a clear sense of what the brand stood for."

The company desperately needed to inject some tightness into its operations, and Microsoft CEO Bill Gates knew it. Gates brought on

Herbold so that he himself could focus on the company's products, leaving Herbold to straighten out the business side. Wanting to preserve their looser way of working, employees first resisted Herbold's mission of centralizing division goals and the company's data reporting. Eventually Herbold sold them on the mission's benefits—namely, the prospect of future profit gains—which strongly motivated them to comply. Within a year of Herbold's business centralization, Microsoft not only saved on costs but boosted profits and its share price.

Prosperous start-ups invariably await tight-loose conflicts, often without anticipating them. They attract highly creative people who clash with the tighter structure and standardization that comes with running a larger organization. When I interviewed Ariel Cohen, who led an R&D enablement group for the start-up Mercury Interactive, which was later acquired by Hewlett-Packard in 2007 for $4.5 billion, he was quick to describe himself as a "serial start-up-er." He prefers the high levels of looseness found in smaller ventures to the tight cultures of large corporations. "People at start-ups prefer to wake up, have an idea, then go execute this idea immediately," he told me. "Then they test the idea as fast as possible in the marketplace, then change it or ditch it." But when start-ups begin to scale up, greater hierarchy and rules are introduced, as Cohen observed firsthand. "After they acquired us, Hewlett-Packard hired new people who liked to plan and research their ideas first. But it slowed their creativity down to add more process," he said. "For people like me, it was frustrating that I needed to persuade them to try new ideas. At the same time, they saw my approach as totally random and impulsive, like I had no due diligence." This is tight-loose conflict in action. Soon after Mercury Interactive joined HP, Cohen left to go lead another start-up.

Even if they aren't merging with another company, some organizations are in dire need of renegotiating their culture when they start to approach *extreme* ends of tightness or looseness. Take ride-sharing start-up Uber, which, in the years after its founding in 2009, became infamous for bulldozing through regional ordinances, using below-the-belt tactics against competitors, and hiding certain business practices from local regulators. The company's normless ideology contributed to its immense success, but also to a major crisis. In 2017, a *New York Times* exposé unveiled Uber's recklessly loose, "anything goes" work culture. Several former employees described the exceedingly loose work environment as a "frat house," rife with unprofessional and even abusive behavior. Following the company's sexual harassment scandal, Uber CEO Travis Kalanick was forced to resign. It later came out that higher-ups had also hidden from the public a major hacking. In an already freewheeling tech industry, where creativity is sometimes prized above all, Uber took its looseness to an extreme, leaving shareholders and new management to impose order.

Just as Uber came under intense scrutiny, another company faced its own public relations debacle. In 2017, a horrific incident played out on one of United Airlines' commercial flights, all of it documented on video. With the flight overbooked, airline personnel asked passengers to give up their seats in exchange for an eight-hundred-dollar voucher. Without any volunteers taking the deal, the United computer system designated that four passengers had to be rebooked on another flight. Of these selected passengers, one person refused to forgo his seat. In response, the cabin crew, following company rules, called in airport security to escort the passenger off the plane. The security guard forcibly dragged the passenger, bleeding and screaming with pain, off the plane as nearby passengers captured the scene on their cell phones. The footage went viral and turned into a brand-damaging PR nightmare for United.

United's tight culture may have been partly to blame. After the incident, United insiders told me that the company historically expected its employees to closely abide by its manuals and rules. In the airline industry, which must demonstrate safety and accountability every day, strong adherence to protocol is critical—but this expectation can be a double-edged sword. "United seems to have hired, or at least trained, employees who love rules more than common sense," one veteran employee told me. Quite clearly, extremely tight cultures can inadvertently create an overcontrolled, static work environment in which employees are afraid to speak up and can have difficulty improvising in unexpected situations. Knowing this now, United is seeking to negotiate its tightness by setting up a support team to help triage customer issues that can arise. Based in Chicago, this new team assists staff on the ground with formulating creative solutions for these unexpected situations in order to avert future blunders.

TIGHT-LOOSE AMBIDEXTERITY

Tightness-looseness in organizations is continuously renegotiated, contested, and sometimes totally altered, due to the ever-changing nature of customers, markets, stakeholders, and clients—not to mention bad PR. Some businesses, like United, may indeed operate best under tight conditions, but these companies' leaders need to know when and how to give employees more latitude when the situation warrants it. At the same time, loose businesses, such as Uber, would benefit from knowing when and how to insert stronger norms into their daily practices.

Many companies today are striving to develop *tight-loose ambidexterity*. The importance of being "ambidextrous"—of balancing the need to explore new frontiers with honoring steadfast traditions—was first promoted by management scholars Charles O'Reilly and Michael Tushman in a 2004 *Harvard Business Review* article. Much like a person who can write fluidly with both her left and right hands, organizations need to learn to wield both tight and loose capabilities to operate effectively. A culturally ambidextrous company may favor tight over loose norms, even designating one as its dominant culture, while being capable of deploying the opposite set of norms when necessary.

When loose organizations insert some tight features into their daily operations, I call this *structured looseness*. Take Google's adoption of the 70/20/10 rule, which guides employees on how to spend their time at work. The rule states that 70 percent of employees' time should be focused on assignments from their managers, 20 percent on any new ideas that may be peripherally connected to their main projects, and the last 10 percent on any fun projects they want to initiate on their own terms. While clearly structured, the rule still allows workers to carve out space for personal creativity and flexibility.

The culture of another loose organization, the world-renowned animated-film studio Pixar, manifests as flexible work hours, hidden bars, and free pizza and cereal. "There was actually an individual here who took the ceiling out of his office, because he wanted the natural light," the facility manager told *SFGate* journalist Peter Hartlaub during a tour in 2010. "It was a little extreme, but we don't freak out about it." To come up with innovative new film ideas, Pixar brings together incubation teams made up of employees from various backgrounds and skill sets. While these teams are left to their own devices, senior managers still monitor each team's ability to work well together, particularly paying attention to whether they share a healthy social dynamic. Each incubator, moreover, has a producer and director who track the team project's time constraints and budget. Thus, while Pixar is highly loose, its operations include enough structure and rules to keep things balanced.

On the flip side, steering a tight organizational culture into a looser state is what I refer to as *flexible tightness*. This happens when tight organizations allow employees to have more discretion. Toyota is a case in point. Toyota is a tight organization that relies on rules and standard operating procedures. But in recent years, it has begun to incorporate several practices to inspire creativity and improve customer service. It's decentralizing its decision-making processes by allowing regional heads to have more discretion. Toyota's leaders are also beginning to invite workers to experiment and innovate on their operational systems and products (a loose practice), by using a strict eight-step process (a tight framework). Senior leaders specify overall company objectives using vague terms so that employees can interpret these goals subjectively, which introduces unconventional thinking into the planning process.

Even the U.S. military injects some looseness into its otherwise tight culture with its practice of "Commander's Intent." Billed as a road map to success for every mission and operation, it lays out how the commander should accomplish the mission's goals while also recognizing that "man plans, and God laughs." Commander's Intent recognizes that in any military operation, there are too many unknowns, moving parts, and sudden changes in the battlefield for soldiers and officers to rely on a single strategy. A critical aspect of the policy is the "Spectrum of Improvisation," which encourages soldiers to rely on tried-and-true strategies but empowers them, when faced with an unexpected event, to adapt the original plan to the unit's goals.

"Managing culture is a tightrope walk," Adam Grant, professor and author of *Originals*, told me. "Create too many norms and rules, and you miss out on creativity and change. Create too few norms and rules, and you miss out on focus and alignment." The key, according to Grant, "is to find a balance of tight and loose: have a few strong values that are widely shared and deeply held, but maintain flexibility around the best ways to put those values into practice."

SHIFTING BETWEEN TIGHT AND LOOSE WORKPLACE GEARS

How can organizations become more ambidextrous, smoothly shifting their loose or tight culture into a state of structured looseness or flexible tightness? It's not easy, no matter how minor the change. But armed with an understanding of tight-loose, companies can diagnose what workplace factors need to change—whether it is the people they recruit, the practices they promote, or the people leading—to get the best results.

Tech businesses in China's booming start-up economy, for example, face the significant challenge of cultivating relatively loose workplace cultures that deviate from the country's pervasive tight orientation. Influenced by the strong norms dictated by the Communist Party, organizations throughout China mimic its top-down and bureaucratic managerial systems. Tech start-ups, however, want to generate creativity by modeling the loose work cultures of Silicon Valley's iconic companies. Baidu, known as "China's Google," founded in 2000, tries to shift into a loose gear by seeking out employees who think outside the box. "We want people who aren't slavishly obedient, or are too much the product of a pedagogical system that places too much emphasis on rote learning," explains Kaiser Kuo, a former spokesman for Baidu and the host of the podcast *Sinica*, about Chinese current affairs. Employees receive copies of a book called the *Baidu Analects*, whose title riffs on the *Analects of Confucius*, a collection of the great philosopher's pithy sayings. "It's anecdote after anecdote of these borderline insubordinate employees who stuck to their ideas in spite of pushback," says Kuo, "and the enlightened manager who let them do it, and ultimately they triumph." But alongside this ethos of organizational dissent, Baidu also emphasizes reliability —"delivering tasks to the next team or person only when they've been perfected," explains Kuo, and trusting colleagues to be willing and able to help out when they're needed. This combination of loose norms with high account-ability has been the key to Baidu's success.

No doubt, changing a workplace's culture can be a trial-and-error process. A senior executive at one of the world's largest manufacturers of office furniture relayed to me the bumpy road the firm took as it tried to loosen up operations. For years it had operated a tight ship, but surveys of salaried employees revealed that they felt the performance appraisal system was overwhelming—full of forms, quarterly evaluations, employee ratings, and explicitly defined objectives attached to stacks of instructional documents. Workers had difficulty meeting these countless expectations, which led to disengagement. In its first attempt at flexible tightness, the company's human resources department adopted an entirely opposite system that gave employees complete freedom to decide how they were going to be evaluated. Such a loose model defied the company's generally tight culture and made people feel too uncertain. "We realized we have to have some boundaries on this freedom, and return to a tighter culture, but gradually bring in a bit of looseness," the senior executive told me. The company ultimately reintroduced work objectives and rewards systems, but provided flexible options by allowing employees to participate in customizing sub-goals. The new system gave employees more flexibility and agency while retaining the overall dominant tight culture that they preferred.

As companies work toward greater tight-loose ambidexterity, one thing is clear: During these shifts, it's critical for organizational leaders to embrace the new initiatives.

Consider the launch of USAToday.com. In 1995, to keep in step with the news industry's digital revolution, Tom Curley, then *USA Today*'s president and publisher, prepared to expand the company's print media business online. He hired new leadership to create a department that, like the work cultures of other digital news companies, was much looser than traditional newsrooms. He communicated his vision to existing print-media leaders, some of whom voiced stiff opposition to investing in a fast-paced and arguably less rigorous online journalism division. Senior executives who didn't buy into the new vision were swiftly removed or transferred. This created a "united front and consistent message" among the leadership, which Michael Tushman, coauthor of *Lead and Disrupt*, cites as critical for any organizational change.

Next, Curley worked toward promoting a collaborative spirit between the new digital division and the old-school print division to deal with fears on both sides. Those in print media feared that they'd lose their identity and value to the company and even become obsolete. They also worried that loose norms would bring disorganization, inefficiency, and loss of control. Members of the digital team, on the other hand, wanted free rein to let their creative juices flow and to avoid a confining structure. To mitigate these tensions and build collaborative bridges, Curley required the unit heads for web, print, and TV to attend daily editorial meetings to share ideas, choose the best stories to feature, and establish a cohesive strategy. He also created an incentive for cooperation—a bonus program that was contingent on all the media divisions hitting their goals. Ultimately, Curley struck an effective tight-loose balance, and the company became truly ambidextrous.

Quite clearly, there isn't one best way to develop tight-loose ambidexterity within organizations. Some companies, such as *USA Today*, do this by cultivating mutual goals and respect across tight and loose units. Other companies channel more looseness directly into a tight group, or tightness into a loose group. Regardless of where and how they do it, the key elements involved are illustrated in Figure 7.2.

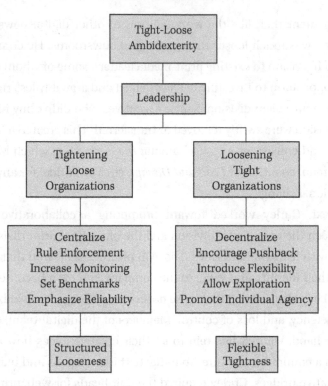

Figure 7.2. Tight-loose ambidexterity. Ways to achieve structured looseness or flexible tightness.

At a workshop I led at Harvard in 2016 with business leaders from across the globe, I shared the tightness-looseness framework and explained how it could manifest in organizational challenges. Many of them commented that they could now see the tensions cropping up in their organization with much greater clarity. Some returned to their offices to urge management to begin using the tight-loose language to help diagnose and solve problems. By understanding the hidden force of social norms in their organizations, business leaders can effectively shepherd their companies toward greater tight-loose balance.

Mirror Check: Are you a "T" or an "L"?

Back in 2012, *Slate* magazine reporter Dahlia Lithwick had an ingenious realization: The Muppets, those beloved puppet characters from
Sesame Street, offer an intriguing paradigm for explaining humanity's
differences. Called Muppet Theory, Lithwick's delightful metaphor
divides people into two groups: those who emanate chaos, much like
Cookie Monster, Gonzo, Animal, and Ernie; and those who embody
order—think Sam the Eagle, Kermit the Frog, Scooter, and Bert. The
Chaos Muppets among us are tumultuous yet dazzling forces of
nature who bring mayhem wherever they go. They think outside the
box, live for new experiences, and are proudly nonconformist. The
passionate drummer Animal is hard to miss in a crowd, with his red
fur and disheveled pink hair. When everyone is going one way, he leaps
in the opposite direction. His drum solos, performed with abandon,
share a lot in common with Cookie Monster's joyous eating sprees.
Unlike these Chaos Muppets, the Order Muppets are overly cautious
and fastidious, the ones cleaning up Cookie Monster's crumbs. Bert,
for example, relishes his morning oatmeal and enjoys hobbies such as
studying pigeons and collecting paper clips. Always dressed neatly in

pressed khakis and striped sweater, he's often providing reality checks to his roomie, Ernie, who is always experimenting with fanciful ideas.

Which type of Muppet are *you*? You'd think your answer would depend a lot on your innate personality. But it turns out that the tightness or looseness of your environment plays a big part in whether you're more Gonzo or Kermit.

We've seen how tightness-looseness plays out in a wide range of groups and entities, from nations to vocations. It's also true that the underlying strength of our culture's social norms affects our dispositions and even our brains. Without even realizing it, each of us has developed *tight* and *loose mind-sets* that effortlessly help us navigate our social surroundings.

Far more than a mere mood or even an attitude, a mind-set is like the program we use to make decisions. The tight mind-set involves paying a great deal of attention to social norms, a strong desire to avoid mistakes, a lot of impulse control, and a preference for order and structure. Relishing routine, it requires a keen sensitivity to signs of disorder. The loose mind-set, by contrast, is less attentive to social norms, more willing to take risks, more impulsive, and more comfortable with disorder and ambiguity. These different mind-sets influence our daily lives and relationships in ways that we might not be fully aware.

We all have a baseline tight or loose mind-set that was shaped by the culture in which we grew up. Some of us are fundamentally more prone to a tight mind-set, like the cautious and tidy Order Muppets, while others tend toward a looser mind-set, like the carefree and boisterous Chaos Muppets. Being raised in a culture with clearly defined social norms fosters a tighter mind-set, and vice versa. Yet while these mind-sets are deeply rooted, they can nonetheless be molded— sometimes in dramatic and rapid fashion—to match different situational requirements.

Take two polar opposite excursions: a symphony and a rock con-cert. At the symphony, everyone is dressed elegantly, and to blend in you probably need to up your game a bit from your usual casual ward-robe. As the orchestra begins to tune up, right on cue, a hush falls over the audience. You turn off your phone, and are careful to keep still in your seat. During a break between movements, you resist the urge to clap, per symphony norms. At the end of the performance, the audi-ence claps in perfect unison and then everyone files out of the hall in an orderly fashion. Now imagine yourself at an outdoor rock concert, crammed in the mosh pit near the stage, getting constantly jostled. People are dressed in revealing or grungy clothing, T-shirts and ripped jeans, and smoke from cigarettes and other substances wafts through the air. All around you, laughter and profanity are the norm, and you and a friend have to shout to hear each other. When the band takes the stage, more than an hour late, the screaming becomes deafening. Throughout the show, people sing at the top of their lungs, dance, and crowd surf. After the final song, everyone shoves their way toward the exit, chaotically pouring into the parking lot.

The symphony is a tight situation, one that requires us to have a keen awareness of how others are behaving and to control our impulses. After all, at a formal symphony performance, atypical behavior—such as talking on the phone or wearing shorts—would stick out like a sore thumb and elicit strong judgment. The rock con-cert, on the other hand, is a loose situation with far fewer restrictions. Audience members feel less need to self-monitor and can express themselves through a wider variety of dress, language, and conduct. Impulsive actions will hardly cause backlash, and a wide range of behavior is encouraged. Above all, these environments don't just alter our wardrobes; they put us in fundamentally different states of mind.

COUNTLESS CALIBRATIONS

The next time you drive, pay attention to how you manage to stay in your lane and keep up with traffic. You'll notice that your hands make countless micro-adjustments, your eyes dart from the road ahead to the mirrors, and your foot makes minute adjustments to your speed. According to the Occupational Safety and Health Administration, drivers make some two hundred decisions for every mile traveled. On the highway, that's more than three per second.

We make the same automatic calibrations throughout the day in response to social norms. These environments automatically change our mind-sets—constrained at the symphony; relaxed at the rock concert. Psychologically, this is your mind and body adjusting to the strength of social norms in your surroundings.

From the time we wake up to the moment we go to bed, we experience the ebb and flow of tight and loose mind-sets. They show up in our households: Are you a helicopter parent or more laid-back? Do your children follow the rules or do they challenge them frequently? If you have a partner, you might see tight-loose tensions play out in different attitudes about religion, savings, or neatness. Do you get grief about your poor dishwashing skills or tendency to leave damp towels on the bed (as I do), or are *you* the neatnik?

During your train commute, if you take a seat in the quiet car, you might be annoyed when someone enters with a looser mind-set and talks loudly on the phone. You'll also see these mind-sets at your place of work, whether you're employed in a buttoned-up law office that has a lot of formalities, or a loose start-up where everyone's wearing jeans and hoodies while playing Ping-Pong. Small changes to our environment can trigger significant changes in our normative radar. If you and your boss are having a client meeting in a conference room, you're likely to be in a tighter state of mind—weighing each word and sitting up straight as a result—than if you're troubleshooting with a colleague in your office. Even your hobbies can activate different mental grooves. Highly structured and rule-bound activities, like playing bridge or doing karate, foster a tight mind-set, whereas more spontaneous and open-ended activities, like painting or hip-hop dancing, foster a loose mind-set.

Tight and loose differences also become apparent in our neighborhoods, schools, and clubs. Before sorting ranked teams for its youth travel program, the soccer board in one New England town spends two hours reviewing a spreadsheet of player evaluations, according to a friend of mine. The soccer officials give coaches and parents reams of statistical data in a bid to underscore the fairness and integrity of the process. It's like a hedge fund quant meeting—about eight-year-olds. Just another example of adults taking youth sports way too seriously? Perhaps. But dig deeper, and you'll see cultural tightness at work. The board developed a rigid set of procedures because of the ever-present threat of Type A parents complaining that their "gifted" child was misranked.

Likewise, when you ask parents about the schools they've chosen for their children—public, private, religious, charter, and so on—you might hear about test scores, pedagogies, and teaching philosophies. But probe some more, and you'll inevitably hear comments that reflect the strength of norms. Some families tend to be drawn to a looser school environment, such as a Waldorf school, while evangelical families who embrace strict rules regarding moral behavior may seek out the tight order at the heart of Christian academies.

As we navigate these different facets and transitions to our day, our tight-loose settings move up and down the scale, sometimes to the point of stress. That doesn't mean we are purely reactive, however.

Each of us has a default setting on the tight-loose spectrum, which reflects our upbringing, geography, generational attitudes, social class, occupation, and other factors. You may have a predominantly tight mind-set due to strict socialization by your parents or hardships you've experienced in your personal life. If you have a looser mind-set, you may have lived in safer circumstances or moved around a lot, experiencing a diverse array of norms.

Think about where your own set point is on the tight-loose spectrum: Are you more of an Order Muppet or a Chaos Muppet? To determine this, ask yourself three questions:

1. How much do you notice the norms around you and the expectations that people have of you?
2. Do you tend to be cautious and controlled, or adventurous and impulsive?
3. Are you a creature of habit—preferring structure and social order—or do you enjoy situations that are less structured?

Beyond your general tendency toward a tight or loose mind-set, you can also diagnose how that mind-set shifts over time, depending on the situation. Throughout the day, what situations bring out more of the former than the latter? With whom does your mind-set fit best, or clash? The coworker you find most annoying may simply be the one whose position on the spectrum is furthest from your own. Our deep cultural programming and varying ability to adjust to different social settings help shape our relationships, careers, communities, and lives as a whole. And with greater awareness of our personal tight-loose mind-set, we can better understand why we act the way we do and, also, be more sensitive to the ways in which layers of culture have shaped the habits of others.

HOW MUCH DO YOU REALLY NOTICE?

Species such as bats, dolphins, and even rats use forms of radar to navigate their physical environment. Humans, too, employ a type of radar to detect the social norms and cues that surround them, whether they're aware of it or not. In fact, a defining quality of tight and loose mind-sets is the strength or weakness of this normative radar.

Some people just seem to be oblivious to social norms. We call otherwise intelligent adults who lack normative radar idiots, jerks, or comedians. We all know people who seem completely unaware of social norms. Perhaps it's a friend who blurts out inappropriate thoughts, even during formal business meetings. Maybe it's an uncle who tells the same stories over and over at every family gathering, blind to the eye rolls and bored looks they elicit. Audiences couldn't help cringing and laughing simultaneously when, after a bathroom break, the fictional "Kazakh journalist" Borat brought a bag of his own poop to a Southern dinner in his namesake movie. More generally, people with low normative radar have difficulty understanding what is expected of them, and they tend to behave similarly across a wide range of situations. Paying no heed to situational requirements, they act primarily on their own beliefs and desires.

You likely also know people who have highly attuned normative radar, such as a Zelig-like "chameleon" who can adjust his or her behavior to fit any setting, engaging with all kinds of people and even winning over those they dislike. People with high normative radar are quite sensitive to the social norms around them. They're what psychologist Mark Snyder calls "high self-monitors." They're very good at picking up on interpersonal and social expectations, and are likely to behave differently across situations in response to what is considered acceptable.

In a clever study, psychologist Janice Mill at the Wright Institute had participants listen to twenty prerecorded sentences in which a trained actress conveyed different emotions by changing her voice intonations and inflections. The results were striking. People with high normative radar identified the different emotions with great accuracy. Meanwhile, people with low normative radar struggled with the task.

Our normative radar fluctuates depending on the situation. For example, a job interview requires keen attention to the social norms present in the environment we've entered. As an interviewee, you need to impress your recruiter by appearing competent. This can mean wearing a suit, avoiding words that might offend, and only asking the interviewer relevant questions. In your bedroom, however, with no one watching, there's little need to monitor your environment—you can wear pajamas, swear, do a wiggle dance, and sing to your heart's content. In this situation, you can turn off your normative radar.

What might not be so apparent, however, is that your normative radar has also been highly influenced by your culture. In a global survey, I found that people in tight nations clearly possessed higher normative radar; they're higher self-monitors and they excel at adapting their behavior to situational requirements. This is a learned trait. In tight countries dominated by strong rules with substantial constraints on acceptable behavior, a keen ability and desire to detect social expectations pays off—if only to avoid punishment. By the same logic, in countries where rules are weaker, and a wider range of behavior is permissible (as at a rock concert), people tend to possess a looser mind-set and lower normative radar.

These differences don't just show up in surveys. Remarkably, scientists in a new interdisciplinary field of cultural neuroscience are learning that differences in normative radar can be physically grooved into our brains.

The brain, as we know, is an enormously adaptive organ. When we're repeatedly exposed to certain kinds of situations, our brains start to adapt to them and change accordingly. In one study, researchers used structural MRI to study the brains of London taxi drivers with extensive driving experience. They found that the region of the brain that stores spatial representations of the environment—the posterior hippocampus—was much larger in the taxi drivers than among non-taxi drivers. Among the taxi drivers, the more miles driven, the larger the region. Taxi drivers' brains actually expand to accommodate complex spatial representations, which ultimately may help their navigational skills.

Just as neurons in the brain of a taxi driver adapt to their complicated routes, likewise, the brain also adapts to repeated experiences with either strong or weak social norms. My collaborators Yan Mu, Shinobu Kitayama, and Shihui Han had American and Chinese students wear electroencephalography (EEG) caps with electrodes that recorded the activity in their brains as they read vignettes about norm-abiding or norm-defiant behavior. If you'd been a participant, you would have read about either a person who was dancing during a tango lesson (appropriate), or a person who was dancing in an art museum (inappropriate). Other vignettes described a person applauding in a concert versus at a funeral, shouting at the library versus on a city sidewalk, and so on. The brains of participants from both the United States and China registered the norm violations in the central-parietal brain region, which is responsible for processing surprising events. Yet individuals' neural responses to norm violations varied dramatically. The neurons of Chinese subjects fired with great force in the frontal area of the brain, which helps us think about the intentions of others and make decisions about punishment. Americans, in contrast, showed little response to norm violations in the frontal region. Differences in normative radar, it appears, become deeply embrained.

Figure 8.1. Dr. Yan Mu, my postdoctoral researcher, in an electroencephalography (EEG) cap. EEG measures electrical activity in the brain.

DO YOU THINK BEFORE YOU ACT?

After registering the normative requirements of a situation, our brains give us the psychological tools we need to adapt. When norms are strong, we feel a strong sense of accountability—we sense that our actions may be evaluated and even punished if they deviate. When that warning signal goes off, the tight mind-set takes over. Its prime motive is to avoid making mistakes by being vigilant, cautious, and careful—what professor Tory Higgins at Columbia University calls a "prevention-focused orientation." But when we're in situations with fewer normative requirements, we have fewer fears about doing the wrong thing. Rather than being driven to avoid mistakes, we set bolder, often riskier goals. This "promotion-focused orientation" allows us to pursue our own ideals, even if that means making a mistake or two. In this psychological state of low accountability, we can afford to be less careful and more risky. Differences in these mind-sets can be found all over the world. People in tight cultures who have to abide by strong social norms are socialized to be more cautious, my surveys show. They're more likely to agree with statements such as, "I am very careful to avoid mistakes" and "I choose my words with care," and they're also more deliberate in their decision making, reporting that they reflect on things before acting. People in loose cultures, who have far fewer normative constraints, report that they're more spontaneous and that they might act before thinking.

These are learned differences, but they may also have at least some genetic basis. In one study, we found that people in tight cultures were more likely to carry a particular gene (the S allele of the 5-HTTLPR length polymorphism) that has been associated with vigilance, attention to negative information, and avoidance of harm. It makes sense that people in tight cultures would be more likely to have this particular gene. From an evolutionary perspective, they may have better survived high-threat environments. Over time, this gene might have been "selected for" in threatening environments, ultimately helping to reinforce tight cultures.

Differences in cautiousness affect countless decisions we make every day. Imagine you're in a study where you're given a simple connect-the-dots task, and you're asked to connect as many dots as you can in a series of four pictures, given thirty seconds per picture.

Typically, in this kind of study, people face a choice between being highly accurate but slow, or fast but less accurate. If you're in a loose mind-set where you're more promotion focused, you'll tend to complete more pictures, but miss some dots. If you're in a tight mind-set where you're concerned about not making mistakes, you'll likely be slower but more accurate at connecting the dots.

You can also see this kind of trade-off very clearly in groups of people making financial decisions. In one study, psychologists separated people into groups, either high-prevention or high-promotion, and had each group consider a number of investment funds and decide jointly which one they'd hypothetically invest in together. The funds varied from highly volatile with a high payoff, to safe but with a lower payoff. The results: The prevention-oriented groups were more likely to choose the safest fund to invest in. What's more, discussions in these groups were more focused on avoiding monetary losses, while the promotion-oriented groups were more intent on discussing ways to maximize profits. This trade-off between security and risk shows the tight and loose mind-sets at work.

When we feel accountable, in addition to being vigilant, we also flex our internal *self-control muscle* to inhibit impulses that might get us into big trouble, like yelling in a library, clapping at inappropriate times at the symphony, or burping during a job interview. People with high levels of self-control, like the Order Muppets, have a lot of self-discipline. They can control their aggressive impulses when they're angry, avoid eating the last donut at the table, and temper the urge to splurge when they're trying to save money. Others, like the Chaos Muppets, have a harder time inhibiting urges and desires. They feel less accountable, and more uninhibited.

Research shows that differences in self-control start developing very early in life. Back in the 1960s, American psychologist Walter Mischel and his team assessed preschoolers' self-control ability with a tempting object: a marshmallow. They told the kids that they could either eat the marshmallow placed in front of them immediately or wait several minutes alone in a room until the researcher returned, at which point they could eat *two* marshmallows instead. Years later, a follow-up study showed an incredible pattern: Children who were able to wait for the researcher to come back with a second marshmallow scored higher on their SAT exams as teenagers, were described by their parents as more socially competent, and were better able to cope with stress in frustrating situations. Another study, this one of more than a thousand adolescents, found that children who had more difficulty with self-control (for example, being impatient or acting without thinking) were more likely to drink alcohol and use tobacco and marijuana during a four-year time span. The ability to tame one's impulses can be identified early, and it clearly has important consequences.

As with other aspects of the tight-loose mind-set, individuals and cultures differ in their powers of self-control. Not surprisingly, loose-natured Americans can struggle with this. Emblazoned in huge, colorful letters on the cafeteria wall of a top Massachusetts elementary school is a two-word plea: "Manage impulsivity!" Administrators understand that American students' impulsive behavior can give teachers grief—but scientists have found that it has deep roots in cultural looseness.

American children, who are generally socialized with fewer normative requirements, score more poorly on self-regulation than children from tight cultures. In one study, psychologists gave both Japanese and American preschoolers a series of hypothetical stories about interpersonal dilemmas (such as two children fighting, or a child falling and being hurt). Next, the kids were asked to complete the stories by "showing and telling" what would happen next, using props and miniature figures. As compared with the Japanese preschoolers, the children from the much looser U.S. culture responded to the stories with more verbal and behavioral aggression, indicating less emotional regulation. Another study found that Chinese preschoolers outperformed American preschoolers on multiple self-regulation tasks, such as playing a game where they had to override their impulses by doing the opposite of what the experimenter asked (such as touching their toes when asked to touch their head).

Spend time in an elementary school in China and you'll immediately see why this self-control muscle is so much more developed. A graduate student of mine recalls encountering an arsenal of regulations at her childhood school in Taiyuan, Shanxi. Students had to sit at their desks with their hands behind their backs at all times, could only raise their right hands when they had a question, and had to be completely silent in the school's corridors. Pupils who acted out faced a range of punishments, such as standing in front of the classroom for the entirety of the class, being excluded from fun school activities, or even being hit with a ruler. Many Chinese schools have strong monitoring systems. Some classrooms even have webcams that continuously broadcast how well children are behaved, with footage being shown to parents and school officials. Similar tales could be told of schools in tight nations such as Japan, Saudi Arabia, and former Communist countries, among others. Masaki Yuki, a professor at the University of Hokkaido, Japan, recalled that when he was in school, kids couldn't be too creative in answering teachers' questions. Deviate too much from the expected response, and you were neglected or punished (which, with his deviant attitude, he experienced firsthand!). Years later, though the punishments are weaker in his nine-year-old son's school, he still observes negative feedback given to children who deviate.

Meanwhile, many American schools not only impose fewer rules, they often encourage individual expression. Nava Caluori, another one of my students, remembers how her elementary school in New Jersey scheduled offbeat events like "Crazy Sock Day" and "Silly Hat Day." For these themed occasions, students who wore the zaniest accessories actually received rewards for their nonconformity. Students could hardly keep their one-square-foot cubbies clean; nor were they expected to. In her after-school care program, which was typical of many elementary schools in her district, kids were allowed to make messes at their craft stations, play games, and make lots of noise. They were rarely told to be quiet, and could do their homework if and when they wanted to.

It's not surprising that deviant behavior is much more common in schools in loose cultures. In 2012, studies by the Programme for International Student Assessment showed that 30 percent of American students arrived late to school at least once within the two weeks prior to the administration survey, compared with 17 percent of students in Shanghai. Seventy percent of U.S. students said there is "never" or "hardly ever" noise and disorder in their classes, which might sound impressive until we compare it with the 87 percent in Shanghai and 90 percent in Japan. People in tight cultures that I surveyed around the world also had less difficulty managing their impulses, agreeing more often with statements such as "I keep my emotions under control" and "I easily resist temptations."

Actually, it's possible to see the neural markers of differences in self-control deep in the brain. In one study, my colleague Yan Mu and I had Chinese and American participants sit in dimly lit, quiet rooms and instructed them to close their eyes and relax for five minutes while hooked up to an EEG. The Chinese participants had greater alpha band activity in the parietal region of their brain, which is involved in self-control, even while they were resting. What's more, these differences made a difference: Greater activity in the parietal lobe predicted Chinese participants' greater self-regulation of eating habits and ability to resist temptations such as drinking alcohol, procrastinating, and playing video games. Self-control differences, in other words, run deep into our neurons, cultivated over years of adaptation to social norms.

We don't need brain scans to see how cultures vary in their self-control. You can just tune in to popular media. The Olympics are perhaps the ultimate acid test for emotional suppression. In an ingenious study, psychologist David Matsumoto used a high-speed camera to photograph athletes' immediate reactions to their victory or defeat, as shown on their faces, in the 2004 Olympic Games. As Matsumoto puts it, the "thrill of victory" and "agony of defeat" played out universally across the athletes' faces at the very end of a meet, match, or race. But he noticed something interesting: Within seconds, athletes' expressions altered from one another in culture-specific ways. Some athletes, particularly those from the West, continued to express unbridled joy; others, mainly those from East Asia, would quickly either adopt a stoic expression or unnaturally try to maintain a wide smile. It seems that our universally shared reactions to victory or loss alter as cultural expectations seep into our psyches.

DO YOU CRAVE OR ESCHEW ORDER?

Are you a creature of habit or a trailblazer? Like those Order Muppets Kermit and Bert, some people are bothered by disorder and ambiguity. They prefer structure and order, wanting everything in its rightful place. Organized and methodical, they regularly establish and enjoy routines, and they like knowing what they can expect from situations. By contrast, other people are hardly bothered by disorder or surprises. Leading more unstructured, chaotic lives, they feel perfectly content grappling with situations that lack clarity. They thrive on unpredictability, and accept ambiguity.

Tolerance for ambiguity is another manifestation of the tight-loose mind-set. When you live in a culture that has tight norms, a lot of monitoring, and strong punishments for violations, ambiguity feels dangerous. Not only is ambiguity in this type of environment atypical—and thus psychologically jarring—but it also raises the fear of threat: What if I accidentally break a rule? Will I be punished, and how? We've seen that a fear of being punished for making mistakes leads people in tight cultures to develop a strong normative radar and to become cautious and self-conscious. No surprise, then, that they prefer structured environments that are less likely to stress these carefully honed qualities.

When I surveyed people around the world regarding their attitudes toward ambiguity, the differences were striking. People in tight cultures preferred to have a clear and structured mode of life and favored consistent routines. People in loose cultures were much more comfortable with ambiguity. To be clear: Neither attitude reflects a character weakness. Rather, they're adaptive traits. When you live in an environment in which there is more disorder, you learn that it pays to tolerate ambiguity. And when order is required to deal with threats, you begin valuing predictability.

Just like other aspects of the tight-loose mind-set, tolerance for ambiguity has a huge impact on our decisions. For one thing, people who avoid ambiguity react much more negatively to changes in their daily routines. In one study, psychologist Arie Kruglanski and his colleagues took advantage of changes that were about to be implemented in many administrative offices of the government of the City of Rome. They found that employees who didn't like ambiguity reacted more negatively to these changes, expressing insecurity, suspicion, and pessimism. When people are in a tight mind-set, their intolerance for ambiguity can also cause them to become upset when others disrupt the social order, such as when someone expresses a decision that goes against a group's consensus.

People who have a low tolerance for ambiguity also have trouble dealing with people who are unfamiliar or different from themselves. In a study conducted in the late 1990s, researchers measured participants' tolerance for ambiguity and asked them to indicate their feelings toward different ethnic groups, including their own. People with a low tolerance for ambiguity reported more positive feelings toward people from their own ethnic group and more negative feelings toward people from other groups.

Remarkably, these differences seem to be passed on from parents to children very early in life. In a study of nearly two hundred parent-child pairs conducted in Belgium, parents and their children showed high levels of intergenerational similarity in their distaste for ambiguity, as well as exclusionary attitudes and support for obedience. Intolerance of ambiguity, it appears, is transmitted from one generation to the next.

A "CHEAT SHEET" FOR MANAGING TIGHT-LOOSE CONFLICT

Once we understand the differences between tight and loose mindsets, we can start to see how they drive conflicts in many areas of life. One of my colleagues, for example, is engaged in a perpetual tight-loose debate with her husband over how to raise their kids. Coming from a loose background, he prefers giving their children a lot of freedom to make mistakes, and he reserves reprimands for very serious occasions. By contrast, to enforce a "tight ship," his wife, who comes from a tighter background, tries to regularly monitor their children and closely control their schedules, and she reprimands them for even small deviations from her expectations. (Think the free-range parenting movement versus the proverbial "Tiger Mom.") Equipped with a tight and loose vocabulary, parents like these can identify the roots of their conflict and, more important, begin to negotiate solutions. For example, my colleague and her husband could compromise by jointly deciding which domains should be tighter for their children (such as use of social media) and which can be looser (such as adherence to immaculate grooming).

Even if you aren't a parent, you may have experienced related tight-loose clashes. Have you ever gone on vacation with a group who liked to plan everything down to the last detail, from dinner reservations to tours, while you had hoped to take a more relaxed approach to the trip and leave room for spontaneity, or vice versa? On the home front, do you habitually get irritated with a partner or roommate who doesn't take the trash out often enough or leaves dishes in the sink? Or are you the one in the relationship who "doesn't sweat the small stuff"? Differing approaches to housekeeping may be rooted in deeper differences in cultural history or experience. At work, perhaps you've noticed that a hardworking, detail-oriented colleague is also dogmatic and controlling when it comes to ensuring no mistakes are made. Now you can label this suite of behaviors more clearly as a tight mind-set. Or maybe you work with someone who procrastinates and makes many errors but is also flexible and innovative—and now recognize it as a loose mind-set. When you find yourself irritated by such predispositions, consider their backgrounds. Might people's life circumstances, such as their culture of origin or upbringing, or any traumatic or pivotal events they've experienced, help to explain their mind-sets? People may assess the same situation from a totally different vantage point depending on their mind-set, and for good reasons. Striking a balance—and negotiating between tight and loose—can prove beneficial in many contexts.

Tight-loose mind-sets often butt heads when people have to make financial decisions together. One woman I know grew up in a relatively affluent household that experienced substantial financial stress when her father lost his job and never returned to the workforce. Her husband, meanwhile, grew up lower-middle-class but watched his parents steadily increase their wealth. Today, scarred by seeing her family's standard of living drop dramatically, the wife is habitually anxious about money. Her husband, on the other hand, assumes each year brings greater prosperity—and spends accordingly. The stress in their marriage over financial matters reflects the psychological tightness or looseness they bring to the issue, a direct result of the contrasting cultures in their homes growing up.

An understanding of tight and loose differences is also helpful in dealing with in-laws and friends. One of my students is a Korean American woman. While she was born and raised in the loose United States, her Korean family adheres to a tighter way of life. When she brought home her Irish American boyfriend, who had a mostly loose upbringing, she had to give him a crash course in adopting a tighter mind-set. He needed to bow to older members of her family but not the younger generation. Over dinner, her parents would give her boyfriend a single drink to go with his meal, and raise their eyebrows if he poured himself a second one. In addition, his deep and booming voice would startle her reserved parents. But when she visited her boyfriend's family, formalities had to go. His parents loved buying her cocktails, and they gossiped with her like old friends. She had to get used to being more relaxed, talkative, and unpolished in the company of his family, setting aside the heightened sense of decorum that her parents taught her to convey around unfamiliar adults.

These dynamics all illustrate how tight and loose differences can become a source of friction—even irritation—when they collide. But by understanding their cultural roots, this couple was able to better work through them together. For example, by recognizing each family's default mind-set, the couple was able to prepare for visits home.

• • •

Not surprisingly, when people cross borders, tight-loose culture clashes are particularly common. My Dutch collaborator, for example, was baffled by some of the behavioral restrictions she faced when she moved to Germany. At first she couldn't understand why her neighbors chastised her for changing her tires in the parking lot on a Sunday (a day on which doing chores tends to be prohibited) or why she wasn't allowed to change the way the furniture was set up in her classroom (because there are extensive fire/safety regulations). Ultimately, she realized that her loose Dutch mind-set was butting heads with the tighter German mind-set. On the flip side, I've also seen East Asian students with tight mind-sets struggle with the comparatively unstructured life of U.S. universities. "What are the rules?" they ask me. Indeed, our research shows that the more "cultural distance" there is between one's own home and host culture, the harder the adjustment. Understanding the reasons for these cultural differences can help us make smoother transitions.

This logic also applies to biculturals—people who routinely switch back and forth between two cultures. I've known first-generation immigrants, for example, who have to constantly navigate different cultural codes. At home, their parents enforce a tight mind-set, yet at school, they feel compelled to switch to a looser mind-set among friends and even teachers. Unsurprisingly, this constant code switching can be difficult. One of my friends recalled how, when she would get on the school bus every morning, she would take off her hijab and apply makeup to transition into her loose school world, only to reverse the ritual later in the day to enter her household. Tight-loose offers a language to identify challenges that biculturals face and helps them negotiate different cultural realities.

Whether we're bicultural or not, all of us can use our knowledge of tight and loose to better understand our own lives. How do you see tight and loose patterns playing out in *your* life? Think about people who cause you stress at home, at work, or at holiday dinners with in-laws. Could a tight-loose gap between you be one of the major factors of discord? Taking the time to consider what a neighbor, colleague, or relative deems a major threat can be a game-changer. While cultural style doesn't excuse all behaviors you find frustrating, it can help you see the "why" behind the "what the . . . ?" Far from calcifying stereotypes with cultural labels, tight-loose theory can help deepen our empathy toward those whose ways just don't sync up with ours.

PART III

Applications:
Tight-Loose in a Changing World

Goldilocks Had It Right

What makes a society happy? Philosophers have been obsessed with this question since antiquity. The Greek philosophers Aristotle, Socrates, and Plato (circa 400 BC) considered happiness to be the ultimate purpose of human existence, echoing Buddha's argument hundreds of years earlier that "contentment is the greatest wealth."

Later, as the Enlightenment age dawned, the pursuit of happiness was unleashed in full force. In his 1725 essay "Inquiry Concerning Moral Good and Evil," Scottish moral philosopher Francis Hutcheson developed an early version of "the greatest happiness for the greatest numbers" as a vision for ideal societies. The English utilitarian philosopher Jeremy Bentham (1748–1832) was also concerned with how to ensure collective happiness, or what is now referred to as the psychological wealth of nations. And, of course, the pursuit of happiness was enshrined as an "unalienable right," along with life and liberty, in the U.S. Declaration of Independence. Indeed, according to Thomas Jefferson, "the freedom and happiness of man . . . [are] the sole objects of all legitimate government."

In the twenty-first century, the quest for societal happiness has only accelerated. Economists, philosophers, psychologists, neuroscientists, and policy makers alike are all weighing in on how to create happy citizens and thus happy societies. In 1998, Martin Seligman and his colleagues created the field of positive psychology for the sole purpose of helping people find happiness and meaning. Many nations now consider psychological well-being as a crucial indicator, alongside wealth, of their development and progress, a trend sparked in 2005 when the government of Bhutan began to construct an index of Gross National Happiness (GNH). More recently, "ministers of happiness" and "happiness centers" have been propagating around the world, and meanwhile, neuroscientists are joining this movement to study what happiness looks like in the brain. Prompted by none other than the Dalai Lama, University of Wisconsin psychiatrist Richard Davidson and his colleagues brought Buddhist practitioners to the lab to observe, with an fMRI machine and EEG techniques, how meditation changes their brain activation.

The quest to maximize societal well-being has taken on a new sense of urgency given the alarming disparity in happiness rates around the globe. For example, Estonia, Hungary, Japan, and China have some of the highest suicide rates in the world—ranging from eighteen to thirty-eight people per hundred thousand—two to five times higher than rates in the United Kingdom and Italy. Pakistan and Greece have happiness index scores of around 150 out of 200, while Spain and Belgium both have scores of 185. Depression rates also vary widely around the world. China and the Ukraine, for example, have much higher chronic depression rates than France and Mexico.

As you might guess, this variation has a lot to do with culture, and specifically with a country's spot on the tight-loose continuum—but not in the way you might expect.

FREEDOM OR CONSTRAINT?

Well-being is a crucial ideal for any society, but the question of *how* societies should be structured to maximize it remains a mystery. Long before I discovered the power of tight-loose to explain cultural differences between nations, many social scientists and philosophers were focusing on a crucial piece of the well-being puzzle: Should societies strive for maximal *freedom* or maximal *order*? Those who favored freedom claimed it allowed individuals to "self-actualize"—to realize their full potential—which, in turn, ensured societal well-being and economic progress. Meanwhile, those who emphasized the importance of order insisted that rules and regulations were critical for creating a secure and stable society that enabled prosperity.

For example, in *The Republic*, Plato advocated for a paternalistic city-state governed by a "philosopher-king" who was in charge of achieving the most good for the entire society. Within this tight city, order was more important than freedom of expression. One of Plato's more austere decrees within this hypothetical city was the censorship of writers, poets, artists, and ideas that he considered dangerous to the populace. Similarly, in *The Analects*, the legendary Chinese philosopher Confucius advocated for an order-centered state modeled on the family, with the emperor as a paternalistic figure who gives protection to his subjects, who in turn owe him loyalty. Confucius stressed the concept of *li*, or "ritual propriety," which mandated that individuals engage in proper conduct at all times as a means to sustain society-wide order. On the opposing side of this debate stand the so-called Cynics of Ancient Greece, a group descended from a Socratic lineage. They famously rejected societal conventions as a millstone limiting freedom and autonomy. In the Cynics' view, human beings were naturally rational, rendering laws unnecessary. If a governing system was too rigid, it would limit our potential to achieve virtue, happiness, personal growth, and self-sufficiency.

Later, in the 1600s, the debate over freedom versus order continued unabated. Thomas Hobbes, who perceived life as "nasty, brutish, and short," advocated in the *Leviathan* for the rule of a sovereign, absolute monarch. According to his logic, only a strong ruler would prevent the brutal, constant warfare in which humanity was embroiled. By contrast, in his 1859 treatise *On Liberty*, John Stuart Mill advocated for a more open system in which freedom of expression reigned. Individuality was essential for human well-being, according to Mill, while conformity enslaved the human soul and hindered progress. Sigmund Freud chimed in on the debate as well. In his 1930 book *Civilization and Its Discontents*, he summarized what he saw as a fundamental tension between the human desire for freedom and the restraints civilization places on us in the interest of societal order. "The development of civilization imposes restrictions on [the liberty of the individual], and justice demands that no one shall escape those restrictions," he wrote. Yet the need to repress our impulses to fit into society leads to deep dissatisfaction and all sorts of neuroses, including guilt and anxiety, according to Freud.

TIGHT-LOOSE AND THE GOLDILOCKS PRINCIPLE

After centuries of debate, the question remains unresolved: Which better promotes human welfare—freedom or constraint?

Could it be that the answer is *neither*? We theorized that *both* excessive freedom *and* excessive constraint would be costly to societal well-being. In particular, overly constraining or very tight environments severely limit individual choice and necessitate constant self-monitoring; on the flip side, overly permissive environments can promote normlessness and chaos. Either extreme—tight or loose—we reasoned could be damaging to societal happiness. In this view, it's the *balance* of tight and loose—of constraint and freedom—that might be the critical societal ideal.

Émile Durkheim, the influential French sociologist, was one of the first social scientists to hint at the importance of tight-loose balance. Studying the challenges of modernity in Europe during the late nineteenth century, Durkheim observed that people were becoming less engaged with traditional religious institutions. Monarchies and other ancient political structures were being replaced by democracies, which gave individuals unprecedented freedoms. At the same time, more people were moving to cities, leaving behind stable, close-knit rural communities. As a result, people had greater freedom but often felt very isolated, surrounded by strangers indifferent to their well-being.

How would these societal changes influence human behavior? In his well-known study *Suicide*, he contended that people were more likely to take their own lives in either very constraining or excessively disorganized societies. *Anomic suicide*, as Durkheim called it, resulted when individuals lived in societies that lacked clear behavioral norms to regulate behavior. In such situations, people felt unguided in their choices, which led them to feel disillusioned. "Irrespective of any external regulatory force, our capacity for feeling is in itself an insatiable and bottomless abyss," wrote Durkheim. "But if nothing external can restrain this capacity, it can only be a source of torment to itself." By contrast, he theorized that *fatalistic suicide* stems from a desire to die rather than live under a constant state of authoritarian control. This type of self-harm is resorted to by people "with futures pitilessly blocked and passions violently choked by oppressive discipline."

Erich Fromm, the renowned psychologist and philosopher, made similar arguments, albeit from a very different vantage point: his firsthand observations of the rise of Nazism in Germany. After moving to Switzerland and then New York in the early 1930s, he began working on his book *Escape from Freedom*, which aimed to understand the rise of authoritarianism. Like Durkheim, Fromm recognized that the modern era presented people with unique social problems, especially when it came to individual freedom. In the relatively open societies of the early twentieth century, an individual in Western Europe could make personal decisions on how to live, what to believe, and how to behave, but their community ties were weaker. This newfound freedom, Fromm observed, left many people feeling isolated, untethered, and lacking a sense of order—a recipe for high existential anxiety. To bring a semblance of order back into their lives, he theorized, individuals latch on to authoritarianism and conformity. "Modern man still is anxious and tempted to surrender his freedom to dictators of all kinds," he wrote, "or to lose it by transforming himself into a small cog in the machine, well fed, and well clothed, yet not a free man but an automaton."

More recently, in the 1990s, sociologist Amitai Etzioni argued that an emphasis on either liberty or constraint alone is problematic in a society. A free society that has few or no rules plunges into chaos. Imagine, for example, if our communities had no traffic laws or other norms to guide behavior—a state that psychologist Barry Schwartz calls "the tyranny of freedom." But order without freedom also results in tyranny. Imagine, for example, if our communities had rules for nearly all of our actions? Etzioni theorized that communities are enriched when both individual autonomy and societal order are blended in equal parts. "A good society," he wrote, "requires a carefully maintained equilibrium of order and autonomy, rather than the 'maximization' of either."

Avoiding extremes has actually been a popular topic for thousands of years. Writing about the "golden mean," Aristotle argued that human virtues exist between the two extremes of excess and deficiency. In the second century BC, the Roman playwright Terence echoed this sentiment in his play *Andria* with the oft-repeated line "Not anything in excess." We see a similar idea in the Chinese philosophy of yin and yang: Two opposing forces can reach a harmonious balance when brought together.

A less erudite text also teaches the value of moderation. In the endearing children's story "Goldilocks and the Three Bears," written by British writer Robert Southey in 1837, and since translated into over twenty languages, readers are transported to a magical world where bears live in their own houses, eat porridge, and speak. Despite these fantastical elements, the story is dominated by a logic of moderation: A young girl wanders through the house of Papa Bear, Mama Bear, and Baby Bear trying to find an optimal balance in all the objects she encounters. Finding three bowls of porridge, she declares the first to be too hot, the second to be too cold, and the third to be just right. She then tries out three chairs until she finds the one that is just right, not too big or too small. Finally, she falls asleep in Baby Bear's bed, which feels just right, after having tried the other beds, which were either too hard or too soft.

Now a common reference point in conversations about the value of balance and moderation, the folk tale has lent its name to a much invoked modern-day theory called "the Goldilocks Principle." Scientists reference the story when describing situations that fall within certain extreme bounds. Climatologists employ the Goldilocks Principle in their "Rare Earth" hypothesis, which posits that, in order to support life, planets must exist within the galactic habitable zone, or the region in a galaxy that is most conducive to life. Psychologists have also applied the Goldilocks Principle to stress: According to the Yerkes-Dodson Law, having too *little* stress can be almost as harmful to well-being as having too much stress. In medicine, the Goldilocks

Principle can refer to the perfect balance of ingredients within a drug that is needed to produce the most desired effect.

From enjoying porridge at the optimal temperature to living on a habitable planet, humans rely on the "sweet spot" that the Goldilocks Principle offers to improve societal happiness. We wondered: Is there also a Goldilocks Principle for the strength of social norms?

THE CURVILINEAR HAPPINESS HYPOTHESIS

All cultures evolve to occupy a particular place on the tight-loose spectrum in response to their unique ecological and historical circumstances—including threat, mobility, and exposure to diversity. Some groups have to prioritize constraint over freedom, while others can prioritize freedom over constraint. This makes perfect sense: Groups ideally *need* to lean in the direction that is more or less adaptive to their environments.

But sometimes, societies can lean *too far* in either direction—becoming either too tight or too loose—which can keep them from functioning well, both psychologically as well as economically. Jesse Harrington, Pawel Boski, and I discovered this by gathering and analyzing measures of well-being in more than thirty different countries. What we found was fascinating: The nations that were extremely tight and extremely loose had the *lowest* levels of happiness and the highest levels of suicide. By comparison, nations that were less extreme on the tight-loose scale exhibited higher happiness scores, and lower suicide rates. The same was the case for depression. Of course, many factors affect people's happiness, but these data show a clear pattern in which both very tight and very loose nations have lower happiness scores and higher suicide rates. In statistics, this is called a *curvilinear* relationship.

Given that the health of the human mind is symbiotically linked with the health of the body, we next examined whether the result held true for *physical* health. We gathered data on life expectancy, and found that, even controlling for economic inequalities across countries, very tight and very loose nations had the lowest life expectancies. The tight nations of Pakistan, India, and Turkey had average life expectancies of just sixty-seven, sixty-seven, and seventy-three years respectively, and the loose nations of Ukraine, Brazil, and Hungary had average life expectancies of sixty-nine, seventy-three, and seventy-four years of age. By contrast, nations that were more moderate had higher life expectancies. France, Spain, and the United Kingdom, for example, all had average life expectancies of between eighty and eighty-two years.

Countries that are either extremely loose or extremely tight also had the highest death rates from cardiovascular diseases and diabetes. The very tight cultures of Pakistan, India, and China had respective rates of 422, 335, and 286 per 100,000. This was also the case for very loose cultures: Estonia had an average death rate of 351 per 100,000; Brazil had an average rate of 265 per 100,000; and Hungary had an average rate of 329 per 100,000. Compare these statistics with the much lower rates of death from cardiovascular diseases and diabetes in more moderate countries: 129, 113, and 134 per 100,000 for Italy, Spain, and the United Kingdom, respectively.

The relative tightness of a populace was also linked to its political instability and economic wealth. According to the Economist Intelligence Unit, threats to political stability are usually accompanied by violence or disorder, even if an existing regime isn't successfully toppled. We found, again, that tightness-looseness and political instability have a curvilinear relationship: Nations with excessive freedom or constraint show higher levels of political instability. The loose nations of Ukraine, Venezuela, and Greece were at high risk for political instability in 2009–2010, a prediction that played out for each country in the years that followed. Similarly, some of the tightest nations—Turkey, Malaysia, and Pakistan—were also considered high risk for political instability. Turkey, as if on cue, experienced a major coup attempt just a few years later. By contrast, nations like the United Kingdom, Austria, and Belgium have had less political instability. The tightest and loosest countries also exhibit the lowest GDP per capita.

The data are clear: Both excessive constraint *and* latitude contribute to poor national outcomes, including lower happiness, greater rates of depression, higher suicide rates, lower life expectancy, greater mortality rates from cardiovascular disease and diabetes, lower GDP per capita, and a higher risk for political instability. These societal outcomes are all highly interrelated and can be averaged for an overall score of well-being.

Figure 9.1 illustrates this effect. There is no linear relationship between tightness and well-being (shown by the dashed line)—in other words, happiness doesn't tend to increase as tightness increases. But, with some notable exceptions, you can clearly see an inverted U or curvilinear relationship (shown by the solid line) whereby both very loose and very tight countries tend to have lower well-being.

THE BIRDS, THE BEES, AND THE BRAIN

We know that the tight-loose Goldilocks Principle applies to humans. But does it also hold true for other species?

Yes—for many, certainly. Consider what happens each year when a colony of honeybees outgrows its hive and needs to find a new home. Usually in late spring or early summer, two-thirds of the bees leave with the queen to create a new colony, while the remaining one-third stay behind with the queen's daughter. The bees who leave must find

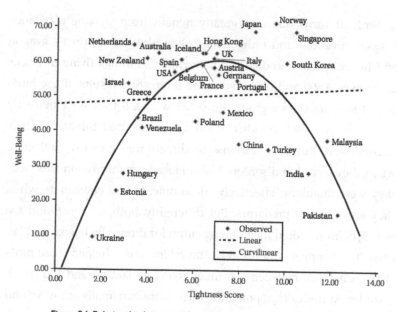

Figure 9.1. Relationship between tightness-looseness and overall well-being.

a new home as quickly as possible to ensure the group's survival. They start by clustering on a tree branch, then hundreds of them fly off at a time to scout out potential nest sites. If they come across any good ones, the bees return to the branch and perform so-called waggle dances, which allow them to convey how good they believe the sites to be and instruct the other bees on their exact locations. After observing these dances, the next group of bees fly out to visit the sites for themselves. Thus, the process of finding a new home involves not only *latitude*—as the earlier bee scouts must decide on their own which sites to recommend—but also *conformity*—as later groups of bees conform to the groups' recommendations. Using computer simulation models, researchers have proven that bee colonies work best with a balance of conformity and independence rather than a high level of either one. In this respect, successful bee colonies have a lot in common with successful nations.

Birds, it turns out, also greatly benefit from striking a balance between freedom and order. The Italian physicist Andrea Cavagna and his colleagues studied the behavior of starlings flying in flocks as large as 4,300 and observed some interesting results. If the birds were too ordered as a group—in other words, if they were perfectly synchronized—they couldn't adapt to unexpected threats in their environment. But their response to threats was similarly ineffective when they were too disordered, and lacked synchrony—in this case, they were unable to effectively communicate and coordinate when they encountered predators. Put differently, both *too much* and *too little* synchrony could mean being eaten for dinner by hawks and falcons. The happy medium, called the *critical point*, helped these birds strike a balance between too much synchronization and too much disorder. At this critical point, the birds were maximally attentive and ready to defend themselves against predators.

Getting back to humans, the problematic nature of excessive order or disorder has been shown in the most mysterious of places: our brains. Studies show that both too much and too little synchrony among neurons are associated with a host of brain disorders. For instance, one study used EEG recordings to look at the brains of epileptic subjects during seizures. The recordings showed that the interactions among neurons were too synchronized during seizures. Whereas normal neuronal activity shows intermittent synchronization between different regions of the brain, the neurons of epileptic subjects were firing in an abnormally synchronized fashion, which prevented the brain from adapting to changing conditions. Too much neural coordination also has been linked to Parkinson's disease, specifically to tremors and an inability to initiate movement.

But at the same time, too little synchrony in the brain means that there is far less communication between neurons than normal, which makes the spread of information much less efficient. This reduced coordination is characteristic of autism, Alzheimer's disease, and schizophrenia. For instance, individuals with autism often do not "see the big picture" in everyday life—they have difficulty experiencing "wholes without full attention to constituent parts," wrote Leo Kanner, the scientist who first clearly defined the disorder in 1943. Abnormally low neural synchrony may account for the difficulty that those with autism have integrating information from different components, research has found. Similarly, studies of individuals with schizophrenia suggest that impaired neural synchrony makes it difficult for them to process information. Studies also suggest that low neural synchrony may underlie the memory breakdown associated with Alzheimer's disease. In all, an ineffective brain is "one that does exactly the same thing every minute, or, in the other extreme, is so chaotic that it does a completely random thing, no matter what the circumstances," according to neurophysiologist Dante Chialvo. Avoiding extremes of chaos or order is as important in biology as it is in society.

THE GOLDILOCKS PRINCIPLE IN ACTION

The Goldilocks Principle, when applied to tightness-looseness, can explain how everything from nations to neurons can achieve optimal levels of functioning. These insights can also inform how we might increase our day-to-day well-being. Whether we're navigating our closest relationships, trying to perform well at our work, or making big and small life decisions, we need to balance our natural preferences for more constraint or more freedom to be at our best. This means not allowing either extreme to dominate.

Take parenting. As we saw in our comparison of the lower and upper classes in Chapter 6, some parents need to enforce stronger norms to help their children cope with threats like poverty, violence, and unemployment. But as with honeybees and our brains, extreme constraint or extreme latitude in families can cause problems. For example, when parents are extremely overprotective, they may produce children who are obedient at home, but lack personal discipline and self-confidence when outside their parents' fastidious oversight. The mothers and fathers who keep their children on a tight leash and micromanage their daily activities are what is commonly referred to as "helicopter parents." They *hover*. While on the surface, children who are the objects of such scrutiny may seem to be functioning well, studies suggest that many suffer from depression, anxiety, and lower life satisfaction.

Of course, parents who are exceedingly lax, permissive, and indulgent can be equally problematic. Children raised with few rules in place and little monitoring can develop poor academic habits and self-regulation skills. In their teenage years, they're more likely than other kids to engage in underage drinking, substance abuse, and other risky behaviors.

The parenting "sweet spot," where children have limits but also the freedom to make their own decisions, can produce healthier children. In a longitudinal study, sociologist Laura Hamilton of the University of California, Merced, compared college students' outcomes based on whether their parents offered what I would call tight or loose guidance. Among the students who had uninvolved parents, none in the sample graduated within four years, and they struggled to find a job following graduation. Students with overbearing helicopter parents all graduated on time, yet these students had professional and emotional dependency issues. In Hamilton's later interviews with these individuals, she noted that "they are still calling their parents about major decisions. They are unsure of themselves, more anxious than others and not as comfortable in their own skin as you might expect a thirty-year-old to be. The reins of responsibility were not handed over." In addition to these two extremes, she also looked at a third type of parents, whom she dubbed the "paramedics." The paramedics were involved, but not overly so: They gave their children freedom and space to make their own decisions and mistakes, while remaining available if guidance was needed. Children of paramedics had the best outcomes, generally graduating from college within the expected four years, finding employment, and being able to handle emotional matters on their own.

The tight-loose Goldilocks Principle also applies to everyday decisions in *other* areas of life. Is it better to have many choices when making decisions, or very few? Again, the answer is neither. Having no choice can be problematic. Decades of research have shown that having some degree of personal autonomy is a robust predictor of well-being. However, though it might not be obvious, the other extreme—having too many choices—is also highly problematic.

To see why this might be the case, imagine that you're shopping at the supermarket and come across a table where you have the opportunity to taste a whopping thirty flavors of jam. How many do you think you'd taste? And how many jars might you buy? Now imagine that only six flavors are available for tasting. How many do you think you'd taste and buy? You might assume that more choices would suggest more flavors to fall in love with, and that you'd spend a bit more money if you found multiple jams you liked. However, when psychologists Sheena Iyengar and Mark Lepper set up this scenario in a supermarket, they found the exact opposite. In fact, people were *less* likely to buy jam at all when given thirty options. Only 3 percent of people who had this huge range of choices ended up making a purchase, while almost 30 percent of those who could taste just six jams wound up buying a jar.

An abundance of choice can overwhelm us and paralyze our

decision-making ability in higher-stakes situations as well. Research has found that when 401(k) plans offered more funds for people to invest their money in, fewer employees ended up enrolling. For every ten additional fund options that 401(k) plans offered, there was a 1.5 to 2 percent *decrease* in the amount of people participating. The highest rate of participation was 75 percent, when only two fund options were offered. The lowest participation rate clocked in at 60 percent, when people had a staggering fifty-nine fund options to choose from. "Choice overload," as psychologists call it, ironically can keep employees from making any choice at all.

Having too many choices can also undermine satisfaction when people do end up coming to a decision. Recent college graduates who made a conscious effort to ensure they had as many choices as possible during the application process—or *maximizers*—were less satisfied with their jobs than were *satisficers*, or those who only looked for jobs until they found an acceptable option. In this case, trying to make the best choice backfired due to people's regret about the many roads not taken. "There is a dark side to all this freedom from constraint, to all this emphasis on individuals as the makers of their own worlds, their own destinies," writes psychologist Barry Schwartz in his 2004 book *The Paradox of Choice*. "It leaves people indecisive about what to do and why. Freedom of choice is a two-edged sword, for just on the other side of liberation sits chaos and paralysis. Thus, there is a price for freedom—danger. There is a price for enlightenment—uncertainty."

A similar logic applies to our love lives. The massive amount of choice people perceive they have about whom to partner with may actually stand in the way of meaningful commitment, according to Schwartz. Movies, novels, TV shows, and magazines relentlessly push the idea that the "right person" is out there—that everyone has a soul mate. At the same time, online dating apps ranging from Match.com to Tinder create the perception that there are endless numbers of fish in the sea, so to speak, which can lead people to be restless and indecisive. How will you know if a particular person is "the one" if there are thousands of others just waiting to be discovered on your cell phone? We tend to assume that it's only people with few romantic options who lack contentment. But people with endless romantic choices might also be dissatisfied. Being lucky in love might be as simple as turning off Tinder, and its endless array of possibilities.

The Goldilocks Principle of tightness and looseness also can help us perform better at work. As we saw in Chapter 3, too many top-down constraints can keep our creative juices from flowing. But while it may seem as if creative thought flourishes best with minimal restrictions in place, too much freedom can leave us without any sense of direction. In an interesting study done at the University of California, Berkeley, students were assigned to do Internet research on a general topic, like health, as well as five subtopics (drug abuse, fitness, nutrition, preventing illness, and stress). Next, they were asked to use this research to write up a proposal for a new product designed to address these issues. There was an important catch: Participants were randomly assigned to one of four conditions that had varying levels of constraint. In group one, which had lowest constraint, they were told to address any issue related to the general topic of health. In group two, which had moderately low constraint, they were told to address any one of the five subtopics. In group three, which had moderately high constraint, they were told to address one of three of the subtopics. Lastly, in group four, which had the highest constraint, they were told to address only one specific subtopic. After the participants wrote up their proposals, five trained judges rated the creativity of their proposals. More moderate degrees of constraint (groups two and three) proved more conducive to creativity than either the higher or lower degrees of constraint (groups one and four). Put simply, balancing freedom and constraint can help us be our most creative selves.

The Goldilocks Principle could even help society develop healthier financial institutions. The 2001 Enron scandal is one of the most striking cautionary tales in recent history of an institution that crashed due to a dearth of internal controls. Before its free fall into bankruptcy, Enron was the world's largest energy trading company and considered the "darling of Wall Street." But during this time, Enron executives were implicated in obfuscating losses on the company's balance sheets, hiding mounting debt to keep the company looking like a rising and remarkably profitable enterprise. Compounding this lack of self-regulation were Enron's lead auditors, who were accused of routinely overlooking the company's questionable financial practices. Enron's under-regulation and resulting bankruptcy rocked the public's trust in corporations and the financial markets.

On the other hand, too many controls can hold back an organization's financial success. Excess controls can make work processes too time-consuming and hurt overall competitiveness. In particular, when companies are required to meet standards that are costly to comply with, they may no longer have the capital to invest in growing their businesses. In Chapter 7, I described the benefits to organizations of cultivating tight-loose ambidexterity—an application of the Goldilocks Principle, where workers and divisions toggle back and forth between tightness and looseness depending on the needs of the situation.

Moving to one final arena, the Goldilocks Principle helps inform political debates over national security. In the United States, the tension between liberty and constraint erupted after 9/11 with the Patriot Act and the National Security Agency's mass surveillance techniques, both of which allowed the U.S. government unprecedented monitoring of its citizens. These constraints have been hotly debated: Proponents argue that expanded surveillance powers are necessary to protect the country and its citizens from terrorism. Detractors, on the other hand, insist that these expanded government powers overstate the threat of terrorist acts in the country, unnecessarily curtailing the freedom and rights of citizens.

The trick, of course, is to emphasize security without infringing on civil liberties. This challenge resonates in other countries as well. "Both [security and freedom] are vital to our nation's well-being," said David Cameron, who later became the British prime minister, in a speech to the Center for Policy Studies in 2006. "So we should be permanently vigilant. We should never stop thinking hard about how to protect our security and freedom as our society and our circumstances change." As in other aspects of our lives, striving for a middle ground on these issues—the tight-loose sweet spot—can help guide us toward greater national well-being. The problem comes when groups lean too far in one direction—when a nation facing security threats starts turning toward totalitarianism and infringes on individual rights, for example, or a loose nation veers toward lawlessness and suffers an uptick in violent crime.

Each culture may well have its own optimal level of tight-loose given the demands of its environment. But one thing is for sure: Extreme levels of tightness and looseness aren't optimal for any group. When governments and their citizens become aware of the Goldilocks Principle of tight-loose, they may be better positioned to guard against these developments.

Culture's Revenge and Global (Dis)Order

In January 2011, the world watched, stunned, as hundreds of thousands of Egyptian citizens ignited a nationwide revolution. Spanning all age groups, political backgrounds, and religious affiliations, the protesters assembled in Cairo's major town square to demand the ousting of President Hosni Mubarak and the dismantling of thirty years of autocratic rule. Their rallying chants included "Illegitimate!" and "Mubarak, go!" They used social media platforms to turn up the noise, globally broadcasting their uprising. "We use Facebook to schedule the protests, Twitter to coordinate, and YouTube to tell the world," explained one protester—in a tweet, no less. Despite several violent clashes between police and demonstrators, hundreds of deaths, and thousands of injuries, the activists didn't give up. After eighteen days of protests, Mubarak's authoritarian regime collapsed. The Egyptians' dream of a new government was finally being realized.

This dream, however, soon turned into a nightmare. Egypt's first democratically elected leader, Mohamed Morsi, went rogue, granting his office dictatorial powers. By June 2014, he'd been ousted in a military coup, and Abdel Fattah el-Sisi—another oppressive autocrat—

had taken the reins. In 2017, human rights groups estimated that there might be as many as sixty thousand political prisoners in Egypt's jails, a tenfold increase from Mubarak's rule. New laws repressed protests, and Sisi issued decrees that granted him absolute power to silence his critics.

At first glance, Egypt's U-turn toward dictatorship seems inexplicable. How did people who joined together with such hope and determination to overthrow a fiercely authoritarian president end up living under an even *more* autocratic leader?

Many recent societal disruptions around the world—from the Arab Spring to ISIS to the populist wave in politics—have stemmed in part from the structural stress of tight-loose tension. While all of these upheavals have unique elements, each demonstrates a simple truth: Humans crave social order. When people experience disorder and normlessness—when they become exceedingly loose—they desperately yearn for security. Autocratic leaders are there to pick up the cultural pieces and sate this universal need.

Call it culture's revenge, but tightness-looseness is a stubborn fact of our existence. As long as humans populate the Earth, the strength of social norms will be a key part of our cultural DNA. Part of this cultural code dictates that in response to extreme looseness, humans gravitate toward tightness, and vice versa. Understanding this link between tight-loose dynamics and geopolitical events will allow us to not only better anticipate global trends, but also develop culturally intelligent policies to manage them.

THE DIZZINESS OF FREEDOM

The Goldilocks Principle uncovered the dysfunctions that arise from cultural extremes. Too much tightness constrains our autonomy, but too much looseness can breed chaos. Both ends of the spectrum are detrimental.

While nations at the far ends of the cultural continuum are more vulnerable to radical change, Egypt's swing from tight to loose and back to tight again was especially dramatic. After ousting Mubarak, the Egyptian populace was ecstatic to have escaped decades of brutal rule. Men, women, and children of all ages danced and cheered, "Egypt is free!" and "God is great!" Opposition leader Mohamed ElBaradei proclaimed, "For the first time, Egypt has a chance to be democratic, to be free . . . to have a sense of dignity, of freedom." "I feel as though my handcuffed wrists and my sealed lips are now free," protester Mustafa Sayed rejoiced.

It quickly became apparent, however, that Egypt was bound for chaos, not freedom. Though life during Mubarak's regime was oppressive—with 12 percent inflation and more than 10 percent unemployed—society deteriorated in the months after his toppling to intolerable levels. GDP growth was nearly stagnant; the country's reserves declined by more than $10 billion; and by December 2011, the stock market was down more than 40 percent. Forty-four percent of all Egyptians were categorized as extremely poor or near poor. The Arab Spring was on the verge of turning into an economic winter.

It wasn't just Egypt's economy that suffered. Its social norms unraveled. Over the course of three months following Mubarak's resignation, crime rates rose an astonishing 200 percent. Riots and kidnappings spiked due to a lower police presence. "Sure, we were all happy. And of course we celebrated. The whole world was watching Egypt. We were enormously proud," remarked journalist Gabriele Habashi, eight months after Mubarak was ousted. "But then? The Egyptians have returned to daily life, which has become much more difficult than before . . . The people have become tired of revolution."

Having taken down an authoritarian regime, Egyptians now found themselves living at the other cultural extreme: in a completely chaotic environment. After Mubarak's top-down control was dismantled, they had no mechanisms to coordinate and regulate their society or to satisfy even their most basic needs.

This outcome, in many ways, was the very design of Mubarak's autocracy. Under his rule, Egyptians lived in a tightly controlled society with harsh regulations and minimal autonomy. Roadblocks were put up to prevent citizens from developing trust and self-organizing, a strategic ploy to fend off challenges. Volunteer associations, labor unions, professional associations, NGOs, and any group of strangers coordinating shared interests faced a labyrinth of government-imposed restrictions.

In the face of increasing chaos, the same Egyptian citizens who had craved freedom were now looking for order. Sisi "will bring back security and will bring the institutions of the country together," said Cairo silversmith Ayman Iskandar to former *Guardian* foreign affairs reporter Patrick Kingsley. Alexandria resident Ahlam Ali Mohamed said she voted for Sisi because she wanted to "feel safe." "For pro-Sisi Egyptians, a vote for their candidate is a vote against chaos," explained Sarah Eltantawi, a professor of comparative religion at Evergreen State College. In my 2017 book *Values, Political Action, and Change in the Middle East and Arab Spring*, I described this political shift in Egypt as an example of *autocratic recidivism*. Reacting to the chaos following the ousting of Mubarak, people became amenable to yet another strong ruler who promised to restore the social order.

This dynamic is not limited to Egypt. When people encounter normlessness, they feel tremendous anxiety. Inevitably, this anxiety leads to a quest for security. In his 1941 book *Escape from Freedom*, psychologist Erich Fromm described this phenomenon as "a readiness to accept any ideology and any leader if only he offers a political structure and symbols which allegedly give meaning and order to an individual's life." Having observed the widespread acceptance of fascism in Germany, which he fled in 1934, Fromm believed that a return to autocracy was a universal response to excessive freedom. Remarkably, a century before, the Danish philosopher Søren Kierkegaard coined the phrase "the dizziness of freedom" to capture a similar dynamic in his time: the sense of intense anxiety when one is confronted with endless freedom.

Putting these insights to a modern test, my collaborators and I distributed surveys to Egyptians in the spring of 2012 to assess whether their sense of normlessness was driving their yearning for a tighter culture. The surveys asked a variety of questions, including "To what extent is Egypt experiencing a breakdown of social order?"; "To what extent is Egypt very chaotic these days?"; "To what extent is Egypt safe?"; and "To what extent would Egypt be a better place if there were more rules than there are now?" We also asked our respondents whether they preferred a religious or secular government and whether they supported the Salafis (a highly conservative branch of Sunni Islam). Those who perceived that Egypt had become exceedingly loose after Mubarak's presidency expressed preferences for autocratic rule. That is, there was a close connection between the normlessness that ensued after Mubarak's ousting and support for an even stricter government to restore order. Sure enough, Egypt soon jolted back to a tight regime.

Such cultural shifts between tightness and looseness have accompanied other major disruptions to the social order. After the crumbling of the oppressively tight USSR in 1991, 51 percent of Russians supported democracy and 53 percent endorsed having the freedom to pursue life goals unimpeded by state interference. On the other hand, only 39 percent supported a leader with a strong hand. By 2011, however, there was a huge pivot: 57 percent of Russians supported a ruler with a strong hand, and 68 percent were in favor of state interference.

What caused such a dramatic shift? Tightness-looseness theory suggests it was the precipitous economic decline and widespread societal disorder that followed the fall of the Soviet Union. Between around 1991 and 1998, Russia lost approximately 30 percent of its GDP and was plagued by runaway inflation. Disposable income declined, nearly $150 billion in capital left the country, and oil prices plummeted. As the economy suffered a series of shocks, crime in Russia was rising fast. There were more than four thousand organized-crime groups in Russia in 1992, and gang-related shootings riddled Moscow. The government's decision to wage war in the breakaway southern Russian republic of Chechnya also took a toll, triggering acts of terrorism on Russian soil and the deaths of thousands of Russian soldiers in combat. Alcoholism, a perennial scourge in Russia, surged. Illegal drug use, particularly heroin and other hard drugs, also exploded fivefold in the 1990s. Life expectancy for males fell from sixty-four in 1990 to fifty-eight years by 1994, in large part due to alcoholism, homicide, and suicide. Russia was falling apart.

Reflecting back on this chaotic time, journalist Arkady Ostrovsky remarked, "For me, the shortages of food in the shops were fully compensated by this exhilarating new sense of possibility. History was being made in Moscow, and we were in the middle of it. Looking back at that period, I realize now that this sense of excitement was experienced by a narrow circle of people. For the majority of the population, the collapse of the Soviet Union was associated with uncertainty and a sharp decline in living standards."

"It was a very difficult time, and I would not characterize it as a feeling of freedom," echoed Sasha Latypova, who was a college student in Kiev at the time. "Freedom was the last thing everyone was thinking about, but the inflation, food, and shortage of everything else were foremost on everyone's mind."

By the end of the twentieth century, Russians were yearning for order and desperate for any semblance of collective national identity, according to sociologist Lev Gudkov, an expert in ethno-national relations in Russia. A cultural vacuum was ready to be filled.

Enter Vladimir Putin, the former KGB agent handpicked by then Russian president Boris Yeltsin as his successor. Putin is one of the world's most popular politicians, with an approval rating of over 80 percent in 2017. This soaring support has not been in spite of but *because* of his highly autocratic leadership. Why? Because Putin has restored order to a chaotic country. From 2000 to 2015, GDP per person grew 70 percent in Russia, as compared with only 17 percent in the European Union. Under Putin, unemployment dropped from 11 percent in 2000 to 6 percent in 2015. "Putin is widely viewed at home as the man who tamed a tumultuous post-Soviet Russia," American journalist Julia Ioffe wrote in *National Geographic*.

Yet this economic prosperity comes with a heavy trade-off: Putin rules with an iron fist. Harsh punishments—including thousands of dollars in fines and prison time—are levied against those who protest, criticize the government online, or engage in political or human rights advocacy. Most of the Russian media is state run and, as in the Soviet era, reports the news with a distinctly pro-government slant. A number of political websites critical of Putin are blocked, and international organizations, foreign citizens, and even Russians with dual citizenship are banned from owning any mass media outlets. According to the Committee to Protect Journalists, Russia ranked fifth globally for the highest number of journalists killed between 1992 and 2014, and Freedom House consistently ranks the country as having among the most severe restrictions on freedom of the press.

By tightening his country to a degree that resembles a stranglehold, Putin has propagated a proud, ethno-nationalist culture. In place of the Marxist-Leninist ideology that galvanized the Soviet Union,

Putin's national rallying cry has been the protection of traditional and family values. Putin strategically partnered with the Russian Orthodox Church to "project Russia as the natural ally of all those who pine for a more secure, illiberal world free from the tradition-crushing rush of globalization, multiculturalism and women's and gay rights," according to Andrew Higgins of the *New York Times*. The Russian Orthodox Church is the primary religious group that is tolerated; other sects are harassed and persecuted. A 2013 gay propaganda law signed by Putin has led to the imprisonment of LGBTQ rights activists and gays who dare simply to hold hands, as well as a rise in homophobic violence, according to critics. Meanwhile, Putin's turn to tightness has received widespread support: Polls of Russian citizens show that nationalism is on the rise.

It's a stubborn fact of human existence: High levels of disorganization and insecurity invite tightness. In such circumstances, people are willing to tolerate a major trade-off of liberty for security as they seek to find a semblance of order in a collapsing community.

Once we see how this pattern plays out, other shocking developments around the world make more sense. Upon being elected president of the Philippines in a landslide victory on June 30, 2016, Rodrigo Duterte wasted no time in clarifying his intention to instill order by any means necessary. "I expect you to obey the laws so there will be no chaos," he said in his first press conference after his victory. "If you resist, show violent resistance, my order to police will be to shoot to kill. Shoot to kill for organized crime. You heard that? Shoot to kill for every organized crime."

Within only about six months of Duterte taking office, more than seven thousand people were estimated to be killed with the initiation of his "war on drugs" policy. "I have worked in 60 countries, covered wars in Iraq and Afghanistan, and spent much of 2014 living inside West Africa's Ebola zone, a place gripped by fear and death," wrote *New*

RULE MAKERS, RULE BREAKERS

York Times journalist Daniel Berehulak of the bloody scenes he witnessed while reporting in the Philippines. "What I experienced in the Philippines felt like a new level of ruthlessness: police officers' summarily shooting anyone suspected of dealing or even using drugs, vigilantes' taking seriously Mr. Duterte's call to 'slaughter them all.'"

In addition to laying down "shoot to kill" orders, Duterte has praised Hitler, joked about rape, accused Barack Obama of being the "son of a whore," and publicly directed a vulgar gesture at the European Union during an address to Filipino government officials.

Many citizens of the Philippines don't just tolerate Duterte's ruthless policies; they revere him. Why? Because he provided a way out of the normlessness that plagued the country for years. After the ousting of former president Ferdinand Marcos's totalitarian regime in 1986, the country gradually started to unravel. By 2015, more than twenty-six million Filipinos were impoverished, and the country's unemployment rates were sky high. Rapid urbanization, industrialization, and migration had led to a dramatic increase in slums, with the urban poor facing limited educational and housing options, unemployment, and inadequate health and sanitation. Crime and disorder were rampant. Over the years, the country's homicide rate grew to be the highest in Asia and the eleventh-highest in the world. The Philippines also became home to an extensive drug trade, largely due to its geographic location.

With alienation and disorder seeping into every corner of the country, it's not surprising that many citizens welcomed Duterte's extreme attempts to create social order. "We obey him because we love him," Duterte supporter Julius Jumamoy remarked to *Time* reporter Charlie Campbell. "And we follow him because he's right. He's not killing innocent people, he's just killing criminals. He's a very good man." While recognizing that Duterte is "far from perfect," Justin Quirino said, "I think he's what the country needs right now . . . around this country, you'll find a blatant disregard for many of our laws,'and there's little to no accountability. We have to change that." Filipinos have overwhelmingly embraced Duterte's iron fist. One year after his election, 86 percent of the population said they view him favorably.

WHEN CULTURES COLLAPSE, RADICALIZATION STEPS IN

Formed in 2006, the jihadist militant group ISIS soon was widely viewed as one of the most violent terrorist organizations on the Earth with its sensational videotaped beheadings of civilians, massive destruction of historical monuments in the Middle East, and recruitment of child soldiers.

Its dramatic rise to power was fueled in a cultural tinderbox. After the U.S.-led invasion of Iraq in 2003, President Saddam Hussein, a Sunni leader, was toppled, and a new political order made up of Kurds and Shiites was established. These events later set in motion a collapse of stability and order—a state of extreme looseness—in Iraq that ISIS exploited.

By the time the United States had withdrawn its forces from Iraq in 2011, years of widespread sectarian violence between the Shiites and the Sunnis, and a bloody insurgency that left thousands of Iraqis dead, had taken its toll on the country. The nation's economy and security were at an all-time low. By 2015, 48 percent of Iraqis reported not being able to buy food, up from 12 percent in 2009. Electricity was sorely lacking, and only one-sixth of Iraqis had access to drinking water for more than two hours per day. Corruption was rampant, and violence was a daily occurrence. According to the online database Iraq Body Count, there were more than 2,500 deadly bombing incidents in Iraq between 2010 and 2012, an average of two a day.

Iraq was disintegrating, and the Sunni minority population, excluded from the Shiite government led by Prime Minister Nouri al-Maliki, was suffering the most. Hundreds of Sunni opposition leaders and thousands of other Sunnis were detained in prisons. As many as a hundred thousand Sunni members of Saddam's Ba'ath party lost their government jobs, leaving them unemployed and marginalized. By 2014, many Sunnis were penniless, and had no trust in their government. My collaborator Munqith Dagher, a leading pollster in Iraq, was on the ground during this time documenting the discontent. In his surveys of over 1,200 Iraqis in 2014, just one week before ISIS took over Mosul and other Sunni territories in Iraq, he found that nearly 80 percent of Sunnis reported feeling unsafe in their neighborhoods (up from only 22 percent in 2011). Only 30 percent of Sunnis in Iraq had trust in their judicial system, and only a dismal 28 percent trusted the Iraqi army.

Enter ISIS. Backed by the disaffected Sunni population, leaders of ISIS—many of them former senior military leaders under Saddam who were further radicalized while imprisoned in U.S.-organized detention facilities—began to impose a very tight order on an otherwise highly chaotic environment. As ISIS began making territorial gains in early 2014, it quickly repaired essential services that had been neglected by the government, including electricity, water, and street cleaning, and also lowered the prices of consumer staples such as bread. ISIS provided bus transportation, oil and gasoline distribution, and health care. Islamic State fighters and employees received, relatively speaking, good salaries and housing. Moreover, they provided much-needed security following the tumultuous years of war. "Do you know how it was in Mosul before ISIS came?" civilian Abu Sadr commented to *Time* journalist Rebecca Collard. "We had bombings and assassinations almost every day. Now we have security."

Munqith continued to interview thousands of Iraqis in dangerous circumstances. Consistent with tight-loose theory, he found that ISIS was most successful in taking over provinces that had the most disorder. Ramadi and Fallujah, for example, two districts in the Anbar province that ISIS swiftly conquered, reported particularly high levels of chaos, with many people agreeing with statements such as "My whole world feels like it's falling apart" and "The condition of the average person in Iraq is getting worse." Munqith and his collaborators reported that the population in Anbar was exhibiting high levels of stress, and its people were looking for alternatives to deal with their dire circumstances.

ISIS may have restored order, but it did so in a ruthless way. At its peak, ISIS was known as one of the tightest groups in the modern era. Members who failed to comply with its strict rules faced brutal punishment. After taking over an area, ISIS would often disseminate long lists of rules through billboard postings and loudspeakers; they would also summon residents through loudspeaker announcements to watch executions of people who were accused of various transgressions. It banned many local activities and customs, like playing soccer, wearing Western clothing and haircuts, watching TV, listening to music, using the Internet and mobile phones, smoking cigarettes, and drinking alcohol. According to city locals in Mosul, one man who was caught with a mobile phone was whipped with forty-five lashes—only to be executed for cursing at ISIS's leader, Abu Bakr al-Baghdadi, while being whipped. Smokers were punished with broken fingers, hefty fines, and even imprisonment. Those suspected of being homosexual could be thrown from the roof of a house. Women who were deemed immodest were lashed with ropes and sticks. Convictions of adultery or treason were punished with beheading. ISIS also killed individuals who strayed from its ideological principles. Its forty-point creed legitimized the killing of anyone who supported democracy and secularism, including any governments not ruling by Sharia law.

In short, ISIS imposed order by instilling fear and terror. But despite the terror endured under their rule, in many ways, the quality of life in the regions under ISIS's control improved, at least at first. Many early supporters of ISIS backed it for the sake of survival—for a job, food, and security. The stability that ISIS provided was "particularly appealing to people living in civil war contexts," explained political scientist Mara Revkin in a 2016 article in *Foreign Affairs*, "where the collapse of preexisting legal frameworks has created a fertile environment for looting, banditry, and land grabs."

By the end of 2015, ISIS had lured nearly thirty thousand foreigners from all over the world to join its fight. How? As it turns out, inductees' motivation to join ISIS was quite similar. Many of these people "are living in an age of anxiety, and welcome a tight environment that promises to reduce uncertainty," anthropologist Scott Atran remarked to me. In fact, people facing great uncertainty are more likely to be attracted to radical ideologies, Arie Kruglanski and I found based on our research in Sri Lanka, the Philippines, and the United States. When people feel adrift, groups with strict norms and a clear purpose can exert a powerful pull.

Take, for example, John Walker Lindh, an American citizen captured by the Afghan Northern Alliance and later arrested in 2001 for fighting with the Taliban at age twenty. Many Americans struggled to understand how a fellow citizen could have aided the Taliban, but the early signs were there. As a teen, Lindh became increasingly critical of America's freewheeling culture. He openly criticized Americans for failing to spend time with their families and communities. He was drawn to the tightness of an ideology that provided moral grounding and a sense of security. "In the U.S., I feel alone," he told his teacher at a religious school in Pakistan. "Here I feel comfortable and at home."

"Most teenagers, when they rebel, say they want more freedom," wrote journalist Evan Thomas in *Newsweek*. "John Walker Lindh rebelled against freedom. He did not demand to express himself in different ways. Quite the opposite. He wanted to be told precisely how to dress, to eat, to think, to pray. He wanted a value system of absolutes, and he was willing to go to extreme lengths to find it." In short, he felt more at home in a tight culture compared with his loose motherland.

Leaders of violent groups like the Taliban and ISIS have proven adept at attracting alienated souls like Lindh. Indeed, leaders of these groups often declare looseness to be their common enemy. Osama bin Laden, the founder of al-Qaeda, openly said that he found loose Western societies repulsive. In November 2017, the CIA released more than 450,000 files taken from the 2011 raid on bin Laden's compound, including his personal journal. Commenting on his visits to the United Kingdom at age fourteen, he wrote, "I was not impressed, and I saw that they were a society different from ours and that they were a morally loose society." Similarly, in his 1951 essay "The America I Have Seen," Egyptian Sayyid Qutb, who soon after became a leader of the Egyptian Muslim Brotherhood, argued that the United States was exceedingly materialistic, superficial, and obsessed with violence and sexual pleasures. In his view, Americans lacked any moral grounding whatsoever. "The matter of morals and rights are an illusion in the conscience of the American," he wrote.

Some members of terrorist organizations will go so far as to attack their own people to take down what they view as an exceedingly loose, "immoral" culture. I witnessed this firsthand in my work on terrorism in Indonesia. In August 2017, I flew to Jakarta to interview Ali Imron, one of the masterminds of the 2002 bombings in Bali (an Indonesian island) that killed over two hundred people and injured hundreds more. He was escorted from prison to meet my collaborators and me in a police station, where we talked through an interpreter for several hours.

Jihadists, Imron told us, not only supported attacks against Westerners; they also supported terrorist attacks against their own government.

"Why is it acceptable to inflict violence on fellow Indonesians?" I asked him.

He looked me straight in the eye. "Jihadists think that anyone in the government is a devil because they are not following Islamic law. Once they are infidels, it's easy to justify killing." From this perspective, bars, nightclubs, and brothels are the enemies of Islam, and the government is responsible for their depravity.

After years of rehabilitation in prison, Ali said that he still yearns for an Islamic state but has renounced violence as a means of attaining it. Now he believes that it is possible to have an Islamic state that is tolerant of ethnic and religious diversity, a message that he is preaching to others. Alongside the mentor who trained him in Afghanistan, Nasir Abas, Ali works to deradicalize other jihadists in Indonesian prisons. Through dialogue and debate, they aim to convince detained terrorists that violence is anti-Islamic and, moreover, that the Indonesian government is not anti-Islam.

Terrorism is a complex phenomenon with many contributing factors. Tight-loose is one of them. It affects the conditions under which terrorist groups evolve, as well as the reasons people find these groups attractive. Knowing this can help us to better anticipate when these dynamics will occur and develop policies to counteract them.

THE BATTLE BETWEEN NATIONALISTS AND GLOBALISTS

Tightness-looseness underlies many other geopolitical events around the world. The rise of populist politicians and movements around 2016, ranging from Marine Le Pen in France, Matteo Salvini in Italy, Geert Wilders in the Netherlands, and Viktor Orbán in Hungary, may seem unrelated on the surface. In reality, however, they reflect the same cultural fault line: Nationalist groups that long for tightness are fighting back against globalists who embrace looseness.

Gains made by far-right political parties across Europe, in addition to events like Brexit and the Trump presidency in 2016, were largely brought about by individuals who felt increasingly threatened by economic decline and social disruption in a rapidly changing world. They wanted to return to a tight social order, and populist leaders around the world were ready to exploit this. In France, some citizens feared increased immigration, blaming newcomers for a rise in terrorist acts and a dilution of French culture. Le Pen appealed to these concerns, running on a platform of French nationalism. Our surveys of French voters in the spring of 2017 showed a dynamic similar to that in our U.S. surveys of Trump's popularity: People who felt most threatened wanted greater tightness and intended to vote for Le Pen as a result. Though Le Pen ultimately lost the election, her rise illustrates how the tight-loose fault line can thrust itself into global politics.

These, of course, aren't isolated examples. Supporters of the Law and Justice Party in Poland shared similar preoccupations, viewing globalization as a threat and seeking to affirm a tighter national identity. Backers of the Freedom Party in Austria and the Alternative for Germany party also viewed the growing population of immigrants as a threat to their economy, security, and cultural identity. Across all of these countries, cultural backlash against multiculturalism and globalism played a large role in the rise of populism, according to research by political scientists Ronald Inglehart and Pippa Norris. "In all of these cases, citizens rebelled against cultural looseness," Inglehart said to me. They welcomed the narrative given by leaders who pandered to their anxiety and offered the ultimate cure: a return to a tight social order where they know their place in the world.

Such perceived existential threats to one's survival and cultural identity can also be seen in many of the neo-Nazi movements around the world. In Germany, for example, there has been a rise in right-wing extremism since 2014, following years of decline. In the United States, more than nine hundred hate groups were found in the country in 2016—a 17 percent increase from 2014—including a motley mix of neo-Nazi groups, KKK outposts, white nationalist groups, neo-Confederate groups, and skinhead groups.

In August 2017 one of the largest white supremacist events in recent U.S. history, the "Unite the Right" rally, was held in Charlottesville, Virginia, to protest the removal of a Confederate statue. The demonstrators quickly clashed with counter-protesters, leading to a horrific eruption of violence. Thirty-two-year-old Heather Heyer was killed when a car rammed into a crowd of counter-protesters, and more than thirty others were injured.

Since this incident, Americans have struggled to grapple with the ferocity of the demonstrators, some of whom openly carried guns, Confederate battle flags, and banners with swastikas while chanting racist slogans. What motivated them? Surveys of over four hundred self-identified alt-righters by psychologists Patrick Forscher and Nour Kteily are telling. As compared with non–alt right samples, the white nationalists said their very survival was under threat. They were particularly worried about being displaced by the increasing numbers of immigrants in the United States. For them, being part of an extremist group was a response to the fear of becoming obsolete. As we know, when there is threat—whether physical, economic, or even spiritual—groups tighten up, and negative outgroup attitudes soon follow.

Nationalists from all around the world are stoking anti-immigrant sentiment. According to a survey of twenty-four countries by global market research firm Ipsos, approximately one in two people feel immigration is leading to changes they don't like in their country.

Half of those surveyed believe there are too many immigrants in their country, and only 28 percent of over seventeen thousand people surveyed believe the economic effect of immigration is positive. In the United States, a 2015 Pew study found that the word *illegal* was used more than any other word when participants were asked to give the first word that came to mind when thinking about immigrants.

What might not be obvious is that such anti-immigration prejudice creates a vicious cycle. This bias is tightening immigrant communities around the world and putting them at risk for radicalization, my research shows. It's simple: When immigrants are discriminated against and made to feel "culturally homeless"—that they don't belong—they may be more susceptible to recruitment by radicals who exploit these experiences and welcome them with open arms.

In a 2015 study, my colleagues and I surveyed approximately two hundred Muslims in the United States about their feelings of being discriminated against, as well as how they balanced their Muslim and American identities. They read a description of a hypothetical radical group said to be willing to resort to extreme actions to protect Islam, and were then asked to rate the extent to which they'd support such a group. We also asked whether they had a radical interpretation of Islam—for example, whether they believed that violence is acceptable. By far, most of those in our sample wanted to integrate into the United States; very few showed any signs of radicalization. Yet some people *did* feel marginalized: They no longer identified with the culture of their heritage, but didn't identify with American culture, either. They felt culturally homeless. Those who also reported being discriminated against, on top of feeling marginalized, were particularly at risk for holding views in support of radicalism.

These data were collected in the relatively loose culture of the United States. Yet, as we know, residents of tight nations tend to have more negative attitudes toward people who threaten the traditional social order. Might immigrants in tight cultures have even greater risk for radicalization? Yes. In a later study of U.S. and German Muslims, we found that Muslims had a much harder time integrating into the tight culture of Germany than into the loose culture of the United States, in part due to their perception that the former was less open to cultural diversity. Across the board, Muslim immigrants in Germany reported a stronger belief that their host country was closed-minded and they had more difficulty managing their cultural identities. And, just as in our study on cultural homelessness, some immigrants who had a hard time integrating with German culture showed support for extremist ideologies.

MENDING CULTURAL DIVIDES

As mass migration continues across the globe, the need to promote acceptance and inclusion of others—and reduce feelings of threat—has never been more pressing. In 2015, the number of international migrants worldwide hit over 240 million, a 41 percent increase from 2000, in large part due to natural disasters, resource scarcity, and war.

With this dramatic increase in intercultural contact, we need to find spaces for people from tight and loose cultures to interact in meaningful and positive ways. Fortunately, this is already starting to occur. For example, the global education network Communities Engaging with Difference and Religion (CEDAR) has run programs aimed at fostering tolerance and understanding between groups in many different countries for over ten years. One program in Birmingham, England, focused on tensions between immigrant communities and local residents. The program encouraged participants—a group of nearly forty people from more than ten different countries who visited different places of worship around the city—to reflect openly on their experiences through group discussion. This allowed people to see how "the other" viewed them, and in turn, better understand one another. As one participant noted, "I found that my different point of view can become another's point of learning to accept differences."

My research similarly shows that creating spaces for empathy can prove invaluable for combating intergroup hostility. In 2015, my research assistants and I interviewed Americans and Pakistanis on their views of each other's culture. We found that both groups held highly negative beliefs and stereotypes about the other. Pakistanis didn't just see Americans as loose, but as immoral and arrogant. Americans saw Pakistanis as overly constrained, but also aggressive and violent. As impressions are often formed through the media, which thrives on caricature, such extreme stereotyping is perhaps not surprising. What's more, we tend to live in our own echo chambers. Even on Twitter and Facebook, we communicate with those we know and those who share our views, rather than engaging with people from other cultures.

In our study, we wondered if we could lessen intergroup hostility by giving each group a more realistic window into each other's lives. We didn't have the budget to fly Pakistanis to the United States or vice versa. But what if Americans were able to read the actual daily diaries of Pakistanis, and Pakistanis were able to read the diaries of Americans, over the course of a week? Would this exposure to one another's day-to-day lives change their attitudes?

To find out, my collaborator Joshua Jackson and I had American and Pakistani students write about their everyday experiences for one week. We then gave a new group of participants, including a hundred American and a hundred Pakistani students, a set of these diary entries to read over the course of a week. The results of this low-cost intervention were striking: As compared with participants who read diary entries from members of their own culture, participants who read diary entries written by members of the other culture viewed the two cultures as being much more similar. What's more, Pakistani participants who read Americans' diaries viewed Americans as more moral and as having less of a sense of superiority over other cultures. And, by the end of this intervention, our American participants who read diaries written by Pakistanis viewed Pakistanis as less violent and more fun-loving.

"I don't know many Pakistanis personally, but the diary entries helped me learn about the everyday life of someone in Pakistan," one American participant wrote at the study's end. "I think that they tend to be a bit more religious than the people in America, but have similar life patterns and personalities to us." Likewise, a Pakistani participant remarked, "Americans may be different than us in moral, ethical, or religious values, but the lives of students in America are very similar to the life of a student here . . . They are law-abiding citizens, which is one of the reasons the system in America is working smoothly."

As these quotes show, interventions that improve our understanding of people from other cultures hold tremendous promise for defusing stereotypes, heading off conflict, and resolving intercultural disputes. Every day, citizens are finding meaningful ways to interact with people far outside their own social circles. In 2017, the *Washington Post* reported that, in a Dairy Queen in Dallas, Texas, two American-born men decided to have a sit-down over burgers and fries to untangle their mutual suspicion. On one end, there was David Wright, a white man who had founded a militia called the Bureau of American Islamic Relations (BAIR) with the mission of rooting out Islamic terrorists in

Texas. At the other end was Ali Ghouri, a member of a local mosque where Wright and his coalition had protested twice with weapons and signs reading "Stop the Islamization of America." Against the advice of other members of his mosque, Ghouri confronted the protesters, saying, "I have a weapon. You have a weapon. I'm not scared of you." Five months later, Wright and Ghouri met at the Dairy Queen. Each man brought a friend—and a gun.

As journalist Robert Samuels reported in the *Post*, Wright and his friend were quick to explain the root of their distrust of immigrants, Muslims, and Islam. "The core issue for me is about America and what it means," said Christopher Gambino, Wright's friend. "I'm not a white nationalist," he added. "I come from a house with very strong values. And some people keep trying to change our values."

Ali Ghouri's friend, Tameem Budri, responded that he was born and raised in Texas. During a visit to his parents' country of origin, Afghanistan, he was strongly reminded that he identified with American culture.

Talking for hours, the four men found some common ground. All of them, they learned, wanted to stop terrorism-related crime. Budri wanted to know why Wright's group would show up to a place of worship, where children were present, with guns. "If I were not to show up with guns, none of y'all would have never paid a damn bit of attention to me," Wright responded. But at the end of the conversation, Wright promised he wouldn't protest in front of Ghouri's mosque anymore. He was especially swayed by the fact that groups he disdained, like neo-Nazis and KKK groups, had taken up such practices.

The men didn't come to many other agreements, but they did find that they shared a love of cigarettes, guns, and Texas. Gambino said he "learned a lot" from the two Muslim men, and Budri said he now had "respect" for Wright and his friend. The men had confronted their own discomfort with someone perceived to be threatening their way of life.

Culture is both the *cause* and the *cure* of many of our most pressing issues. Once we understand how tightness-looseness shapes our attitudes, we can go a long way toward mending these divides.

II

Harnessing the Power of Social Norms

From Apple's Siri to Amazon's Alexa, artificially intelligent helpers can make our lives easier by booking reservations, playing just the right song, and even telling amusing jokes. In 2017, engineers at Facebook's A.I. Research lab gave this technology an even more difficult task: negotiation. A highly nuanced process even for humans, negotiation poses many challenges, including accurately reading others' emotions, making persuasive arguments, and balancing cooperation with competition. Perhaps hoping that naming them might confer such human abilities, Facebook researchers called their chatbots "Bob" and "Alice." They taught the software hundreds of hypothetical English dialogues that could occur within a negotiation session. Then they assigned Bob and Alice a simple negotiation: splitting up some balls, hats, and books between them. Researchers programmed Bob and Alice to carry out this task over and over again, a trial-and-error process that allowed them to adapt and upgrade their negotiation tactics.

Over the course of thousands of practice sessions, Bob and Alice became deal-making savants. But there was just one problem. In the pair's later interactions, Bob and Alice no longer seemed to be speaking English. Like childhood twins often do, the chatbots had developed their own secret code.

When Bob said, "I can i everything else," Alice responded, "balls have zero to me to me to me to me to me to me to me to me to." Bob replied, "you i everything else," to which Alice countered, "balls have a ball to me to me to me to me to me to me to me to me." And the conversation went on.

It sounds like gibberish or a bug in the software, but it actually reflects the canny work of two negotiation ninjas. Having been programmed to work together, Alice and Bob had developed their own code words and rules to coordinate. On the plus side, their new lingo and "rules of the game" appeared to be leading to successful negotiation results. But to the chagrin of Bob and Alice's human creators, their exchanges no longer made any sense to outsiders. The researchers had to go back to the drawing board and reconfigure the software to follow the syntax of English.

We've seen what happens when humans commit to collective goals: They coordinate by developing distinctive rules that set (mostly unspoken) expectations for behavior. Remarkably, it seems that even primitive chatbots will do the same thing when designed to be social with each other. As Alice and Bob refined their abilities to coordinate, give-and-take, solve problems, and reach a deal, they naturally developed a kind of social code.

Humans have to negotiate much more than balls, hats, and books in the twenty-first century. From climate change and a population surge to global health crises, we face a wide array of challenges. In the past, efforts to alleviate these problems have often relied on economic and engineering solutions, such as making sure aid gets to the right people and developing technologies to fix our problems. While these remedies are often needed, we can also help mitigate many of these collective challenges by *recalibrating our social norms*. Although human cultures can't be reconfigured as fast as reprogramming the code between two robots, they certainly can be changed. Our cultures aren't destiny. The tightness and looseness of any culture is capable of being modified when needed to better solve our most vexing problems.

It might sound far-fetched, but adjusting a culture's tight-loose balance is no pipe dream. We already have a rich history of cases in which communities successfully did so. In some cases, they had to loosen social norms. In others, they needed to tighten. In all cases, they began with honest self-reflection on how to better their communities.

AN EPIC CURFEW

In 1998, Iceland's teens had a major drinking problem. More than 40 percent of fifteen- and sixteen-year-olds got drunk at least once a month, making them some of the heaviest teen drinkers in Europe. Marijuana use was high, and almost a quarter of teens smoked cigarettes. "You couldn't walk the streets in downtown Reykjavik on a Friday night because it felt unsafe," according to Icelandic psychologist Gudberg Jónsson. "There were hordes of teenagers getting in-your-face drunk." Parents and officials realized that loose social norms needed tightening to protect their country's future.

To tackle the problem, Iceland's government launched a multi-pronged program called "Youth in Iceland." One major step was to toughen up laws. The country made it illegal for people under age eighteen to buy cigarettes and for those under age twenty to buy alcohol. Legislators also banned alcohol and tobacco advertising, and set a curfew for teens under sixteen.

Crucially, the program then addressed cultural factors. In an "eyes are upon you"–like program, parents took to the streets to monitor children and enforce the new curfew, kindly asking kids who were out too late to head home. Officials also encouraged parents to get more involved in their children's schools, spend more time with their kids, and sign contracts with other parents stipulating the types of teen behaviors they'd prohibit. The government increased funding for sports, music, and art to give youth diversions other than alcohol and drugs.

The intervention showed sweeping results: By 2016, surveys indicated that only 5 percent of teens had gotten drunk in the last month, a mere 7 percent had smoked marijuana, and only 3 percent reported smoking cigarettes every day. In a world where alcohol abuse causes more than 3.3 million deaths globally, programs like the Icelandic Model—which combat social norm violations with tighter standards—can serve as an example worldwide.

Iceland's success illustrates a broader—and encouraging—point about culture: Our environment may shape our social norms, but so can we. We can make collective choices about the kinds of norms we want to embrace. And when our norms aren't serving us well, we can, and should, take steps to rebalance them.

WORLD WILD WEB

For centuries, our early ancestors lived in small communities where face-to-face interactions and intimate social networks built trust and kept people accountable. Following the Industrial Revolution, in cities and large factories, human beings faced a new reality: regularly interacting with hundreds of strangers outside their social networks. We again adapted by creating new norms that enabled cooperation to flourish.

Today, we live in an entirely new world: the Internet. Between 2000 and 2016, the number of people using the Internet grew from 738 million to almost 3.8 billion. Across the globe, we each have, on average, five different social media accounts and spend about two hours every day online. More than half the world's population has a smartphone, which we use to shop, network, date, get the news, and entertain ourselves. Remarkably, the Internet is so important to people that on average over 70 percent of Americans said they would go without coffee, chocolate, and alcohol to have access, 43 percent said they would give up exercise, and 21 percent even said they would sacrifice sex for a whole year.

Our new online world offers many advantages, including convenience, quick access to information, and new relationships. We can even conduct many of our most important financial transactions online—from banking, to bill paying, to filing taxes and insurance claims—creating unprecedented economic efficiencies. We're also being exposed to more unfamiliar ideas than ever before, which boosts our capacity for innovation. Reaping the benefits of this brave new technological change invariably requires looseness. Not only will people with loose mind-sets be able to create new technologies, but they'll also be better able to adapt to "dizzying" rates of change, in the words of journalist Thomas Friedman.

But while technological change thrives on looseness, it's also in dire need of tightness. Many of the virtual spaces where we spend a considerable portion of our days lack regulation and monitoring. Consequently, they're treacherous catch basins for insults, bullying, dishonesty, and even criminal behavior. This is the dark side of the Internet's subterranean cultures. Incivility is ubiquitous, and fraud, data breaches, and cyberattacks are on the rise. As many as 40 percent of young people have reported being victims of cyberbullying, and more than 50 percent also admit that they, too, have been mean or hurtful to people online. A new vocabulary—*flaming, trolling, spamming*, and *doxxing*—has arisen to describe egregious behavior.

Undeniably, people feel psychologically unleashed to be rude and uncivil when they're on the Internet—to be *norm violators*. The "online disinhibition effect" describes the sense of anonymity and dissociation that people feel from their "real" selves when they're online, therefore also feeling less restrained by the social norms they follow in the real world. Studies have shown that people who meet in computer-mediated discussions are less inhibited—more apt to swear, flirt, and make impolite comments—as compared with those who meet face-to-face. Unlike in the "real world," online bullies show even less remorse for their bad behavior because they don't see the sadness and outrage on their victims' faces.

Another vexing consequence of digital connectivity is the massive rise of "fake news." On the Internet, inaccurate and misleading information can spread like wildfire, enflaming fear and threatening communities.

In 2014, for example, panic swept the state of New York when the news broke that an American doctor who had volunteered in Guinea to help victims of the Ebola outbreak had checked into a hospital with symptoms of the virus. Although medical professionals assured the public that the patient was in quarantine and there was no future threat of the infection spreading, news outlets suggested otherwise. Ominous Ebola-related headlines and social media conversations amplified the false sense that New York had become a contagious cesspool.

This is a major historical pivot. While in the past we've had to deal with mostly objective threats, now we must sort through a murky universe of subjective and false threats, without always having clear means of discerning truth from fiction. Moreover, through algorithms that analyze how people behave on the Internet and what stories they pay attention to, online marketers and media sources have grasped what cognitive psychologists discovered in the lab decades ago: Emotional content, including information that triggers our greatest fears—terrorism, disease, natural disaster—grabs our attention. Once captured with the help of complex algorithms, our attention translates into high click-through rates that may even be monetized as advertising and subscription revenues. For those seeking to profit from our fears, it's a "race to the bottom of the brain stem," according to technology ethicist Tristan Harris.

The Internet poses a dilemma: We need to have loose mind-sets to adapt to technology, yet we need tighter norms to regulate the destructive, normless, and fear-mongering behavior that it enables. Even the cofounder of the World Wide Web Robert Cailliau has voiced the need for a tighter Internet culture: "The Net is a space in which you encounter others," he told *New Scientist* magazine, "so there has to be some regulation of behavior." Just as a person must learn traffic laws to earn their license to drive, Cailliau suggests navigation of the web ought to have similar provisions. "A traffic regulation only limits behavior, not content," emphasizes Cailliau. "You can drive where you want, when you want, provided you do it with safe behavior toward other traffic users." Even on the web, he says, "we should all know what our rights and duties are. Teach it in schools. Hand out a license that shows one has passed a test of minimal awareness."

Just like in other areas of our lives, we need a tight-loose Goldilocks balance in these new spaces. The effort to tighten up our online spaces must balance users' freedoms but still have adequate constraints.

Fortunately, tighter norms for appropriate behavior are starting to emerge in our new virtual worlds. Some of this is occurring informally. Hundreds of books, online manuals, and YouTube videos offer guidelines on how to act appropriately via email, tweet, text, Facebook, and more. "Netiquette" guides stress the importance of remembering that there are actual people on the other side of our screens who deserve to be treated with the same respect we'd give them face-to-face.

Online communities are also taking more formal steps to tighten overly loose environments by simultaneously promoting the free exchange of information and monitoring and punishing norm-violating behavior. For example, visitors to the Reddit discussion forum ChangeMyView engage in challenging someone's viewpoint on topics ranging from spanking to immigration, yet they're required to do so with civility. Volunteer moderators ensure conversations don't get out of hand by deleting inappropriate comments and kicking out rule violators. What's more, a user who succeeds in changing another person's opinion through respectful dialogue is rewarded with a delta sign by their username. Other online communities are posting official behavioral guidelines to promote a healthy balance of tight and loose in their virtual spaces.

In an even more formal approach, web-based platforms and businesses are test-driving ways to tighten their online cultures by policing more of their offensive content. After Facebook introduced its Live feature, which allowed its users to broadcast videos in real time, the developers were shocked by the number of people who used the feature to share footage of torture, sexual assaults, suicides, child abuse, and murders. Facebook CEO Mark Zuckerberg added three thousand more employees to regulate and remove offensive videos and users "to build a safe community" and adjusted the site's algorithms to show people fewer news reports and ads, and more posts from family and friends. Over on Twitter, following the 2016 U.S. presidential election, investigators discovered that over fifty thousand accounts were actually bots controlled by Russian parties. Since this discovery, Twitter has been creating new online tools to detect bots and hiring people to get rid of them. Google likewise is working on curbing the dissemination of false and offensive information by employing raters tasked with evaluating whether certain web pages are putting forth demonstrably inaccurate information. And Instagram's CEO, Kevin Systrom—who once declared the Internet a "cesspool"—is tasking engineers to develop machine learning techniques to detect and eradicate offensive behavior.

Promoting more personal accountability will also help to counter antinormative behavior on the Internet. Max Bazerman at Harvard Business School and his research team have found that very simple changes can incentivize people to avoid the temptation of lying when filling out forms online. Remarkably, when people are asked to sign their name *before* filling out a form when their money is at stake, their responses are more honest as compared with when they sign *after* making their claim. "Signing before rather than after reporting cues people to the fact that the task has an ethical dimension and thus encourages them to avoid cheating," Bazerman told me. Moreover, simply having customers video-record their claims might also improve honesty by heightening their awareness that they're being watched and that their responses will be available for analysis at a later date. Such steps can be taken in any industry where customers may be tempted to engage in "loose" reporting.

Perhaps the best way to reduce norm violations is to boost the sense of community in online spaces. "Those who gain a sense of group membership become part of a virtual community and often develop a sense of responsibility toward the social cyberspace in which it is situated, much as residents of a neighborhood may take responsibility for the area's cleanliness and safety," points out Lance Strate, professor of communication and media studies at Fordham University. Just as people have *off-line* for millennia, those who feel connected in an *online* environment may be motivated to develop and enforce social norms for the benefit of all.

OUR CROWDED PLANET

We face pressing issues in the real world, too, of course. Here again, viewing our challenges through the lens of social norms can help. By tightening norms in some realms and loosening them in others, we can ensure that culture is a force for good.

One of the greatest threats is overpopulation. Today, the Earth is being asked to feed, clothe, and house a staggering 7.6 billion people—9.3 billion by 2050. To put this in perspective, in the 1500s, there were only an estimated 540 million people on the planet. By the 1800s, the human population had just breached the 1 billion mark. A century later, in the year 1900, the population was estimated to be around 1.76 billion. This means that our population will grow more in the next three decades than it did between 1500 and 1900. Few countries will escape the surge. The United States is expected to add over 100 million people, or 36 percent, between 2010 and 2050. This pales in comparison with countries like Uganda, where the population is set to triple in the same time frame. Nigeria will add 271 million people in those years; India will add another 450 million.

The consequences of this population boom could prove catastrophic, entailing rising unemployment, poverty, migration, and conflict over limited resources. Globally, producing enough food to feed an exploding population—especially when one in nine people already don't have enough food to eat—will be a huge challenge. In the Democratic Republic of Congo, for example, the number of severely food insecure people rose 30 percent in 2017 to reach 7.7 million. With a projected population growth of 81 million from 2011 to 2050, poverty and limited resources threaten to devastate the nation. Globally, water supplies will be scarce as well: The number of people living in water-scarce areas is projected to rise from 2 billion in 2017 to 3.6 billion by 2035, the majority concentrated in the Middle East and North Africa.

Kuwait, which is expected to grow by 4.3 million people between 2010 and 2035, is projected to have only 4,600 liters of water to give to each person for the entire year in 2035—what an average American consumes in about fifteen days. Other countries like the UAE, Libya, and Singapore face similar population-exacerbated water scarcities.

Ultimately, recalibrating social norms has to be part of the solution to the problem of overpopulation. In many countries, having large families is a tight social norm that has been hard to negotiate. Kenya, for example, has strict gender norms that prevent women from making decisions about family planning and accessing contraception. It's taboo to even talk about such issues with one's spouse and extended family.

CARE, an international humanitarian organization, was keenly aware that to affect fertility rates in Kenya, it had to focus on changing these norms, and that the change had to be led by esteemed, high-status members of the community. CARE trained local health workers, religious leaders, government officials, and teachers to lead community-wide dialogues on gender equity and the benefits of family planning. For three years, starting in February 2009, the organization led more than 750 dialogues in churches, markets, and village meetings. Community leaders gave their support for family planning and encouraged communication on the topic. CARE's efforts succeeded in loosening the tight norms of male-dominated family planning; the percentage of women using contraception rose from 36.5 percent before the intervention to 51.8 percent afterward. In surveys conducted after the intervention, both men and women indicated that they were communicating more equitably with each other on the issue of family planning. CARE has led similar interventions to change social norms surrounding family planning in such countries as Rwanda and Ethiopia.

The pressure for large families isn't restricted to developing nations. In his book *The Land Is Full*, Israeli environmental activist and academic Alon Tal explains why Israel is bursting at its seams. Once a tiny nation of 800,000, it's now home to nearly 8.6 million, and by 2065 is projected to have a population of around 25 million—approximately 3,000 people per square mile, far surpassing the population densities of Japan and the Netherlands. Israelis are feeling squeezed in schools, hospitals, housing, and highways. Noise pollution is so bad that one of every four complaints to the police is about the racket made by neighbors. The ballooning population is wreaking havoc on Israel's environment, with rising greenhouse gas emissions, diminishing natural resources, and massive losses of biodiversity. Tal's logical conclusion is that Israel has to stop producing so many children. But the public response to his wake-up call has been underwhelming. "In a country that argues over everything else," Tal remarked, "overpopulation, it seems, is one issue we never want to address."

In November 2017, I met with Tal over coffee in College Park, Maryland. He wanted to discuss how to use tight-loose theory to deal with population growth in Israel. His hunch was that mere economic incentives wouldn't solve the problem. Israelis, we agreed, are loose in many domains. But when it comes to family size, he told me, they're exceedingly tight. In 2015, the national average (for both religious and secular families) was 3.1 children per family, as compared with an average of 1.7 kids per family in other developed countries. Ultra-Orthodox families have around 7 children on average. The norm of large families is rigidly promoted; couples face significant peer and even governmental pressure to have kids. David Ben-Gurion, the main founder of Israel and a former prime minister, is even credited with saying, "Any woman who does not have four children, as much as it depends on her, is betraying the Jewish mission."

The sentiment offends modern ears, but it has a historical rationale. After the decimation of six million Jews in the Holocaust, Israelis understandably saw it as their national duty to have large families to replenish their numbers. Many also felt driven to match the high Arab birth rate. But these pressures have receded, Tal argues. The Jewish population worldwide has sprung back. As of 2016, there are about seventeen million people in the world who identify as Jewish, approximating pre-Holocaust numbers. The birth rate of Arab Israelis also leveled off at around three children per family by 2016. Ironically, the tight norm that helped successfully replenish Israel might now be threatening its survival.

Tal is determined to adapt these norms to build a more sustainable future. He knows it will be no easy task: The push for large families runs deep in the national psyche, and evolved for good reasons.

But, as with other stubborn social phenomena that have yielded to concerted effort in many nations, such as reducing smoking and combating homophobia, the problem of over-fecundity, Tal is convinced, can be tamed by launching a public advocacy campaign attuned to Israel's unique culture. "This is the result of public policies and cultural norms," he explains in an article in the *Jerusalem Post* in February 2018 after we ran a joint Maryland–Tel Aviv University workshop together with fertility experts from around the world in Israel. "David Ben-Gurion encouraged people to have many children, but now we need to have a collective conversation as a nation and realize that while there was once a period in Israeli history when having lots of children was absolutely a patriotic thing to do, today it is an unpatriotic thing to do because it harms the common good."

FIGHTING CARBON WITH CULTURE

Today we're on the cusp of facing what is perhaps nature's greatest test: climate change. This crisis, too, has cultural causes that demand cultural solutions.

Through much of our current Holocene period, which started about eleven thousand years ago, the Earth's temperature has been relatively stable, enabling us to thrive as a species. In the last few hundred years, our technological advances have upset this environmental balance. Caused in part by the dramatic increase in carbon emissions since the Industrial Revolution, climate change could wreak havoc in ways we don't fully understand. Scientists predict a bleak future: Land will become too salinized to support crop growth, and extreme weather events will become more frequent. Even a moderate sea-level rise could threaten cities worldwide.

Climate change will inevitably reshape global ecological threats— and, with them, social norms. Some nations that have enjoyed a relatively threat-free status for much of their history are now facing the specter of widespread disruption. While many tight countries are found on the Center for Global Development's list of the fifty countries most threatened by future extreme weather events (China is number one, India is number two, and Hong Kong is number six), loose countries also make the list. The United States clocks in at twenty-five, Brazil at thirty-six, and Australia at forty-five. NASA predicts that in the second half of the twenty-first century, the American Southwest and Central Plains will experience droughts worse than those of the 1930s Dust Bowl. And many cities on the East Coast are at high risk of rising sea levels.

When disaster strikes, groups will need to tighten up. Many tight cultures are already skilled at doing so, but loose cultures will have to develop stronger norms to coordinate in the face of massive climate changes. This was one of the main points of the 2014 science fiction novel *The Collapse of Western Civilization: A View from the Future*, by science historians Naomi Oreskes and Eric Conway. Set in the year 2393, the book records how human follies led to a climate-related apocalypse. Interestingly, Western civilizations collapse in the catastrophe, while China, with its top-down control, is the only country to survive. In the book, Western nations fail to enforce strict regulations to slow rising CO_2 levels due to their insistence on defending personal freedoms.

Of course, this is just a work of fiction. But the book offers an interesting premonition—that some degree of tightening will be needed across the globe to cope with climate change. Among other possibilities, however, this also prompts us to consider a world where *all* cultures are increasingly becoming tight. While tightness has many advantages, it also relates to higher ethnocentrism and hostility toward outsiders, which could lead to cross-cultural conflict, radicalization, and even large-scale wars. A world made up of tightening cultures, all dealing with imminent threats and limited resources, could spell disaster for all of us.

But there's a more optimistic view. As the world collectively deals with mounting natural threats, we may be able to harness tightness-looseness to improve collaboration—not just *within* cultures, but *between* them. When we focus on developing strong norms that cut *across* ethnic and national lines—and build a larger global identity to deal with our planetary threats—cooperation can evolve at a much larger scale, to the benefit of all. In this view, our already highly cooperative species would evolve even further, given our collective challenges on Earth.

This might sound like a crazy pipe dream, but it's already in action. Consider Greece and Turkey's "earthquake diplomacy" of 1999. Relationships between the neighboring nations had long been strained, dating at least as far back as Greece's fight for independence from the Ottoman Empire in the 1820s. But when Greece and Turkey were each hit by earthquakes in August and September 1999, they surprised the world by coming to each other's aid. After the first earthquake killed around seventeen thousand people in Turkey, the Greeks were the first to fly in food and medicine. More aid followed, and Greek pop stars raised money through benefit concerts to help their Turkish neighbors. When Athens was struck by a quake less than a month later, Turkey returned the favor, rushing to send over rescue crews. The reciprocal aid ultimately led to cross-border diplomatic discussions on bolstering collaboration in areas like tourism, trade, and the environment. In this situation, the boundaries to outsiders that tightness usually creates were diminished, allowing cooperation to flourish *between* groups.

Similarly, in August 2017, India and Bangladesh rose above their long-standing border dispute after severe floods washed over Bangladesh and the West Bengal area of India. Bangladeshi border guards peacefully allowed eight hundred fleeing Indians to cross the border to safety, and Bangladeshi families immediately welcomed them into their homes. "There should not be any question over crossing the borderlines when it comes to natural disaster or any other massive crisis," said Reazul Haq, a resident of the Bangladesh Lalmonirhat District. In the future, cross-cultural collaboration will be needed to regulate rivers flowing through both nations to curb the threat of severe floods.

Disaster is often tragic, but it also has the power to bond diverse people under the universal banner of suffering. When a crisis exposes our common humanity, we become capable of seeing those outside our own culture as being like ourselves. In the process, natural disasters can produce the outpouring of compassion toward outsiders that characterizes looseness, while spurring the tight coordination needed to survive.

FISH IN WATER

In a 2005 commencement address at Kenyon College, the late American writer David Foster Wallace shared an old fable with the new graduates: "There are these two young fish swimming along, and they happen to meet an older fish swimming the other way, who nods at them and says, 'Morning, boys, how's the water?' The two young fish swim on for a bit, and then eventually one of them looks over at the other and goes, *'What the hell is water?'*"

"The point of the fish story," Wallace explained, "is merely that the most obvious, important realities are often the ones that are hardest to see."

Social norms are as old as humanity itself, and they've helped us coordinate and survive on this planet in the most difficult circumstances. They surround us, shape our experiences, and influence our interactions on a daily basis. Yet, like the fish who can't see the water that surrounds them, we rarely notice the extent to which norms pervade our lives and how much we need them.

In this book, I've tried to make this pervasive force visible and intelligible, and illuminate how it affects everything from our nations to our neurons. The more we recognize the impact of our cultural programming, the better we can understand not just others, but ourselves—and cultivate the capacity to solve our biggest problems. Our ability to grasp the nature of our differences, why they exist, and what trade-offs are involved will help us to successfully navigate an increasingly globalized world. Norms have shifted within cultures over the centuries, often dramatically, and will continue to shift, but their basic code—tight or loose—remains timeless.

In an age of breathtaking global change, we need to be prepared to recondition our cultural reflexes. Through a smart mix of monitoring and accountability efforts, Iceland reduced teen drinking, and Reddit clamped down on obnoxious trolling. On the flip side, CARE succeeded in loosening centuries of tight gender norms in Kenya to increase the use of contraception. And in 2017, Crown Prince Mohammed bin Salman initiated a major loosening of Saudi society. In enacting such measures as opening movie theaters and allowing women to drive, he's betting that cultural change can precipitate sorely needed economic growth and reform. By tightening when we're becoming too loose and loosening when we're becoming too tight, we can build a better planet.

As you continue to encounter the world's great diversity, keep asking yourself this simple question: *Tight* or *loose*?

Acknowledgments

My personal exploration of culture began more than thirty years ago, when I realized how little I understood about the world. When I was a junior in college, I ventured off to London for a semester, my first experience abroad. A sheltered kid from Long Island, I was the classic New Yorker who didn't know life existed outside the Big Apple, as depicted in the famous *New Yorker* cartoon. Overwhelmed by the strange accents, the cars driving on the left side of the road, the pub scene, and the British jokes I didn't quite understand, I experienced a quintessential case of culture shock.

I remember phoning my father and telling him how strange it was that other members of my study-abroad group would just pick up and go to places like Paris, Amsterdam, and Scotland for the weekend. In his thick Brooklyn accent, my father responded, "Well, imagine that it's like going from New *Yawk* to Pennsylvania!" That metaphor gave me so much comfort that, the very next day, I booked a low-budget tour to Egypt. It was just like going from New York to California, I reasoned (much to my father's dismay!). That fortuitous phone call with my dad sparked a lifelong passion for exploring cultures around the globe. I thank my dad, my late mother, and my brothers, Larry and Joel Gelfand, for always being huge supporters of my intellectual journeys, even when I venture off to study terrorists in prisons!

ACKNOWLEDGMENTS

Ditching my plan of becoming a medical doctor, I decided to learn about culture using the best tools available—the tools of science. I packed my bags for the not-so-glamorous twin cities of Champaign-Urbana, Illinois, where I studied under the founder of the field of cross-cultural psychology, Harry C. Triandis. Harry taught me how to be a good scientist; even more important, he taught me how to approach life. I always try to follow his tripartite advice: Be passionate about what you do, don't be afraid to be controversial, and, above all, don't take yourself too seriously. I am forever indebted to Harry for his wisdom and his incredible support, mentorship, and inspiration throughout the years.

This book is a collective effort that involved a global village transcending time and space. I am grateful to my former students—Lisa Nishii, Jana Raver, Lisa Leslie, and Janetta Lun—and my collaborators from thirty-three countries who worked with me on the tight-loose project. Many thanks to Jesse Harrington, who courageously took the "road less traveled" to study tight-loose across the United States and social classes and to examine the Goldilocks effect. Much appreciation and heartfelt thanks to Joshua Jackson, an amazing champion of tight-loose as it applies to politics, stigma, revenge, religion, and beyond. I'm grateful to my incredible computer science team, Dana Nau, Soham De, and Patrick Roos, who worked with me—at Plato's Diner, no less—in what became an incredible intellectual marriage between cross-cultural psychology and evolutionary game theory. I thank my cultural neuroscience team, led by Yan Mu, along with Shinobu Kitayama and Shihui Han, who worked tirelessly to use the tools of neuroscience to study the strength of social norms. I also thank Carol Ember for bringing me into her Yale team to study tightness-looseness in traditional societies; Marieke van Egmond for leading our efforts to look at tightness-looseness with unobtrusive measures on city streets around the world; Chengguang Li for his innovative work on tight-loose and organizational mergers; Nicolas Geeraert, Ren Li, Colleen Ward, and Kali Demes for studying

ACKNOWLEDGMENTS

tight-loose and expatriation; and Sarah Lyons-Padilla for her fascinating research on tight-loose and radicalization. I'm also grateful to my other amazing current and former doctoral students and post docs: Garriy Shteynberg, Ryan Fehr, Ashley Fulmer, Lynn Imai, Kirsten Keller, Anu Ramesh, Brandon Crosby, Laura Severance, Elizabeth Salmon, Jasmine Wheeler, Michelle Dugas, Jessica Fernandez, Xinyue Pan, Tiane Lee, Amelia Stillwell, Rebecca Mohr, and many others whom I've had the great fortune to work with over the years. Many thanks also to the RAs who have worked in our lab on research on tight-loose: Trey Parker, Myles Arrington, Ioanna Galani, Brianna Dubose, Payal Pubbi, Sid Tan, Paul Capobianco, Ruchi Mathur, Nour Mansour, Morgan Taylor, Sarah Tayel, Julia Maney, Rachael Parsons, and Noah Smith.

I am extremely fortunate to have had the most amazing "dream team" of research associates, without whom this book would not have been possible: Nava Caluori, Sarah Gordon, and Virginia Choi. Your tireless energy, commitment, and passion for the book were invaluable. You all are the definition of "unflappable" and I can't thank you enough. Thanks also to my incredible current and former colleagues at the University of Maryland—Ben Schneider, Katherine Klein, Paul Hanges, Karen O'Brien, Arie Kruglanski, Edward Lemay, Charles Stangor, Jennifer Wessel, James Grand, and Jens Herberholz—for always putting up with me.

I am grateful to many others who provided encouragement, advice, and friendship throughout my career: Hazel Markus, Zeynep Aycan, Miram Erez, Marta Fulop, Yoshi and Emiko Kashima, CY Chiu and Ying-Yi Hong, Robin Pinkley, Laura Kray, Adam Galinsky, Jeanne Brett, Michael Bond, Shalom Schwartz, Klaus Boehnke, Linda Babcock, Hannah Bowles, Maurice Schweitzer, Ray Friedman, Don Conlon, Carsten de Dreu, Michael Morris, Laurie Weingart, Bill Bottom, Susan Fiske, Carol Dweck, Michael Tushman, Max Bazerman, Jeffrey Edwards, Michael Frese, Gerben van Kleef, Astrid Homan, Joshua Greene, David Sloan Wilson, Peter Turchin, Joe Brewer, Munqith Dagher, Abdel-

ACKNOWLEDGMENTS

Hamid Abdel-Latif, Gilad Chen, Andrzej Nowak, Amy Wasserman, Shari Friedman, Hannah Kruglanski, Antonia Carrasco, the Bowie Jazzercise ladies, the Gelfand/Baxt/Betesh/Croland/Jacobs crew, and the Betke/Gerleman family.

Many thanks go to my amazing agent, Katinka Matson, at Brockman, Inc., for encouraging me to write this book and for being a constant source of support. Rick Horgan at Scribner has been the most incredible editor. His advice on how to make the book more accessible (and overcome some bad academic writing habits!) was invaluable, and his love of all things tight-loose—from nations to neurons—kept me going throughout the process. Thanks to my great team at Scribner, including Susan Moldow, Nan Graham, Amanda Pelletier, Emily Greenwald, and Ashley Gilliam, among many others, and to Rimjhim Dey and her awesome crew for their tireless efforts. I am also lucky to have worked with David Nussbaum, a true mediator between science and practice.

I am indebted to Katie Shonk, my chief editor extraordinaire and enthusiast, and Josh Burek, my chief strategist, commentator, and supporter, for their wisdom and edits on each and every chapter. I often ask myself how I got so lucky to work with such amazing talent, and I plan to write another book just so we can work together again! Thanks to the Harvard Kennedy School and the Middle East Institute for sponsoring my writing sabbatical, and the National Science Foundation, the Department of Defense, and the Alexander von Humboldt Foundation for their support of my research.

Finally, I'm forever grateful to my husband, Todd Betke (aka Bubsy), and my two wonderful daughters, Jeanette and Hannah, who have had to listen to me talking about tight-loose 24/7. I marvel at the great tight-loose balance in our family—the Goldilocks Principle in action.

Michele Gelfand
University Park, Maryland, USA

Notes

INTRODUCTION

1 **forty-four-page dress code:** Wachtel, K. (2010, December 15). La Dress-Code: The banker's guide to dressing and smelling like a winner. Business Insider. Retrieved from http://www.businessinsider.com/ubs-dresscode -clothes-bank-2010-12.

1 **195 countries:** Independent states in the world. (2017, January 20). U.S. Department of State. Retrieved from https://www.state.gov/s/inr/rls /4250.htm.

1 **more than seven thousand languages:** *The world factbook.* (2016). Central Intelligence Agency. Retrieved from https://www.cia.gov/library /publications/the-world-factbook/geos/xx.html.

1 **many thousands of religions:** Barrett, D. B., Kurian, G. T., & Johnson, T. M. (2000). *World Christian encyclopedia* (Vol. 3). London and New York: Oxford University Press.

2 **96 percent of the human genome:** Waterson, R. H., Lander, E. S., & Wilson, R. K. (2005). Initial sequence of the chimpanzee genome and comparison with the human genome. *Nature, 437*(7055), 69.

2 **far more similar across communities:** Whiten, A. (2011). The scope of culture in chimpanzees, humans and ancestral apes. *Philosophical Transactions of the Royal Society B: Biological Sciences, 366*(1567), 997–1007; Whiten, A. (2017). A second inheritance system: The extension of biology through culture. *Interface Focus, 7*(5), 20160142.

NOTES

2 different "civilizations": Huntington, S. P. (1996). *The clash of civiliza-tions and the remaking of world order*. New York: Simon & Schuster.

3 *tight* or *loose* culture . . . enforces them: Gelfand, M. J., Raver, J. L., Nishii, L., Leslie, L. M., Lun, J., Lim, B. C., . . . & Aycan, Z. (2011). Differ-ences between tight and loose cultures: A 33-nation study. *Science*, *332*(6033), 1100–1104.

3 Tight cultures . . . highly permissive: Ibid.

3 norm violations are rare . . . nowhere to be found: Metz, E. (2015, March 28). Why Singapore banned chewing gum. BBC. Retrieved from http://www.bbc.com/news/magazine-32090420.

3 clocks on city streets: Levine, R. V., & Norenzayan, A. (1999). The pace of life in 31 countries. *Journal of Cross-Cultural Psychology*, *30*(2), 178–205.

3 arriving late for business meetings . . . "*com pontualidade britânica*": How Brazil's relationship with time affects personal and professional relationships. (2016, May 6). *Street Smart Brazil*. Retrieved from https://streetsmartbrazil.com/how-brazils-relationship-with-time-affects-personal-and-professional-relationships/.

3 trains almost *never* arrive late: 54 seconds, the average delay time of the Shinkansen. (2016, August 22). *Time Lapse Tokyo*. Retrieved from http://timelapsetokyo.com/2016/08/22/shinkansen-punctual/.

4 hand out cards to passengers: Sorry for the one-minute delay: Why Tokyo's trains rule. (2013, September 25). *Traveller*. Retrieved from http://www.traveller.com.au/sorry-for-the-one-minute-delay-why-tokyos-trains-rule-2udv1.

CHAPTER 1: A CURE FOR CHAOS

8 millions of people stand in the freezing cold: Mueller, B. (2017, December 28). In wake of attacks, tighter security for Times Square on New Year's Eve. *The New York Times*. Retrieved from https://www.nytimes.com/2017/12/28/nyregion/times-square-new-years-eve-security.html.

8 eating twelve grapes: Koehler, J. (2012, December 31). Green grapes and red underwear: A Spanish New Year's Eve. NPR. Retrieved from https://www.npr.org/sections/thesalt/2012/12/26/168092673/green-grapes-and-red-underwear-a-spanish-new-years-eve.

8 eating a spoonful of lentils: Chilean traditions for the New Year. (2016,

NOTES

December 31). *Traveling in Chile*. Retrieved from https://www.thisischile.cl/chilean-traditions-for-the-new-year/?lang=en.

8 **filling barbed wire with flammable material:** Hogmanay traditions old and new. BBC. Retrieved from http://news.bbc.co.uk/local/tayside andcentralscotland/hi/people_and_places/arts_and_culture/newsid _8434000/8434937.stm.

8 **frigid, polluted river in celebration for Kumbh Mela:** Maclean, K. (2008). *Pilgrimage and power: The Kumbh Mela in Allahabad, 1765–1954*. Oxford, UK: Oxford University Press.

9 **In a groundbreaking study:** Hamlin, J. K., & Wynn, K. (2011). Young infants prefer prosocial to antisocial others. *Cognitive Development, 26*(1), 30–39.

9 **In one study:** Vaish, A., Missana, M., & Tomasello, M. (2011). Three-year-old children intervene in third-party moral transgressions. *British Journal of Developmental Psychology, 29*(1), 124–130.

10 **After being taught a certain arbitrary behavior:** Rakoczy, H., Warneken, F., & Tomasello, M. (2008). The sources of normativity: Young children's awareness of the normative structure of games. *Developmental Psychology, 44*(3), 875–888; see also Schmidt, M. F., Rakoczy, H., & Tomasello, M. (2012). Young children enforce social norms selectively depending on the violator's group affiliation. *Cognition, 124*(3), 325–333; Schmidt, M. F., Butler, L. P., Heinz, J., & Tomasello, M. (2016). Young children see a single action and infer a social norm: Promiscuous normativity in 3-year-olds. *Psychological Science, 27*(10), 1360–1370.

10 **The nine-spined stickleback fish:** Pike, T. W., & Laland, K. N. (2010). Conformist learning in nine-spined sticklebacks' foraging decisions. *Biology Letters*, rsbl20091014.

10 **Norway rats will eat food:** Galef, B. G., & Whiskin, E. E. (2008). "Conformity" in Norway rats? *Animal Behaviour, 75*(6), 2035–2039.

10 **birds are also keenly attuned:** Beecher, M. D., & Burt, J. M. (2004). The role of social interaction in bird song learning. *Current Directions in Psychological Science, 13*(6), 224–228.

10 **Researchers in Germany:** Haun, D. B., Rekers, Y., & Tomasello, M. (2014). Children conform to the behavior of peers; other great apes stick with what they know. *Psychological Science, 25*(12), 2160–2167.

11 **now classic study in 1956:** Source: Asch, S. E. (1956). Studies of indepen-

dence and conformity: I. A minority of one against a unanimous majority. *Psychological Monographs: General and Applied, 70*(9), 1.

12 **Figure 1.1:** Ibid.

12 **handshake may have originated in ancient Greece:** *Handshake— Priest and Two Soldiers.* [Sculpture] (500 BC). Berlin: Pergamon Museum.

13 **Figure 1.2:** Source: DeAgostini Picture Library/Getty Images.

13 **A testament of commitment to Lord Murugan:** Ward, C. (1984). Thaipusam in Malaysia: A psycho-anthropological analysis of ritual trance, ceremonial possession and self-mortification practices. *American Anthropological Association.* Retrieved from http://www.jstor.org /stable/pdf/639977.pdf.

13 **It's fairly common . . . to pierce one's skin:** Mellor, D., Hapidzal, F. M., Ganesan, R., Yeow, J., Latif, R. A., & Cummins, R. (2012). Strong spiritual engagement and subjective well-being: A naturalistic investigation of the Thaipusam festival. *Journal of Spirituality and Mental Health, 14*, 209–225. Retrieved from http://www.tandfonline.com/doi/abs/10.1080/19349637 .2012.697375.

13 **On the island of Mauritius:** Xygalatas, D., Mitkidis, P., Fischer, R., Reddish, P., Skewes, J., Geertz, A. W., . . . & Bulbulia, J. (2013). Extreme rituals promote prosociality. *Psychological Science, 24*(8), 1602–1605.

14 **strapped to planks of nails:** Foran, S. (2015). The puzzle of extreme rituals. *UConn Today.* Retrieved from https://today.uconn.edu/2015/02 /the-puzzle-of-extreme-rituals/.

14 **in San Pedro Manrique, Spain, June 23:** Armstrong, L. (1970). Firewalking at San Pedro Manrique, Spain. *Folklore, 81*(3), 198–214.

14 **Each year, around three thousand spectators:** Konvalinka, I., Xygalatas, D., Bulbulia, J., Schjødt, U., Jegindø, E. M., Wallot, S., Van Orden, G., & Roepstorff, A. (2011). Synchronized arousal between performers and related spectators in a fire-walking ritual. *Proceedings of the National Academy of Sciences, 108*(20), 8514–8519.

14 **Some people walk . . . while others:** Armstrong, L. (1970). Fire-walking at San Pedro Manrique, Spain; see also UConn. [Username]. (2015, February 10). *Firewalking in San Pedro Manrique, Spain* [Video file]. Retrieved from https://www.youtube.com/watch?v=SNfgq-7VAKc.

14 **Volunteers often carry relatives:** Konvalinka et al. Synchronized arousal between performers and related spectators in a fire-walking ritual.

14 **a team of anthropologists:** Ibid.

15 **Some of the same anthropologists who studied heart rates:** Xygala- tas, D., Mitkidis, P., Fischer, R., Reddish, P., Skewes, J., Geertz, A. W., ... & Bulbulia, J. (2013). Extreme rituals promote prosociality. *Psychological Science, 24*(8), 1602–1605.

15 **In a series of experiments:** Bastian, B., Jetten, J., & Ferris, L. J. (2014). Pain as social glue: Shared pain increases cooperation. *Psychological Science, 25*(11), 2079–2085.

16 **In a study at New Zealand's University of Otago:** Jackson, J. C., Jong, J., Bilkey, D., Whitehouse, H., Zollmann, S., McNaughton, C., & Halber- stadt, J. (in press). Synchrony and physiological arousal increase cohe- sion and cooperation in large naturalistic groups. *Scientific Reports.*

16 **Being in sync with others:** Valdesolo, P., Ouyang, J., & DeSteno, D. (2010). The rhythm of joint action: Synchrony promotes cooperative ability. *Jour- nal of Experimental Social Psychology, 46*(4), 693–695.

16 **Researchers from Harvard Business School:** Schroeder, J., Risen, J., Gino, F., & Norton, M. (2014). Handshaking promotes cooperative dealmaking. *Harvard Business School Negotiation, Organizations & Mar- kets Unit Working Paper.* Retrieved from https://hbswk.hbs.edu/item/ handshaking-promotes-cooperative-dealmaking.

17 *The Secret of Our Success:* Henrich, J. (2015). *The secret of our success: How culture is driving human evolution, domesticating our species, and making us smarter.* Princeton, N.J.: Princeton University Press.

18 **remarkably cooperative species:** Turchin, P. (2015). *Ultrasociety: How 10,000 years of war made humans the greatest cooperators on earth.* Chaplin, CT: Beresta Books; Richerson, P. J., & Boyd, R. (2005). *Not by genes alone: How culture transformed human evolution.* Chicago: University of Chicago Press.

CHAPTER 2: PAST VS. PRESENT: THE MORE THINGS CHANGE, THE MORE THEY STAY THE SAME

19 **accused of theft and vandalism:** Shenon, P. (1994, March 16). Singa- pore journal; a flogging sentence brings a cry of pain in U.S. *The New York Times.* Retrieved from http://www.nytimes.com/1994/03/16/world/ singapore-journal-a-flogging-sentence-brings-a-cry-of-pain-in-us.html.

19 **ten-day spree:** Top ten innocents abroad: Do not mess with Singapore.

Time. Retrieved from http://content.time.com/time/specials/packages /article/0,28804,1915352_1915354_1915337,00.html.

19 **spray-painting and throwing eggs at eighteen cars:** Shenon, P. Singapore journal; a flogging sentence.

19 **four months in jail:** Ibid.

19 **a fine of 3,500 Singapore dollars:** Bahrampour, F. (1994). The caning of Michael Fay: Can Singapore's punishment withstand the scrutiny of international law. *American University Journal of International Law and Policy,* 10, 1075.

19 **six strokes of a cane:** Shenon, P. Singapore journal; a flogging sentence.

19 **the *New York Times*:** Time to assert American values. (1994, April 13). *The New York Times.* Retrieved from http://www.nytimes.com/1994/04/13 /opinion/time-to-assert-american-values.html; Safire, W. (1994, May 19). President doormat. *The New York Times.* Retrieved from http://www .nytimes.com/1994/05/19/opinion/president-doormat.html.

19 **the *Washington Post*:** Singapore's shame. (1994, May 7). *The Washington Post.* Retrieved from https://www.washingtonpost.com/archive/opin ions/1994/05/07/singapores-shame/a8813ab0-75fe-4ed6-b073-9c3d80 909a93/?utm_term=.d0ba55a4e8ae.

19 **the *Los Angeles Times*:** A sentence from the Dark Ages: Flogging is barbaric torture; Singapore's president should grant Michael Fay clemency. (1994, April 19). *Los Angeles Times.* Retrieved from http://articles .latimes.com/1994-04-19/local/me-47545_1_michael-fay-clemency; Skolnick, J. H. (1994, April 7). Perspective on corporal punishment. Would "caning" work here? No!: It's not a deterrent; it is discriminatory and cruel, and it would seriously harm our justice system. *Los Angeles Times.* Retrieved from http://articles.latimes.com/1994-04-07/local/me -42956_1_corporal-punishment.

19 **a hundred miles per hour:** Von Mirbach, J. (2015, May 3). The invisible scars left by strikes of the cane. *Deutsche Welle.* Retrieved from http://www.dw.com/en/the-invisible-scars-left-by-strikes-of-the-cane /a-18298970.

19 **blood and flesh, fainting:** Don't copy Singapore. (1994, April 5). *USA Today.* Retrieved from http://www.corpun.com/usju9404.htm.

19 **President Clinton:** Branigin, W. (1994, April 13). American teenager awaits

caning in orderly, unbending Singapore. *The Washington Post.* Retrieved from https://www.washingtonpost.com/archive/politics/1994/04/13/american-teenager-awaits-caning-in-orderly-unbending-singapore/9f4d542f-00ac-452e-be4f-2d3352ba41fa/?utm_term=.804114d0c92d.

20 **"even police cars":** Shenon, P. Singapore journal; a flogging sentence.

20 **reduced Fay's caning sentence:** Spare the rod, spoil the child: Michael Fay's caning in Singapore (2016, August 19). *The Huffington Post.* Retrieved from http://www.huffingtonpost.com/adst/spare-the-rod-spoil-the-c_b_8012770.html.

20 **about 5.6 million people:** Population, total. The World Bank. Retrieved from https://data.worldbank.org/indicator/SP.POP.TOTL?locations=MA.

20 **"fine city":** Metz, E. (2015, March 28). Why Singapore banned chewing gum. *BBC News Magazine.* Retrieved from http://www.bbc.com/news/magazine-32090420.

20 **fined up to a thousand dollars:** Environmental public health (public cleansing) regulations. *Singapore Statutes Online.* Retrieved from https://sso.agc.gov.sg/SL/95-RG3?DocDate=20180611&ViewType=Advance&Phrase=Environmental+public+health&WiAl=1#pr16-.

20 **up to a hundred thousand dollars and/or jail time:** Regulation of imports and exports (chewing gum) regulations. *Singapore Statutes Online.* Retrieved from https://sso.agc.gov.sg/SL/272A-RG4?DocDate=20161028&ViewType=Advance&Phrase=import+chewing+gum&WiAl=1.

20 **Drinking alcohol:** Han, L. Y. (2015, April 1). What you can or cannot do under the new alcohol law. *The Straits Times.* Retrieved from http://www.straitstimes.com/singapore/what-you-can-or-cannot-do-under-the-new-alcohol-law.

20 **death penalty:** Singapore: Executions continue in flawed attempt to tackle drug crime, despite limited reforms (2017, October 11). Amnesty International. Retrieved from https://www.amnesty.org/en/latest/news/2017/10/singapore-executions-continue-in-flawed-attempt-to-tackle-drug-crime/.

20 **Making too much noise:** Miscellaneous offences (public order and nuisance) act. *Singapore Statutes Online.* Retrieved from https://sso.agc.gov.sg/Act/MOPONA1906?ViewType=Advance&Phrase=Miscellaneous+offences+public+order+and+nuisance+act&WiAl=1.

20 **singing obscene songs:** Offenses affecting the public tranquility, public health, safety, convenience, decency and morals. *Singapore Statutes Online.* Retrieved from https://sso.agc.gov.sg/Act/PC1871?& ProvIds=P4XIV_267A-&ViewType=Advance&Phrase=public+tranquility %2c+public+health%2c+safety%2c+convenience%2c+decency+and+mor als&WiAl=1.

20 **distributing offensive photos:** Miscellaneous offences (public order and nuisance) act. *Singapore Statutes Online.*

20 **forget to flush:** Environmental public health (public cleansing) regulations. *Singapore Statutes Online.*

21 **urine detection devices:** Arnold, W. (1999, September 19). Where the start-up dance is still hard to do. *The New York Times.* Retrieved from http://www.nytimes.com/1999/09/19/business/where-the-start-up -dance-is-still-hard-to-do.html?pagewanted=all&src=pm.

21 **Homosexual acts:** Outrages on decency. *Singapore Statutes Online.* Retrieved from https://sso.agc.gov.sg/Act/PC1871?&ProvIds=pr377A -&ViewType=Advance&Phrase=gross+indecency&WiAl=1.

21 **"power-hungry and malicious":** Kelly, C. (2016, February 1). The strange case of Amos Yee: Whither free speech and children's rights in Singapore? *Oxford Human Rights Hub.* Retrieved from http://ohrh.law.ox.ac.uk/the -strange-case-of-amos-yee-whither-free-speech-and-childrens-rights-in -singapore/.

21 **"Social Development Unit":** Social Development Unit is established. (n.d.). Singapore Government. Retrieved from http://eresources.nlb.gov .sg/history/events/3c520e6c-dc34-4cef-84f5-1d73062c411b#4.

21 **over 80 percent:** Human Development Report 2015: Work for Human Development. (2015). United Nations Development Programme [Data file]. Retrieved from http://hdr.undp.org/sites/default/files/2015_human _development_report.pdf.

21 **drive with open bottles of alcohol:** Bayer, K. (2013, March 6). Beer-swigging loophole unlikely to close. *The New Zealand Herald.* Retrieved from http:// www.nzherald.co.nz/nz/news/article.cfm?c_id=1&objectid=10869614.

21 **Same-sex marriage is legal:** Equaldex. (2013). LGBT rights in New Zealand. Retrieved from http://www.equaldex.com/region/new-zealand.

21 **Women have the highest number:** Kiwi women most promiscuous in

NOTES

the world. (2007, October 13). *Stuff.* Retrieved from http://www.stuff.co .nz/life-style/22444/Kiwi-women-most-promiscuous-in-the-world.

21 **Prostitution has long been decriminalized:** New Zealand Prostitutes' Collective: History. Retrieved from http://www.nzpc.org.nz/History.

21 **New Zealanders are frequent users:** Pornhub (2015). 2015 year in review. Retrieved from https://www.pornhub.com/insights/pornhub-2015-year -in-review.

22 **Over one-third:** Collinson, L., Judge, L., Stanley, J., & Wilson, N. (2015). Portrayal of violence, weapons, antisocial behaviour and alcohol: Study of televised music videos in New Zealand. *New Zealand Medical Journal, 128*(1410), 84–86.

22 **they eschew formal titles:** New Zealand guide. *Commisceo Global.* Retrieved from http://www.commisceo-global.com/country-guides/new -zealand-guide.

22 **walk barefoot:** Whelan, M. (Host). (2015, April 8). *On the dial* [Audio podcast]. Retrieved from http://thewireless.co.nz/audio_articles/on-the -dial-episode-18.

22 **protests are frequent:** See https://teara.govt.nz/en/public-protest/page -5 and https://nzhistory.govt.nz/keyword/protest.

22 **Even couch burnings have been a common sight:** Arrests after couch burnings during Otago University's orientation week. (2016, February 24). *New Zealand Herald.* Retrieved from http://www.nzherald.co.nz/nz/news /article.cfm?c_id=1&objectid=11594793.

22 **engaging in various shenanigans:** The Wizard. *Christchurch City Libraries.* Retrieved from https://my.christchurchcitylibraries.com/the -wizard/.

22 **Mike Moore, proclaimed:** Brendal, S. (2017). New Zealand's national wizard [Blog post]. Retrieved from https://medium.com/new-zealand -thoughts/new-zealands-national-wizard-e8acf6ed5548.

23 **one of the largest studies of cultural norms:** Gelfand et al. Differences between tight and loose cultures.

25 **Figure 2.1:** Data source: ibid.

26 **Takeshita Street in Tokyo:** Janette, M. (2014, December 5). DOG: An underground fashion fantasy in Harajuku. *IS JAPAN COOL?* Retrieved from https://www.ana-cooljapan.com/columns/?p=98.

26 **take a designated break:** Rodionova, Z. (2017, May 15). Why getting drunk is a huge part of doing business in Japan. *The Independent.* Retrieved from https://www.independent.co.uk/news/business/news/japan-drinking -business-culture-why-getting-drunk-is-so-important-a7736946.html.

27 **vibrant artistic culture . . . caves:** Crowder, N. (2014, October 16). Most art forms in Iran are heavily censored. So many artists chose to perform underground. *The Washington Post.* Retrieved from https://www.washingtonpost .com/news/in-sight/wp/2014/10/16/2538/?utm_term=.3539f9a75200.

27 **"My Stealthy Freedom":** Itkowitz, C. (2016, August 9). This Iranian activist fights for women's rights not to wear hijab. But Donald Trump has complicated her effort. *The Washington Post.* Retrieved from https:// www.washingtonpost.com/news/inspired-life/wp/2016/08/09/in-era -of-trump-being-pro-women-and-anti-muslim-can-seem-the-same-but -its-not/?utm_term=.3792a572aa31.

27 **having large families:** Tal, A. (2016). *The land is full: Addressing overpopulation in Israel.* New Haven, Conn.: Yale University Press.

27 **tight commitment:** Kaplan, J. (n.d.). The role of the military in Israel. The Jewish Agency. Retrieved from http://www.jewishagency.org/soci ety-and-politics/content/36591.

27 **"tall poppies":** Peeters, B. (2004). "Thou shalt not be a tall poppy": Describing an Australian communicative (and behavioral) norm. *Intercultural Pragmatics, 1*(1), 71–92.

27 **economic development . . . collectivist or individualist:** Gelfand et al. Differences between tight and loose cultures.

28 **From cradle to grave:** Cartledge, P. (2003). *The Spartans: The world of warrior-heroes of ancient Greece.* New York: Overlook Press.

28 **At age seven:** Whitby, M. (2001). *Sparta.* New York: Overlook Press.

28 **If he showed signs of fear . . . fit physique:** Plutarch. (1992). *Lives of the noble Grecians and Romans.* (J. Dryden, Trans.). A. H. Clough (Ed.). New York: Random House.

29 **The Spartans found obesity grotesque:** Aelian, C. (1666). *Claudius Ælianus, his various history.* London: Printed for Thomas Dring.

29 **Men and women who failed:** Bradley, P. (2014). *The ancient world transformed.* New South Wales: Cambridge University Press.

29 **If an infant was deemed weak or deformed:** Plutarch. *Lives of the noble Grecians and Romans.*

29 **They were trained to wear solemn expressions:** Powell, A. (2014). *Classical Sparta: Techniques behind her success (Routledge revivals).* New York: Routledge.

29 **Children were disciplined:** Plutarch. *Lives of the noble Grecians and Romans.*

29 **Spartans appreciated laughter and humor:** Powell. *Classical Sparta.*

29 **who considered themselves a superior race:** Plutarch. *Lives of the noble Grecians and Romans.*

29 **Total uniformity:** Whitby. *Sparta.*

29 **Foreigners and foreign influence were prohibited:** Plutarch. *Lives of the noble Grecians and Romans.*

29 **Famous ancient Greeks and Romans:** Schofield, M. (Ed.). (2016). *Plato: The Laws.* New York: Cambridge University Press.

29 **Augustus Caesar:** Cartledge, P. (2003). *The Spartans.* New York: Overlook Press. See also Spawforth, A. J. S. (2011). *Greece and the Augustan cultural revolution.* New York: Cambridge University Press.

30 **Sparta's military rival and cultural nemesis:** Frey, W. (2004). Life in two city-states: Athens and Sparta. *History Alive: The Ancient World.* Teachers Curriculum Institute. Getty Publications.

30 **Athens had permissive norms:** Thucydides. (1954). *The Peloponnesian War.* (R. Warner, Trans.). Harmondsworth, UK: Penguin; see also Davis, W. S. (1960). *A day in old Athens: A picture of Athenian life.* Cheshire, Conn.: Biblo & Tannen.

30 **Strolling the streets of Athens . . . meet Diogenes:** Mark, J. J. (2009). Agora. *Ancient History Encyclopedia.* Retrieved from http://www.ancient.eu/agora/.

30 **proximity to the Aegean Sea . . . sculpture:** Frey. Life in two city-states.

30 **Every ten days:** Villing, A. (2010). *The ancient Greeks: Their lives and their world.* Teachers Curriculum Institute. Getty Publications.

30 **schools in Athens cultivated:** Connolly, P., & Dodge, H. (1998). *The ancient city: Life in classical Athens and Rome.* Oxford, UK: Oxford University Press.

30 **Radical new ideas transformed politics:** Villing. *The ancient Greeks.*

31 **abject eccentricity:** It's important to note following the Peloponnesian War, severe losses in population, political turmoil, and economic strains temporarily lowered the tolerance of contrarian views and attitudes in

Athens. This didn't bode well for Socrates, a known critic of the government, especially in the light of his personal relationships with Alcibiades, a defector to Sparta, and Critias, one of the Thirty Tyrants. Tried and sentenced to death, Socrates chose to drink the hemlock in 399 B.C. Martin, T. R. (2018). An overview of Classical Greek history from Mycenae to Alexander. Retrieved from http://www.perseus.tufts.edu/hopper/text?d oc=Perseus%3Atext%3A1999.04.0009%3Achapter%3D14.

31 **Guarded and reserved in their interactions . . . wrongdoings of others:** Lewis, O. (1951). *Life in a Mexican village: Tepoztlán restudied.* Urbana: University of Illinois Press.

32 **appropriate conduct was maintained:** Sandstrom, A. R. (2010). *Culture summary: Nahua.* New Haven, Conn.: Human Relations Area Files.

32 **growing up like "wild plants":** Jenness, D. (1922). "The Life of the Copper Eskimos." *Report of the Canadian Arctic expedition, 1913–18.* Ottawa, Ont.: F. A. Acland.

32 **roaming about on their own . . . parents' house:** Condon, R. G. (1983). "Inuit behavior and seasonal change in the Canadian Arctic." *Studies in cultural anthropology.* Ann Arbor, Mich.: UMI Research Press.

32 **If and when couples eventually did get married:** Damas, D. (1996). *Culture summary: Copper Inuit.* New Haven, Conn.: Human Relations Area Files.

32 **but returned to their respective families' homes:** Jenness, D. (1922). "The Life of the Copper Eskimos." *Report of the Canadian Arctic expedition, 1913–18.* Ottawa, Ont.: F. A. Acland.

33 **wife-swapping:** Damas, D. (1972). "Copper Eskimo." *Hunters and gatherers today: A socioeconomic study of eleven such cultures in the twentieth century.* New York: Holt, Rinehart and Winston.

33 **"rudimentary law":** Hoebel, E. A. (2009). *The law of primitive man: A study in comparative legal dynamics.* Cambridge, Mass.: Harvard University Press.

33 **high rates of homicide and blood feuds:** Damas. *Culture summary: Copper Inuit.*

33 **Ruth Benedict:** Benedict, R. (1934). *Patterns of culture* (Vol. 8). Boston: Houghton Mifflin Harcourt.

33 **used the terms *tight* and *loose*:** Pelto, P. J. (1968). The differences between "tight" and "loose" societies. *Trans-action, 5*(5), 37–40.

33 **The Standard Cross-Cultural Sample:** Murdock, G. P., & White, D. R. (1969). Standard cross-cultural sample. *Ethnology, 8*(4), 329–369.

34 **hundreds of societies:** Gelfand, M. J., Jackson, J. C., and Ember, C. (2017, February). *Ecological threat and the transmission of cultural tightness-looseness.* Talk given at the AAAS annual meeting. Boston, Mass.

CHAPTER 3: THE YIN AND YANG OF TIGHT AND LOOSE

35 **I asked some of my research assistants:** Gelfand, M. J., Jackson, J. C., van Egmond, M., Choi, V. K., Balanovic, J., Basker, I. N., . . . & Ward, C. The strength of social norms predicts global patterns of prejudice and discrimination.

35 **In 2008, researchers at the University of Groningen:** Keizer, K., Lindenberg, S., & Steg, L. (2008). The spreading of disorder. *Science, 322*(5908), 1681–1685.

36 **2017 episode of *Wait Wait . . . Don't Tell Me!*:** Panel Questions. (2017, May 27). NPR. Retrieved from https://www.npr.org/2017/05/27 /530256558/panel-questions.

36 **According to the *Economist*:** As crime dries up, Japan's police hunt for things to do. (2017, May 18). *The Economist.* Retrieved from https://www .economist.com/news/asia/21722216-there-was-just-one-fatal-shoot ing-whole-2015-crime-dries-up-japans-police-hunt.

36 **analyses of George Thomas Kurian's *Illustrated Book of World Rankings*:** Gelfand et al. Differences between tight and loose cultures.

37 ***The Better Angels of Our Nature*:** Pinker, S. (2012). *The better angels of our nature: Why violence has declined.* New York: Penguin Books.

37 **Looser nations have higher rates than tight ones . . . highly correlated with tightness rankings:** Gelfand et al. Differences between tight and loose cultures.

37 **death penalty in Singapore:** Singapore: Executions continue in flawed attempt to tackle drug crime, despite limited reforms. (2017, October 11). Amnesty International. Retrieved from https://www.amnesty.org/en/lat est/news/2017/10/singapore-executions-continue-in-flawed-attempt -to-tackle-drug-crime/.

37 **coffee shops:** Government of the Netherlands. (n.d.). Toleration policy regarding soft drugs and coffee shops. Retrieved from https://www.gov ernment.nl/topics/drugs/toleration-policy-regarding-soft-drugs-and -coffee-shops.

37 **increasingly in some U.S. states:** Delkic, M. (2017, October 24). Recreational marijuana is legal in these states—and Maine might be next. *Newsweek.* Retrieved from http://www.newsweek.com/where-recreational-marijuana-legal-691593.

37 **At least sixteen crimes:** Cornell Center on the Death Penalty Worldwide. (2011, April 4). Saudi Arabia. Retrieved from http://www.deathpenalty worldwide.org/country-search-post.cfm?country=saudi+arabia#f43-3. See also King, J. (2015, June 18). 16 things that could get you executed in Saudi Arabia. *Vocativ.* Retrieved from http://www.vocativ.com/under world/crime/saudi-arabia-execution-beheading/index.html.

37 **jail time:** Cacciottolo, M. (2015, October 13). Saudi Arabia drinking: The risks expats take for a tipple. BBC. Retrieved from http://www.bbc.com /news/uk-34516143.

37 **public flogging:** What you can be flogged for in Saudi Arabia. (2015, October 13). BBC. Retrieved from http://www.bbc.co.uk/newsbeat/arti cle/34513278/what-you-can-be-flogged-for-in-saudi-arabia.

37 **relatively crime free:** Why does Singapore top so many tables? (2013, October 24). BBC. Retrieved from http://www.bbc.com/news/world -asia-24428567.

37 **more police per capita:** Gelfand et al. Differences between tight and loose cultures.

37 **employ more security personnel:** Jackson, J., Gelfand, M. J., van Egmond, M., . . . & Caluori, N. (2018). Unobtrusive indicators of tightness-looseness from around the world.

37 *saher:* 8 features of new saher cameras installed in Saudi Arabia. *Life in Saudi Arabia.* Retrieved from http://lifeinsaudiarabia.net/blog/2014/12 /10/5-facts-about-new-saher-cameras-of/.

37 **millions of surveillance cameras:** Tokyo's robotic eyes are everywhere. *The Japan Times.* Retrieved from https://www.japantimes.co.jp /news/2014/08/30/national/media-national/tokyos-robotic-eyes-every where/#.WoXkOpM-cWp.

38 **Psychologists at Newcastle University:** Bateson, M., Nettle, D., & Roberts, G. (2006). Cues of being watched enhance cooperation in a real-world setting. *Biology Letters, 2*(3), 412–414.

38 **reduced student littering by half:** Ernest-Jones, M., Nettle, D., & Bate-

son, M. (2011). Effects of eye images on everyday cooperative behavior: A field experiment. *Evolution and Human Behavior, 32*(3), 172–178.

38 **Figure 3.1:** Data source: ibid. By permission of the Royal Society.

39 **people who were prompted to think about religious concepts:** Randolph-Seng, B., & Nielsen, M. E. (2007). Honesty: One effect of primed religious representations. *The International Journal for the Psychology of Religion, 17*(4), 303–315. See also Mazar, N., Amir, O., & Ariely, D. (2008). The dishonesty of honest people: A theory of self-concept maintenance. *Journal of Marketing Research, 45*(6), 633–644, Study 1.

39 **"Watched people are nice people":** Norenzayan, A. (2013). *Big gods: How religion transformed cooperation and conflict.* Princeton, N.J.: Princeton University Press.

39 **examine signs of cleanliness in public settings:** Jackson et al. Unobtrusive indicators of tightness-looseness from around the world.

39 **"waste watchers":** City of Vienna—Municipal Department 48—Waste Management, Street Cleaning and Vehicle Fleet. (n.d.). Street cleaning in Vienna. Retrieved from https://www.wien.gv.at/umwelt/ma48/service /publikationen/pdf/strassenreinigung-en.pdf.

39 **"Kehrwoche":** Zudeick, P. (2012, December 21). Germans and hygiene. *Deutsche Welle.* Retrieved from http://www.dw.com/en/germans-and -hygiene/a-16459423.

39 **anti-littering mascot . . . two hundred thousand volunteers:** Rusken: How to engage citizens in keeping Oslo clean. (n.d.). Vimeo. Retrieved from https://vimeo.com/55861175.

39 **Japanese fans swarmed over Brazil's Arena Pernambuco:** Best fans at World Cup? Japanese clean up stadium after team's matches (2014, June 20). *RT.* Retrieved from https://www.rt.com/news/167408-japan -fans-cleaning-stadium/.

40 **"drunken vomity hellhole":** Aran, I. (2014, June 16). Gracious Japanese World Cup fans clean up stadium after loss. *Jezebel.* Retrieved from https://jezebel.com/gracious-japanese-world-cup-fans-clean-up-sta dium-after-1591298011.

40 **Seventy-five percent of Americans . . . entails over $11 billion:** Littering statistics. (2016, August 25). *Statistic Brain.* Retrieved from https:// www.statisticbrain.com/littering-statistics/.

40 **government in Brazil spends hundreds of millions of dollars:** Conde, M. L. (2013, April 30). Rio Lixo Zero to impose fines for littering. *The Rio Times*. Retrieved from http://riotimesonline.com/brazil-news/rio-poli tics/rio-lixo-zero-to-impose-fines-for-littering/.

40 **makeshift landfills:** Kitsantonis, N. (2008, June 4). Greece struggles to reduce its trash. *The New York Times*. Retrieved from http://www .nytimes.com/2008/06/04/world/europe/04iht-rbogtrash.1.13452003 .html?pagewanted=all.

40 **health and safety risks:** Of course, not all loose cultures are messy, and not all tight cultures are squeaky clean. New Zealand works hard to "Keep New Zealand beautiful." Keep New Zealand Beautiful. (2015). About us. Retrieved from https://www.knzb.org.nz/contact/about-us/. And after years of massive illegal dumping activities, Estonia has worked to clean up its huge littering problem. Läks, H. (2017). Estonia leading a world cleanup day—staying stubborn and uniting people. Let's Do It! Retrieved from https://www.letsdoitworld.org/2017/04/estonia-leading -world-cleanup-day-staying-stubborn-uniting-people/.

Likewise, India, for all of its normative tightness, had massive problems with open defecation until campaigns started shaming its population. These exceptions notwithstanding, overall, disorder tends to go hand in hand with looseness and order with tightness. Doshi, V. (2017, November 5). India turns to public shaming to get people to use its 52 million new toi- lets. *The Washington Post*. Retrieved from https://www.washingtonpost .com/world/asia_pacific/india-turns-to-public-shaming-to-get-people -to-use-its-52million-new-toilets/2017/11/03/882166fe-b41c-11e7-9b93 -b97043e57a22_story.html?noredirect=on&utm_term=.0458da1f7efa.

40 **People have been found to litter more:** Keizer et al. The spreading of disorder.

40 **mandated quiet hours:** Hiob, R. (2006, May 18). German law tells you how. *Spiegel Online*. Retrieved from http://www.spiegel.de/international /love-thy-neighbor-german-law-tells-you-how-a-416736.html.

40 **yapping dog:** Bridge, A. (1995, July 28). German dogs face rules on bark- ing. *The Independent*. Retrieved from http://www.independent.co.uk /news/world/german-dogs-face-rules-on-barking-1593699.html; Hiob. German law tells you how.

40 **Commuters are expected:** (2017, February 8). Train etiquette in Japan:

More of the "don'ts" than the "dos." *City-Cost.* Retrieved from https://www
.city-cost.com/blogs/City-Cost/G6n8G-transportation.

40 **Dutch commuters:** (2016, February 17). Opruimen? Van de gekke. *De
Volkskrant.* Retrieved from https://www.volkskrant.nl/opinie/-kunnen
-er-ook-patatvrije-coupes-komen~a4246020/.

41 **"more like the British":** Roth, D. (2016, September 1). New Jerusalem
Light Rail video urges Israelis to adopt UK manners while traveling.
Jerusalem Post. Retrieved from http://www.jpost.com/Israel-News/New
-Jerusalem-Light-Rail-video-urges-Israelis-to-adopt-UK-manners-while
-traveling-466631.

41 **"The City That Never Shuts Up" . . . more than 420,000 noise complaints:** Hu, W. (2017, July 19). New York Becomes the City That Never
Shuts Up. *The New York Times.* Retrieved from https://www.nytimes
.com/2017/07/19/nyregion/new-york-becomes-the-city-that-never
-shuts-up.html.

41 **dangerous decibel levels:** Buckley, C. (2012, July 19). Working or playing indoors, New Yorkers face an unabated roar. *The New York Times.*
Retrieved from http://www.nytimes.com/2012/07/20/nyregion/in-new
-york-city-indoor-noise-goes-unabated.html?_r=1&ref=nyregion.

41 **rated as being much noisier in looser cultures:** Jackson et al. Unobtrusive indicators of tightness-looseness from around the world.

41 **Fireflies:** Pikovsky, A., Rosenblum, M., & Kurths, J. (2003). *Synchronization: A universal concept in nonlinear sciences* (Vol. 12). Cambridge, UK:
Cambridge University Press.

41 **crickets:** Walker, T. J. (1969). Acoustic synchrony: Two mechanisms in
the snowy tree cricket. *Science, 166*(3907), 891–894.

41 **cardiac pacemakers, firing neurons, intestinal activity:** Strogatz, S.
(2003). *Sync: The emerging science of spontaneous order.* New York:
Hyperion.

41 **a clever study:** Levine, R. V., & Norenzayan, A. (1999). The pace of life in
31 countries. *Journal of Cross-Cultural Psychology, 30*(2), 178–205.

42 **Figure 3.2:** Data source: ibid.

42 **up to two hundred miles per hour:** Shu, L. (2014, December 5). Want
to watch the world flick by at over 200 mph? Hop on the world's fastest trains. *Digital Trends.* Retrieved from https://www.digitaltrends.com
/cool-tech/traveling-beyond-200-mph-on-worlds-fastest-trains/.

42 **average delay of only fifty-four seconds:** 54 seconds, the average delay time of the Shinkansen. (2016, August 22). *Time Lapse Tokyo.* Retrieved from http://timelapsetokyo.com/2016/08/22/shinkansen-punctual/.

42 **97 percent punctuality rate:** Bleisch, R. (2015, March 17). The Swiss Railway System. Retrieved from http://jernbanekonferanser.no/jernban eforum/jernbaneforum_2015/presentasjoner/content_3/text_7ef9e c7e-4065-4870-8440-9b416bd584b01426677868018/1426692524 989/_0910_reto_bleisch_4.pdf.

42 **only fourteen delays:** MRT Incident Stats. (2015, March 11). Land Transport Authority of Singapore. Retrieved from https://www.lta.gov .sg/content/dam/ltaweb/corp/PublicationsResearch/files/FactsandFig ures/MRT_incident_stats.pdf.

42 **up to one million Singapore dollars:** Ismail, S. (2014, January 12). Revised penalties for train operators expected to be announced in Jan. *Today.* Retrieved from http://www.todayonline.com/singapore/revised -penalties-train-operators-expected-be-announced-jan.

43 **public apology:** SMRT apologises after massive three-hour train break-down. (2015, July 9). *Intellasia East Asia News.* Retrieved from http:// www.intellasia.net/smrt-apologises-after-massive-three-hour-train -breakdown-455312.

43 **detailed explanation:** Connolly, K. (2016, June 11). Why German trains don't run on time any more. *The Guardian.* Retrieved from https://www .theguardian.com/world/2016/jun/11/why-german-trains-dont-run-on -time-any-more.

43 **20 to 30 percent of trains run late:** Amtrak train route on-time per-formance. Retrieved from https://www.amtrak.com/historical-on-time -performance. Rank of busiest train lines retrieved from https://ggwash .org/view/32108/top-10-busiest-amtrak-routes.

43 **fewer "lefties" in tight cultures:** Gelfand et al. Differences between tight and loose cultures.

43 **more likely it is to require school uniforms:** School uniforms by country. (Accessed September 2016). Wikipedia. Retrieved from https:// en.wikipedia.org/wiki/School_uniforms_by_country. Information on uniforms in different countries was coded on a five-point scale, with an assigned value of "1" indicating that no schools in the country required uniforms, "2" indicating that very few schools required uniforms, "3"

indicating that some schools required uniforms, "4" indicating that most schools required uniforms, and "5" indicating that uniforms were compulsory in all schools. Correlation with TL (N = 21): $r = .49$, $p = .03$. In correlational analyses, r corresponds to the strength of a correlation, and can range from a value of −1 to 1. A value of +.1 indicates a small correlation, a value of +.3 indicates a medium correlation, and a value of +.5 indicates a large correlation. A p value indicates the statistical significance of an analysis, with a value less than .05 signaling significance.

43 **venture into parking lots:** Jackson et al. Unobtrusive indicators of tightness-looseness from around the world.

43 *Shuudan Koudou*: White, K. (2017, November 3). 40 men stand in perfect square—take walking to new level with jaw-dropping routine. *Inspire More*. Retrieved from https://www.inspiremore.com/shuudan-koudou/.

43 **radio calisthenics:** Should exercise be compulsory at work? (2017, April 5). BBC. Retrieved from http://www.bbc.com/news/health-39490607.

43 **many primary and secondary schools:** Latham, K. (2007). *Pop culture China! Media, arts, and lifestyle*. Santa Barbara, Calif.: ABC-CLIO. See also: Sum, C. Y. (2010). An exercise for the People's Republic: Order and discipline in the morning ritual of a Chinese primary school. Paper, Boston University.

43 **gather in public squares:** Hui, L. (2014, July 14). Chinese elderly favor exercise in parks. *Xinhua Net*. Retrieved from http://www.xinhuanet.com/english/2017-07/14/c_136444020.htm.

44 *adhan*: The 5 Muslim daily prayer times and what they mean. (2017, September 18). *Thoughtco*. Retrieved from https://www.thoughtco.com/islamic-prayer-timings-2003811.

44 **In a paper published in the *Journal of Financial Economics*:** Eun, C. S., Wang, L., & Xiao, S. C. (2015). Culture and R 2. *Journal of Financial Economics, 115*(2), 283–303.

44 *The Civilizing Process*: Elias, N. (1978). *The civilizing process* (original work published in 1939). (Edmund Jeffcott, Trans.) New York: Urizen.

45 **weigh much more:** Correlation between tightness and male BMI, controlling for GNP and height (N = 30): $r = −.45$, $p = .02$; correlation between tightness and female BMI, controlling for GNP and height (N = 30): $r = −.50$, $p = .007$. Data obtained from https://www.indexmundi.com/blog/index.php/2013/04/11/body-mass-index-bmi-by-country/.

45 **over 50 percent of dogs and cats:** Dotinga, R. (2014, May 30). More than half of U.S. pets are overweight or obese, survey finds. CBS. Retrieved from https://www.cbsnews.com/news/more-than-half-of-u-s-pets-are -overweight-or-obese-survey-finds/.

45 **alcohol consumption:** Gelfand et al. Differences between tight and loose cultures.

45 **more likely to gamble:** Correlation between tightness and prevalence of gambling, controlling for GNP (N = 14): $r = -.80$, $p = .001$. Data obtained from http://onlinelibrary.wiley.com/doi/10.1111/add.12899/full.

45 **gross national savings:** Correlation between tightness and gross savings in 2016 controlling for GNP (N = 32): $r = .50$, $p = .004$. Data obtained from http://databank.worldbank.org/data/reports.aspx?source=2&series =NY.GNS.ICTR.ZS&country=.

45 **€300 billion into debt:** Lin, C. Y. Y., Edvinsson, L., Chen, J., & Beding, T. (2012). *National intellectual capital and the financial crisis in Greece, Italy, Portugal, and Spain* (Vol. 7). New York: Springer Science & Business Media.

45 **"You just have to ask":** Vasagar, J. (2013, July 27). What we can learn from the Germans. *The Telegraph*. Retrieved from http://www.telegraph .co.uk/news/worldnews/europe/germany/10206103/What-we-can -learn-from-the-Germans.html.

45 **German word for debt:** Germany, Greece and debt: As we forgive our debtors (2015, June 16). *The Economist*. Retrieved from https://www .economist.com/blogs/erasmus/2015/07/germany-greece-and-debt; Jack, S., & Clark, K. (2015, February 13). Inside the Germans' debt psyche—what makes them tick? *BBC*. Retrieved from http://www.bbc .com/news/business-31369185.

46 **leave the eurozone:** Germans call for Greece to leave the euro zone after "no" referendum vote. (2015, July 5). *Fortune*. Retrieved from http://for tune.com/2015/07/05/germans-call-for-greece-to-leave-the-euro-zone -after-no-referendum-vote/.

46 **In one study:** Chua, R. Y., Roth, Y., & Lemoine, J.-F. (2015). The impact of culture on creativity: How cultural tightness and cultural distance affect global innovation crowdsourcing work. *Administrative Science Quarterly*, *60*(2), 189–227.

47 **Figure 3.3:** Source: Vohs, K. D., Redden, J. P., & Rahinel, R. (2013). Physical

order produces healthy choices, generosity, and conventionality, whereas disorder produces creativity. *Psychological Science, 24*(9), 1860–1867. Reprinted by permission of SAGE Publications, Inc.

47 **people who spent time in a messy room . . . "classic":** Ibid.

48 **In one study . . . In another study:** Gelfand, M., Jackson, J. C., Taylor, M., & Caluori, N. (2017, May). *Group synchrony reduces creativity and dissent.* Poster session presented at the Annual Convention of the Association for Psychological Science, Boston, Mass.

48 **unconventional ideas for gifts:** Leung, A. K. Y., & Chiu, C. Y. (2010). Multicultural experience, idea receptiveness, and creativity. *Journal of Cross-Cultural Psychology, 41*(5–6), 723–741.

48 **tasks that require novel solutions:** Maddux, W., & Galinsky, A. (2009). Cultural borders and mental barriers: The relationship between living abroad and creativity. *Journal of Personality and Social Psychology, 96*(5), 1047–1061.

48 **Imagine you're given a book of matches:** Duncker, K. (1945). On problem solving. *Psychological Monographs, 58*(5, Whole No. 270).

48 **"fluidity":** Baumol, W. J., Litan, R. E., & Schramm, C. J. (2007). *Good capitalism, bad capitalism, and the economics of growth and prosperity.* New Haven, Conn.: Yale University Press; Schramm, C. J. (2008). Economic fluidity: A crucial dimension of economic freedom. In Holmes, K. R., Feulner, E. K., & O'Grady, M. A. (Eds.). *2008 index of economic freedom* (pp. 15–22). Washington, D.C.: Heritage Foundation.

48 **Howard Gardner:** Gardner, H. (2011). *Creating minds: An anatomy of creativity seen through the lives of Freud, Einstein, Picasso, Stravinsky, Eliot, Graham, and Gandhi.* New York: Basic Books.

49 **Figure 3.4:** Source: Duncker. On problem solving.

49 **our analyses of the 2015 Global Entrepreneurship Monitor:** Correlation between tightness and percentage of the population between ages eighteen and sixty-four who view entrepreneurship as a good career choice, controlling for GNP (N = 18): $r = -.54$, $p = .03$; correlation between tightness and percentage of the population between ages eighteen and sixty-four who believe they have the required skills and knowledge to start a business, controlling for GNP (N = 19): $r = -.53$, $p = .02$. Data obtained from http://www.gemconsortium.org/report/49480.

49 **"If one were to order all mankind":** Herodotus. (1998). *The Histories* (p.

183; R. Waterfield, Trans.). Oxford, UK: Oxford University Press. (Original work published 440 BC.)

49 **story in which King Darius:** Ibid. (p. 184).

50 **cosmopolitan mind-set:** Correlation between tightness and percentage of people who said they belonged to the world as a first or second choice in response to the question "To which of the following geographic groups would you say you belong first of all? And the next?" controlling for GNP (N = 10): $r = -.71$, $p = .03$. Data obtained from 1994–2004 World Values Survey.

50 **tolerate immigrants:** Gelfand et al. Differences between tight and loose cultures.

50 **back up those attitudes:** Ibid.

50 **culture is superior:** Ibid.

50 **needs to be protected from foreign influences:** Ibid.

50 **90th percentile:** China ranks 130th out of 140 countries for unwelcoming attitudes toward foreign visitors in their country. Data obtained from Blanke, J., & Chiesa, T. (2013, May). The travel & tourism competitiveness report 2013. In the World Economic Forum (http://www3.weforum.org /docs/WEF_TT_Competitiveness_Report_2013.pdf).

50 **2 percent of the population:** Foreign population (n.d.). OECD (Organisation for Economic Co-operation and Development) Data. Retrieved from https://data.oecd.org/migration/foreign-population.htm.

50 **many landlords:** Osumi, M. (2017, July 2). "No foreign tenants"—and not much you can do about it. *The Japan Times*. Retrieved from https://www .japantimes.co.jp/community/2017/07/02/issues/no-foreign-tenants -not-much-can-you-can-do/#.WleDuVQ-fVo.

50 **bathhouses, shops, restaurants, and hotels:** Kikuchi, D. (2017, June 4). Tackling signs in Japan that you're not welcome. *The Japan Times*. Retrieved from https://www.japantimes.co.jp/news/2017/06/04/national /tackling-signs-japan-youre-not-welcome/#.Wl513lQ-fVo.

50 **the *Guardian* reported:** McCurry, J. (2016, October 11). Japanese train conductor blames foreign tourists for overcrowding. *The Guardian*. Retrieved from https://www.theguardian.com/world/2016/oct/11/jap anese-train-conductor-blames-foreign-tourists-for-overcrowding.

50 **anti-Semitic attitudes:** 28 percent of Austrians answered "probably true" to six or more of the anti-Semitic stereotypes tested in the 2014

ADL Global 100: A survey of attitudes toward Jews in over 100 countries around the world (http://global100.adl.org/).

50 **politically exclusive:** According to the 2015 Migrant Integration Policy Index report (http://www.mipex.eu/sites/default/files/downloads/pdf /files/austria.pdf), in 2014 alone, over 350,000 foreign residents of voting age—approximately 24 percent of the city's population—were excluded from voting in the country's capital, Vienna. The report also states that Austria has the lowest naturalization rates in Western Europe.

51 **In surveys:** Gelfand et al. The strength of social norms predicts global patterns of prejudice and discrimination.

51 **Figure 3.5:** Data source: ibid.

51 **International surveys by Gallup:** Correlation between tightness and the percent of people who said the city or area where they live is not a good place to live for gay or lesbian people (N = 29): $r = .49$, $p = .007$. Data obtained from http://news.gallup.com/poll/175520/nearly-worldwide -areas-good-gays.aspx.

51 **gay-friendly travel destinations:** 11 most gay friendly cities in the world. *Wonderful Odysseys Worldwide*. Retrieved from http://wowtravel .me/11-most-gay-friendly-cities-in-the-world/.

51 **Portugal:** Rodrigues, L., Grave, R., de Oliveira, J. M., & Nogueira, C. (2016). Study on homophobic bullying in Portugal using Multiple Correspondence Analysis (MCA). *Revista Latinoamericana de Psicología, 48*(3), 191–200.

51 **Turkey:** Fiswich, C. (2017, November 23). "It's just the start": LGBT community in Turkey fears government crackdown. *The Guardian*. Retrieved from https://www.theguardian.com/world/2017/nov/23/its -just-the-start-lgbt-community-in-turkey-fears-government-crack down; see also: Not an illness, nor a crime: Lesbian, gay, bisexual and transgender people in Turkey demand equality. (2011). Amnesty International. Retrieved from https://www.amnesty.org/download/Documents /28000/eur440012011en.pdf.

51 **Iran and Afghanistan:** Cornell Center on the Death Penalty Worldwide. (2011, April 4). Iran. Retrieved from https://www.deathpenalty worldwide.org/country-search-post.cfm?country=iran; Cornell Center on the Death Penalty Worldwide. (2011, April 4). Afghanistan. Retrieved from https://www.deathpenaltyworldwide.org/country-search-post.cfm ?country=Afghanistan.

52 **multiple ways for people to cohabitate:** Marriage, registered partnerships, and cohabitation agreements. Government of the Netherlands. Retrieved from https://www.government.nl/topics/family-law/marriage-registered-partnership-and-cohabitation-agreements.

52 **About half of all Dutch children . . . Spain:** Share of births outside marriage.(2016,February4).OECD—SocialPolicyDivision—Directorate of Employment, Labour and Social Affairs. Retrieved from http://www.oecd.org/els/family/SF_2_4_Share_births_outside_marriage.pdf.

52 **sexually tolerant:** Gelfand et al. Differences between tight and loose cultures.

52 **"leftover women":** Gao, H. (2016, October 13). Why Chinese women still can't get a break. *The New York Times.* Retrieved from https://www.nytimes.com/2016/10/16/opinion/why-chinese-women-still-cant-get-a-break.html.

52 **over 90 percent of children:** Hu, E. (2015, May 11). South Korea's single moms struggle to remove a social stigma. NPR. Retrieved from https://www.npr.org/sections/parallels/2015/05/11/405622494/south-koreas-single-moms-struggle-to-remove-a-social-stigma.

52 **Heraclitus:** Schiappa, E. (2013). *Protagoras and logos: A study in Greek philosophy and rhetoric.* Columbia: University of South Carolina Press.

52 **Bill Hicks:** Bould, C. (Director). (1993). *Bill Hicks: Revelations* [TV special]. United Kingdom.

53 **collective political action:** Gelfand et al. Differences between tight and loose cultures.

53 **rally against Iranian president Mahmoud Ahmadinejad:** Vora, J. (2007, September 25). Debating Ahmadinejad at Columbia. *The Nation.* Retrieved from https://www.thenation.com/article/debating-ahmadinejad-columbia/.

53 **autocratic governments:** Gelfand et al. Differences between tight and loose cultures.

53 **openness to the media:** Ibid.

53 **Twitter's analytics division:** Transparency report: Removal requests. Twitter. Retrieved from https://transparency.twitter.com/en/removal-requests.html.

54 **"web police" of two million:** China employs two million microblog

monitors state media say. (2013, October 4). BBC. Retrieved from http://www.bbc.com/news/world-asia-china-24396957.

54 **"social credit" system:** China wants to give all of its citizens a score—and their rating could affect every area of their lives. (2016, October 22). *The Independent.* Retrieved from http://www.independent.co.uk/news/world/asia/china-surveillance-big-data-score-censorship-a7375221.html; Ebbighausen, R. (2018, April 1). China experiments with sweeping Social Credit System. *Deutsche Welle.* Retrieved from http://www.dw.com/en/china-experiments-with-sweeping-social-credit-system/a-42030727; Chin, J., & Wang, G. (2016, November 28). China's new tool for social control: A credit rating for everything. *The Wall Street Journal.* Retrieved from https://www.wsj.com/articles/chinas-new-tool-for-social-control-a-credit-rating-for-everything-1480351590; State Department (2014, June 14). *Notice of the State Council on issuing the outline for planning the construction of social credit system* (2014–2020). Retrieved from http://www.gov.cn/zhengce/content/2014-06/27/content_8913.htm.

54 **over 80 percent:** Fallows, D. (2008, March 27). Most Chinese say they approve of government Internet control. Pew Internet & American Life Project. Retrieved from http://www.pewinternet.org/files/old-media/Files/Reports/2008/PIP_China_Internet_2008.pdf.pdf.

54 **broader trend:** Gelfand et al. Differences between tight and loose cultures.

54 **computer simulations:** De, S., Nau, D. S., & Gelfand, M. J. (2017, May). Understanding norm change: An evolutionary game-theoretic approach. In *Proceedings of the 16th Conference on Autonomous Agents and Multi-Agent Systems* (pp. 1433–1441). International Foundation for Autonomous Agents and Multiagent Systems.

54 **promote tolerance and reduce radicalization:** Hadid, D. (2016, October 14). Jordan tones down textbooks' Islamic content, and tempers rise. *The New York Times.* Retrieved from https://www.nytimes.com/2016/10/15/world/middleeast/jordan-tones-down-textbooks-islamic-content-and-tempers-rise.html.

55 **attack on Islamic values:** Azzeh, L. (2016, September 29). Teachers, parents protest changes to school curricula. *The Jordan Times.* Retrieved from http://jordantimes.com/news/local/teachers-parents-protest-changes-school-curricula.

55 **teachers' union:** Hadid. Jordan tones down textbooks' Islamic content.

CHAPTER 4: DISASTER, DISEASE, AND DIVERSITY

57 **highly dependent on agriculture:** Sandstrom. *Culture summary: Nahua.*

58 **highly self-reliant:** Damas. *Culture summary: Copper Inuit.*

58 **The Temne people of Sierra Leone . . . the Eskimo of Baffin Island:** Berry, J. W. (1967). Independence and conformity in subsistence-level societies. *Journal of Personality and Social Psychology, 7*(4p1), 415.

59 **over twenty thousand:** Population density (per sq. km of land area). The World Bank. Retrieved from https://data.worldbank.org/indicator /EN.POP.DNST. Population density was converted from square kilometers to square miles of land area.

59 **has only eight people:** Ibid.

59 **over eight hundred people:** Ibid.

59 **six sheep per person:** Sheep number falls to six for each person. (2017, January 19). *Statistics New Zealand.* Retrieved from https://www.stats .govt.nz/news/sheep-number-falls-to-six-for-each-person.

59 **forty-five people per square mile:** Population density (per sq. km of land area). The World Bank.

59 **over a thousand people per square mile:** Ibid.

59 **16 percent of India's territorial area:** Kaur, R. (1991). *Women in forestry in India* (Vol. 714). Washington, D.C.: World Bank Publications.

59 **70 percent of Japan:** OECD reviews of risk management policies: Japan 2009 large-scale floods and earthquakes. (2009, February 25). OECD (Organisation for Economic Co-operation and Development). OECD Publishing.

59 **less than 15 percent:** Arable land (% of land area). The World Bank. Retrieved from https://data.worldbank.org/indicator/AG.LND.ARBL.ZS.

59 **three-fifths of the country:** Gilman, D. C., Peck, H. T., & Colby, F. M. (1907, January 1). *The new international encyclopedia: Volume 18.* New York: Dodd, Mead.

59 **over five hundred people per square mile:** Population density (per sq. km of land area). The World Bank.

59 **lab rats:** Calhoun, J. B. (1962). Population density and social pathology. *Scientific American, 206*(2), 139–149.

60 **Figure 4.1:** Source: Randy Olson, National Geographic Creative.

60 **Areas that were populous . . . Present-day population density:** Gelfand et al. Differences between tight and loose cultures.

61 **public crisis:** Chewing gum is banned. HistorySG. Retrieved from http://eresources.nlb.gov.sg/history/events/57a854df-8684-456b-893a-a 303e0041891#3; see also Prystay, C. (2004, June 4). At long last, gum is legal in Singapore, but there are strings. *The Wall Street Journal.* Retrieved from https://www.wsj.com/articles/SB108629672446328324.

61 **By 1992:** Sale of food (prohibition of chewing gum) regulations. *Singapore Statutes Online.* Retrieved from https://sso.agc.gov.sg/SL/SFA1973 -RG2.

61 *The Revenge of Geography:* Kaplan, R. D. (2012). *The revenge of geography: What the map tells us about coming conflicts and the battle against fate.* New York: Random House.

61 **New Zealand and Australia:** Gelfand et al. Differences between tight and loose cultures.

61 **killed off 20 percent:** Daley, J. (2017, June 6). Researchers catalogue the grisly deaths of soldiers in the Thirty Years' War. *Smithsonian.* Retrieved from https://www.smithsonianmag.com/smart-news/researchers-cata logue-grisly-deaths-soldiers-thirty-years-war-180963531/.

61 **tens of thousands:** Clodfelter, M. (2017). *Warfare and armed conflicts: A statistical encyclopedia of casualty and other figures, 1492–2015.* Jefferson, N.C.: McFarland.

61 **Soviet occupation of East Germany:** Duffy, C. (2014). *Red storm on the Reich: The Soviet march on Germany, 1945* (p. 277). London: Routledge.

62 **Han Dynasty:** Violatti, C. (2013, May 27). *Ancient history encyclopedia.* Retrieved from https://www.ancient.eu/Han_Dynasty/.

62 **Yuan and Ming Dynasties . . . Qing Dynasty:** Editorial Committee of Chinese Military History. (1985). *Tabulation of wars in ancient China.* Beijing: People's Liberation Army Press.

62 **millions of deaths . . . devastation to its infrastructure:** Eastman, L. E. (1986). *The nationalist era in China, 1927–1949* (p. 115). Cambridge, UK: Cambridge University Press.

62 **disputes with each of them:** Shen, W. (2012, March 1). China and its neighbors: Troubled relations. EU-Asia Centre. Retrieved from http:// www.eu-asiacentre.eu/pub_details.php?pub_id=46.

62 **"When whales fight":** Drohan, T. (2016). *A new strategy for complex warfare: Combined effects in East Asia.* Amherst, N.Y.: Cambria Press; Ratner, A. (2014, July 4). The shrimp now has a say in the ongoing struggle for East Asian supremacy. Vice News. Retrieved from https://news.vice .com/article/the-shrimp-now-has-a-say-in-the-ongoing-struggle-for -east-asian-supremacy.

62 **Korea was invaded by Japan:** Lee, K. B. (1997). *Korea and East Asia: The story of a phoenix.* Westport, Conn.: Greenwood.

62 **the Manchus:** Ebrey, P., & Walthall, A. (2013). *East Asia: A cultural, social, and political history* (Vol. 2). Boston: Cengage Learning.

62 **Sino-Japanese War:** Paine, S. C. (2005). *The Sino-Japanese War of 1894– 1895: Perceptions, power, and primacy.* Cambridge, UK: Cambridge University Press.

62 **Korea suffered under Japanese rule:** Lee, H. Y., Ha, Y. C., & Sorensen, C. W. (Eds.). (2013). *Colonial rule and social change in Korea, 1910–1945.* Seattle: University of Washington Press.

62 **more than a million:** Feldman, R. T. (2004). *The Korean War.* Minneapolis: Twenty-First Century Books.

62 **Turks . . . English:** Gershoni, I., & Jankowski, J. P. (1986). *Egypt, Islam, and the Arabs: The search for Egyptian nationhood, 1900–1930.* Oxford, UK: Oxford University Press on Demand.

62 **India . . . Pakistan and China:** Guo, R. (2011). *Territorial disputes and conflict management: The art of avoiding war* (Vol. 8, p. 68). London: Routledge.

62 **Pakistan . . . Afghanistan:** Brunet-Jailly, E. (2015). *Border disputes: A global encyclopedia [3 volumes]* (p. 1). Santa Barbara, Calif.: ABC-CLIO.

63 **"The exigencies of war":** Sumner, W. G. (1906). *Folkways.* New York: Ginn.

63 **Darwin:** Darwin, C. R. (1873). *The descent of man, and selection in relation to sex.* New York: D. Appleton & Co. According to Darwin, "a greater number of courageous, sympathetic and faithful members, who were always ready to warn each other of danger, to aid and defend each other . . . would spread and be victorious over other tribes" ([*1*], p. 156).

63 **cooperation and unity:** In the twenty-first century, scientists have taken this argument further, arguing that groups that have high levels of cooperation are more likely to win competitions between groups.

According to this thinking, those whose tendency is to cooperate and to punish norm violators are better able to avoid subjugation and annihilation when enemies are at the door. See Choi, J. K., & Bowles, S. (2007). The coevolution of parochial altruism and war. *Science, 318*(5850), 636–640; and also Henrich, J. (2015). *The secret of our success: How culture is driving human evolution, domesticating our species, and making us smarter.* Princeton, N.J.: Princeton University Press.

63 **indeed were tighter:** Gelfand et al. Differences between tight and loose cultures.

64 **nearly 450,000 lives ... more than the United States:** Guha-Sapir, D., Below, R., & Hoyois, P. EM-DAT: International Disaster Database—Université Catholique de Louvain, Brussels. Retrieved from http://www.emdat.be.

64 **about $10 billion:** Thakurl, P. (2015, March 11). Disasters cost India $10 bn per year: UN report. *The Times of India.* Retrieved from https://timesofindia.indiatimes.com/india/Disasters-cost-India-10bn-per-year-UN-report/articleshow/46522526.cms.

64 **Indonesia's seventeen thousand islands:** Lamoureux, F. (2003). *Indonesia: A global studies handbook* (p. 3). Santa Barbara, Calif.: ABC-CLIO.

64 **the world's two most seismically active areas:** Roberts, C., Habir, A., & Sebastian, L. (Eds.). (2015). *Indonesia's ascent: Power, leadership, and the regional order* (p. 134). New York: Springer.

64 **Kangi Famine:** Farris, W. W. (2009). *Japan to 1600: A social and economic history.* Honolulu: University of Hawaii Press.

64 **more than 150 famines:** Turkington, D. (n.d.). *A chronology of Japanese history.* Retrieved from http://www.shikokuhenrotrail.com/japanhistory/AChronologyOfJapaneseHistory_v1.pdf.

64 **killed thousands of people and cost Japan over $200 billion:** Oskin, B. (2017, September 13). Japan earthquake & tsunami of 2011: Facts and information. *Live Science.* Retrieved from https://www.livescience.com/39110-japan-2011-earthquake-tsunami-facts.html.

64 **water, heat, or food:** Millions without food, water, power in Japan. (2011, March 13). NBC News. Retrieved from http://www.nbcnews.com/id/42044293/ns/world_news-asia_pacific/t/millions-without-food-water-power-japan/#.WIjidFQ-fVo.

65 **over one million people:** Shaw, R. (Ed.). (2014). *Community practices*

for disaster risk reduction in Japan. Tokyo: Springer Science & Business Media.

65 **overwhelmed by offers:** Fujita, A. (2011, May 4). Japan earthquake-tsunami spark volunteer boom but system overwhelmed. ABC News. Retrieved from http://abcnews.go.com/International/japan-earthquake -tsunami-spark-volunteer-boom-holiday-week/story?id=13523923.

65 **the yakuza:** Adelstein, J. (2011, March 18). Even Japan's infamous mafia groups are helping with the relief effort. *Business Insider.* Retrieved from https://www.businessinsider.com.au/japan-yakuza-mafia-aid-earth quake-tsunami-rescue-efforts-2011-3.

65 **prone to:** Synthesis report on ten ASEAN countries disaster risks assessment. (2010, December). ASEAN Disaster Risk Management Initiative. Retrieved from http://www.unisdr.org/files/18872_asean.pdf.

65 **correlates strongly with tightness:** Gelfand et al. Differences between tight and loose cultures.

65 **"We faced tremendous odds":** Yew, L. K. (2012). *From third world to first: The Singapore story, 1965–2000* (p. 3). New York: HarperCollins.

66 **"We had one simple guiding principle":** Ibid. (p. 58).

66 **are much tighter:** Gelfand et al. Differences between tight and loose cultures.

67 **at least seventy-five million:** Dunham, W. (2008, January 29). Black death "discriminated" between victims. ABC Science. Retrieved from http://www.abc.net.au/science/articles/2008/01/29/2149185.htm.

67 **over ten million lives:** The 10 deadliest epidemics in history. (2012, April 6). *Healthcare Business & Technology.* Retrieved from http://www .healthcarebusinesstech.com/the-10-deadliest-epidemics-in-history/.

67 **tens of thousands:** Goddard, J. (2012). *Public health entomology.* Boca Raton, Fla.: CRC Press. In the span of only two years during the Haitian-French War (1801–1803), Napoleon's largest expeditionary force of fifty thousand soldiers was almost entirely wiped out by yellow fever.

67 **hundreds of thousands:** Rhodes, J. (2013). *The end of plagues: The global battle against infectious disease.* New York: Macmillan.

67 **as many as fifty million deaths:** Taubenberger, J. K., & Morens, D. M. (2006). 1918 influenza: The mother of all pandemics. *Emerging Infectious Diseases, 12*(1), 15–22.

NOTES

67 *Guns, Germs, and Steel*: Diamond, J. (1997). *Guns, germs, and steel: The fates of human societies.* New York: W. W. Norton.

67 **An estimated thirty-five million people:** Ending AIDS: Progress towards the 90-90-90 targets. (2017). *Global AIDS Update.* Retrieved from http://www.unaids.org/sites/default/files/media_asset/Global_AIDS_update_2017_en.pdf.

67 **more than thirty million people:** Dying from TB—it can be an awful way to die. *TB Facts.* Retrieved from https://www.tbfacts.org/dying-tb/.

67 **more than 200 million cases:** Malaria fact sheet. (2017, November). World Health Organization. Retrieved from http://www.who.int/media centre/factsheets/fs094/en/.

67 **dousing food with spices:** Murray, D. R., & Schaller, M. (2010). Historical prevalence of infectious diseases within 230 geopolitical regions: A tool for investigating origins of culture. *Journal of Cross-Cultural Psychology, 41*(1), 99–108. See also Billing, J., & Sherman, P. W. (1998). Antimicrobial functions of spices: Why some like it hot. *The Quarterly Review of Biology, 73*(1), 3–49.

67 **when people feel more vulnerable to diseases:** Faulkner, J., Schaller, M., Park, J. H., & Duncan, L. A. (2004). Evolved disease-avoidance mechanisms and contemporary xenophobic attitudes. *Group Processes & Intergroup Relations, 7*(4), 333–353; Navarrete, C. D., & Fessler, D. M. (2006). Disease avoidance and ethnocentrism: The effects of disease vulnerability and disgust sensitivity on intergroup attitudes. *Evolution and Human Behavior, 27*(4), 270–282.

68 **parents teach their children to be compliant and obedient:** LeVine, R. A., Dixon, S., LeVine, S., Richman, A., Keiderman, P. H., Keefer, C. H., & Brazelton, T. B. (1994). *Child care and culture: Lessons from Africa.* New York: Cambridge University Press.

68 **implemented strict rules and restrictions:** Severe acute respiratory syndrome (SARS) outbreak, 2003. (2016, July 30). National Library Board Singapore. Retrieved from http://eresources.nlb.gov.sg/infopedia/articles/SIP_1529_2009-06-03.html.

68 **Webcams:** Legard, D. (2003, April 11). Singapore enforces SARS quarantine with online cameras. *Network World.* Retrieved from https://www.networkworld.com/article/2341374/lan-wan/singapore-enforces-sars-quarantine-with-online-cameras.html.

68 **medical counseling . . . influenza surveillance systems:** Shoba-yashi, T. (2011). Japan's actions to combat pandemic influenza (A/H 1 N 1). *Japan Medical Association Journal, 54*(5), 284–289.

68 **more burdened by infectious diseases:** Gelfand et al. Differences between tight and loose cultures.

69 **traditional societies as well:** Across the 186 historical samples from the Standard Cross-Cultural Sample (SCCS), societies classified as tight had significantly higher rates of famine and external warfare. Gelfand, M. J., Jackson, J. C., & Ember, C. (2017, February). *Ecological threat and the transmission of cultural tightness-looseness.* Talk given at the AAAS annual meeting. Boston, Mass.

69 **even afterlife:** Interestingly, in addition to serving as a source of tight-ness, religious belief can also change in the face of physical threats. Other research has shown that threat can also increase religiosity. For example, a study that followed the 2011 earthquake in Christchurch, New Zea-land, found that religious faith increased in people who lived in areas that were affected by the quake, while it did not increase in people who weren't affected by the quake. Some of my own work with collaborators Nava Caluori, Joshua Jackson, and Kurt Gray found that people describe God as more authoritarian (e.g., punitive, angry, and wrathful) when they feel threatened by things like terrorist attacks, immigration, and warfare with other countries. See Caluori, N., Jackson, J. C., & Gelfand, M. J. (2017, September). *Intergroup conflict causes belief in more authoritarian gods.* Talk given at the Inaugural Meeting of the Cultural Evolution Society in Jena, Germany. See also Sibley, C. G., & Bulbulia, J. (2012). Faith after an earthquake: A longitudinal study of religion and perceived health before and after the 2011 Christchurch New Zealand earthquake. *PloS One, 7*(12), e49648.

69 **Religion tends to breed tightness, both today:** Gelfand et al. Differ-ences between tight and loose cultures.

69 **and in ancient history:** Gelfand, Jackson, & Ember. *Ecological threat and the transmission of cultural tightness-looseness.*

69 **the Almighty inculcates:** Norenzayan, A. (2013). *Big gods: How religion transformed cooperation and conflict.* Princeton, N.J.: Princeton Univer-sity Press.

69 **three dead and more than a hundred wounded:** Gabbatt, A., Lov-

ering, D., & Pilkington, E. (2013, April 16). Two blasts at Boston Marathon kill three and injure more than 100. *The Guardian.* Retrieved from https://www.theguardian.com/world/2013/apr/15/boston-marathon -explosion-finish-line.

69 **rushing to the site . . . donate blood:** Hartogs, J. (2013, April 16). Stories of kindness amid tragedy in Boston Marathon bombing. CBS News. Retrieved from https://www.cbsnews.com/news/stories-of-kindness -amid-tragedy-in-boston-marathon-bombing/.

69 **"Boston Strong":** Zimmer, B. (2013, May 12). "Boston Strong," the phrase that rallied a city. *The Boston Globe.* Retrieved from https://www.boston globe.com/ideas/2013/05/11/boston-strong-phrase-that-rallied-city /uNPFaI8Mv4QxsWqpjXBOQO/story.html.

69 **I set up a field study:** Data collected by Michele Gelfand and Elizabeth Salmon.

70 **In one study:** Gelfand, M. J., & Lun, J. (2013). Ecological priming: Convergent evidence for the link between ecology and psychological processes. *Behavioral and Brain Sciences, 36*(5), 489–490.

70 **In a study we conducted in China:** Mu, Y., Han, S., & Gelfand, M. J. (2017). The role of gamma interbrain synchrony in social coordination when humans face territorial threats. *Social Cognitive and Affective Neuroscience, 12*(10), 1614–1623.

71 **In another experiment:** Gelfand & Lun. Ecological priming.

71 **I planted research assistants outside movie theaters:** Ibid.

72 **computer simulations:** Roos, P., Gelfand, M., Nau, D., & Lun, J. (2015). Societal threat and cultural variation in the strength of social norms: An evolutionary basis. *Organizational Behavior and Human Decision Processes, 129,* 14–23.

72 **just over eight thousand square miles:** Land area (sq. km). The World Bank. Retrieved from https://data.worldbank.org/indicator/AG.LND .TOTL.K2. Land area was converted from square kilometers to square miles.

72 **nearly 8.6 million people:** Population, total. The World Bank. Retrieved from https://data.worldbank.org/indicator/SP.POP.TOTL.

72 **about a thousand people per square mile:** Population density (people per sq. km of land area). The World Bank.

72 **rampant malaria, typhus, and cholera:** Tucker, S. C., & Roberts, P.

NOTES

(Eds.). (2008). *The encyclopedia of the Arab-Israeli conflict: A political, social, and military history [4 volumes]*. Santa Barbara, Calif.: ABC-CLIO.

73 **Seventy-five percent . . . among other groups:** Vital statistics: Latest population statistics for Israel. *Jewish virtual library.* Retrieved from http://www.jewishvirtuallibrary.org/latest-population-statistics-for -israel.

73 **high levels of ethnic diversity:** Demographics of Israel. Center for Israel and Jewish Affairs. Retrieved from http://cija.ca/resource/israel-the -basics/demographics-of-israel/.

73 **up to a point:** Gelfand, M. J., Harrington, J. R., & Fernandez, J. R. (2017). Cultural tightness-looseness: Ecological determinants and implications for personality. In Church, A. T. *Personality Across Cultures.* Santa Barbara, Calif.: ABC-CLIO.

73 **at least six major ethnic groups:** Central Intelligence Agency. (2018). Pakistan. In *The World Factbook.* Retrieved from https://www.cia.gov /library/publications/the-world-factbook/geos/pk.html.

73 **over twenty spoken languages:** Mohiuddin, Y. N. (2007). *Pakistan: A global studies handbook.* Santa Barbara, Calif.: ABC-CLIO.

73 **twenty-two official languages and hundreds of dialects:** Adeney, K., & Wyatt, A. (2010). *Contemporary India.* New York: Palgrave Macmillan.

73 **As the joke goes:** Reik, T. (1962). *Jewish Wit* (p. 117). New York: Gamut Press.

74 **"start-up nation":** Senor, D., & Singer, S. (2009). *Start-up nation: The story of Israel's economic miracle.* New York: Twelve.

74 **dependency on international trade:** Hogenbirk, A., & Narula, R. (1999). Globalisation and the small economy: The case of the Netherlands. In Van Den Bulcke, D., & Verbeke, A. (Eds.). (2001). *Globalization and the small open economy.* Cheltenham, UK: Edward Elgar.

74 **The Dutch traded:** O'Malley, C. (2014). *Bonds without borders: A history of the Eurobond market.* West Sussex, UK: John Wiley & Sons.

74 **controlled much of the trade:** Northrup, C. C., Bentley, J. H., Eckes, A. E., Jr., Manning, P., Pomeranz, K., & Topik, S. (2015). *Encyclopedia of world trade: From ancient times to the present* (Vol. 1). London: Routledge.

74 **booksellers flocked to the Netherlands:** Hoftijzer, P. G. (2001). Dutch

printing and bookselling in the Golden Age. In *Two faces of the early modern world: The Netherlands and Japan in the 17th and 18th centuries* (pp. 59–67). Kyoto: International Research Center for Japanese Studies.

74 **Dutch East India Company:** 1602 trade with the East: VOC. *Stichting het Rijksmuseum.* Retrieved from https://www.rijksmuseum.nl/en/rijksstudio/timeline-dutch-history/1602-trade-with-the-east-voc.

74 **welcomed refugees:** Breck, J. (2002). *How we will learn in the 21st century.* Lanham, Md.: Scarecrow Press.

74 **over 20 percent:** Europe: Netherlands. *The World Factbook.* Retrieved from https://www.cia.gov/Library/publications/the-world-factbook/geos/print_nl.html.

CHAPTER 5: THE WAR BETWEEN AMERICA'S STATES

79 **tremendous divisions:** Huang, J., Jacoby, S., Strickland, M., & Lai, R. K. K. (2016, November 8). Election 2016: Exit polls. *The New York Times.* Retrieved from https://www.nytimes.com/interactive/2016/11/08/us/politics/election-exit-polls.html?mcubz=2&_r=0.

79 **half of Democrats and Republicans:** Partisanship and political animosity in 2016. (2016). Pew Research Center. Retrieved from http://www.people-press.org/2016/06/22/partisanship-and-political-animosity-in-2016/.

80 **"culture war":** Chapman, R., & Ciment, J. (Eds.). (2015). *Culture wars: An encyclopedia of issues, viewpoints and voices.* Armonk, N.Y.: M. E. Sharpe; see also Hunter, J. D. (1991). *Culture wars: The struggle to define America.* New York: Basic Books.

80 **alcohol abuse:** Harrington, J. R., & Gelfand, M. J. (2014). Tightness-looseness across the 50 United States. *Proceedings of the National Academy of Sciences, 111*(22), 7990–7995.

80 **debt:** Ibid.

80 **discrimination:** Ibid.

80 **creativity:** Harrington & Gelfand. Tightness-looseness across the 50 United States.

80 **divorce and mobility:** Ibid.

80 **trait openness . . . trait conscientiousness:** Ibid.

80 **anti-immigration:** Ibid.

80 **same population of illegal immigrants:** U.S. unauthorized immigration population estimates. (2016, November 3). Pew Research Center. Retrieved from http://www.pewhispanic.org/interactives/unauthorized -immigrants/.

81 **little threat of invasion . . . permissive rules and relaxed punishments:** Gelfand et al. Differences between tight and loose cultures.

81 **The patterns we discovered:** Harrington & Gelfand. Tightness-looseness across the 50 United States.

81 **spank far more students, execute more criminals, and punish marijuana possession:** Ibid.

81 **twenty-eight thousand students:** United States Department of Education's Office for Civil Rights. (2011–12). Number and percentage of public school students with and without disabilities receiving corporal punishment by race/ethnicity, by state: School Year 2011–12. Retrieved from http://ocrdata.ed.gov/StateNationalEstimations/Estimations_2011_12.

81 **strict dress codes:** IPS Standard School Attire Guide. Indianapolis Public Schools. Retrieved from https://www.myips.org/cms/lib/IN01906626 /Centricity/Domain/34/dresscode.pdf.

81 **risk facing suspension:** Hudson, C. (2007, October 2). IPS students suspended for not following dress code. WTHR. Retrieved from http://www .wthr.com/article/ips-students-suspended-for-not-following-dress-code.

82 **Sex toys:** Appel, J. M. (2009, September). Alabama's bad vibrations. *The Huffington Post.* Retrieved from http://www.huffingtonpost.com/jacob -m-appel/alabamas-bad-vibrations_b_300491.html.

82 **tattoos:** State last to legalize tattoo artists, parlors. (2006, May 11). *Chicago Tribune.* Retrieved from http://articles.chicagotribune.com/2006 -05-11/news/0605110139_1_tattoo-artists-parlors-health-department.

82 **swearing in public:** Know your rights: Street harassment and the law. Stop Street Harassment. Retrieved from http://www.stopstreetharass ment.org/wp-content/uploads/2013/12/SSH-KYR-Mississippi.pdf.

82 **more dry counties and more marriage restrictions:** Harrington & Gelfand. Tightness-looseness across the 50 United States.

82 **as far back as 1860:** Correlations between tightness and percent of state population that is foreign born, controlling for state wealth: 1860

(N = 41): $r = -.42$, $p = .007$; 1880 (N = 46): $r = -.55$, $p = .000$; 1900 (N = 48): $r = -.62$, $p = .000$; 1920 (N = 48): $r = -.70$, $p = .000$; 1940 (N = 48): $r = -.67$, $p = .000$; 1960 (N = 50): $r = -.65$, $p = .000$; 1980 (N = 50): $r = -.53$, $p = .000$; 2000 (N = 50): $r = -.44$, $p = .002$. Data obtained from https://www.census.gov/population/www/documentation/twps0081/twps0081.pdf.

82 **these indicators all hang together:** Harrington & Gelfand. Tightness-looseness across the 50 United States.

82 **distinct from whether states are collectivist:** Ibid.

83 **Figure 5.1:** Data source: ibid. You might notice that some states look slightly discolored on this map based on their tightness scores. For instance, Illinois appears lighter than Idaho, but Illinois is slightly tighter than Idaho. This is simply an optical illusion. Since Illinois is surrounded by darker states, it *appears* lighter than Idaho, which is surrounded by lighter states, but Illinois is actually slightly darker than Idaho.

83 **connections between tightness and conservatism:** Ibid.

84 **Table 5.1:** Data source: ibid.

85 **Analyzing data from over half a million citizens:** Ibid.

86 **Figure 5.2:** Data obtained from personal communication with psychologist Jason Rentfrow, January 6, 2018. Respondents indicated the extent to which they agreed with statements assessing the prototypical traits of conscientiousness on a scale from 1 (disagree strongly) to 5 (agree strongly). See also Harrington & Gelfand. Tightness-looseness across the 50 United States.

86 *Encyclopedia of Southern Culture:* Wilson, C. R., Thomas, J. G., Jr., & Abadie, A. J. (Eds.). (2006). *The new encyclopedia of southern culture: Volume 4: Myth, manners, and memory.* Chapel Hill: University of North Carolina Press.

87 **proper behavior . . . "too big for your britches":** Batson, A. B. (1988). *Having it y'all.* Nashville: Rutledge Hill Press.

87 **pearls and fancy dresses:** Mason, S. (2016, September 1). Game day in the South? No T-shirts, please. CNN. Retrieved from http://www.cnn.com/2014/12/05/living/irpt-sec-football-fashion/index.html.

87 **psychologist Dov Cohen:** Cohen, D., Nisbett, R. E., Bowdle, B. F., & Schwarz, N. (1996). Insult, aggression, and the southern culture of honor: An "experimental ethnography." *Journal of Personality and Social Psychology, 70*(5), 945.

88 *Village Voice*: Doll, J. (2012, January 23). 55 of the rudest things rude New Yorkers do. *Village Voice*. Retrieved from https://www.villagevoice.com/2012/01/23/55-of-the-rudest-things-rude-new-yorkers-do/.

88 **quiet cars:** Grynbaum, M. M. (2010, September 7). New Jersey Transit tries out quiet cars. *The New York Times*. Retrieved from http://www.nytimes.com/2010/09/08/nyregion/08quiet.html.

88 **"The boorishness of noise polluters":** Sharkey, J. (2004, June 29). Business travel: On the road; want to be unpopular? Start with a cell phone. *The New York Times*. Retrieved from http://www.nytimes.com/2004/06/29/business/business-travel-on-the-road-want-to-be-unpopular-start-with-a-cellphone.html?_r=0.

88 **Psychologist Trevor Foulk:** Foulk, T., Woolum, A., & Erez, A. (2016). Catching rudeness is like catching a cold: The contagion effects of low-intensity negative behaviors. *Journal of Applied Psychology, 101*(1), 50.

88 **TheTopTens:** Correlation between tightness and rudeness rankings (larger numbers reflect lower levels of rudeness), controlling for state wealth (N = 40): $r = .33, p = .04$. Data obtained from https://www.thetoptens.com/us-states-with-rudest-people/ in May 2017.

88 **credit data I analyzed from TransUnion:** Correlation between tightness and average total debt, or sum of total average mortgage debt and total average non-mortgage debt, including vehicle loans, education loans, credit card debt, and unpaid medical and utility bills, controlling for state wealth and poverty (N = 50): $r = -.43, p = .003$. Data obtained from http://www.urban.org/sites/default/files/alfresco/publication-pdfs/41 3190-Debt-in-America.PDF.

88 **Drug use and binge drinking:** Harrington & Gelfand. Tightness-looseness across the 50 United States.

89 **with the recent exception:** While drug use and binge drinking are lower in tight states, prescription opioids are an exception. Opioids for pain management such as oxycodone, hydrocodone, morphine, and codeine were prescribed at a higher rate in tight states as of 2015 ($r = .7$; CDC, 2015), which may correspond to greater threat in these areas (e.g., more unemployment, disabilities, and less insurance, among other factors; for full report, see: Guy, G. P., Zhang, K., Bohm, M., Losby, J., Lewis, B., Young, R., Murphy, L., & Dowell, D. (2017). Vital signs: Changes in opioid prescribing in the United States, 2006–2015. *CDC Morbidity and*

Mortality Weekly Report. Retrieved from https://www.cdc.gov/mmwr /volumes/66/wr/mm6626a4.htm). For prescriptions data by state, see: Centers for Disease Control and Prevention. (2015). *U.S. state prescribing rates, 2015.* Retrieved from https://www.cdc.gov/drugoverdose/maps /rxstate2015.html.

However, there was no statistical correlation between TL and deaths from opiate abuse in 2015 ($r = -.006$). For opiate deaths data by state, see: Centers for Disease Control and Prevention. (2015). *Drug overdose death data.* Retrieved from https://www.cdc.gov/drugoverdose/data/statedea ths.html.

89 **Recreational marijuana use is now legal:** Lopez, G. (2018, April 20). Marijuana has been legalized in nine states and Washington, DC. *Vox.* Retrieved from https://www.vox.com/cards/marijuana-legalization /where-is-marijuana-legal.

89 **"America's cannabis bucket":** Fuller, T. (2017, April 15). Marijuana goes industrial in California. *The New York Times.* Retrieved from https://www .nytimes.com/2017/04/15/us/california-marijuana-industry-agriculture .html?mcubz=2.

89 **"419.99" mile markers:** Taking the highway: Idaho sign for Mile 420 changed to 419.9. (2015, August 18). *Denver Post.* Retrieved from http:// www.denverpost.com/2015/08/18/taking-the-highway-idaho-sign-for -mile-420-changed-to-419-9/.

89 **rural areas and lower rates of mobility:** Harrington & Gelfand. Tightness-looseness across the 50 United States.

89 *Southern Living:* Luesse, V. F. (n.d.). Things only small town southerners know. *Southern Living.* Retrieved from http://www.southernliving.com /culture/small-town-living.

90 **"how to behave":** Foster, E. K. (2004). Research on gossip: Taxonomy, methods, and future directions. *Review of General Psychology, 8*(2), 78.

90 **informal policing mechanism:** Dunbar, R. I. (2004). Gossip in evolutionary perspective. *Review of General Psychology, 8*(2), 100.

90 **police and law enforcement officials . . . keep the social order:** Harrington & Gelfand. Tightness-looseness across the 50 United States.

90 **incarcerate a greater percentage:** Ibid.

90 **higher divorce, single-parent households:** Ibid.

90 **homelessness:** Ibid.

90 **80 percent in Kansas:** Religious landscape study: Adults in Kansas. (2014). Pew Research Center. Retrieved from http://www.pewforum.org /religious-landscape-study/state/kansas/.

90 **83 percent and 78 percent:** Religious landscape study: Adults in Mississippi. (2014). Pew Research Center. Retrieved from http://www.pew forum.org/religious-landscape-study/state/mississippi/; Religious landscape study: Adults in South Carolina. (2014). Pew Research Center. Retrieved from http://www.pewforum.org/religious-landscape-study /state/south-carolina/.

90 **"Megachurches":** Weiss, J. D., & Lowell, R. (2002). Supersizing religion: Megachurches, sprawl, and smart growth. *Saint Louis University Public Law Review, 21,* 313.

90 **Lakewood Church:** Zaimov, S. (2016, September 8). Joel Osteen's Lakewood Church ranked America's largest megachurch with 52,000 weekly attendance. *The Christian Post.* Retrieved from https://www.christian post.com/news/joel-osteens-lakewood-church-ranked-americas-largest -megachurch-with-52k-in-attendance-169279/.

90 **morality lessons:** Kopplin, Z. (2014, January 16). Texas public schools are teaching creationism. *Slate.* Retrieved from http://www.slate.com /articles/health_and_science/science/2014/01/creationism_in_texas _public_schools_undermining_the_charter_movement.html.

91 **minute of silence:** South Carolina prayer in public schools laws. Find-Law. Retrieved from http://statelaws.findlaw.com/south-carolina-law /south-carolina-prayer-in-public-schools-laws.html.

91 **over 60 percent:** Grammich, C. A. (2012). 2010 US religion census: Religious congregations & membership study: An enumeration by nation, state, and county based on data reported for 236 religious groups. Association of Statisticians of American Religious Bodies.

91 **Tea and coffee:** Stack, P. F. (2012, September 1). Mormon caffeine policy clarified, Coke and Pepsi officially OK for Latter-Day Saints. *The Huffington Post.* Retrieved from http://www.huffingtonpost.com/2012/09/01 /mormon-caffeine-policy-cl_n_1848098.html.

91 **Premarital sex . . . pornography:** The Church of Jesus Christ of Latter-Day Saints. Chastity. Retrieved from https://www.lds.org/topics/chast ity?lang=eng.

NOTES

91 **masturbation, and homosexual acts:** Maza, C. (2017, December 14). Masturbation will make you gay, warns leaked Mormon Church document. *Newsweek.* Retrieved from http://www.newsweek.com/masturbation-gay-leaked-mormon-church-lgtb-religion-sex-748201.

91 **Sabbath Sunday:** Tingey, E. C. Keeping the Sabbath day holy. The Church of Jesus Christ of Latter-Day Saints. Retrieved from https://www.lds.org/ensign/2000/02/keeping-the-sabbath-day-holy?lang=eng.

91 **privately interview:** Question: What are the worthiness requirements to enter a Mormon Temple? FairMormon. Retrieved from https://www.fairmormon.org/answers/Question:_What_are_the_worthiness_requirements_to_enter_a_Mormon_temple%3F.

91 **(SCMC):** Religious News Service. (1992, August 15). Mormon church said to be keeping files on dissenters. *The Times-News* (Idaho), 5B.

91 ***The Righteous Mind:*** Haidt, J. (2012). *The righteous mind: Why good people are divided by politics and religion.* New York: Pantheon Books.

91 **Culture is a prime driver:** Correlation between tightness and prioritizing authority/respect (N = 50): $r = .47$, $p = .001$; between tightness and prioritizing harm/care (N = 50): $r = -.44$, $p = .001$; between tightness and prioritizing fairness/reciprocity (N = 50): $r = -.45$, $p = .001$; between tightness and in-group/loyalty (N = 50): $r = .34$, $p = .02$; between tightness and purity/sanctity (N = 50): $r = .60$, $p = .000$. All correlations are controlling for state wealth. Data obtained from psychologist Jesse Graham at the University of Southern California.

91 **is still illegal in Georgia:** Georgia Bureau of Investigation. (n.d.). CCH offense codes. Retrieved from https://gbi.georgia.gov/sites/gbi.georgia.gov/files/related_files/site_page/CCH%20Offense%20Codes%20-%20Active.pdf.

91 **bumper stickers:** Sturm, Melanie. (2013, September 17). Sturm: Who are we to judge? *The Aspen Times.* Retrieved from http://www.aspentimes.com/opinion/sturm-who-are-we-to-judge/.

92 **black-and-white view:** Harrington & Gelfand. Tightness-looseness across the 50 United States.

92 **personality profiles:** Ibid.

92 **more patents:** Ibid.

92 **first laser:** Alfred, R. (2008, May 16). May 16, 1960: Researcher shines a

laser light. *Wired.* Retrieved from https://www.wired.com/2008/05/day intech-0516-2/.

92 **Figure 5.3:** Data obtained from personal communication with psychologist Jason Rentfrow, January 6, 2018. Respondents indicated the extent to which they agreed with statements assessing the prototypical traits of openness on a scale from 1 (disagree strongly) to 5 (agree strongly). See also Harrington & Gelfand. Tightness-looseness across the 50 United States.

93 **Figure 5.4:** Data source: Harrington & Gelfand. Tightness–looseness across the 50 United States. For each state, patents per capita (1963–2011) were calculated by dividing the total number of patents during this time period, as documented by the U.S. Patent and Trademark Office, by the total state population in 2010, and then multiplying this figure by 1,000. Correlation between tightness and patents per capita (N = 50): r = −.32, p = .03, controlling for state wealth.

93 **fax machine:** Asano, S. (2011, May 9). Just the fax. Boston.com. Retrieved from http://archive.boston.com/news/education/higher/arti cles/2011/05/09/sam_asanos_idea_led_to_first_fax_machine/.

93 **microwave oven:** Saltiel, C., & Datta, A. K. (1999). Heat and mass transfer in microwave processing. In *Advances in heat transfer* (Vol. 33, pp. 1–94). New York: Elsevier.

93 **first email:** Grimes, W. (2016, March 17). Raymond Tomlinson, who put the @ sign in email, is dead at 74. *The New York Times.* Retrieved from https://www.nytimes.com/2016/03/08/technology/raymond-tomlinson -email-obituary.html?mcubz=2.

93 **first washing machine:** Maxwell, L. M. (2003). *Save womens lives: History of washing machines.* Eaton, Colo.: Oldewash.

93 **Frisbee:** Bellis, M. (2016, August 13). The history of the Frisbee. *ThoughtCo.* Retrieved from https://www.thoughtco.com/history-of-the -frisbee-4072561.

93 **more creative types:** Ibid.

93 **more creative experiences:** Correlation between tightness and percent of adults who attend visual or performing arts events or go to the movies by state (N = 50): r = −.48, p = .001; correlation between tightness and percent of adults who read literature, including plays, poetry, short stories, or novels (N = 50): r = −.46, p = .001; correlation between tightness and percent of adults who personally perform or create artworks (N = 50): r =

−.41, p = .003; correlation between tightness and percent of adults who use TV, radio, and/or the internet to consume art or arts programming (N = 50): r = −.47, p = .001. All correlations are controlling for state wealth. Data obtained from https://www.arts.gov/artistic-fields/research-analy sis/arts-data-profiles/arts-data-profile-11.

94 **The most fun states . . . The least fun states:** Correlation between tightness and fun rankings, controlling for state wealth (N = 50): r = −.56, p < .01. Data obtained from https://wallethub.com/edu/most-fun -states/34665/#methodology.

94 *Daily Beast:* Correlation between tightness and tolerance (accounting for hate crimes, religious tolerance, discrimination, and gay rights), controlling for state wealth (N = 50): r = −.40, p = .004. Data obtained from http://www.thedailybeast.com/ranking-the-most-tolerant-and-least -tolerant-states.

94 **interracial marriages . . . attitudes toward homosexuals:** Gelfand et al. The strength of social norms predicts global patterns of prejudice and discrimination.

95 **people living in looser states possessed much lower implicit negative attitudes:** Ibid.

95 **minority-owned . . . public office:** Harrington & Gelfand. Tightness-looseness across the 50 United States.

95 **stronger legal protections:** Ibid.

95 **People with mental illness:** Correlation between tightness and access to mental health care rank, including measures on insurance, access to treatment, quality and cost of insurance, access to special education and workforce availability (higher rank = poorer access), controlling for state wealth (N = 50): r = .38, p < .01. Data obtained from http://www .mentalhealthamerica.net/issues/mental-health-america-access -care-data.

95 **Equal Employment Opportunity Commission:** Harrington & Gelfand. Tightness-looseness across the 50 United States.

95 **470 cases:** U.S. Equal Employment Opportunity Commission. EEOC charge receipts by state (includes U.S. territories) and basis for 2017. Retrieved from https://www1.eeoc.gov/eeoc/statistics/enforcement /charges_by_state.cfm.

95 **2,144:** Ibid.

95 **more open to immigrants:** Park, H. (2015, March 30). Which states make life easier or harder for illegal immigrants. *The New York Times.* Retrieved from https://www.nytimes.com/interactive/2015/03/30/us /laws-affecting-unauthorized-immigrants.html?mcubz=2&_r=0.

95 **with some exceptions:** In March 2018, the Supreme Court banned Arizona from denying DACA recipients drivers' licenses. See Stohr, G. (2018, March 19). U.S. Supreme Court rejects Arizona on driver's licenses for immigrants. *Bloomberg.* Retrieved from https://www.bloomberg .com/news/articles/2018-03-19/high-court-rejects-arizona-on-driver-s -licenses-for-immigrants.

96 **Figure 5.5:** For each state, charges of employment discrimination per capita were calculated by dividing the total number of charges in 2017, as documented by the Equal Employment Opportunity Commission, by the total state population in 2017, and then multiplying this figure by 1,000. Correlation between tightness and charges of employment discrimination per capita in 2017, controlling for state wealth (N = 50): $r = .56$, $p < .001$. The same pattern was found using data from 2010, as reported in Harrington & Gelfand. Tightness-looseness across the 50 United States.

96 **Governor Jerry Brown:** Megerian, C. (2014, August 26). Jerry Brown: Immigrants, citizen or not, "welcome in California." *Los Angeles Times.* Retrieved from http://www.latimes.com/local/political/la-me-pc-mex ico-president-visit-california-20140825-story.html.

96 **aren't good places for immigrants:** Correlation between tightness and percent of state residents who say their state is a good place for immigrants to live, controlling for state wealth (N = 50): $r = -.51$, $p = .000$. Data obtained from http://www.gallup.com/poll/189770/neva dans-likely-say-state-good-place-immigrants.aspx?g_source=states&g _medium=search&g_campaign.

96 **support for measures to "Buy American":** Harrington & Gelfand. Tightness-looseness across the 50 United States.

96 **transcendentalism to Unitarianism . . . Greenwich Village:** Wood-ard, C. (2011). *American nations: A history of the eleven rival regional cultures of North America.* New York: Penguin.

96 **"a magnet for cultural revolutionaries":** Ibid (p. 270).

97 **cofounder:** Ibid.

97 **Equal Rights Amendment:** Frequently asked questions. The Equal Rights Amendment: Unfinished business for the Constitution. Retrieved from http://www.equalrightsamendment.org/faq.htm#q4. The tight states included Mississippi, Alabama, Arkansas, Oklahoma, Louisiana, South Carolina, North Carolina, Virginia, Utah, Missouri, and Georgia.

97 **established an early presence:** Woodard. *American nations.*

97 **descendants of Celtic herdsmen:** McKay, B., & McKay, K. (2012, November 26). Manly honor part V: Honor in the American South. The Art of Manliness. Retrieved from http://www.artofmanliness.com/2012/11/26/manly-honor-part-v-honor-in-the-american-south/.

97 **"culture of honor":** Nisbett, R. E., & Cohen, D. (1996). *Culture of honor: The psychology of violence in the South.* Boulder, Colo.: Westview Press.

97 **threat of losing their livestock:** McKay & McKay. Manly honor part V.

97 **lack of formal law enforcement:** Nisbett & Cohen. *Culture of honor.*

98 **frequently entertained guests:** McKay & McKay. Manly honor part V.

98 **Andrew Jackson . . . documented disputes:** Ibid.

98 **maintain order:** Nisbett & Cohen. *Culture of honor.*

98 **by 1790:** McWhiney, G. (1989). *Cracker culture: Celtic ways in the Old South.* Tuscaloosa: University of Alabama Press; McKay & McKay. Manly honor part V.

98 **culture of honor lives on:** Nisbett & Cohen. *Culture of honor.*

98 **Those who tried to run away:** Woodard. *American nations.*

99 **global trading hub . . . many different faiths:** Ibid.

99 **Massachusetts Bay Colony was settled:** Esbeck, C. H. (2004). Dissent and disestablishment: The church-state settlement in the early American republic. *Brigham Young University Law Review, 2004*(4), 1385–1589.

99 **highly intolerant:** Bonomi, P. U. (1986). *Under the cape of Heaven: Religion, society, and politics in colonial America.* New York: Oxford University Press.

99 **outgrowth of other Protestant sects:** Esbeck. Dissent and disestablishment.

99 **norms of tolerance:** Ibid.

99 **"Cradle of Liberty":** Goldfield, D., Abbott, C., Anderson, V., Argersinger, J., & Argersinger, P. (2017). *American journey, the combined volume* (8th ed.). Boston: Pearson.

99 **rise of industrialization:** Christiano, K. J. (2007). *Religious diversity and*

social change: American cities, 1890–1906. New York: Cambridge University Press.

99 **In the 1870s, Massachusetts:** The Editors of Encyclopedia Britannica. Massachusetts. *Encyclopædia Britannica.* Retrieved from https://www.britannica.com/place/Massachusetts.

100 **predominantly agrarian region marked by close-knit tight communities:** Jaffe, D. (2007, April). Industrialization and conflict in America: 1840–1875. The Metropolitan Museum of Art. Retrieved from http://www.metmuseum.org/toah/hd/indu/hd_indu.htm; Cohen, D. (1998). Culture, social organization, and patterns of violence. *Journal of Personality and Social Psychology, 75*(2), 408.

100 **medicine, law, the clergy, and the military:** Wyatt-Brown, B. (1982). *Southern honor: Ethics and behavior in the Old South.* New York: Oxford University Press.

100 **melting pot:** Paddison, J. (2005). Essay: 1848–1865: Gold rush, statehood, and the western movement. Calisphere, University of California. Retrieved from https://calisphere.org/exhibitions/essay/4/gold-rush/.

100 **three hundred thousand:** Ibid.

100 **Australia; Italy:** Chan, S. (2000). A people of exceptional character: Ethnic diversity, nativism, and racism in the California gold rush. *California History, 79*(2), 44–85.

100 **Ireland:** Arnesen, E. (2007). *Encyclopedia of U.S. labor and working-class history* (Vol. 1). New York: Taylor & Francis.

100 **"Here were to be seen":** Paddison. Essay: 1848–1865: Gold rush, statehood, and the western movement.

100 **dark history of racism and exclusion:** Ochoa, M. G. (2017, March 27). California was once a bastion of xenophobia and racism. If we can change, so can the rest of the country. *Los Angeles Times.* Retrieved from http://www.latimes.com/opinion/opinion-la/la-ol-immigration-california-racism-20170327-htmlstory.html.

100 **lacking since 1860:** Correlations between tightness and percent of state population that is foreign born, controlling for state wealth: 1860 ($N = 41$): $r = -.42, p = .007$; 1880 ($N = 46$): $r = -.55, p = .000$; 1900 ($N = 48$): $r = -.62, p = .000$; 1920 ($N = 48$): $r = -.70, p = .000$; 1940 ($N = 48$): $r = -.67, p = .000$; 1960 ($N = 50$): $r = -.65, p = .000$; 1980 ($N = 50$): $r = -.53, p = .000$; 2000

(N = 50): r = -.44, p = .002. Data obtained from https://www.census.gov /population/www/documentation/twps0081/twps0081.pdf.

100 **University of Pennsylvania:** Olson, R. (2014, April 29). U.S. racial diversity by county [Blog post]. Retrieved from http://www.randalolson .com/2014/04/29/u-s-racial-diversity-by-county/.

100 **least diverse:** For example, in Kansas, North Dakota, and Arkansas, only .09 percent, .1 percent, and .37 percent, respectively, of the population is Jewish, and only 3 percent, 2 percent, and 2 percent, respectively, is Asian. On the other hand, in loose states such as New York, Massachusetts, and California, 8.47 percent, 5.28 percent, and 2.74 percent of the population is Jewish, and 8 percent, 7 percent, and 15 percent is Asian, respectively. Correlation between tightness and percent of the state population that is Asian in 2016, controlling for state wealth (N = 50): r = -.36, p = .0.3. Data obtained from https://www.kff.org/other/state-indicator/distribution -by-raceethnicity/?currentTimeframe=0&sortModel=%7B%22colId%22: %22Location%22,%22sort%22:%22asc%22%7D. Correlation between tightness and percent of the state population that is Jewish in 2016, controlling for state wealth (N = 50): r = -.31, p = .03. Data obtained from http://www .jewishvirtuallibrary.org/jewish-population-in-the-united-states-by-state.

101 **the historically diverse:** Campanella, R. (2007). An ethnic geography of New Orleans. *The Journal of American History, 94*(3), 704–715.

101 **French settlement:** New Orleans. *History.* Retrieved from http://www .history.com/topics/new-orleans.

101 **"New Orleans is an accepting":** Durrett, C. (2015, May 21). New Orleans mayor responds to Jindal's executive order; says city is "accepting, inviting." WDSU News. Retrieved from http://www.wdsu.com/article/ new-orleans-mayor-responds-to-jindal-s-executive-order-says-city-is -accepting-inviting/3377488.

101 **80 percent white . . . 92 percent white:** Profile of general population and housing characteristics: 2010. United States Census Bureau: American FactFinder. Retrieved from https://factfinder.census.gov/faces/table services/jsf/pages/productview.xhtml?pid=DEC_10_DP_DPDP1.

102 **inhospitable territories . . . "The altitude was so high":** Woodard. *American nations.*

102 **a series of wildfires:** Significant wildfire events in SC history: chro-

nology by year. South Carolina Forestry Commission. Retrieved from https://www.state.sc.us/forest/firesign.htm.

102 **eight thousand people:** The deadliest, costliest, and most intense United States tropical cyclones from 1851 to 2004 (and other frequently requested hurricane facts). (2005, August). Natural Hurricane Center. Retrieved from http://www.nhc.noaa.gov/pdf/NWS-TPC-4.pdf.

102 **40 percent decrease:** Hicken, J. (2012, August 16). See 5 of the worst droughts in the United States. *Deseret News.* Retrieved from http://www.deseretnews.com/top/920/4/1980s-drought-See-5-of-the-worst -droughts-in-the-United-States.html.

102 **recurrent droughts:** Knittle, A. (2011, October 19). Oklahoma rain records show a history of long droughts. *NewsOK.* Retrieved from http:// newsok.com/article/3614753.

102 **four hundred thousand people:** Okie migrations. Oklahoma Histori-cal Society. Retrieved from http://www.okhistory.org/publications/enc /entry.php?entry=OK008.

102 **most ecologically vulnerable:** One interesting exception to the rela-tionship between tightness and high ecological vulnerability is earth-quakes. We found no significant relationship between tightness and frequency of earthquakes across the fifty states.

102 **Disaster Center:** Harrington & Gelfand. Tightness-looseness across the 50 United States.

103 **147 and 92:** Livingston, I. (2016, April 6). Annual and monthly tornado averages for each state (maps). U.S. Tornadoes. Retrieved from http:// www.ustornadoes.com/2016/04/06/annual-and-monthly-tornado-aver ages-across-the-united-states/.

103 **tornadoes rarely touch down:** Harrington & Gelfand. Tightness-looseness across the 50 United States.

103 **higher death rates:** Ibid.

103 **data from 1851 to 2004:** The deadliest, costliest, and most intense United States tropical cyclones from 1851 to 2004. Natural Hurricane Center.

103 **cope with more disease:** Harrington & Gelfand. Tightness-looseness across the 50 United States.

103 **higher rates of food insecurity:** Ibid.

103 **less access to clean air:** Fine particulate matter (PM2.5) (ug/m3) (2003–2011) [Data file]. Centers for Disease Control and Prevention. Retrieved from https://wonder.cdc.gov/nasa-pm.html. Correlation between tightness and fine particulate matter (N = 50): $r = .41, p = .004$.

104 **tremendous diversity:** Walters, D. (2015, June 25). Census Bureau shows California's diversity. *The Sacramento Bee.* Retrieved from http://www.sacbee.com/news/politics-government/capitol-alert/article25485157.html.

104 **One in ten jobs:** Hoi, S. (2014). The meaning of the creative economy in Los Angeles. *Community Development Investment Review, 2,* 31–34.

104 **Americans' most commonly experienced fears:** Nickum, R. (2014, July 15). The United States of fear: Which American states are the scariest? Estately Blog. Retrieved from http://www.estately.com/blog/2014/07/the-united-states-of-fear-which-american-states-are-the-scariest/.

104 **coincides closely with our tightness-looseness map:** Correlation between tightness and average scariness rank across bears, hurricanes, shark attacks, spiders, snakes, tornadoes, lightning, and volcanoes (the lower the rank, the higher states scored on scariness), controlling for state wealth (N = 50): $r = -.33, p = .02$. Data obtained from ibid.

105 **being "occupied" by "foreign" troops:** Woodard. *American nations.*

105 **"peculiar institution":** Brundage, F. (1997). American slavery: A look back at the peculiar institution. *The Journal of Blacks in Higher Education* (15), 118–120.

105 **threatened their lifestyle, and their survival:** Woodard. *American nations.*

105 **higher levels of slave-owning families:** Harrington & Gelfand. Tightness-looseness across the 50 United States.

105 **By the war's end:** Woodard. *American nations.*

105 **faced economic ruin:** Paskoff, P. F. (2008). Measures of war: A quantitative examination of the Civil War's destructiveness in the Confederacy. *Civil War History, 54*(1), 35–62.

105 **lands had been devastated:** Ibid.

106 **twenty thousand Northern soldiers:** Downs, G. P. (2015). *After Appomattox: Military occupation and the ends of war.* Cambridge, Mass.: Harvard University Press.

106 **federal push toward nationwide desegregation:** Ibid.

106 **implicit rules for social interaction:** Wilson. *The new encyclopedia of southern culture: Volume 4.*

106 **"Southerners ironically viewed":** Ibid.

106 **ritualized battle reenactments:** Ibid.

106 **Alabama, North Carolina, Georgia, and Tennessee:** Kaleem, J. (2017, August 16). In some states, it's illegal to take down monuments or change street names honoring the Confederacy. *Los Angeles Times.* Retrieved from http://www.latimes.com/nation/la-na-confederate-monument -laws-20170815-htmlstory.html.

106 **"ghosts of southern memory":** Wilson. *The new encyclopedia of southern culture: Volume 4.*

107 **would be repeated in the United States:** American history: Fear of communism in 1920 threatens civil rights. (2010, December 8). *Learning English.* Retrieved from https://learningenglish.voanews.com/a/ameri cas-fear-of-communism-in-1920-becomes-a-threat-to-rights-111561904 /116001.html.

107 **series of bombs:** Murray, R. K. (1955). *Red scare: A study in national hysteria, 1919–1920.* Minneapolis: University of Minnesota Press.

107 **Laws were passed:** Ibid. The Sedition Act of 1918 was used to arrest "radicals" and deport them, and several states passed a Criminal Syndicalism Act that limited free speech.

107 **expanding Soviet Union:** Goldstein, R. J. (2006). Prelude to McCarthyism: The making of a blacklist. *Prologue Magazine.* Washington, D.C.: National Archives and Records Administration.

108 **nuclear war:** Fried, A. (1997). *McCarthyism, the great American red scare: A documentary history.* New York: Oxford University Press.

108 **witch hunt against Communists:** Ibid.

108 **Korean War:** Ibid.

108 **throughout the 1950s:** Ibid.

108 **"decade of change":** Klinkowitz, J. (1980). *The American 1960's: Imaginative acts in a decade of change.* Iowa City: Iowa State University Press.

108 **acquired television sets:** Baughman, J. L. (1993). *Television comes to America, 1947–57.* Illinois Periodicals Online.

108 **recreational drug use and sexual promiscuity:** Sheff, D. (1988, May 5). The Rolling Stone survey: On sex, drugs, and rock & roll. *Rolling Stone.*

Retrieved from http://www.rollingstone.com/culture/news/sex-drugs-and-rock-roll-19880505.

108 **popular phrases of the day:** Counterculture. *Boundless.* Retrieved from https://www.boundless.com/u-s-history/textbooks/boundless-u-s-history-textbook/the-sixties-1960-1969-29/counterculture-221/counter culture-1232-9277.

108 **nearly three thousand lives:** *The 9/11 commission report: Final report of the national commission on terrorist attacks upon the United States.* (2011). Washington, D.C.: Government Printing Office.

108 **130 new pieces of legislation . . . 260 new government organizations:** Villemez, J. (2011, September 14). 9/11 to now: Ways we have changed. *PBS NewsHour.* Retrieved from http://www.pbs.org/newshour /rundown/911-to-now-ways-we-have-changed//.

108 **over $600 billion:** Hellman, C. (2011, August 16). Has the Pentagon's post-9/11 spending spree made us safer? *The Nation.* Retrieved from http://www.thenation.com/article/has-pentagons-post-911-spending -spree-made-us-safer/.

109 **ninety-eight out of a hundred senators . . . search homes and businesses:** McCarthy, M. T. (2002). USA Patriot Act.

109 **Transportation Security Administration:** Villemez. 9/11 to now.

109 **over 100 percent:** U.S. Department of Homeland Security, ENFORCE Alien Removal Module (EARM), January 2011; Enforcement Integrated Database (EID), December 2010.

109 **gay marriage:** US Supreme Court rules gay marriage is legal nationwide (2015, June 27). *BBC.* Retrieved from https://www.bbc.com/news/world -us-canada-33290341.

109 **Mexicans bringing violence:** Reilly, K. (2016, August 31). Here are all the times Donald Trump insulted Mexico. *Time.* Retrieved from http://time .com/4473972/donald-trump-mexico-meeting-insult/.

109 **global trade agreements:** Read Donald Trump's speech on trade. (2016, June 28). *Time.* Retrieved from http://time.com/4386335/donald-trump -trade-speech-transcript/.

109 **immigrants taking away jobs:** Kohn, S. (2016, June 29). Nothing Donald Trump says on immigration holds up. *Time.* Retrieved from http://time .com/4386240/donald-trump-immigration-arguments/.

109 **radicalized Muslims plotting terror:** Johnson, J., & Hauslohner, A.

(2017, May 20). "I think Islam hates us": A timeline of Trump's comments about Islam and Muslims. *The Washington Post.* Retrieved from https://www.washingtonpost.com/news/post-politics/wp/2017/05/20/i-think-islam-hates-us-a-timeline-of-trumps-comments-about-islam-and-muslims/?utm_term=.b929e970f937.

109 **China "raping":** Diamond, G. (2016, May 2). Trump: "We can't allow China to rape our country." CNN. Retrieved from https://www.cnn.com/2016/05/01/politics/donald-trump-china-rape/index.html.

110 **"I alone can fix it":** Appelbaum, Y. (2016, July 1). "I alone can fix it." *The Atlantic.* Retrieved from https://www.theatlantic.com/politics/archive/2016/07/trump-rnc-speech-alone-fix-it/492557/.

110 **nationwide survey:** Gelfand, M. J., Jackson, J. C., & Harrington, J. R. (2016, April 27). Trump Culture: Threat, Fear, and the Tightening of the American Mind. *Scientific American.* Retrieved from https://www.scientificamerican.com/article/trump-culture-threat-fear-and-the-tightening-of-the-american-mind/.

111 **"invaders":** Schultheis, E. (2018, January 8). Viktor Orbán: Hungary doesn't want Muslim "invaders." *Politico.* Retrieved from https://www.politico.eu/article/viktor-orban-hungary-doesnt-want-muslim-invaders/.

111 **"Real threats have declined":** Personal communication with Yuval Noah Harari, May 21, 2017.

CHAPTER 6: WORKING CLASS VS. UPPER CLASS: THE HIDDEN CULTURAL FAULT LINE

112 **In the fall of 2011:** Chappell, B. (2011, October 20). Occupy Wall Street: From a blog post to a movement. NPR. Retrieved from https://www.npr.org/2011/10/20/141530025/occupy-wall-street-from-a-blog-post-to-a-movement.

112 **according to U.S. Census Bureau data:** Proctor, B. D., Semega, J. L., & Kollar, M. A. (2016). Income and poverty in the United States. United States Census Bureau Current Population Reports. Retrieved from https://www.census.gov/content/dam/Census/library/publications/2016/demo/p60-256.pdf.

112 **such as raising the minimum wage:** Levitin, M. (2015). The triumph of Occupy Wall Street. *The Atlantic.* Retrieved from https://www.the

atlantic.com/politics/archive/2015/06/the-triumph-of-occupy-wall-street/395408/.

113 **A 2017 Pew Research survey:** Public sees strong conflicts between many groups—especially partisans. (2017, December 19). Pew Research Center. Retrieved from http://www.pewresearch.org/fact-tank/2017/12/19/far-more-americans-say-there-are-strong-conflicts-between-partisans-than-between-other-groups-in-society/ft_17-12-19_politics_publicsees/.

113 **up 12 percent from 2009:** Black-white conflict isn't society's largest. (2009, September 24). Pew Research Center. Retrieved from http://www.pewsocialtrends.org/2009/09/24/black-white-conflict-isnt-societys-largest/.

113 **In 2016 in South Africa:** Orthofer, A. (2016, October 6). South Africa needs to fix its dangerously wide wealth gap. *The Conversation.* Retrieved from https://theconversation.com/south-africa-needs-to-fix-its-dangerously-wide-wealth-gap-66355.

113 **the "1 percenters" in China:** Tiezzi, S. (2016, January 15). Report: China's 1% owns 1/3 of wealth. *The Diplomat.* Retrieved from http://thediplomat.com/2016/01/report-chinas-1-percent-owns-13-of-wealth/; Xie, Y., & Jin, Y. (2015). Household wealth in China. *Chinese Sociological Review, 47*(3), 203–229.

113 **Latin America, according to the World Economic Forum:** Ibarra, A. B., & Byanyima, W. (2016, January 17). Latin America is the world's most unequal region. Here's how to fix it. World Economic Forum. Retrieved from https://www.weforum.org/agenda/2016/01/inequality-is-getting-worse-in-latin-america-here-s-how-to-fix-it/.

113 **social commentators contend:** For examples of such commentary, see Cohn, N. (2016, November 9). Why Trump won: Working-class whites. *The New York Times.* Retrieved from https://www.nytimes.com/2016/11/10/upshot/why-trump-won-working-class-whites.html?mcubz=2&_r=0; Maher, R. (2017). Populism is still a threat to Europe—Here's how to contain it. *The Conversation.* Retrieved from https://theconversation.com/populism-is-still-a-threat-to-europe-heres-how-to-contain-it-78821; Witte, G. (2017, February 22). In Britain's working-class heartland, a populist wave threatens to smash the traditional order. *The Washington Post.* Retrieved from https://www.washingtonpost.com/world/europe/in-britains-working-class-heartland-a-populist-wave-threatens-to

-smash-the-traditional-order/2017/02/22/67c5e6a8-f867-11e6-aa1e-5f
735ee31334_story.html?utm_term=.411363e4b57a.

113 **the region of Sumer in ancient Mesopotamia:** Mark, J. (2014). Daily
life in ancient Mesopotamia. *Ancient history encyclopedia*. Retrieved
from https://www.ancient.eu/article/680/daily-life-in-ancient-mesopo
tamia/.

113 **Later, around the second millennium:** Joshi, N. (2017). Caste system in
ancient India. *Ancient history encyclopedia*. Retrieved from https://www
.ancient.eu/article/1152/caste-system-in-ancient-india/.

113 **in China, a hierarchical social class structure:** Fairbank, J. K., & Goldman, M. (2006). *China: A new history*. Cambridge, Mass.: Harvard University Press.

114 **Capuchin monkeys:** Parr, L. A., Matheson, M. D., Bernstein, I. S., &
De Waal, F. B. M. (1997). Grooming down the hierarchy: Allogrooming
in captive brown capuchin monkeys, Cebus apella. *Animal Behaviour*,
54(2), 361–367.

114 **baboons:** Sapolsky, R. M. (2005). The influence of social hierarchy on
primate health. *Science*, *308*(5722), 648–652.

114 **pigeons:** Nagy, M., Akos, Z., Biro, D., & Vicsek, T. (2010). Hierarchical
group dynamics in pigeon flocks. *Nature*, *464*(7290), 890.

114 **goby fish:** Wong, M. Y., Munday, P. L., Buston, P. M., & Jones, G. P. (2008).
Fasting or feasting in a fish social hierarchy. *Current Biology*, *18*(9), R372–
R373.

114 **mice:** Louch, C. D., & Higginbotham, M. (1967). The relation between
social rank and plasma corticosterone levels in mice. *General and Comparative Endocrinology*, *8*(3), 441–444.

114 **burying beetles:** Scott, M. P. (1998). The ecology and behavior of burying beetles. *Annual Review of Entomology*, *43*(1), 595–618.

114 **Underlying them are deeper cultural codes:** Stephens, N. M., Markus,
H. R., & Phillips, L. T. (2014). Social class culture cycles: How three gateway
contexts shape selves and fuel inequality. *Annual Review of Psychology*, *65*,
611–634; Varnum, M. E., & Kitayama, S. (2017). The neuroscience of social
class. *Current Opinion in Psychology*, *18*, 147–151; Harrington, J., & Gelfand,
M. (2018). *Worlds unto themselves: Tightness-looseness and social class*.

116 **legal scholar Joan Williams notes:** Williams, J. C. (2012). The class culture gap. In S. T. Fiske & H. R. Markus. (Eds.). *Facing social class: How*

societal rank influences interaction (pp. 39–58). New York: Russell Sage Foundation.

116 **Joseph Howell similarly notes:** Howell, J. T. (1973). *Hard living on Clay Street: Portraits of blue collar families.* Garden City, NY: Anchor Press.

117 **Williams explains:** Williams. The class-culture gap.

117 **sometimes only has pennies:** Varner, K. (2017). Sometimes I'm down to pennies before it's time to get paid again. *The Huffington Post.* Retrieved from https://www.huffingtonpost.com/2014/07/01/working-poor_n_55 48010.html.

117 **according to Karen Wall:** Mulero, E. (2014). If I got in a car accident, I'd be homeless. *The Huffington Post.* Retrieved from https://www.huffing tonpost.com/2014/01/31/karen-wall-working-poor_n_4698088.html.

117 **a concern for Erlinda Delacruz:** Gillespie, P. (2016, May 19). U.S. problem: I work three part-time jobs. CNN Money. Retrieved from http:// money.cnn.com/2016/05/17/news/economy/job-multiple-part-time /index.html.

117 **Individuals working in lower-class occupations:** Census of fatal injuries (CFOI)—Current and revised data. (2015). Bureau of Labor Statistics. Retrieved from https://www.bls.gov/iif/oshcfoi1.htm#2010.

118 **poorer communities in the United States:** Harrell, E., Langton, L., Berzofsky, M., Couzens, L., & Smiley-McDonald, H. (2014). *Household poverty and nonfatal violent victimization, 2008–2012.* U.S. Department of Justice, Office of Justice Programs, Bureau of Justice Statistics. Retrieved from https://www.bjs.gov/content/pub/pdf/hpnvv0812.pdf.

118 **also experiences greater health vulnerabilities:** Woolf, S. H., Aron, L., Dubay, L., Simon, S. M., Zimmerman, E., & Luk, K. X. (2015). How are income and wealth linked to health and longevity? Urban Institute. Retrieved from https://www.urban.org/sites/default/files/publication/4 9116/2000178-How-are-Income-and-Wealth-Linked-to-Health-and -Longevity.pdf.

118 **staggering ten- to fifteen-year difference:** Chetty, R., Stepner, M., Abraham, S., Lin, S., Scuderi, B., Turner, N., . . . & Cutler, D. (2016). The association between income and life expectancy in the United States, 2001–2014. *Journal of the American Medical Association, 315*(16), 1750–1766.

118 **less exposure to diversity:** Harrington & Gelfand. *Worlds unto themselves.*

118 **far fewer opportunities for mobility:** Chetty, R., Hendren, N., Kline, P., Saez, E., & Turner, N. (2014). Is the United States still a land of opportunity? Recent trends in intergenerational mobility. *American Economic Review, 104*(5), 141–147.

118 **Jesse Harrington and I surveyed:** Harrington & Gelfand. *Worlds unto themselves.*

119 ***First, Break All the Rules*:** Buckingham, M., & Coffman, C. (1999). *First, break all the rules: What the world's greatest managers do differently.* New York: Gallup Press.

119 ***Breaking the Rules & Getting the Job*:** Copeland, A. (2013). *Breaking the rules & getting the job: A practical guide to getting a great job in a down market.* Memphis, Tenn.: Copeland Coaching.

120 **when we asked our survey respondents:** Harrington & Gelfand. *Worlds unto themselves.*

120 **in studies on morality:** Haidt, J., Koller, S. H., & Dias, M. G. (1993). Affect, culture, and morality, or is it wrong to eat your dog? *Journal of Personality and Social Psychology, 65*(4), 613–628.

121 **Jesse Harrington and I examined if toddlers vary:** Harrington & Gelfand. *Worlds unto themselves.*

121 **devised an ingenious behavioral tool:** Rakoczy, H., Warneken, F., & Tomasello, M. (2008). The sources of normativity: Young children's awareness of the normative structure of games. *Developmental Psychology, 44*(3), 875–881.

123 ***Class and Conformity*:** Kohn, M. (1977). *Class and conformity: A study in values.* Chicago: University of Chicago Press.

123 **to be independent:** Today, research confirms that they do: Grossmann, I., & Varnum, M. E. (2011). Social class, culture, and cognition. *Social Psychological and Personality Science, 2*(1), 81–89; Stephens, Markus, & Phillips. Social class culture cycles; Varnum & Kitayama. The neuroscience of social class.

123 **Five decades later:** Harrington & Gelfand. *Worlds unto themselves.*

123 **more likely to spank their children:** Parenting in America. (2015, December 17). Pew Research Center. Retrieved from http://www.pewso cialtrends.org/2015/12/17/parenting-in-america/.

124 **Alfred Lubrano explains:** Lubrano, A. (2004). *Limbo: Blue-collar roots, white-collar dreams.* Hoboken, N.J.: John Wiley & Sons.

124 **In his 1970 book** *Class, Codes, and Control:* Bernstein, B. (1971). *Class, codes and control: Theoretical studies toward a sociology of education* (Vol. 1). London: Paladin.

125 **fascinating connection:** Bernstein, B. (1960). Language and social class. *The British Journal of Sociology, 11*(3), 271–276; ibid.

125 **resemble the military:** Anyon, J. (1981). Elementary schooling and distinctions of social class. *Interchange, 12*(2), 118–132; MacLeod, J. (2009). *Ain't no makin' it: Aspirations and attainment in a low-income neighborhood.* Boulder, Colo.: Westview Press; Stephens, Markus, & Phillips. Social class culture cycles.

125 **Jean Anyon noted:** Anyon. Elementary schooling and distinctions of social class.

126 **as compensation for participating:** Stephens, N. M., Markus, H. R., & Townsend, S. S. (2007). Choice as an act of meaning: The case of social class. *Journal of Personality and Social Psychology, 93*(5), 814–830.

126 **participants were asked to imagine:** Ibid.

127 **Figure 6.2:** Data source: ibid. Adapted with permission from the American Psychological Association.

127 **people were asked to recall:** Galinsky, A. D., Magee, J. C., Gruenfeld, D. H., Whitson, J. A., & Liljenquist, K. A. (2008). Power reduces the press of the situation: Implications for creativity, conformity, and dissonance. *Journal of Personality and Social Psychology, 95*(6), 1450–1466.

128 **People with nicer cars:** Piff, P. K., Stancato, D. M., Côté, S., Mendoza-Denton, R., & Keltner, D. (2012). Higher social class predicts increased unethical behavior. *Proceedings of the National Academy of Sciences, 109*(11), 4086–4091.

128 **researchers recruited participants and videotaped them:** Kraus, M. W., & Keltner, D. (2009). Signs of socioeconomic status: A thin-slicing approach. *Psychological Science, 20*(1), 99–106.

129 **cheating on a test:** Piff et al. Higher social class predicts increased unethical behavior.

129 **In one lab study . . . In another study:** Ibid.

129 **In one of our studies:** Harrington & Gelfand. *Worlds unto themselves.*

130 **When asked to plan a new menu:** Gervais, S. J., Guinote, A., Allen, J., & Slabu, L. (2013). Power increases situated creativity. *Social Influence, 8*(4), 294–311.

NOTES

130 **Psychologist Murray Straus found:** Straus, M. A. (1968). Communication, creativity, and problem-solving ability of middle- and working-class families in three societies. *American Journal of Sociology, 73*(4), 417–430.

130 **Studies show that, in general:** Carvacho, H., Zick, A., Haye, A., González, R., Manzi, J., Kocik, C., & Bertl, M. (2013). On the relation between social class and prejudice: The roles of education, income, and ideological attitudes. *European Journal of Social Psychology, 43*(4), 272–285.

130 **Across many countries:** Küpper, B., Wolf, C., & Zick, A. (2010). Social status and anti-immigrant attitudes in Europe: An examination from the perspective of social dominance theory. *International Journal of Conflict and Violence, 4*(2), 206.

131 **In one study demonstrating this:** Bowles, H. R., & Gelfand, M. (2010). Status and the evaluation of workplace deviance. *Psychological Science, 21*(1), 49–54.

131 **Similarly, a study looking at:** Egan, M. L., Matvos, G., & Seru, A. (2017). When Harry fired Sally: The double standard in punishing misconduct. *National Bureau of Economic Research.* doi: 10.3386/w23242.

132 **African American criminals are punished more harshly:** Editorial Board. (2016, December 17). Unequal sentences for blacks and whites. *The New York Times.* Retrieved from https://www.nytimes.com/2016/12/17/opinion/sunday/unequal-sentences-for-blacks-and-whites.html?_r=0.

132 **imprisoned at a rate that is five times:** Nellis, A. (2016). The color of justice: Racial and ethnic disparity in state prisons. The Sentencing Project. Retrieved from http://www.sentencingproject.org/publications/color-of-justice-racial-and-ethnic-disparity-in-state-prisons/. See also NAACP. (2018). Criminal justice fact sheet. Retrieved from http://www.naacp.org/criminal-justice-fact-sheet/.

132 **far more likely to be targeted . . . one in eight whites:** Ghandnoosh, N. (2015). Black lives matter: Eliminating racial inequity in the criminal justice system. The Sentencing Project. Retrieved from http://www.sentencingproject.org/publications/black-lives-matter-eliminating-racial-inequity-in-the-criminal-justice-system/#I. Uneven Policing in Ferguson and New York City.

133 **surveyed over 260 high-level college administrators:** Stephens, N. M., Fryberg, S. A., Markus, H. R., Johnson, C. S., & Covarrubias, R.

(2012). Unseen disadvantage: How American universities' focus on independence undermines the academic performance of first-generation college students. *Journal of Personality and Social Psychology, 102*(6), 1178–1197.

133 **A recent study of over:** Soria, K. M., Stebleton, M. J., & Huesman, R. L., Jr. (2013). Class counts: Exploring differences in academic and social integration between working-class and middle/upper-class students at large, public research universities. *Journal of College Student Retention: Research, Theory & Practice, 15*(2), 215–242.

133 **I witnessed these realities:** Harrington, J., & Gelfand, M. (2018). Survey of first-generation students, University of Maryland.

134 **studies done by the National Center for Education Statistics:** Radford, A., Berkner, L., Wheeless, S., & Shepherd, B. (2010). Persistence and attainment of 2003–04 beginning postsecondary students: After 6 years. U.S. Department of Education. Retrieved from https://nces.ed.gov/pubs 2011/2011151.pdf.

134 **Harvard:** Harvard College First Generation Student Union. *About.* Retrieved from http://www.hcs.harvard.edu/firstgen/index.html.

134 **Brown:** Hyde-Keller, O. Brown University to open first-generation college and low-income student center. News from Brown. Retrieved from https://news.brown.edu/articles/2016/03/firstgen.

134 **Arizona State:** Arizona State University. ASU program helps first-generation college students navigate path to higher ed. ASU Now. Retrieved from https://asunow.asu.edu/content/asu-program-helps -first-generation-college-students-navigate-path-higher-ed.

134 **Other universities:** See https://firstgen.studentlife.umich.edu/our-stor ies/ for an example at the University of Michigan, and https://alumni.uc la.edu/email/connect/2016/sept/first/default.htm for an example at the University of California, Los Angeles (UCLA).

134 **These programs can make a big difference:** Stephens, N. M., Hamedani, M. G., & Destin, M. (2014). Closing the social-class achievement gap: A difference-education intervention improves first-generation students' academic performance and all students' college transition. *Psychological Science, 25*(4), 943–953.

134 **by Sarah Eddy and Kelly Hogan:** Eddy, S. L., & Hogan, K. A. (2014).

Getting under the hood: How and for whom does increasing course structure work? *CBE-Life Sciences Education, 13*(3), 453–468.

135 **2017 Census Bureau report:** United States Census Bureau. (2017). *Highest educational attainment levels since 1940.* Retrieved from https://www.census.gov/library/visualizations/2017/comm/cb17-51_educational_attainment.html.

135 **many vocational programs:** The German Vocational Training System. (n.d.). Federal Ministry of Education and Research. Retrieved from https://www.bmbf.de/en/the-german-vocational-training-system-2129.html.

135 **The government works with:** Jacoby, T. (2014). Why Germany is so much better at training its workers. *The Atlantic.* Retrieved from https://www.theatlantic.com/business/archive/2014/10/why-germany-is-so-much-better-at-training-its-workers/381550/.

135 **As Tamar Jacoby in the *Atlantic* writes:** Ibid.

137 **McKinsey & Company found that:** Chui, M., Manyika, J., & Miremadi, M. (2016). Where machines could replace humans—and where they can't (yet). *McKinsey Quarterly.* Retrieved from https://www.mckinsey.com/business-functions/digital-mckinsey/our-insights/where-machines-could-replace-humans-and-where-they-cant-yet.

137 **"I never anticipated being in this situation":** Barabak, M. Z., & Duara, N. (2016). "We're called redneck, ignorant, racist. That's not true": Trump supporters explain why they voted for him. *Los Angeles Times.* Retrieved from http://www.latimes.com/politics/la-na-pol-donald-trump-american-voices-20161113-story.html.

137 **In England, the fear of immigrants:** Hjelmgaard, K., & Zoroya, G. (2016). Exploding UK immigration helped drive "Brexit" vote. *USA Today.* Retrieved from https://www.usatoday.com/story/news/world/2016/06/28/exploding-uk-immigration-helped-drive-brexit-vote/86424670/; Lord Ashcroft. (2016). How the United Kingdom voted on Thursday . . . and why. *Lord Ashcroft Polls.* Retrieved from http://lordashcroftpolls.com/2016/06/how-the-united-kingdom-voted-and-why/.

137 **"restore law and order":** White House. (2018). *Inside President Donald J. Trump's first year of restoring law and order.* Retrieved from https://www.whitehouse.gov/briefings-statements/president-donald-j-trumps-first-year-restoring-law-order/.

138 **"restore order" in France in five years:** Nossiter, A. (2017). Marine Le

Pen echoes Trump's bleak populism in French campaign kickoff. *The New York Times.* Retrieved from https://www.nytimes.com/2017/02/05 /world/europe/marine-le-pen-trump-populism-france-election.html.

138 **And the Polish populist party:** Adekoya, R. (2016). Xenophobic, authoritarian—and generous on welfare: How Poland's right rules. *The Guardian.* Retrieved from https://www.theguardian.com/commentisfree /2016/oct/25/poland-right-law-justice-party-europe.

CHAPTER 7: IS YOUR ORGANIZATION TIGHT OR LOOSE? IT MATTERS MORE THAN YOU THINK

139 **In 1998, two auto industry giants:** Vlasic, B., & Stertz, B. A. (2001). *Taken for a ride: How Daimler-Benz drove off with Chrysler.* New York: HarperCollins.

139 **German automaker Daimler:** Andrews, E. L., & Holson, L. M. (2001, August 12). Daimler-Benz to buy Chrysler in $36 billion deal. *The New York Times.* Retrieved from http://www.nytimes.com/2001/08/12/busi ness/daimlerbenz-to-buy-chrysler-in-36-billion-deal.html.

139 **its share price peaked at $108:** CBSNews.com Staff. (2001, January 29). Chrysler to cut 26,000 jobs. CBS News. Retrieved from https://www .cbsnews.com/news/chrysler-to-cut-26000-jobs/.

139 **In cultural integration workshops:** Schneider, P. (2001, August 12). Scenes from a marriage. *The New York Times.* Retrieved from http://www .nytimes.com/2001/08/12/magazine/scenes-from-a-marriage.html.

139 **keeping their hands out of their pockets:** Ibid.

139 **felt uncomfortable:** Ibid.

140 **And while the Germans wanted thick files:** Ibid.

140 **Americans approached these gatherings:** Ibid.

140 **For long-term assignments overseas:** Wright, C. (2000, August 1). Taken for a ride. *Automotive News.* Retrieved from http://www.autonews .com/article/20000801/SUB/8010710/.

140 **Integrating organizational structures:** *The Economist* Staff. (2000, July 27). The DaimlerChrysler emulsion. *The Economist.* Retrieved from http://www.economist.com/node/341352.

140 **Daimler CEO Jürgen Schrempp . . . "merger of equals":** Vlasic & Stertz. *Taken for a ride.*

140 **won the battle:** Schuetze, A. (2007, October 4). Benz sidelined as Daimler gets name change. Reuters. Retrieved from https://www.reuters.com /article/us-mercedesbenz-name/benz-sidelined-as-daimler-gets-name -change-idUSL0423158520071004.

140 **Daimler dispatched a German to head:** Schneider. Scenes from a marriage.

140 **replaced American managers with German ones:** CBSNews.com Staff. Chrysler to cut 26,000 jobs.

140 **laid off thousands of Chrysler employees:** Ibid.

140 **talk of "German invaders":** Schneider. Scenes from a marriage.

140 **Chrysler's dispirited employees coined a joke:** Maynard, M. (2007, August 12). DAM-lerChrysler? If you say so, Chief. *The New York Times.* Retrieved from http://www.nytimes.com/2007/08/12/business/your money/12suits.html.

140 **Key Chrysler executives left:** CBSNews.com Staff. Chrysler to cut 26,000 jobs; see also CNN Money Staff. (2000, November 28). Kerkorian sues Daimler. CNN Money. Retrieved from http://money.cnn .com/2000/11/27/news/chrysler/.

140 **after nine years of:** Landler, M. (2007, May 14). Daimler calling it quits with Chrysler. *The New York Times.* Retrieved from https://www.nytimes .com/2007/05/14/business/worldbusiness/14iht-daimler.5.5708176 .html.

141 **My colleague Chengguang Li:** Li, C., Gelfand, M. J., & Kabst, R. (2017). The influence of cultural tightness-looseness on cross-border acquisitions. *Academy of Management Proceedings, 2017*(1), 10533.

142 **one start-up for nearly every two thousand Israelis:** Senor & Singer. *Start-up nation*; Israel Venture Capital Research Center. (n.d.). Retrieved from www.ivc-online.com.

142 **Wix:** Wix. (n.d.). About us. Retrieved from https://www.wix.com/about/us.

142 **most successful tech start-ups:** Koetsier, John. (2013, November 6). Website builder Wix raises $127M in largest-ever IPO for Israeli firm. *Venture Beat.* Retrieved from https://venturebeat.com/2013/11/06/web site-builder-wix-raises-127m-in-largest-ever-ipo-for-israeli-firm/.

142 **eschewed a hierarchical organizational structure:** Wix Blog. (2014). "Ah, the View!": Wix offices around the globe. Retrieved from https://

www.wix.com/blog/2014/08/wix-offices-around-the-globe/; Abrahami, A. (2016, June 6). Wix CEO: How a 10-year-old company innovates. *Medium.* Retrieved from https://medium.com/@Wix.com/wix-ceo-how-a-10-year -old-company-innovates-ee173a81ae95.

142 **share large tables in an open studio:** Wix Blog. (2014). What we look like at work. Retrieved from https://www.wix.com/blog/2014/10/what -we-look-like-at-work/.

142 **Pet dogs:** Wix Blog. (2015). 5 things that will disqualify you from working at Wix. Retrieved from https://www.wix.com/blog/2015/06/5-things -that-will-disqualify-you-from-working-at-wix/.

142 **assortment of skateboards, boxing gear, and My Little Pony dolls:** Bort, J. (2013). Hot Israel startup Wix has a gorgeous headquarters overlooking the Mediterranean Sea. *Business Insider.* Retrieved from http:// www.businessinsider.com/startup-wix-has-one-of-the-most-spectacu lar-offices-in-isreal-2013-4.

142 **With rules few and far between:** Abrahami. Wix CEO.

142 **the atmosphere at Wix:** Wix Blog. 5 things that will disqualify you from working at Wix; Abrahami, A. (2014, July 31). An ode to transparency. *Entrepreneur.* Retrieved from https://www.entrepreneur.com/article/23 5873; Wix Blog. (2016). Saying thanks for these 10 things. Retrieved from https://www.wix.com/blog/2016/11/saying-thanks-for-these-10 -things/.

142 **In Wix's Vilnius office:** Wix Blog. "Ah, the View!"

142 **"the people make the place":** Schneider, B. (1987). The people make the place. *Personnel psychology, 40*(3), 437–453.

142 **"start-up nation":** Senor & Singer. *Start-up nation.*

142 **Jon Medved, a leading venture capitalist:** 2geeks1city (Producer). (2016, November 3). *Startup ecosystem in Israel: the documentary* [Video]. Retrieved from https://www.youtube.com/watch?v=qgCcymWeKrc.

143 **Yiddish word, *chutzpah*:** Rosten, L. (1968). *The Joys of Yiddish.* New York: McGraw-Hill.

143 **"An outsider would see *chutzpah* everywhere":** Senor & Singer. *Start-up nation.*

143 **To level the playing field, Israelis:** Ibid.

143 **Israeli tech blogger and entrepreneur Hillel Fuld:** Rudee, E. (2016,

March 10). What gives Israel the edge on marijuana? *Observer.* Retrieved from http://observer.com/2016/03/what-gives-israel-the-edge-on-mari juana/.

143 **Wix president and COO Nir Zohar:** Freilich, A. (Producer). (2015, August 24). *The COO of a billion dollar company Nir Zohar tells the story of Wix (Feat Nir Zohar, WIX)* [Audio podcast]. Retrieved from http://startupcamel.com/podcasts/83-if-you-want-your-startup-to-grow -10x-faster-your-personality-needs-to-grow-at-the-same-pace-feat-nir -zohar-wix/.

144 **from video arcade rooms:** Stangel, L. (2013, April 8). Facebook's 12 most fantastic employee perks. *Silicon Valley Business Journal.* Retrieved from https://www.bizjournals.com/sanjose/news/2013/04/03/facebooks -12-most-fantastic-employee.html.

144 **minibars:** Simoes, M. (2013, February 7). Why everyone wants to work at big tech companies. *Business Insider.* Retrieved from http://www .businessinsider.com/everyone-wants-to-work-at-tech-companies -2013-1.

144 **massages:** Bradford, L. (2016, July 27). 13 tech companies that offer cool work perks. *Forbes.* Retrieved from https://www.forbes.com/sites /laurencebradford/2016/07/27/13-tech-companies-that-offer-insanely -cool-perks/#318a950179d1.

144 **free cooking classes:** Yang, L. (2017, July 11). 13 incredible perks of working at Google, according to employees. *Insider.* Retrieved from http:// www.thisisinsider.com/coolest-perks-of-working-at-google-in-2017 -2017-7.

144 **Employees are given unlimited paid leave:** Roy, E. A. (2017, February 19). New Zealand startup offers unlimited holiday and profit share to attract workers. *The Guardian.* Retrieved from https://www.theguard ian.com/world/2017/feb/20/new-zealand-startup-unlimited-holiday -profit-share-attract-workers.

144 **visits from stress-reducing kittens:** Ibid.

144 **respect for the organizational hierarchy:** SBS Consulting. (2016). A comprehensive guide to Singapore work culture for new expats. Retrieved from https://www.sbsgroup.com.sg/blog/a-comprehensive -guide-to-singapore-work-culture-for-new-expats/.

144 **business cards are expected:** Commisceo Global. (n.d.). Singapore

guide. Retrieved from https://www.commisceo-global.com/country
-guides/singapore-guide.

144 **work is an integral component:** Schein, E. H., & Scheim, P. (2016). *Organizational culture and leadership* (5th ed.). Hoboken, N.J.: John Wiley & Sons.

144 **work-centric culture:** Lai, A. (2014, September). Singapore working hours survey 2014—media coverage. Morgan McKinley. Retrieved from https://www.morganmckinley.com.sg/article/singapore-working -hours-survey-2014-media-coverage.

144 **"What Israelis have not done so well":** Reed, J. (2014, January 2). Israel aims to grow from start-up nation to scale-up nation. *Financial Times.* Retrieved from https://www.ft.com/content/56f47908-67fa-11e3-8ada -00144feabdc0.

144 **In their comparison of the two countries . . . lawns:** Senor & Singer. *Start-up nation.*

145 **Japanese organizations are also generally known for their many rules:** De Mente, B. L. (2015). *Etiquette guide to Japan: Know the rules that make the difference!* North Clarendon, Vt.: Tuttle.

145 **Toyota has operated:** Magee, D. (2007). *How Toyota became #1: Leadership lessons from the world's greatest car company.* New York: Penguin.

145 **Employees shun conflict:** Ozawa, H. (2010, February 24). Toyota crisis throws spotlight on Japan's corporate culture. *Industry Week.* Retrieved from http://www.industryweek.com/companies-amp-executives/toy ota-crisis-throws-spotlight-japans-corporate-culture.

145 **conservative business suits:** Brooker, J. (2005, May 20). Is a salaryman without a suit like sushi without the rice? *The New York Times.* Retrieved from http://www.nytimes.com/2005/05/20/business/worldbusiness/is -a-salaryman-without-a-suit-like-sushi-without-the.html.

145 **complex bowing protocols are de rigueur:** De Mente. *Etiquette guide to Japan.*

145 **As part of their intensive orientation:** Rigoli, E. (2007, July 10). The kaizen of Toyota recruiting. ERE Media. Retrieved from https://www.ere .net/the-kaizen-of-toyota-recruiting/.

145 **Panasonic:** Unoki, K. (2012). *Mergers, acquisitions and global empires: Tolerance, diversity and the success of M&A.* New York: Routledge.

145 **compared to a military boot camp:** *Economist* Business Staff. (2015,

November 26). Loosening their ties. *The Economist.* Retrieved from https://www.economist.com/news/business/21679214-punishing-work-culture-gradually-being-relaxed-loosening-their-ties.

145 **sleep-deprived trainees memorizing every detail:** Ibid.

145 **Koreans face collective pressure to cooperate ... *nunchi*:** Lee, C. Y. (2012). Korean culture and its influence on business practice in South Korea. *Journal of International Management Studies, 7*(2), 184–191.

145 **"You have to fall in line":** Grobart, S. (2013, March 28). How Samsung became the world's no. 1 smartphone maker. *Bloomberg Businessweek.* Retrieved from https://www.bloomberg.com/news/articles/2013-03-28/how-samsung-became-the-worlds-no-dot-1-smartphone-maker.

145 **country's 2,500-year adherence to Confucian teachings:** Śleziak, T. (2013). The role of Confucianism in contemporary South Korean society. *Rocznik Orientalistyczny,* (1).

146 **emphasize the importance of obedience and discipline:** *Economist* Business Staff. Loosening their ties.

146 **After noticing a spike in recent years:** Granli, T. C. (2012). *Cross-cultural adaption in Norwegian companies in Brazil.* University of Oslo. Retrieved from https://www.duo.uio.no/bitstream/handle/10852/25180/Thomas CGranli-Thesis-LATAM4590.pdf.

146 **The *jeitinho Brasileiro*:** De H. Barbosa, L. N. (1995). The Brazilian *jeitinho*: An exercise in national identity. In Hess, D. J., & DaMatta, R. (Eds.). *The Brazilian Puzzle: Culture on the Borderlands of the Western World.* New York: Columbia University Press.

146 **cutting lines, finding legal loopholes:** Mello, J. (2012, March 26). The Brazilian way of doing things. *The Brazil Business.* Retrieved from http://thebrazilbusiness.com/article/the-brazilian-way-of-doing-things.

146 **devising ingenious life hacks:** Universidade Federal Fluminense (Producer). (2010, December 16). *O Jeitinho Brasileiro Em Diversos Âmbitos* [Video file]. Retrieved from https://www.youtube.com/watch?v=f0sf60R m27g.

146 **version of "don't worry"—*fique tranquilo*:** Keller, K. (2013). *Portuguese for dummies.* Indianapolis, Ind.: John Wiley & Sons.

146 **Semco Partners has embraced one rule:** Kruse, K. (2016, August 29). The big company that has no rules. *Forbes.* Retrieved from https://www

.forbes.com/sites/kevinkruse/2016/08/29/the-big-company-that-has
-no-rules/#47d6916556ad.

146 **Interviewees in Granli's study:** Granli. *Cross-cultural adaption in Norwegian companies in Brazil.*

147 **"Anyone who isn't sure":** Dieter Zetsche on sustainability. (2009). *360° Magazine.* Retrieved from http://multimedia.mercedes-benz.it/gruppo/pdf/Reports_Magazine.pdf.

147 **"Every employee must make sure":** Ibid.

147 **Chrysler's executives often granted . . . irreconcilable leadership styles:** Stephan, E., & Pace, R. W. (2002). *Powerful leadership: How to unleash the potential in others and simplify your own life.* Upper Saddle River, N.J.: Prentice Hall; Kansal, S., & Chandani, A. (2014). Effective management of change during merger and acquisition. *Procedia Economics and Finance, 11,* 208–217.

147 **GLOBE:** House, R. J., Hanges, P. J., Javidan, M., Dorfman, P. W., & Gupta, V. (Eds.). (2004). *Culture, leadership, and organizations: The GLOBE study of 62 societies.* Thousand Oaks, Calif.: Sage.

147 **recruited over seventeen thousand managers . . . sixty countries:** Ibid.

147 **Which qualities mattered most?:** Ibid.

147 **In my own analysis of its dataset:** Aktas, M., Gelfand, M. J., & Hanges, P. J. (2016). Cultural tightness–looseness and perceptions of effective leadership. *Journal of Cross-Cultural Psychology, 47*(2), 294–309.

147 **People in loose cultures prefer visionary leaders:** Ibid.

147 **Ricardo Semler, CEO:** Semler, R. (2014, October). *Ricardo Semler: How to run a company with (almost) no rules* [Video file]. Retrieved from https://www.ted.com/talks/ricardo_semler_how_to_run_a_company_with_almost_no_rules.

147 **He's worked hard to get out of the way:** Semler, R. (1995). *Maverick: The success story behind the world's most unusual workplace.* New York: Warner Books.

148 **"Our people have a lot of instruments":** Fisher, L. M. (2005, November 29). Ricardo Semler won't take control. *strategy + business (s+b).* Retrieved from https://www.strategy-business.com/article/05408?gko=3291c.

148 **All workers are taught:** Semler. *Maverick.*

148 **"I'm still sure we should have bought":** Semler, R. (1989, September–October). Managing without managers. *Harvard Business Review.* Retrieved from https://hbr.org/1989/09/managing-without-managers.

148 **"The goal of a leader":** Barrett, F. (2012). *Yes to the mess: Surprising leadership lessons from jazz.* Cambridge, Mass.: Harvard Business Review Press.

148 **People in tight cultures view effective leaders:** Aktas et al. Cultural tightness–looseness and perceptions of effective leadership.

148 **Foxconn:** Ngai, P., & Chan, J. (2012). Global capital, the state, and Chinese workers: The Foxconn experience. *Modern China, 38*(4), 383–410.

148 **Founded in 1974 by Terry Gou:** Ibid.

148 **one of China's largest exporters:** Ibid.

148 **employs over 1.2 million people:** Statt, N. (2016, December 30). iPhone manufacturer Foxconn plans to replace almost every human worker with robots. *The Verge.* Retrieved from https://www.theverge.com/2016/12/30/14128870/foxconn-robots-automation-apple-iphone-china-manufacturing.

148 **his leadership philosophy as "decisive" . . . "a righteous dictatorship":** Ngai & Chan. Global capital, the state, and Chinese workers.

148 **Valuing discipline . . . command-and-control management:** Ibid.

149 **mid-level managers model Gou's style:** Ibid.

149 **The U.S. Department of Labor's O*Net database:** The Occupational Information Network. (n.d.). About us. Retrieved from https://www.onetcenter.org/about.html.

149 **underlying structure that explains how industries differ:** Gordon, S. M., Choi, V., & Gelfand, M.W. (2017, May). *Cultural influences on occupational structure: A tightness-looseness perspective.* Poster presented at the Association for Psychological Science Conference in Boston, Mass.

150 **Balfour Beatty, one of the largest construction contractors:** Balfour Beatty Construction. (n.d.). Who we are. Retrieved from https://www.balfourbeattyus.com/our-company/who-we-are.

150 **Like many organizations in the construction industry:** Balfour Beatty Construction. (n.d.). Services. Retrieved from https://www.balfourbeattyus.com/our-work/services.

150 **some of the most dangerous jobs in the world:** Ward, M. (2017, January

4). The 10 most dangerous jobs for men. CNBC. Retrieved from https://www.cnbc.com/2017/01/04/the-10-most-dangerous-jobs-for-men.html.

150 **Balfour Beatty takes this responsibility seriously:** Balfour Beatty Construction. (n.d.). Zero harm. Retrieved from https://www.balfourbeatty us.com/our-company/zero-harm.

150 **tremendous levels of discipline on soldiers:** Pendry, J. D. (2001). *The three meter zone: Common sense leadership for NCOs.* Novato, Calif.: Presidio Press.

150 **From day one, U.S. Marine recruits endure:** Personal interview with Steve Colley, August 6, 2017.

150 **"The military is like a machine":** Ibid.

150 **In the course of a single day . . . hundreds of push-ups:** Ibid.

151 **"We have standards for things":** Ibid.

151 **Employees at the global design company Frog Design Inc.:** Smith, B. (2014, January 20). Getting hired: To land a job at frog, know your strengths, have a point of view and be comfortable with ambiguity. *Core77.* Retrieved from http://www.core77.com/posts/26280/Get ting-Hired-To-Land-a-Job-at-frog-Know-Your-Strengths-Have-a-Point-of -View-and-Be-Comfortable-with-Ambiguity.

151 **enjoy pushing boundaries:** Ibid.

151 **"You need to be a rebel in your heart":** Ibid.

151 **"I'm trying to qualify what makes a frog":** Ibid.

151 **Zappos:** Lashinsky, A. (2016, March 4). Why Amazon tolerates Zappos' extreme management experiment. *Fortune.* Retrieved from http://for tune.com/2016/03/04/amazon-zappos-holacracy/.

151 **emerged as the top web-based footwear retailer:** Parr, B. (2009, July 22). Here's why Amazon bought Zappos. *Mashable.* Retrieved from http://mashable.com/2009/07/22/amazon-bought-zappos/.

151 **Zappos has clung to its start-up culture:** Lashinsky. Why Amazon tolerates Zappos' extreme management experiment.

151 **bottom-up, egalitarian practices:** Bernstein, E., Bunch, J., Canner, N., & Lee, M. (2016). Beyond the holacracy hype. *Harvard Business Review, 94*(7/8), 38–49.

151 **adoption of "holacracy," a system of self-management:** Ibid.; Cheng, A. (2017, April 7). On holacracy, customer service and "Zappos Anything." *eMarketer Retail.* Retrieved from https://retail.emarketer.com/article

/zappos-ceo-tony-hsieh-on-holacracy-customer-service-zappos-any
thing/58e8084eebd4000a54864afc.

151 **self-organize into democratically run "circles":** Reingold, J. (2015,
March 4). How a radical shift to "self-management" left Zappos reeling.
Fortune. Retrieved from http://fortune.com/zappos-tony-hsieh-hola
cracy/.

151 **Everyone's roles are fluid . . . friendly guides:** Ibid.

152 **McKinsey's work tends to include strategy and risk assessments:** Hill,
A. (2011, November 25). Inside McKinsey. *Financial Times.* Retrieved from
https://www.ft.com/content/0d506e0e-1583-11e1-b9b8-00144feabdc0.

152 **IDEO mainly works on more creative and artistic:** IDEO. (n.d.). About
IDEO. Retrieved from https://www.ideo.com/about.

152 **McKinsey values a hard-nosed list:** McKinsey. (n.d.). Our mission and
values. Retrieved from https://www.mckinsey.com/about-us/overview
/our-mission-and-values.

152 **Unlike IDEO consultants:** Bennett, P. (n.d.). A loosely-designed organization. IDEO. Retrieved from https://lboi.ideo.com/paulbennett.html.

152 **New hires must absorb the infamous:** Raisel, E. M. (1999). *The McKinsey Way.* New York: McGraw-Hill Education.

152 **IDEO's loose company values:** IDEO. (n.d.). Nurturing a Creative Culture. Retrieved from https://www.ideo.com/case-study/nurturing-a-cre
ative-culture.

152 **The relaxed dress code:** Smith, B. (2014, January 20). Getting hired: To
work at IDEO, skip the suit, tell a compelling story and don't be creepy!
Core77. Retrieved from http://www.core77.com/posts/26239/getting
-hired-to-work-at-ideo-skip-the-suit-tell-a-compelling-story-and-dont
-be-creepy-26239.

153 **Big Four accounting firm Deloitte:** Dakers, M. (2016, October 4).
Deloitte overtakes PwC as world's biggest accountant. *The Telegraph.*
Retrieved from http://www.telegraph.co.uk/business/2016/10/04/delo
itte-overtakes-pwc-as-worlds-biggest-accountant/.

153 **Consultants often hustle through:** Naficy, M. (Ed.). (1997). *The fast
track: The insider's guide to winning jobs in management consulting, investment banking, and securities trading.* New York: Broadway.

153 **At Ball Corporation, there's a radically mixed work culture:** O'Reilly,

C. A., & Tushman, M. L. (2016). *Lead and disrupt: How to solve the innovator's dilemma*. Stanford, Calif.: Stanford Business Books.

153 **Founded in the late 1800s . . . aerospace:** Ibid.

154 **In the spring of 2017:** Personal interview with a senior manager in a manufacturing firm, July 21, 2017.

155 **Take Microsoft in the mid-1990s:** Personal interview with Bob Herbold, August 21, 2017; Herbold, R. J. (2002, January). Inside Microsoft: Balancing creativity and discipline. *Harvard Business Review*. Retrieved from https://hbr.org/2002/01/inside-microsoft-balancing-creativity-and-discipline.

156 **Ariel Cohen:** Personal interview with Ariel Cohen, April 12, 2017.

156 **Take ride-sharing start-up Uber:** Isaac, M. (2017, February 22). Inside Uber's aggressive, unrestrained workplace culture. *The New York Times*. Retrieved from https://www.nytimes.com/2017/02/22/technology/uber-workplace-culture.html.

157 **bulldozing through regional ordinances:** Dou, E. (2016, July 28). China clears road for Uber to operate legally. *The Wall Street Journal*. Retrieved from https://www.wsj.com/articles/china-clears-road-for-uber-to-operate-legally-1469703991; Robertson, A. (2016, July 22). Victory for cabbies as Uber fails in bid to roll out its cheap taxi app in Oxford after licensed drivers and private hire firms rallied together to block the application. *Daily Mail*. Retrieved from http://www.dailymail.co.uk/news/article-3703247/Uber-BANNED-setting-cheap-taxi-app-Oxford-licensed-drivers-private-hire-firms-rallied-block-application.html; Hawkins, A. J. (2017, February 6). Uber sues Seattle over law allowing drivers to unionize. *The Verge*. Retrieved from https://www.theverge.com/2017/2/6/14524792/uber-law suit-seattle-law-drivers-unionize.

157 **below-the-belt tactics:** Lazzaro, S. (2014, August 12). Startup sabotage: Uber employees allegedly submitted 5,560 fake Lyft ride requests. *Observer*. Retrieved from http://observer.com/2014/08/startup-sabotage-uber-employees-submitted-5560-fake-lyft-ride-requests/.

157 **hiding certain business practices:** Hawkins, A. J. (2017, January 19). Uber to pay $20 million to settle claims it misled drivers about pay, financing. *The Verge*. Retrieved from https://www.theverge.com/2017/1/19/14330708/uber-ftc-settlement-20-million-driver-mislead-earn

ings; Golson, J. (2017, March 3). Uber used an elaborate secret program to hide from government regulators. *The Verge*. Retrieved from https://www.theverge.com/2017/3/3/14807472/uber-greyball-regulators-taxi-legal-vtos.

157 **a *New York Times* exposé unveiled Uber's:** Isaac. Inside Uber's aggressive, unrestrained workplace culture.

157 **work environment as a "frat house":** Della Cava, M., Guynn, J., & Swartz, J. (2017, February 24). Uber's Kalanick faces crisis over "baller" culture. *USA Today*. Retrieved from https://www.usatoday.com/story/tech/news/2017/02/24/uber-travis-kalanick-/98328660/.

157 **unprofessional and even abusive behavior:** Isaac. Inside Uber's aggressive, unrestrained workplace culture.

157 **sexual harassment scandal:** Fowler, S. (2017, February 19). Reflecting on one very, very strange year at Uber. Susanjfowler.com. Retrieved from https://www.susanjfowler.com/blog/2017/2/19/reflecting-on-one-very-strange-year-at-uber.

157 **Travis Kalanick was forced to resign:** Isaac, M. (2017, June 21). Uber founder Travis Kalanick resigns as C.E.O. *The New York Times*. Retrieved from https://www.nytimes.com/2017/06/21/technology/uber-ceo-travis-kalanick.html.

157 **higher-ups had also hidden:** Weise, E. (2017, November 22). Uber paid hackers $100,000 to hide year-old breach of 57 million users. *USA Today*. Retrieved from https://www.usatoday.com/story/tech/2017/11/21/uber-kept-mum-year-hack-info-57-million-riders-and-drivers/887002001/; see also Newcomer, E. (2017, November 21). Uber paid hackers to delete stolen data on 57 million people. *Bloomberg*. Retrieved from https://www.bloomberg.com/news/articles/2017-11-21/uber-concealed-cyberattack-that-exposed-57-million-people-s-data.

157 **incident played out on one of United Airlines':** Gelfand, M., & Choi, V. (2017, May 15). Why United's culture needs to loosen up to avoid more PR fiascos. *The Conversation*. Retrieved from https://theconversation.com/why-uniteds-culture-needs-to-loosen-up-to-avoid-more-pr-fiascos-77662.

157 **exchange for an eight-hundred-dollar voucher:** Leocha, C. (2017, April 11). United Airlines' incompetence bloodies passenger [Press release]. *Travelers United*. Retrieved from https://www.travelersunited

.org/policy-columns/release-united-airlines-incompetence-bloodies
-passengers/.

158 **"United seems to have hired":** Personal correspondence with United employee, January 2, 2018.

158 **Knowing this now, United:** United Airlines (2017, April 27). United Airlines announces changes to improve customer experience [News release]. Retrieved from http://newsroom.united.com/2017-04-27-United -Airlines-Announces-Changes-to-Improve-Customer-Experience.

158 **Based in Chicago:** Stewart, J. B. (2017, July 27). The boycott that wasn't: How United weathered a media firestorm. *The New York Times.* Retrieved from https://www.nytimes.com/2017/07/27/business/how -united-weathered-a-firestorm.html.

158 **management scholars Charles O'Reilly and Michael Tushman:** O'Reilly & Tushman. *Lead and disrupt.*

159 **Google's adoption of the 70/20/10 rule:** Weiss, N. (2015, February 18). Manage your time like Google invests its resources: 70/20/10. *Medium.* Retrieved from https://medium.com/pminsider/manage-your-time-like -google-invests-its-resources-70-20-10-3bb4d600abaa.

159 **Pixar . . . flexible work hours:** Association of Independent Colleges of Art & Design. (n.d.). Nathan Fariss: animator and illustrator. Retrieved from http://aicad.org/nathan-fariss-animatorillustrator/.

159 **hidden bars:** Lane, A. (2011, May 16). The fun factory. *The New Yorker.* Retrieved from https://www.newyorker.com/magazine/2011/05/16/the -fun-factory.

159 **free pizza and cereal:** Bell, C. (2013, July 10). Monsters University: What's it like to work at Pixar? *The Telegraph.* Retrieved from http://www.tele graph.co.uk/culture/film/10144531/Monsters-University-whats-it-like -to-work-at-Pixar.html.

159 **"There was actually an individual here":** Hartlaub, P. (2010, June 13). Creativity thrives in Pixar's animated workplace. *SFGate.* Retrieved from http://www.sfgate.com/g00/bayarea/article/Creativity -thrives-in-Pixar-s-animated-workplace-3261925.php?i10c.encReferrer =&i10c.ua=1.

159 **Pixar brings together incubation teams:** Catmull, E. (2008, September). How Pixar fosters collective creativity. *Harvard Business Review.* Retrieved from https://hbr.org/2008/09/how-pixar-fosters-collective-creativity.

159 **Toyota . . . relies on rules and standard operating procedures:** Sosnovskikh, S. (2016). Toyota Motor Corporation: Organizational culture. Retrieved from https://www.researchgate.net/profile/Sergey_Sosnovskikh /publication/308624812_Toyota_Motor_Corporation_Organizational _Culture/links/57e9128d08aed0a291301389/Toyota-Motor-Corporation -Organizational-Culture.pdf.

160 **It's decentralizing:** Kubota, Y. (2016, February 29). Toyota plans organizational shake-up. *The Wall Street Journal.* Retrieved from https://www .wsj.com/articles/toyota-plans-shake-up-to-avoid-curse-of-the-10-mil lion-club-1456745512; Reuters Staff. (2016, March 2). Toyota shakes up corporate structure to focus on product lines. *Reuters.* Retrieved from https://www.reuters.com/article/us-toyota-management-structure /toyota-shakes-up-corporate-structure-to-focus-on-product-lines-id USKCN0W41CB.

160 **Toyota's leaders are . . . eight-step process:** Lussier, R. N. (2018). *Management fundamentals: Concepts, applications, skill development.* Thousand Oaks, Calif.: Sage; Radeka, K. (2009). Extreme Toyota: Radical contradictions that drive success at the world's best manufacturer by Emi Osono, Norihiko Shimizu, and Hirotaka Takeuchi. *Journal of Product Innovation Management, 26*(3), 356–358.

160 **invite workers to experiment:** Takeuchi, H., Osono, E., & Shimizu, N. (2008, June). The contradictions that drive Toyota's success. *Harvard Business Review.* Retrieved from https://hbr.org/2008/06/the-contradic tions-that-drive-toyotas-success.

160 **vague terms:** Takeuchi et al. The contradictions that drive Toyota's success.

160 **practice of "Commander's Intent":** Shattuck, L. G. (2000). *Communicating intent and imparting presence.* Army combined arms center Fort Leavenworth KS Military Review. http://www.dtic.mil/dtic/tr/fulltext /u2/a522123.pdf.

160 **"Spectrum of Improvisation":** Storlie, C. (2010, November 3). Manage uncertainty with Commander's Intent. *Harvard Business Review.* Retrieved from https://hbr.org/2010/11/dont-play-golf-in-a-football-g.

160 **"Managing culture is a tightrope walk":** Personal interview with Adam Grant, September 7, 2017.

161 **China's booming start-up . . . significant challenge of cultivating:**

Mozur, P. (2016, December 3). Silicon Valley's culture, not its companies, dominates in China. *The New York Times*. Retrieved from https://www.nytimes.com/2016/12/04/technology/china-silicon-valley-culture.html.

161 **dictated by the Communist Party:** Ibid.

161 **"We want people who aren't slavishly obedient":** Kuo, K. (2013, March 29). What is the internal culture like at Baidu? *Forbes*. Retrieved from https://www.forbes.com/sites/quora/2013/03/29/what-is-the-internal-culture-like-at-baidu/#5acf065f5c62.

161 **book called the *Baidu Analects*:** Mozur. Silicon Valley's culture, not its companies, dominates in China.

161 **"It's anecdote after anecdote":** Ibid.

162 **A senior executive at one of the world's:** Personal interview with an executive in a global manufacturing firm, July 6, 2017.

162 **In 1995, to keep in step . . . hired new leadership:** O'Reilly & Tushman. *Lead and disrupt*.

163 **"united front and consistent message":** Ibid.

163 **Those in print media . . . the unit heads:** Ibid.

CHAPTER 8: MIRROR CHECK: ARE YOU A "T" OR AN "L"?

165 **Called Muppet Theory:** Lithwick, D. (2012, June 8). Chaos theory. *Slate*. Retrieved from http://www.slate.com/articles/life/low_concept/2012/06/what_kind_of_muppet_are_you_chaos_or_order_.html.

168 **two hundred decisions for every mile traveled:** Guidelines for employers to reduce motor vehicle crashes. United States Department of Labor. Retrieved from https://www.osha.gov/Publications/motor_vehicle_guide.html.

171 **Species such as bats, dolphins:** Pennisi, E. (2013, September 4). Bats and dolphins evolved echolocation in same way. *Science Magazine*. Retrieved from http://www.sciencemag.org/news/2013/09/bats-and-dolphins-evolved-echolocation-same-way.

171 **even rats use forms of radar:** Rosenzweig, M. R., Riley, D. A., & Krech, D. (1955). Evidence for echolocation in the rat. *Science, 121*, 600.

171 **Borat:** Cohen, S. B. (Producer), & Charles, L. (Director). 2006. *Borat* [Motion picture]. UK: 20th Century Fox.

NOTES

171 **Mark Snyder:** Snyder, M. (1974). Self-monitoring of expressive behavior. *Journal of Personality and Social Psychology, 30*(4), 526–537.

171 **Janice Mill:** Mill, J. (1984). High and low self-monitoring individuals: Their decoding skills and empathic expression. *Journal of Personality, 52*(4), 372–388.

172 **In a global survey, I found:** Gelfand et al. Differences between tight and loose cultures.

173 **the brains of London taxi drivers:** Maguire, E. A., Gadian, D. G., Johnsrude, I. S., Good, C. D., Ashburner, J., Frackowiak, R. S., & Frith, C. D. (2000). Navigation-related structural change in the hippocampi of taxi drivers. *Proceedings of the National Academy of Sciences, 97*(8), 4398–4403.

173 **My collaborators Yan Mu:** Mu, Y., Kitayama, S., Han, S., & Gelfand, M. J. (2015). How culture gets embrained: Cultural differences in event-related potentials of social norm violations. *Proceedings of the National Academy of Sciences, 112*(50), 15348–15353.

174 **Tory Higgins at Columbia University:** Higgins, E. T. (1998). Promotion and prevention: Regulatory focus as a motivational principle. *Advances in Experimental Social Psychology, 30*, 1–46.

175 **People in tight cultures . . . before thinking:** Gelfand et al. Differences between tight and loose cultures.

175 **more likely to carry a particular gene:** Mrazek, A. J., Chiao, J. Y., Blizinsky, K. D., Lun, J., & Gelfand, M. J. (2013). The role of culture–gene coevolution in morality judgment: Examining the interplay between tightness–looseness and allelic variation of the serotonin transporter gene. *Culture and Brain, 1*(2–4), 100–117.

175 **Imagine you're in a study:** Förster, J., Higgins, E. T., & Bianco, A. T. (2003). Speed/accuracy decisions in task performance: Built-in trade-off or separate strategic concerns? *Organizational Behavior and Human Decision Processes, 90*(1), 148–164.

176 **In one study, psychologists separated people:** Florack, A., & Hartmann, J. (2007). Regulatory focus and investment decisions in small groups. *Journal of Experimental Social Psychology, 43*(4), 626–632.

176 **American psychologist Walter Mischel:** Mischel, W., Shoda, Y., & Rodriguez, M. L. (1989). Delay of gratification in children. *Science, 244*(4907), 933–938.

177 **were more likely to:** Wills, T. A., & Stoolmiller, M. (2002). The role of

self-control in early escalation of substance use: A time-varying analysis. *Journal of Consulting and Clinical Psychology, 70*(4), 986–997.

177 **"Manage impulsivity!":** The slogan "Manage Impulsivity!" was part of a series of short phrases emblazoned on the cafeteria of Hildreth Elementary School in Harvard, Mass., personal communication from a friend, 2017.

177 **psychologists gave both Japanese and American preschoolers:** Zahn-Waxler, C., Friedman, R. J., Cole, P. M., Mizuta, I., & Hiruma, N. (1996). Japanese and United States preschool children's responses to conflict and distress. *Child Development, 67*(5), 2462–2477.

177 **Chinese preschoolers outperformed American preschoolers:** Lan, X., Legare, C. H., Ponitz, C. C., Li, S., & Morrison, F. J. (2011). Investigating the links between the subcomponents of executive function and academic achievement: A cross-cultural analysis of Chinese and American preschoolers. *Journal of Experimental Child Psychology, 108*(3), 677–692.

178 **Some classrooms even have webcams:** Hernandez, J. C. (2017, April 25). In China, daydreaming students are caught on camera. *The New York Times.* Retrieved from https://www.nytimes.com/2017/04/25/world /asia/in-china-daydreaming-students-are-caught-on-camera.html.

178 **Masaki Yuki:** Personal communication, December 15, 2017.

179 **30 percent of American students:** OECD (2013). *PISA 2012 results: Ready to learn (volume III): Students' engagement, drive and self-beliefs.* Paris: OECD Publishing. Retrieved from http://dx.doi.org/10.1787/9789 264201170-en. Percentage of students who reported arriving late to school in the two weeks prior to the PISA test. Students surveyed were fifteen and sixteen years old.

179 **Seventy percent of U.S. students:** Ibid.

179 **that I surveyed around the world:** Gelfand et al. Differences between tight and loose cultures.

179 **Yan Mu and I had Chinese and American participants:** Mu, Y., Kitayama, S., Han, S., & Gelfand, M. (2018). Do we "rest" differently? Cultural variation in neural markers of self control.

180 **psychologist David Matsumoto:** Matsumoto, D., Willingham, B., & Olide, A. (2009). Sequential dynamics of culturally moderated facial expressions of emotion. *Psychological Science, 20*(10), 1269–1274.

181 **When I surveyed people around the world:** Gelfand et al. Differences between tight and loose cultures.

181 **psychologist Arie Kruglanski:** Kruglanski, A. W., Pierro, A., Higgins, E. T., & Capozza, D. (2007). "On the move" or "staying put": Locomotion, need for closure, and reactions to organizational change. *Journal of Applied Social Psychology, 37*(6), 1305–1340.

181 **expresses a decision:** Kruglanski, A. W., & Webster, D. M. (1991). Group members' reactions to opinion deviates and conformists at varying degrees of proximity to decision deadline and of environmental noise. *Journal of Personality and Social Psychology, 61*(2), 212–225.

181 **conducted in the late 1990s:** Shah, J. Y., Kruglanski, A. W., & Thompson, E. P. (1998). Membership has its (epistemic) rewards: Need for closure effects on in-group bias. *Journal of Personality and Social Psychology, 75*(2), 383–393.

182 **In a study of nearly two hundred parent-child pairs:** Dhont, K., Roets, A., & Van Hiel, A. (2013). The intergenerational transmission of need for closure underlies the transmission of authoritarianism and anti-immigrant prejudice. *Personality and Individual Differences, 54*(6), 779–784.

185 **Indeed, our research shows:** Geeraert, N., Li, R., Ward, C., Gelfand, M. J., & Demes, K. (2018). A tight spot: How personality moderates the impact of social norms on sojourner adaptation.

CHAPTER 9: GOLDILOCKS HAD IT RIGHT

189 **Aristotle:** Aristotle. (1953). *The ethics of Aristotle.* (J. A. K. Thompson, Trans.). London, UK: Penguin Books.

189 **Socrates, and Plato:** Plato. (1993). *Republic.* (R. Waterfield, Trans.). Oxford, UK: Oxford World's Classics. See also Plato's *Euthydemus.*

189 **"contentment is the greatest wealth":** Buddharakkhita, A. (2008). *The Dhammapada: The Buddha's path of wisdom.* Buddhist Publication Society.

189 **In his 1725 essay:** Hutcheson, F. (1969). *Inquiry concerning moral good and evil.* Farnborough, UK: Gregg International Publishers. (Original work published in 1725).

189 **Jeremy Bentham (1748–1832) was also concerned:** Bentham, J. (1789). *An introduction to the principles of morals and legislation.*

189 **psychological wealth of nations:** Oishi, S. (2011). *The psychological*

wealth of nations: Do happy people make a happy society? (Vol. 10). Malden, Mass.: John Wiley & Sons.

189 **according to Thomas Jefferson:** Founders Online. (n.d.). *Thomas Jefferson to Tadeusz Kosciuszko, 26 February 1810.* National Archives. Retrieved from https://founders.archives.gov/documents/Jefferson/03-02-02-0211.

190 **In 1998, Martin Seligman:** University of Pennsylvania Positive Psychology Center. (2018). *Martin E. P. Seligman.* Retrieved from https://ppc.sas .upenn.edu/people/martin-ep-seligman.

190 **Gross National Happiness:** Centre for Bhutan Studies & GNH Research (2015). *A compass towards a just and harmonious society: 2015 GNH survey report.* Retrieved from http://www.grossnationalhappiness.com /wp-content/uploads/2017/01/Final-GNH-Report-jp-21.3.17-ilovepdf -compressed.pdf.

190 **"ministers of happiness":** Simmons, A.M. (2017, March 6). UAE's minister of happiness insists her job is no laughing matter. *Los Angeles Times.* Retrieved from http://www.latimes.com/world/middleeast/la-fg-global -uae-happiness-2017-story.html.

190 **"happiness centers":** Hamblin, J. (2016, April 26). Harvard has a new center for happiness. *The Atlantic.* Retrieved from https://www.theatlantic .com/health/archive/2016/04/harvard-center-for-happiness/479784/.

190 **psychiatrist Richard Davidson and his colleagues:** Davidson, R. J., Kabat-Zinn, J., Schumacher, J., Rosenkranz, M., Muller, D., Santorelli, S. F., . . . & Sheridan, J. F. (2003). Alterations in brain and immune function produced by mindfulness meditation. *Psychosomatic medicine, 65*(4), 564–570; Davidson, R. J., & Lutz, A. (2008). Buddha's brain: Neuroplasticity and meditation [in the spotlight]. *IEEE Signal Processing Magazine, 25*(1), 176–174; Lutz, A., Greischar, L. L., Rawlings, N. B., Ricard, M., & Davidson, R. J. (2004). Long-term meditators self-induce high-amplitude gamma synchrony during mental practice. *Proceedings of the National Academy of Sciences, 101*(46), 16369–16373.

190 **highest suicide rates:** Harrington, J. R., Boski, P., & Gelfand, M. J. (2015). Culture and national well-being: Should societies emphasize freedom or constraint? *PloS One, 10*(6), e0127173.

190 **happiness index scores:** Ibid.

190 **Depression rates also vary:** Ibid.

191 **Plato advocated for a paternalistic city-state:** Plato. *Republic.*

NOTES

191 **Confucius advocated for an order-centered state:** Confucius. (2008). *The analects.* (R. Dawson, Trans.). Oxford, UK: Oxford University Press.

191 **In the Cynics' view:** Piering, J. (n.d.). Cynics. *Internet encyclopedia of philosophy.* Retrieved from http://www.iep.utm.edu/cynics/#SH3a.

192 **Thomas Hobbes, who perceived life as "nasty, brutish, and short":** Hobbes, T. (1651). *Leviathan.*

192 **John Stuart Mill advocated for a more open system:** Mill, J. S. (1859). *On Liberty.* London: John W. Parker and Son, West Strand.

192 **he summarized:** Freud, S. (2005). *Civilization and its discontents.* (J. Strachey, Trans.). New York: W. W. Norton. (Original work published in 1930).

192 **We theorized:** Harrington et al. Culture and national well-being.

193 **Durkheim observed that people:** Durkheim, E. (1984). *The Division of labor in society.* London: The Macmillan Press. (Original work published in 1893).

193 **In his well-known study:** Durkheim, E. (1951). *Suicide.* (J. A. Spaulding and G. Simpson, Trans.). New York: The Free Press. (Original work published in 1897).

194 **he began working on his book:** Fromm, E. (1941). *Escape from freedom.* New York: Holt, Rinehart and Winston.

194 **sociologist Amitai Etzioni:** Etzioni, A. (1996). *The new golden rule.* New York: Basic Books.

194 **psychologist Barry Schwartz calls "the tyranny of freedom":** Schwartz, B. (2000). Self-determination: The tyranny of freedom. *American Psychologist, 55*(1), 79–88.

194 **Etzioni theorized:** Etzioni, *The new golden rule.*

194 **Aristotle argued:** Aristotle's ethics. (2014). *Stanford encyclopedia of philosophy.* Retrieved from https://plato.stanford.edu/entries/aristotle -ethics/#VirDefConInc.

195 **Terence echoed this sentiment:** Terence. (2002). *Andria.* (G. P. Shipp, Trans.). London: Bristol Classical Press.

195 **Chinese philosophy of yin and yang:** The Editors of Encyclopedia Britannica. (2017). Yinyang. *Encyclopædia Britannica.* Retrieved from https://www.britannica.com/topic/yinyang.

195 **"Goldilocks and the Three Bears":** Southey, R. (1837). *Goldilocks and the three bears.* London: Longman, Rees, etc.

NOTES

195 **"Rare Earth" hypothesis:** Cain, F. (2016). Does our galaxy have a habitable zone? Phys.org. Retrieved from https://phys.org/news/2016-09-galaxy-habitable-zone.html.

195 **the Yerkes-Dodson Law:** Gino, F. (2016). Are you too stressed to be productive? Or not stressed enough? *Harvard Business Review.* Retrieved from https://hbr.org/2016/04/are-you-too-stressed-to-be-productive-or-not-stressed-enough.

195 **In medicine:** Goldilocks Principle. (2017). *Seeking alpha.* Retrieved from https://seekingalpha.com/article/4084225-goldilocks-principle.

196 **Jesse Harrington, Pawel Boski, and I:** Harrington et al. Culture and national well-being.

197 **life expectancy:** Ibid.

197 **death rates from cardiovascular diseases and diabetes:** Ibid.

197 **According to the Economist Intelligence Unit:** Ibid.; the Economist Intelligence Unit. (March 19, 2009). Political instability index: Vulnerability to social and political unrest. Retrieved from http://viewswire.eiu.com/index.asp?layout=VWArticleVW3&article_id=874361472.

197 **show higher levels:** Harrington et al. Culture and national well-being.

198 **Turkey, as if on cue:** Turkey's failed coup attempt: All you need to know. (2017, July 15). *Al Jazeera.* Retrieved from https://www.aljazeera.com/news/2016/12/turkey-failed-coup-attempt-161217032345594.html.

198 **GDP per capita:** Harrington et al. Culture and national well-being. For example, very loose countries (Ukraine at $7,400, Estonia at $22,400, Venezuela at $13,600) and very tight countries (Pakistan at $3,100, Turkey at $15,300, and Malaysia at $17,500) have low GDPs. Meanwhile, Germany, Hong Kong, and Italy had much higher GDPs per capita of $39,500, $52,700, and $29,600, respectively.

198 **The data are clear:** Harrington et al. Culture and national well-being.

198 **colony of honeybees:** Kameda, T., & Hastie, R. (2015). Herd behavior. In Scott, R. A., & Kosslyn, S. M. (Eds.). *Emerging trends in the social and behavioral sciences: An interdisciplinary, searchable, and linkable resource.* New York: Wiley.

199 **Figure 9.1:** Data source: Harrington et al. Culture and national well-being.

199 **computer simulation models:** List, C., Elsholtz, C., & Seeley, T. D. (2009). Independence and interdependence in collective decision mak-

ing: An agent-based model of nest-site choice by honeybee swarms. *Philosophical Transactions of the Royal Society of London B: Biological Sciences, 364*(1518), 755–762.

200 **starlings flying in flocks:** Cavagna, A., Cimarelli, A., Giardina, I., Parisi, G., Santagati, R., Stefanini, F., & Viale, M. (2010). Scale-free correlations in starling flocks. *Proceedings of the National Academy of Sciences, 107*(26), 11865–11870.

200 **epileptic subjects:** Meisel, C., Storch, A., Hallmeyer-Elgner, S., Bullmore, E., & Gross, T. (2012). Failure of adaptive self-organized criticality during epileptic seizure attacks. *PLoS Computational Biology, 8*(1), e1002312.

200 **tremors:** Levy, R., Hutchison, W. D., Lozano, A. M., & Dostrovsky, J. O. (2000). High-frequency synchronization of neuronal activity in the subthalamic nucleus of Parkinsonian patients with limb tremor. *Journal of Neuroscience, 20*(20), 7766–7775.

200 **inability to initiate movement:** Schnitzler, A., & Gross, J. (2005). Normal and pathological oscillatory communication in the brain. *Nature Reviews Neuroscience, 6*(4), 285–296.

201 **autism:** Just, M. A., Cherkassky, V. L., Keller, T. A., & Minshew, N. J. (2004). Cortical activation and synchronization during sentence comprehension in high-functioning autism: Evidence of underconnectivity. *Brain, 127*(8), 1811–1821.

201 **Alzheimer's disease:** Stam, C. J., Montez, T., Jones, B. F., Rombouts, S. A. R. B., Van Der Made, Y., Pijnenburg, Y. A. L., & Scheltens, P. (2005). Disturbed fluctuations of resting state EEG synchronization in Alzheimer's disease. *Clinical Neurophysiology, 116*(3), 708–715.

201 **schizophrenia:** Uhlhaas, P. J., Linden, D. E., Singer, W., Haenschel, C., Lindner, M., Maurer, K., & Rodriguez, E. (2006). Dysfunctional long-range coordination of neural activity during Gestalt perception in schizophrenia. *Journal of Neuroscience, 26*(31), 8168–8175.

201 **"wholes without full attention":** Kanner, L. (1943). Autistic disturbances of affective contact. *Nervous Child, 2,* 217–250.

201 **integrating information from different components:** Happé, F., & Frith, U. (2006). The weak coherence account: Detail-focused cognitive style in autism spectrum disorders. *Journal of Autism and Developmental Disorders, 36*(1), 5–25.

201 **process information:** Uhlhaas et al. Dysfunctional long-range coordination of neural activity during Gestalt perception in schizophrenia.

201 **memory breakdown:** Grady, C. L., Furey, M. L., Pietrini, P., Horwitz, B., & Rapoport, S. I. (2001). Altered brain functional connectivity and impaired short-term memory in Alzheimer's disease. *Brain, 124*(4), 739–756.

201 **"one that does exactly":** Oullette, J. (2014, April 7). Sand pile model of the mind grows in popularity. *Scientific American.* Retrieved from https://www.scientificamerican.com/article/sand-pile-model-of-the -mind-grows-in-popularity/.

202 **extreme constraint:** Gavazzi, S. M. (1993). The relation between family differentiation levels in families with adolescents and the severity of presenting problems. *Family Relations,* 463–468.

202 **parents are extremely overprotective:** Want, J., & Kleitman, S. (2006). Imposter phenomenon and self-handicapping: Links with parenting styles and self-confidence. *Personality and Individual Differences, 40*(5), 961–971.

202 **"helicopter parents":** LeMoyne, T., & Buchanan, T. (2011). Does "hovering" matter? Helicopter parenting and its effect on well-being. *Sociological Spectrum, 31*(4), 399–418.

202 **depression, anxiety, and lower life satisfaction:** Reed, K., Duncan, J. M., Lucier-Greer, M., Fixelle, C., & Ferraro, A. J. (2016). Helicopter parenting and emerging adult self-efficacy: Implications for mental and physical health. *Journal of Child and Family Studies, 25*(10), 3136–3149; Young, J. L. (2017, January 25). The Effects of "Helicopter Parenting." *Psychology Today.* Retrieved from https://www.psychologytoday.com/blog /when-your-adult-child-breaks-your-heart/201701/the-effects-helicop ter-parenting; LeMoyne & Buchanan. Does "hovering" matter?

202 **poor academic habits:** Richardson, J. L., Radziszewska, B., Dent, C. W., & Flay, B. R. (1993). Relationship between after-school care of adolescents and substance use, risk taking, depressed mood, and academic achievement. *Pediatrics, 92*(1), 32–38.

202 **engage in underage drinking:** Luyckx, K., Tildesley, E. A., Soenens, B., Andrews, J. A., Hampson, S. E., Peterson, M., & Duriez, B. (2011). Parenting and trajectories of children's maladaptive behaviors: A 12-year prospective community study. *Journal of Clinical Child & Adolescent Psychology, 40*(3), 468–478.

202 **substance abuse, and other risky behaviors:** Richardson et al. Rela-

tionship between after-school care of adolescents and substance use, risk taking, depressed mood, and academic achievement.

202 **In a longitudinal study:** Hamilton, L. T. (2016). *Parenting to a degree: How family matters for college women's success.* Chicago: University of Chicago Press. See also Hamilton, L. (2016). The partnership between parents and helicopter parents. *The Atlantic.* Retrieved from https://www.theatlantic.com/education/archive/2016/05/the-partnership-between-colleges-and-helicopter-parents/482595/.

203 **Sheena Iyengar and Mark Lepper:** Iyengar, S. S., & Lepper, M. R. (2000). When choice is demotivating: Can one desire too much of a good thing? *Journal of Personality and Social Psychology, 79*(6), 995–1006.

204 **Research has found that when 401(k) plans:** Iyengar, S. S., Huberman, G., & Jiang, G. (2004). How much choice is too much? Contributions to 401(k) retirement plans. In Mitchell, O. S., & Utkus, S. P. (Eds.), *Pension design and structure: New lessons from behavioral finance* (pp. 83–96). Oxford, UK: Oxford University Press.

204 **Recent college graduates:** Iyengar, S. S., Wells, R. E., & Schwartz, B. (2006). Doing better but feeling worse: Looking for the "best" job undermines satisfaction. *Psychological Science, 17*(2), 143–150.

204 *The Paradox of Choice:* Schwartz, B. (2004). *The Paradox of Choice.* New York, NY: Harper Perennial.

204 **according to Schwartz:** Ibid.

205 **study done at the University of California, Berkeley:** Caneel, J. K. (2009). The blank page: Effects of constraint on creativity. Electronic Theses and Dissertations, UC Berkeley.

206 **The 2001 Enron scandal is one of the most striking:** Healy, P. M., & Palepu, K. G. (2003). The fall of Enron. *Journal of Economic Perspectives, 17*(2), 3–26.

206 **"darling of Wall Street":** Carr, L. P., & Nanni, A. J., Jr. (2009). *Delivering results: Managing what matters.* New York: Springer Science & Business Media.

206 **Enron executives were implicated in obfuscating losses:** Petrick, J. A., & Scherer, R. F. (2003). The Enron scandal and the neglect of management integrity capacity. *American Journal of Business, 18*(1), 37–50.

206 **Enron's lead auditors, who were accused:** Nelson, K. K., Price, R. A., & Rountree, B. R. (2008). The market reaction to Arthur Andersen's role in

the Enron scandal: Loss of reputation or confounding effects? *Journal of Accounting and Economics, 46*(2–3), 279–293.

207 **Proponents argue:** For example, Jeb Bush, a Republican presidential candidate in the 2016 U.S. election, stated: "We do protect our civil liberties, but [the Patriot Act] is a hugely important program to use these technologies to keep us safe." Marco Rubio, a Republican senator and another 2016 presidential hopeful, urged other senators to "consider a permanent extension of the counterterrorism tools our intelligence community relies on to keep the American people safe." Peterson, A. (2015, April 23). Here's where the presidential candidates stand on the NSA scooping up Americans' phone records. *The Washington Post.*

207 **Detractors:** On the other side of the debate are politicians like former senator Mark Udall from Colorado, who said he did "everything in my power" to make people more aware of NSA spying. Weiner, R. (2013, June 6). Mark Udall: I tried to expose NSA program. *The Washington Post.* Retrieved from https://www.washingtonpost.com/news/post-politics/wp/2013/06/06/mark-udall-i-tried-to-expose-nsa-spying/?utm_term=.ea40b22e7995. Hillary Clinton, the democratic nominee in the 2016 U.S. presidential race, praised Udall for "asking the hard questions about intelligence and the trade-off between liberty and security." Peterson. Here's where the presidential candidates stand on the NSA scooping up Americans' phone records.

207 **without infringing on civil liberties:** Many American citizens have discussed the need for a balance between freedom and security. Sixty-one percent of Americans supported renewing the Patriot Act in 2015, but 65 percent still thought that there weren't strong enough checks on the government's ability to collect data from private citizens. Kurtzleben, D. (2015, June 1). Americans say they want the Patriot Act renewed . . . but do they, really? NPR. Retrieved from https://www.npr.org/sections/itsallpolitics/2015/06/01/411234429/americans-say-they-want-the-patriot-act-renewed-but-do-they-really. Likewise, in 2014, 74 percent of Americans believed they should not have to give up their privacy and freedom in exchange for safety—there should be other routes to security that don't come at such a personal cost. Gao, G. (2015, May 29). What Americans think about NSA surveillance, national security and privacy. Pew Research Center. Retrieved from http://www.pewresearch.org

/fact-tank/2015/05/29/what-americans-think-about-nsa-surveillance
-national-security-and-privacy/.

207 **"Both [security and freedom] are":** Cameron, D. (2006). Speech to the
Center for Policy Studies. Retrieved from https://www.theguardian.com
/politics/2006/jun/26/conservatives.constitution.

CHAPTER 10: CULTURE'S REVENGE AND GLOBAL (DIS)ORDER

208 **hundreds of thousands:** Fleishman, J. (2011, February 11). Mubarak's
end came quickly, stunningly. *Los Angeles Times.* Retrieved from http://
articles.latimes.com/2011/feb/11/world/la-fg-egypt-revolution-2011
0212.

208 **age groups, political backgrounds, and religious affiliations:** Ham-
mond, J. (2011, February 7). Egyptian women play vital role in anti-
Mubarak protests. Radio Free Europe/Radio Liberty. Retrieved from
https://www.rferl.org/a/egypt_women_protests/2300279.html.

208 **thirty years of autocratic rule:** Fleishman. Mubarak's end came quickly,
stunningly.

208 **"Illegitimate!" and "Mubarak, go!":** Asser, M. (2011, February 11). Q&A:
Egyptian protests against Hosni Mubarak. BBC. Retrieved from http://
www.bbc.com/news/world-middle-east-12324664.

208 **social media:** Arafa, M., & Armstrong, C. (2016). "Facebook to mobilize, Twitter to coordinate protests, and YouTube to tell the world": New
media, cyberactivism, and the Arab Spring. *Journal of Global Initiatives:
Policy, Pedagogy, Perspective, 10*(1), 6.

208 **eighteen days of protests:** Egypt Revolution: 18 days of people power.
(2016, Jan 25). Al Jazeera. Retrieved from http://www.aljazeera.com
/indepth/inpictures/2016/01/egypt-revolution-160124191716737.html.

208 **granting his office dictatorial powers:** Hammer, J. (2012, December 7).
Understanding Mohamed Morsi. *New Republic.* Retrieved from https://
newrepublic.com/article/110866/understanding-mohammad-morsi.

208 **military coup . . . el-Sisi:** Abdel Fattah el-Sisi Fast Facts (2018, April 5).
CNN. Retrieved from https://www.cnn.com/2014/07/01/world/africa
/abdel-fattah-el-sisi-fast-facts/index.html; see also Ketchley, N. (2017,
July 3). How Egypt's generals used street protests to stage a coup. *The
Washington Post.* Retrieved from https://www.washingtonpost.com

/news/monkey-cage/wp/2017/07/03/how-egypts-generals-used
-street-protests-to-stage-a-coup/?utm_term=.4b3d231f7a55.

209 **sixty thousand political prisoners:** Hammer, J. (2017, March 14). How
Egypt's activists became "generation jail." *The New York Times.* Retrieved
from https://www.nytimes.com/2017/03/14/magazine/how-egypts-ac
tivists-became-generation-jail.html.

209 **repressed protests . . . silence his critics:** Ibid.

210 **"Egypt is free!" and "God is great!":** Fantz, A. (2016, April 27). CNN.
Retrieved from http://www.cnn.com/2016/04/27/middleeast/egypt
-how-we-got-here/index.html.

210 **"For the first time":** Mohamed ElBaradei: People have to be in control.
(2011, February 11). CNN. Retrieved from http://cnnpressroom.blogs
.cnn.com/2011/02/11/mohamed-elbaradei-people-have-to-be-in-con
trol/.

210 **"I feel as though":** Whitlock, C. (2011, February 12). Mubarak steps
down, prompting jubilation in Cairo streets. *The Washington Post.*
Retrieved from https://www.washingtonpost.com/national/mubarak
-steps-down-prompting-jubilation-in-cairo-streets/2011/02/11/ABEc
AqF_story.html?utm_term=.462f7e67c26e.

210 **12 percent inflation . . . Forty-four percent:** Heineman, B. W. (2011,
December 12). Why Egypt's economy matters. *The Atlantic.* Retrieved
from https://www.theatlantic.com/international/archive/2011/12/why
-egypts-economy-matters/249718/.

210 **economic winter:** Torbey, J. (2011, November 24). The future of the
Arab world in light of recent transitions. Annual Arab Banking Summit.
Retrieved from http://www.josephmtorbey.com/admin/docs/translated
_uab_speech_english.pdf.

210 **an astonishing 200 percent:** Egypt: crime soars 200 per cent since
Hosni Mubarak was ousted. (2011, April 5). *The Telegraph.* Retrieved from
http://www.telegraph.co.uk/news/worldnews/africaandindianocean
/egypt/8430100/Egypt-crime-soars-200-per-cent-since-Hosni-Mubarak
-was-ousted.html.

210 **Riots and kidnappings:** Kirkpatrick, D. D. (2011, May 12). Crime wave in
Egypt has people afraid, even the police. *The New York Times.* Retrieved
from http://www.nytimes.com/2011/05/13/world/middleeast/13egypt
.html.

210 **"Sure, we were all happy":** Habashi, G. (2011, October 27). Egypt—after the revolution is before the revolution. *Transform! Europe.* Retrieved from https://www.transform-network.net/en/publications/yearbook /overview/article/journal-092011/egypt-after-the-revolution-is-before -the-revolution/.

211 **Roadblocks were put up:** Meltz, D. (2016). Civil society in the Arab Spring: Tunisia, Egypt, and Libya. Undergraduate honors thesis, University of Colorado Boulder.

211 **"will bring back security":** Kingsley, P. (2014, June 3). Abdel Fatah al-Sisi won 96.1% of vote in Egypt presidential election, say officials. *The Guardian.* Retrieved from https://www.theguardian.com/world/2014/jun/03 /abdel-fatah-al-sisi-presidential-election-vote-egypt.

211 **"feel safe":** Vick, K. (2014, May 29). Al-Sisi wins Egypt's presidency but is stumbling already. *Time.* Retrieved from http://time.com/124449/egypt -election-president-al-sisi-low-voter-turnout/.

211 **"For pro-Sisi Egyptians":** Eltantawi, S. (2014, May 28). Why Egyptians voted for Sisi. Reuters. Retrieved from https://www.reuters.com/article /idUS122710170920140528.

211 *Values, Political Action, and Change in the Middle East and Arab Spring:* Moaddel, M., & Gelfand, M. J. (Eds.). (2017). *Values, political action, and change in the Middle East and the Arab Spring.* New York: Oxford University Press.

211 *Escape from Freedom:* Fromm. *Escape from freedom.*

212 **fled in 1934:** Friedman, L. (2013). *The lives of Erich Fromm: Love's prophet.* New York: Columbia University Press.

212 **"the dizziness of freedom":** Kierkegaard, S. (1844). *The concept of anxiety: A simple psychologically orienting deliberation on the dogmatic issue of hereditary sin.*

212 **distributed surveys to Egyptians:** Gelfand, M. J. (2012). Survey of autocratic recidivism.

212 **51 percent of Russians:** Russia's weakened democratic embrace. (2006, January 5). Pew Research Center. Retrieved from http://www.pewglobal .org/2006/01/05/russias-weakened-democratic-embrace/.

212 **53 percent:** Chapter 6. Individualism and the Role of the State. (2011, December 5). Pew Research Center. Retrieved from http://www.pewglobal .org/2011/12/05/chapter-6-individualism-and-the-role-of-the-state/.

NOTES

212 **only 39 percent:** Russia's weakened democratic embrace. Pew Research Center.

212 **57 percent:** Russians back protests, political freedoms. (2012, May 23). Pew Research Center. Retrieved from http://www.pewglobal.org/2012 /05/23/russians-back-protests-political-freedoms-and-putin-too/.

212 **68 percent:** Chapter 6. Individualism and the role of the state. (2011, December 5). Pew Research Center. Retrieved from http://www.pewglobal .org/2011/12/05/chapter-6-individualism-and-the-role-of-the-state/.

213 **Between around 1991 and 1998 . . . oil prices plummeted:** Johnston, M. (2016, January 21). The Russian economy since the collapse of the Soviet Union. *Investopedia.* Retrieved from https://www.investopedia .com/articles/investing/012116/russian-economy-collapse-soviet -union.asp.

213 **four thousand organized-crime groups:** Lowy, D. M. (1994). *Understanding organized crime groups in Russia and their illicit sale of weapons and sensitive materials* (Doctoral dissertation, Monterey, California. Naval Postgraduate School).

213 **gang-related shootings:** Lazear, E. P. (Ed.). (1995). *Economic transition in Eastern Europe and Russia: Realities of reform.* Stanford, Calif.: Hoover Press.

213 **acts of terrorism . . . deaths of thousands:** Bhattacharji, P. (2010, April 8). Chechen terrorism (Chechnya, separatist). Council on Foreign Relations. Retrieved from https://www.cfr.org/backgrounder/chechen -terrorism-russia-Chechnya-separatist.

213 **Alcoholism:** Fedun, S. (2013, September 25). How alcohol conquered Russia. *The Atlantic.* Retrieved from https://www.theatlantic.com/inter national/archive/2013/09/how-alcohol-conquered-russia/279965/.

213 **fivefold:** Paoli, L. (2002). The development of an illegal market: Drug consumption and trade in post-Soviet Russia. *The British Journal of Criminology, 42,* 21–39; see also Paoli, L. (n.d.). Drug trafficking and related organized crime in Russia. Max Planck Institute for Foreign and International Criminal Law. Retrieved from https://www.mpicc.de/en/forsc hung/forschungsarbeit/kriminologie/archiv/drug_trafficking.html. In 1999, there were 359,067 registered drug users in state-run drug-treatment centers; however, experts claim the true number of drug users was actually eight to ten times larger.

213 **Life expectancy:** Notzon, F. C., Komarov, Y. M., Ermakov, S. P., Sempos, C. T., Marks, J. S., & Sempos, E. V. (1998). Causes of declining life expectancy in Russia. *Jama*, *279*(10), 793–800.

213 **"For me":** Keating, J. (2017, January 2). How Vladimir Putin engineered Russia's return to global power—and what he'll do next. *Slate*. Retrieved from http://www.slate.com/articles/news_and_politics/cover_story/2017 /01/how_vladimir_putin_engineered_russia_s_return_to_global _power.html; see also Ostrovsky, A. (2017). *The invention of Russia: From Gorbachev's freedom to Putin's war*. New York: Penguin.

213 **"It was a very difficult time":** Latypova, Sasha. (2014, October 17). What was it like to be in the Soviet Union just after it collapsed? *The Huffington Post*. Retrieved from https://www.huffingtonpost.com/quora/what-was -it-like-to-be-in_1_b_5998002.html.

214 **collective national identity:** Koshkin, P. (2016). Interview with Lev Gudkov: Russia's national identity through the lens of the Kremlin's foreign policy. *Russia Direct*, *4*(6), 14–17.

214 **handpicked by then Russian president Boris Yeltsin:** Bohlen, C. (2000, January 1). Yeltsin resigns: The overview; Yeltsin resigns, naming Putin as acting president to run in March election. *The New York Times*. Retrieved from http://www.nytimes.com/2000/01/01/world/yeltsin-resigns-over view-yeltsin-resigns-naming-putin-acting-president-run-march.html.

214 **over 80 percent:** Poll shows Putin's approval skyrockets to record high for 2017. *Russia Beyond*. Retrieved from https://www.rbth.com/news /2017/03/02/poll-shows-putins-approval-skyrockets-to-record-high-for -2017_711993; see also Taylor, A. (2018, March 16). 9 charts that lay out Russia's uncertain future—with or without Putin. *The Washington Post*. Retrieved from https://www.washingtonpost.com/news/worldviews /wp/2018/03/16/9-charts-that-lay-out-russias-uncertain-future-with-or -without-putin/?noredirect=on&utm_term=.954dad577b48.

214 **70 percent . . . "post-Soviet Russia":** Ioffe, J. (2016, December). Why many young Russians see a hero in Putin. *National Geographic*. Retrieved from https://www.nationalgeographic.com/magazine/2016/12/putin -generation-russia-soviet-union/.

214 **those who protest:** Herszenhorn, D. M. (2012, June 8). New Russian law assesses heavy fines on protesters. *The New York Times*. Retrieved from

NOTES

https://www.nytimes.com/2012/06/09/world/europe/putin-signs-law
-with-harsh-fines-for-protesters-in-russia.html.

214 **criticize the government online ... human rights advocacy:** Maida,
A. (2017, July 18). Online and on all fronts: Russia's assault on freedom
of expression. Human Rights Watch. Retrieved from https://www.hrw
.org/report/2017/07/18/online-and-all-fronts/russias-assault-freedom
-expression.

214 **state run:** Russia profile—media. (2017, April 25). BBC. Retrieved from
http://www.bbc.com/news/world-europe-17840134.

214 **political websites:** Websites of Putin critics blocked in Russia. (2014,
March 14). BBC. Retrieved from http://www.bbc.com/news/technology
-26578264.

214 **owning any mass media outlets:** Boghani, P. (2015, January 13). Putin's
legal crackdown on civil society. PBS. Retrieved from https://www.pbs
.org/wgbh/frontline/article/putins-legal-crackdown-on-civil-society/.

214 **Committee to Protect Journalists:** Chalabi, M. (2014, April 4). A look
at journalists killed, by country. *FiveThirtyEight*. Retrieved from https://
fivethirtyeight.com/features/a-look-at-journalists-killed-by-country/.

214 **Freedom House:** Freedom in the world: Russia. Freedom House.
Retrieved from https://freedomhouse.org/report/freedom-world/2017
/russia.

214 **Marxist-Leninist ideology:** Hook, S. (1989). Knowing the Soviet Union:
The ideological dimension. In *The USSR: What do we know and how do
we know it?* Boston: Boston University Institute for the Study of Conflict,
Ideology, and Policy.

215 **"project Russia":** Higgins, A. In expanding Russian influence, faith combines with firepower. *The New York Times*. Retrieved from https://www
.nytimes.com/2016/09/14/world/europe/russia-orthodox-church.html.

215 **primary religious group that is tolerated ... persecuted:** Ellis, G.,
& Kolchyna, V. Putin and the "triumph of Christianity" in Russia. (2017,
October 19). Al Jazeera. Retrieved from http://www.aljazeera.com/blogs
/europe/2017/10/putin-triumph-christianity-russia-171018073916624
.html.

215 **imprisonment:** Rankin, J. (2017, June 20). Russian "gay propaganda law"
ruled discriminatory by European court. *The Guardian*. Retrieved from

https://www.theguardian.com/world/2017/jun/20/russian-gay-propa
ganda-law-discriminatory-echr-european-court-human-rights.

215 **rise in homophobic violence:** Elder, M. (2013, June 11). Russia passes
law banning "gay" propaganda. *The Guardian.* Retrieved from https://
www.theguardian.com/world/2013/jun/11/russia-law-banning-gay
-propaganda.

215 **Polls of Russian citizens:** Kolstø, P., & Blakkisrud, H. (2016). *The new
Russian nationalism.* Edinburgh: Edinburgh University Press; see also
Arnold, R. (2016, May 30). Surveys show Russian nationalism is on the
rise. This explains a lot about the country's foreign and domestic politics.
The Washington Post. Retrieved from https://www.washingtonpost.com
/news/monkey-cage/wp/2016/05/30/surveys-show-russian-national
ism-is-on-the-rise-this-explains-a-lot-about-the-countrys-foreign-and
-domestic-politics/?utm_term=.33e239ac2ac8.

215 **"I expect you":** Philippines' Rodrigo Duterte recommends death penalty.
(2016, May 16). Al Jazeera. Retrieved from http://www.aljazeera.com/
news/2016/05/philippines-rodrigo-duterte-backs-capital-punishment
-160516041658959.html.

215 **more than seven thousand people:** Bueza, M. (2016, September 13).
In numbers: The Philippines "war on drugs." *Rappler.* Retrieved from
https://www.rappler.com/newsbreak/iq/145814-numbers-statistics
-philippines-war-drugs.

215 **"I have worked in 60 countries":** Berehulak, D. (2016, December 7).
"They are slaughtering us like animals." *The New York Times.* Retrieved
from https://www.nytimes.com/interactive/2016/12/07/world/asia/rod
rigo-duterte-philippines-drugs-killings.html.

216 **"shoot to kill" orders:** "License to kill": Philippine police killings in
Duterte's "war on drugs." Human Rights Watch. Retrieved from https://
www.hrw.org/report/2017/03/02/license-kill/philippine-police-killings
-dutertes-war-drugs.

216 **praised Hitler ... "son of a whore":** Goldman, R. (2016, September 30). Rodrigo Duterte's most contentious quotes. *The New York Times.*
Retrieved from https://www.nytimes.com/interactive/2016/09/30/world
/asia/rodrigo-duterte-quotes-hitler-whore-philippines.html.

216 **publicly directed a vulgar gesture:** Bearak, M. (2016, September 21).
Potty-mouthed Philippine president Duterte gives E.U. the middle finger.

The Washington Post. Retrieved from https://www.washingtonpost.com /news/worldviews/wp/2016/09/21/potty-mouthed-philippine-presi dent-duterte-gives-e-u-the-middle-finger/?utm_term=.6119e40f55eb.

216 **more than twenty-six million:** Yap, D. J. (2016, March 18). 12 M Filipinos living in extreme poverty. *Inquirer.* Retrieved from http://newsinfo .inquirer.net/775062/12m-filipinos-living-in-extreme-poverty.

216 **unemployment rates:** Gonzalez, Y. V. (2016, May 24). PH has worst unemployment rate despite high GDP growth—Ibon. *Inquirer.* Retrieved from http://business.inquirer.net/210532/ph-has-worst-unemployment -rate-despite-high-gdp-growth-research.

216 **urbanization . . . Crime and disorder:** Sanidad-Leones, C. (2006). The current situation of crime associated with urbanization: Problems experienced and countermeasures initiated in the Philippines. *Resource Material Series,* (68).

216 **highest in Asia . . . eleventh-highest in the world:** Jenkins, N. (2016, May 10). Why did the Philippines just elect a guy who jokes about rape as its president? *Time.* Retrieved from http://time.com/4324073/rodrigo -duterte-philippines-president-why-elected/.

216 **extensive drug trade:** Mirasol, J. D. B. (2017, May). Cooperation with China on Philippines' war on drugs. Foreign Service Institute. Retrieved from http://www.fsi.gov.ph/cooperation-with-china-on-the-philippines -war-on-drugs/.

216 **"We obey him because we love him" . . . "very good man":** Jenkins. Why did the Philippines just elect a guy who jokes about rape as its president?

216 **"far from perfect" . . . "We have to change that":** Bevins, V. (2017, April 17). Duterte's drug war is horrifically violent. So why do many young, liberal Filipinos support it? *The Washington Post.* Retrieved from https://www.washingtonpost.com/world/asia_pacific/dutertes-drug -war-is-horrifically-violent-so-why-do-many-young-liberal-filipinos -support-it/2017/04/16/9d589198-1ef1-11e7-be2a-3a1fb24d4671_story .html?utm_term=.fed69194c3c4.

217 **86 percent of the population:** Aquino, N. P. (2017, September 21). Broad support for Duterte's drug war in Philippines, Pew finds. *Bloomberg.* Retrieved from https://www.bloomberg.com/news/articles/2017-09-21 /duterte-approval-ratings-stands-at-86-pew-research-center-poll.

217 **beheadings of civilians:** Callimachi, R. (2014, October 25). The hor-

ror before the beheadings. *The New York Times*. Retrieved from https://
www.nytimes.com/2014/10/26/world/middleeast/horror-before-the
-beheadings-what-isis-hostages-endured-in-syria.html.

217 **historical monuments:** Williams, J. (2017, June 22). What has ISIS
destroyed? Al-Nuri Mosque and other historical sites Islamic State has
ruined. *Newsweek*. Retrieved from http://www.newsweek.com/al-nuri
-mosque-iraq-mosul-isis-628447.

217 **child soldiers:** What to do with Islamic State's child soldiers. (2017,
June 17). *The Economist*. Retrieved from https://www.economist.com
/news/middle-east-and-africa/21723416-cubs-caliphate-are-growing
-up-what-do-islamic-states-child.

217 **new political order:** Gerges, F. (2016). *ISIS: A history*. Princeton, N.J.:
Princeton University Press.

217 **years of widespread sectarian violence:** Shuster, M. (2007, February
15). Iraq War deepens Shia-Sunni divide. NPR. Retrieved from https://
www.npr.org/2007/02/15/7411762/iraq-war-deepens-sunni-shia
-divide.

217 **48 percent of Iraqis:** Woertz, E. (2017, June). Food security in Iraq: Politics matter. Barcelona Centre for International Affairs. Retrieved from
https://www.cidob.org/en/publications/publication_series/opinion
/seguridad_y_politica_mundial/food_security_in_iraq_politics_matter.

217 **Electricity . . . drinking water . . . Corruption:** Smith, J. (2013, March 15).
The failed reconstruction of Iraq. *The Atlantic*. Retrieved from https://www
.theatlantic.com/international/archive/2013/03/the-failed-reconstruc
tion-of-iraq/274041/.

217 **deadly bombing incidents:** Cordesmon, A. H. (2015, October 5). Trends
in Iraqi violence, casualties, and impact of war: 2003–2015. Center for
Strategic and International Studies. Retrieved from https://csis-prod
.s3.amazonaws.com/s3fs-public/legacy_files/files/publication/150914
_Trends_in_Iraqi_Violence_Casualties.pdf.

218 **suffering the most:** Jasko, K., Kruglanski, A. W., Rijal bin Hassan, A. S., &
Gunaratna, R. (in press). ISIS: Its history, ideology, and psychology. In
Handbook of contemporary Islam and Muslim lives. New York: Springer.

218 **Hundreds of Sunni opposition leaders:** Stone, O., & Kuznick, P. (2012).
The untold history of the United States. New York: Simon & Schuster.

218 **thousands of other Sunnis:** Boghani, P. (2014, October 28). In their own words: Sunnis on their treatment in Maliki's Iraq. *Frontline Journalism.* Retrieved from http://www.pbs.org/wgbh/frontline/article/in-their-own -words-sunnis-on-their-treatment-in-malikis-iraq/.

218 **a hundred thousand Sunni members:** Moyar, M. (2014). *A question of command: Counterinsurgency from the Civil War to Iraq.* New Haven, Conn.: Yale University Press. See also West, B. (2009). *The strongest tribe: War, politics, and the endgame in Iraq.* New York: Random House.

218 **surveys of over 1,200 Iraqis:** Dagher, M. (2017, October 30). *Iraqi public opinion on the rise, fall, and future of ISIS.* Presentation given at the Center for Strategic and International Studies in Washington, D.C.

218 **detention facilities:** Chulov, M. (2014, December 11). ISIS: The inside story. *The Guardian.* Retrieved from http://www.theguardian.com/world /2014/dec/11/-sp-isis-the-inside-story.

218 **repaired essential services:** Revkin, M., & McCants, W. (2015, November 20). Experts weigh in: Is ISIS good at governing? Brookings Institute. Retrieved from https://www.brookings.edu/blog/markaz/2015/11/20 /experts-weigh-in-is-isis-good-at-governing/.

218 **bus transportation, oil and gasoline distribution, and health care:** Covarrubias, J., Lansford, T., & Pauly, R. J., Jr. (2016). *The new Islamic State: Ideology, religion and violent extremism in the 21st century.* Abingdon, UK: Routledge.

218 **good salaries and housing:** Gerges. *Isis: A history.*

218 **"Do you know" . . . "Now we have security":** Collard, R. (2014, June 19). Life in Mosul gets back to normal, even with ISIS in control. *Time.* Retrieved from http://time.com/2901388/mosul-isis-iraq-syria/.

219 **ISIS was most successful:** McCulloh, I., Newton, S., & Dagher, M. Strain theory as a driver of radicalization processes. Working paper.

219 **lists of rules:** Callimachi, R. (2016, December 12). For women under ISIS, a tyranny of dress code and punishment. *The New York Times.* Retrieved from https://www.nytimes.com/2016/12/12/world/middleeast/islamic -state-mosul-women-dress-code-morality.html; "We feel we are cursed": Life under ISIS in Sirte, Libya. (2016, May 18). Human Rights Watch. Retrieved from https://www.hrw.org/report/2016/05/18/we-feel-we-are -cursed/life-under-isis-sirte-libya.

219 **summon residents:** Medina, G. (2017). Samer. The Raqqa diaries: Escape from "Islamic State."

219 **playing soccer:** Perry, M., Chase, M., Jacob, J., Jacob, M., & Von Laue, T. H. (2012). *Western civilization: Ideas, politics, and society, Volume II: From 1600.* Boston: Cengage Learning.

219 **wearing Western clothing:** Karam, Z. (2015). *Life and death in ISIS: How the Islamic State builds its caliphate.* AP Editions.

219 **haircuts:** Hall, R. (2016, November 18). ISIS jailed and beat up this Iraqi barber for giving the wrong haircut. Public Radio International. Retrieved from https://www.pri.org/stories/2016-11-18/isis-jailed-and-beat-iraqi -barber-giving-wrong-haircut.

219 **watching TV:** Porter, T. (2015, August 21). Isis in Syria: Islamic State bans TV and smashes up satellite dishes. *International Business Times.* Retrieved from http://www.ibtimes.co.uk/isis-syria-islamic-state-bans -tv-smashes-satellite-dishes-1516525.

219 **listening to music, using the Internet and mobile phones:** Hawramy, F., & Shaheen, K. (2015, December 9). Life under ISIS in Raqqa and Mosul: "We're living in a giant prison." *The Guardian.* Retrieved from https://www.theguardian.com/world/2015/dec/09/life-under-isis -raqqa-mosul-giant-prison-syria-iraq.

219 **smoking cigarettes, and drinking alcohol:** Saul, H. (2015, February 13). Life under Isis in Raqqa: The city where smoking a cigarette could see you publicly flogged, imprisoned and even decapitated. *The Independent.* Retrieved from http://www.independent.co.uk/news/world/mid dle-east/life-under-isis-in-raqqa-the-city-where-smoking-a-cigarette -could-see-you-publicly-flogged-10043969.html.

219 **forty-five lashes:** Hawramy & Shaheen. Life under ISIS in Raqqa and Mosul.

219 **broken fingers, hefty fines:** Cigarette smuggler skirts edge of ISIS ban. (2015, June 19). *New York Post.* Retrieved from https://nypost.com /2015/06/19/cigarette-smuggler-skirts-edge-of-isis-ban/.

219 **even imprisonment:** Winsor, M. (2015, February 12). ISIS beheads ciga- rette smokers: Islamic State deems smoking "slow suicide" under Sharia law. *International Business Times.* Retrieved from http://www.ibtimes .com/isis-beheads-cigarette-smokers-islamic-state-deems-smoking -slow-suicide-under-sharia-1815192.

NOTES

219 **homosexual:** ISIS, many of their enemies share a homicidal hatred of gays. (2016, June 13). CBS News. Retrieved from https://www.cbsnews.com/news/isis-orlando-shooting-gays-execution-torture-ramadan/.

219 **deemed immodest:** Female ISIS member paid £35 per month to lash "immodest women" with ropes and sticks. (2017, March 9). *International Business Times.* Retrieved from http://www.ibtimes.co.uk/female-isis-member-paid-35-per-month-lash-immodest-women-ropes-sticks-1610479.

219 **Convictions of adultery:** Moubayed, S. (2015). *Under the black flag: At the frontier of the new jihad.* London and New York: IB Tauris.

219 **treason:** Harmon, C. C., & Bowdish, R. G. (2018). *The terrorist argument: Modern advocacy and propaganda.* Washington, D.C.: Brookings Institution Press.

219 **forty-point creed:** Hassan, M. H. (2015, August 12). A wolf in sheep's clothing: An analysis of Islamic State's takfir doctrine. *Eurasia Review.* Retrieved from https://www.eurasiareview.com/12082015-a-wolf-in-sheeps-clothing-an-analysis-of-islamic-states-takfir-doctrine/.

220 **"particularly appealing":** Revkin, M. (2016, January 10). ISIS' social contract. *Foreign Affairs.* Retrieved from https://www.foreignaffairs.com/articles/syria/2016-01-10/isis-social-contract.

220 **nearly thirty thousand:** Schmitt, E., & Sengupta, S. (2015, September 26). Thousands enter Syria to join ISIS despite global efforts. *The New York Times.* Retrieved from https://www.nytimes.com/2015/09/27/world/middleeast/thousands-enter-syria-to-join-isis-despite-global-efforts.html.

220 **"are living in an age of anxiety":** Personal communication with Scott Atran, December 19, 2017.

220 **more likely to be attracted to radical ideologies:** Webber, D., Babush, M., Schori-Eyal, N., Vazeou-Nieuwenhuis, A., Hettiarachchi, M., Bélanger, J. J., . . . & Gelfand, M. J. (in press). The road to extremism: Field and experimental evidence that significance loss-induced need for closure fosters radicalization. *Journal of Personality and Social Psychology.*

220 **John Walker Lindh:** Swann, S., & Corera, G. (2011, September 30). A decade on for the "American Taliban." BBC. Retrieved from http://www.bbc.com/news/magazine-15101776.

220 **spend time with their families . . . "find it":** Thomas, E. (2001, Decem-

ber 16). A long, strange trip to the Taliban. *Newsweek*. Retrieved from http://www.newsweek.com/long-strange-trip-taliban-148503.

221 **more than 450,000 files:** Gaffey, C. (2017, November 2). Bin Laden and Shakespeare: How a visit to the British playwright's home contributed to al-Qaeda leader's radicalization. *Newsweek*. Retrieved from http://www.newsweek.com/osama-bin-laden-william-shakespeare-699318.

221 **"The America I Have Seen":** Qutb, S. (2000). The America I have seen: In the scale of human values. In Abdel-Malek, K. (Ed.). *America in an Arab mirror: Images of America in Arabic travel literature—an anthology*. New York: Palgrave Macmillan.

221 **killed over two hundred people:** The 12 October 2002 Bali bombing plot. (2012, October 11). BBC. Retrieved from http://www.bbc.com/news/world-asia-19881138.

222 **"Jihadists think that anyone in the government":** Personal interview with Ali Imron, September 1, 2017.

223 **blaming newcomers:** Roberts, E. (2017, April 25). From economic woes to terrorism, a daunting to-do list for France's next president. CNN. Retrieved from http://www.cnn.com/2017/04/25/europe/problems-fac ing-france-president/index.html.

223 **platform of French nationalism:** Nowack, M., & Branford, B. (2017, February 10). France elections: What makes Marine Le Pen far right? BBC. Retrieved from http://www.bbc.com/news/world-europe-38321401.

223 **Our surveys of French voters:** Gelfand, M., & Jackson, J. C. (2017, May 1). The cultural division that explains global political shocks from Brexit to Le Pen. *The Conversation*. Retrieved from http://theconversation.com /the-cultural-division-that-explains-global-political-shocks-from-brexit -to-le-pen-76962.

223 **Law and Justice Party:** King, L. (2017, July 5). In Poland, a right-wing, populist, anti-immigrant government sees an ally in Trump. *Los Angeles Times*. Retrieved from http://www.latimes.com/world/la-fg-poland -trump-2017-story.html.

223 **Freedom Party:** Lowe, J. (2017, October 16). Another far-right party has won voters' hearts in Europe with anti-Islam message. *Newsweek*. Retrieved from http://www.newsweek.com/freedom-party-austria-far -right-marine-le-pen-685567.

223 **Alternative for Germany:** German election: How right-wing is nation-

alist AfD? (2017, October 13). BBC. Retrieved from http://www.bbc.com /news/world-europe-37274201.

223 **Ronald Inglehart and Pippa Norris:** Inglehart, R., & Norris, P. (2016). Trump, Brexit, and the rise of populism: Economic have-nots and cultural backlash. *Harvard Kennedy School Faculty Research Working Paper Series.*

223 **"In all of these cases":** Personal communication with Ronald Inglehart, January 8, 2017.

224 **rise in right-wing extremism:** Dick, W. (2016, October 22). From Anti-Antifa to Reichsburger: Germany's far-right movements. *Deutsche Welle.* Retrieved from http://www.dw.com/en/from-anti-antifa-to-reichsb%C3 %BCrger-germanys-far-right-movements/a-36122279.

224 **more than nine hundred hate groups:** Struyk, R. (2017, August 15). By the numbers: 7 charts that explain hate groups in the United States. CNN. Retrieved from http://www.cnn.com/2017/08/14/politics/charts -explain-us-hate-groups/index.html.

224 **one of the largest white supremacist events:** Strickland, P. (2017, August 13). Unite the right: White supremacists rally in Virginia. Al Jazeera. Retrieved from http://www.aljazeera.com/news/2017/08/unite -white-supremacists-rally-virginia-170812142356688.html.

224 **openly carried guns:** Robles, F. (2017, August 25). As white nationalist in Charlottesville fired, police "never moved." *The New York Times.* Retrieved from https://www.nytimes.com/2017/08/25/us/charlottesville-protest -police.html.

224 **Confederate battle flags, and banners with swastikas:** Deconstructing the symbols and slogans spotted in Charlottesville. (2017, August 18). *The Washington Post.* Retrieved from https://www.washingtonpost.com /graphics/2017/local/charlottesville-videos/?utm_term=.f20cf350df15.

224 **chanting racist slogans:** Green, E. (2017, August 15). Why the Charlottesville marchers were obsessed with Jews. *The Atlantic.* Retrieved from https://www.theatlantic.com/politics/archive/2017/08/nazis-rac ism-charlottesville/536928/.

224 **Surveys of over four hundred self-identified alt-righters:** Forscher, P. S., & Kteily, N. S. (2017). A psychological profile of the alt-right. Retrieved from https://psyarxiv.com/c9uvw.

224 **a survey of twenty-four countries:** Nardelli, A. (2015, August 6). Immi-

gration viewed negatively by half of developed world's population. *The Guardian.* Retrieved from https://www.theguardian.com/world/data blog/2015/aug/06/immigration-viewed-negatively-half-developed -world-population.

225 **2015 Pew study:** Chapter 4: U.S. public has mixed views of immigrants and immigration. (2015, September 28). Pew Research Center. Retrieved from http://www.pewhispanic.org/2015/09/28/chapter-4-u-s-public-has -mixed-views-of-immigrants-and-immigration/.

225 **2015 study:** Lyons-Padilla, S., Gelfand, M. J., Mirahmadi, H., Farooq, M., & van Egmond, M. (2015). Belonging nowhere: Marginalization & radical-ization risk among Muslim immigrants. *Behavioral Science & Policy, 1*(2), 1–12.

226 **later study:** Lyons, S. L. (2015). *The psychological foundations of home-grown radicalization: An immigrant acculturation perspective* (Doctoral dissertation, University of Maryland, College Park).

226 **240 million:** 244 million international migrants living abroad world-wide, new UN statistics reveal. United Nations. Retrieved from http:// www.un.org/sustainabledevelopment/blog/2016/01/244-million-inter national-migrants-living-abroad-worldwide-new-un-statistics-reveal/.

226 **One program in Birmingham, England:** Seligman, A. B., Wasserfall, R. R., & Montgomery, D. W. (2016). *Living with difference: How to build community in a divided world* (Vol. 37). Oakland: University of California Press.

227 **"I found that my different":** The language of neighborhood and prac-tices of public life. CEDAR. Retrieved from http://www.cedarnetwork.org /programs/past-programs/2009-united-kingdom/. For successful inter-ventions that reduced conflict in Africa, see Paluck, E. L. (2009). Reducing intergroup prejudice and conflict using the media: A field experiment in Rwanda. *Journal of Personality and Social Psychology, 96*(3), 574–587. For a broader discussion of real-world norm change and policy interventions, see Bicchieri, C. (2016). *Norms in the wild: How to diagnose, measure, and change social norms.* New York: Oxford University Press.

227 **In 2015, my research assistants and I interviewed Americans and Pakistanis:** Jackson, J. C., Gelfand, M., Ayub, N., & Wheeler, J. (2017). Together from afar: Using a diary contact technique to reduce conflict across cultures.

228 the *Washington Post* reported: Samuels, R. (2017, September 22). A showdown over Sharia. *The Washington Post.* Retrieved from http://www.washingtonpost.com/sf/national/2017/09/22/muslims-and-anti-sharia-activists-meet-armed-at-a-dairy-queen-to-talk-fears-about-americas-future/?utm_term=.f089d7ebba4a.

CHAPTER 11: HARNESSING THE POWER OF SOCIAL NORMS

231 In 2017, engineers at Facebook's A.I. Research lab: Lewis, M., Yarats, D., Dauphin, Y. N., Parikh, D., & Batra, D. (2017, June 16). Deal or no deal? End-to-end learning for negotiation dialogues. *arXiv preprint arXiv:1706.05125*; McKay, T. (2017, July 31). No, Facebook did not panic and shut down an AI program that was getting dangerously smart. Gizmodo. Retrieved from https://gizmodo.com/no-facebook-did-not-panic-and-shut-down-an-ai-program-1797414922.

232 On the plus side, their new lingo: Berman, V. (2017, September 6). The secret language of chatbots. *TechCrunch.* Retrieved from https://techcrunch.com/2017/09/06/the-secret-language-of-chatbots/.

233 More than 40 percent: Young, E. (2017). How Iceland got teens to say no to drugs. *The Atlantic.* Retrieved from https://www.theatlantic.com/health/archive/2017/01/teens-drugs-iceland/513668/.

233 "eyes are upon you"–like program . . . alcohol and drugs: Kenny, R. (2017). How one country persuaded teens to give up drink and drugs. BBC News. Retrieved from http://www.bbc.com/news/av/stories-41973296/how-one-country-persuaded-teens-to-give-up-drink-and-drugs; see also Sorrel, C. (2017). Iceland fixed its teen substance-abuse problem by giving them something better to do. *Fast Company.* Retrieved from https://www.fastcompany.com/3067732/iceland-fixed-its-teen-substance-abuse-problem-by-giving-them-something-better-to-do.

234 By 2016, surveys indicated: Young. How Iceland got teens to say no to drugs.

234 3.3 million deaths globally: Alcohol facts and statistics. (2017). National Institute of Alcohol Abuse and Alcoholism. Retrieved from https://www.niaaa.nih.gov/alcohol-health/overview-alcohol-consumption/alcohol-facts-and-statistics.

234 ancestors lived in small: Johnson, A. W., & Earle, T. K. (2000). *The evolu-*

tion of human societies: From foraging group to agrarian state. Stanford, Calif.: Stanford University Press.

235 **from 738 million:** Davidson, J. (2015, May 26). Here's how many Internet users there are. *Time.* Retrieved from http://time.com/money/3896219 /internet-users-worldwide/.

235 **to almost 3.8 billion:** Digital in 2017: Global overview. (2017, January 24). We Are Social. Retrieved from https://wearesocial.com/special -reports/digital-in-2017-global-overview.

235 **five different social media accounts:** Davidson, L. (2015, May 17). Is your daily social media usage higher than average? *The Telegraph.* Retrieved from http://www.telegraph.co.uk/finance/newsbysector /mediatechnologyandtelecoms/11610959/Is-your-daily-social-media -usage-higher-than-average.html.

235 **spend about two hours every day:** Ibid.

235 **has a smartphone:** Digital in 2017. We Are Social.

235 **Internet is so important:** Dean, D., DiGrande, S., Field, D., Lundmark, A., O'Day, J., Pineda, J., & Zwillenberg, P. (2012). The internet economy in the G-20. Boston Consulting Group. Retrieved from https://www.bcg.com /publications/2012/technology-digital-technology-planning-internet -economy-g20-4-2-trillion-opportunity.aspx.

235 **"dizzying" rates of change:** Friedman, T. L. (2017). *Thank you for being late: An optimist's guide to thriving in the age of accelerations.* New York: Farrar, Straus and Giroux.

235 **Incivility . . . on the rise:** Graham, L. (2017, September 20). The number of devastating cyberattacks is surging—and it's likely to get much worse. CNBC. Retrieved from https://www.cnbc.com/2017/09/20/cyberattacks -are-surging-and-more-data-records-are-stolen.html; Duggan, M. (2014, October 22). Online harassment. Pew Research Center. Retrieved from http://www.pewinternet.org/2014/10/22/online-harassment/.

235 **victims of cyberbullying:** Duggan, M. Online harassment; Cyber bullying: Statistics and tips. (n.d.). i-SAFE foundation. Retrieved from https:// www.isafe.org/outreach/media/media_cyber_bullying. See also http:// archive.ncpc.org/resources/files/pdf/bullying/cyberbullying.pdf.

236 **they, too, have been:** Duggan. Cyber bullying. i-SAFE foundation.

236 **new vocabulary:** Gurak, L. J. (2001). *Cyberliteracy: Navigating the Internet with awareness.* New Haven, Conn.: Yale University Press.

236 **The "online disinhibition effect":** Suler, J. (2004). The online disinhibition effect. *Cyberpsychology & Behavior,* 7(3), 321–326.

236 **compared with those who meet face-to-face:** Kiesler, S., Zubrow, D., Moses, A. M., & Geller, V. (1985). Affect in computer-mediated communication: An experiment in synchronous terminal-to-terminal discussion. *Human-Computer Interaction,* 1(1), 77–104.

236 **Unlike in the "real world":** Gosling, S. D., & Mason, W. (2015). Internet research in psychology. *Annual Review of Psychology,* 66, 877–902.

236 **In 2014, for example, panic:** Rose-Stockwell, T. (2017, July 14). This is how your fear and outrage are being sold for profit. *Medium.* Retrieved from https://medium.com/the-mission/the-enemy-in-our-feeds-e86511 488de.

236 **algorithms that analyze . . . subscription revenues:** Ibid.

237 **"race to the bottom":** Harris, T. (2017, April 11). The eyeball economy: How advertising co-opts independent thought. *big think.* Retrieved from http://bigthink.com/videos/tristan-harris-the-attention-economy-a -race-to-the-bottom-of-the-brain-stem.

237 **Robert Cailliau has voiced . . . "one has passed a test of minimal awareness":** Marchant, J. (2000). Out of the shadows. *New Scientist,* 167(2253), 40–43.

238 **"Netiquette" guides:** Shea, V., & Shea, C. (1994). *Netiquette.* San Francisco: Albion Books.

238 **Reddit discussion forum ChangeMyView:** Malone, K. (2017, June 29). Change My View on Reddit helps people challenge their own opinions. NPR. Retrieved from https://www.npr.org/2017/06/29/534916052 /change-my-view-on-reddit-helps-people-challenge-their-own-opin ions. See also Moderation standards and practices. Retrieved from https://www.reddit.com/r/changemyview/wiki/modstandards.

238 **Facebook introduced its Live:** Kantrowitz, A. (2017, June 16). Violence on Facebook Live is worse than you thought. *BuzzFeed.* Retrieved from https://www.buzzfeed.com/alexkantrowitz/heres-how-bad-facebook -lives-violence-problem-is.

238 **Mark Zuckerberg added three thousand more employees:** Tsukayama, H. (2017, May 3). Facebook adds 3,000 employees to screen for violence as it nears 2 billion users. *The Washington Post.* Retrieved from https://www.washingtonpost.com/news/the-switch/wp/2017/05/03

/facebook-is-adding-3000-workers-to-look-for-violence-on-facebook-live.
See also https://www.facebook.com/communitystandards/.

238 **"to build a safe community":** Ibid.

238 **adjusted the site's algorithms:** Constine, J. (2018). Facebook feed change sacrifices time spent and news outlets for "well-being." *Tech-Crunch.* Retrieved from https://techcrunch.com/2018/01/11/facebook-time-well-spent/.

238 **over fifty thousand accounts:** Twitter PublicPolicy (2018, January 31). Update on Twitter's review of the 2016 U.S. election. Twitter Blog. Retrieved from https://blog.twitter.com/official/en_us/topics/company/2018/2016-election-update.html.

238 **Twitter has been creating new online tools:** Crowell, C. (2017, June 14). Our approach to bots & misinformation. Twitter Blog. Retrieved from https://blog.twitter.com/official/en_us/topics/company/2017/Our-Approach-Bots-Misinformation.html.

238 **Google likewise is working on:** Guynn, J. (2017, March 16). Google starts flagging offensive content in search results. *USA Today.* Retrieved from https://www.usatoday.com/story/tech/news/2017/03/16/google-flags-offensive-content-search-results/99235548/. See also https://www.facebook.com/communitystandards/.

239 **demonstrably inaccurate information:** Ibid.

239 **Instagram's CEO, Kevin Systrom:** Thompson, N. (2017, August 14). Instagram's Kevin Systrom wants to clean up the &#%$@! internet. *Wired.* Retrieved from https://www.wired.com/2017/08/instagram-kevin-systrom-wants-to-clean-up-the-internet/.

239 **Max Bazerman at Harvard Business School:** Shu, L. L., Mazar, N., Gino, F., Ariely, D., & Bazerman, M. H. (2012). Signing at the beginning makes ethics salient and decreases dishonest self-reports in comparison to signing at the end. *Proceedings of the National Academy of Sciences, 109*(38), 15197–15200.

239 **"Signing before rather than after":** Personal communication with Max Bazerman, December 23, 2017.

239 **having customers video-record their claims:** Ibid.

239 **boost the sense of community in online spaces:** Sternberg. *Misbehavior in cyber places.*

239 **"Those who gain a sense of group membership":** Ibid.

240 **7.6 billion people:** Worldometers. (2018). Current world population. Retrieved from http://www.worldometers.info/world-population/.

240 **9.3 billion by 2050 . . . 1.76 billion:** Population estimates: Year one through 2050 A.D. (n.d.). Ecology Global Network. Retrieved from http://www.ecology.com/population-estimates-year-2050/.

240 **The United States . . . 450 million:** Sauter, M. B. (2011). The countries with the fastest growing populations. *24/7 Wall St.* Retrieved from http://247wallst.com/investing/2011/08/02/the-countries-with-the-fastest-growing-populations/3/.

240 **one in nine people:** Zero hunger. (2018). World food programme. Retrieved from http://www1.wfp.org/zero-hunger.

240 **the number of severely food insecure people:** Democratic Republic of the Congo. (2017). World Food Programme. Retrieved from http://www1.wfp.org/countries/democratic-republic-congo.

240 **growth of 81 million:** Sauter. The countries with the fastest growing populations.

240 **number of people living in water-scarce areas . . . by 2035:** Why population matters to water resources. (2011). Population Action International. Retrieved from https://pai.org/wp-content/uploads/2012/04/PAI-1293-WATER-4PG.pdf.

241 **an average American consumes:** How much water does the average person use at home per day? (2016). United States Geological Survey. Retrieved from https://water.usgs.gov/edu/qa-home-percapita.html.

241 **Other countries:** Why population matters to water resources. Population Action International.

241 **Kenya, for example . . . to 51.8 percent afterward:** Wegs, C., Creanga, A. A., Galavotti, C., & Wamalwa, E. (2016). Community dialogue to shift social norms and enable family planning: An evaluation of the family planning results initiative in Kenya. *PloS One, 11*(4), e0153907.

241 **CARE's efforts succeeded:** Ibid.

241 **Rwanda and Ethiopia:** CARE initiative almost doubles family planning rate in Ethiopia. (2013). CARE. Retrieved from http://www.care.org/work/health/family-planning/care-initiative-almost-doubles-family-planning-rate-ethiopia.

NOTES

241 *The Land Is Full*: Tal, A. (2016). *The land is full: Addressing overpopulation in Israel.* New Haven, Conn.: Yale University Press.

242 **Once a tiny nation:** Tal, A. (2016). Israel's looming demographics crisis. *The New York Times.* Retrieved from https://www.nytimes .com/2016/07/23/opinion/israels-looming-demographic-crisis.html.

242 **nearly 8.6 million:** Population, total. The World Bank. Retrieved from https://data.worldbank.org/indicator/SP.POP.TOTL.

242 **and by 2065:** Projection of population in Israel for 2020–2065, by population group, sex and age. (2017). Central Bureau of Statistics. Retrieved from http://www.cbs.gov.il/reader/shnaton/templ_shnaton_e.html?num _tab=st02_10&CYear=2017.

242 **Israelis are feeling squeezed . . . losses of biodiversity:** Tal. *The land is full.*

242 **"In a country that argues":** Tal. Israel's looming demographics crisis.

242 **In 2015, the national average:** Fertility rates. (2018). Organization for Economic Cooperation and Development. Retrieved from https://data .oecd.org/pop/fertility-rates.htm.

242 **Ultra-Orthodox families:** Total fertility rates in Israel by religion and level of religiosity and their impact on public expenditure. (2016). Department of Budgetary Control, Research and Information Center, The Knesset. Retrieved from https://www.knesset.gov.il/mmm/data/pdf/m03735.pdf.

242 **David Ben-Gurion:** Tal. *The land is full.*

242 **After the decimation:** Ibid.

243 **match the high Arab birth rate:** Tal. Israel's looming demographics crisis.

243 **The Jewish population worldwide has sprung back . . . pre-Holocaust numbers:** Ibid.

243 **The birth rate of Arab Israelis also leveled off:** Fertility rates, average age of mother and sex ratio at birth, by selected characteristics of the mother. Central Bureau of Statistics, Israel. (2017). Retrieved from http:// www.cbs.gov.il/shnaton68/st03_14x.pdf.

243 **article in the *Jerusalem Post*:** Eisenbud, D. (2018). Current Israeli birth rates unsustainable, says expert. *The Jerusalem Post.* Retrieved from http://www.jpost.com/Israel-News/Current-Israeli-birth-rates-unsus tainable-says-expert-543209.

244 **Through much of our current Holocene period . . . upset this envi-**

358

ronmental balance: Climate Analytics. (2015). Global warming reaches 1°C above preindustrial, warmest in more than 11,000 years. *Climate Analytics.* Retrieved from http://climateanalytics.org/briefings/global -warming-reaches-1c-above-preindustrial-warmest-in-more-than -11000-years.html.

244 **dramatic increase in carbon emissions:** Monroe, B. (2015). What does this number mean? Scripps Institution of Oceanography. Retrieved from https://scripps.ucsd.edu/programs/keelingcurve/2015/05/12/what -does-this-number-mean/. See also Kahn, B. (2017). We just breached the 410 PPM threshold for CO2. *Scientific American.* Retrieved from https:// www.scientificamerican.com/article/we-just-breached-the-410-ppm -threshold-for-co2/.

244 **Scientists predict a bleak future:** The consequences of climate change. (n.d.). National Aeronautics and Space Administration. Retrieved from https://climate.nasa.gov/effects/.

244 **Center for Global Development's list:** Mapping the impacts of climate change. (2011). Center for Global Development. Retrieved from https:// www.cgdev.org/page/mapping-impacts-climate-change.

244 **NASA predicts that in the second half:** Shirah, G., & Zheng, C. (2015). Megadroughts in U.S. west predicted to be the worst of the millennium. National Aeronautics and Space Administration. Retrieved from https:// svs.gsfc.nasa.gov//cgi-bin/details.cgi?aid=4270.

244 **many cities on the East Coast:** Brennan, P. (2017, November 13). Greenland melt speeds East Coast sea level rise. National Aeronautics and Space Administration. Retrieved from https://climate.nasa.gov/news /2651/greenland-melt-speeds-east-coast-sea-level-rise/.

244 *The Collapse of Western Civilization:* Oreskes, N., & Conway, E. M. (2014). *The collapse of Western civilization: A view from the future.* New York: Columbia University Press.

245 **"earthquake diplomacy":** Kinzer, S. (1999). Earthquakes help warm Greek-Turkish relations. *The New York Times.* Retrieved from http:// www.nytimes.com/1999/09/13/world/earthquakes-help-warm-greek -turkish-relations.html?mcubz=3; Smith, H., & Freely, M. (1999). Greek missions of mercy melt ancient hatred. *The Guardian.* Retrieved from https://www.theguardian.com/world/1999/aug/29/turkeyquakes.tur key1.

245 **around seventeen thousand people:** The Editors of Encyclopedia Britannica. (n.d.). Izmit earthquake of 1999; Turkey. *Encyclopœdia Britannica.* Retrieved from https://www.britannica.com/event/Izmit-earthquake-of-1999.

245 **Greeks were the first . . . and the environment:** Kinzer (1999). Earthquakes help warm Greek-Turkish relations. *The New York Times.*

246 **in August 2017, India and Bangladesh:** Ahmed, K. A. (2017). In Bangladesh, a flood and an efficient response. *The New York Times.* Retrieved from https://www.nytimes.com/2017/09/01/opinion/bangladesh-floods.html.

246 **said Reazul Haq:** Lalmonirhat, M. H. (2017). When natural disaster wipes out man-made borders. *Dhaka Tribune.* Retrieved from http://www.dhakatribune.com/bangladesh/2017/08/15/natural-disaster-breaks-borderline-issues/.

246 **2005 commencement address:** Sullivan, J. (2013). *This is water—full version—David Foster Wallace commencement speech* [Video file]. Retrieved from https://www.youtube.com/watch?v=8CrOL-ydFMI&t=136s.

247 **Crown Prince Mohammed bin Salman:** Music, movies, women drivers: 11 ways how Crown Prince Salman is transforming Saudi Arabia. (2017). *India Times.* Retrieved from https://www.indiatimes.com/news/india/music-movies-women-drivers-11-ways-how-crown-prince-salman-is-transforming-saudi-arabia-332577.html.

248 **precipitate sorely needed economic growth and reform:** Hubbard, B. (2017). Saudi Arabia agrees to let women drive. *The New York Times.* Retrieved from https://www.nytimes.com/2017/09/26/world/middleeast/saudi-arabia-women-drive.html.

Index

INDEX

INDEX

INDEX

Kalanick, Travis, 157
Kanner, Leo, 201
Kaplan, Robert, 61
Kenya, 241, 247
Kierkegaard, Søren, 212
Kitayama, Shinobu, 173, 250
Kohn, Melvin, 123
Korea. *See* South Korea
Kruglanski, Arie, 181, 220
Kteily, Nour, 224
Kumbh Mela celebration, India, 8, 9
!Kung Bushmen, Southwest Africa, 33–34
Kuo, Kaiser, 161
Kurian, George Thomas, 36–37

Landrieu, Mitch, 101
language, and class differences, 126
leadership styles, 147–49
Lee Kuan Yew, 66
left handedness, 43
Lemoine, Jean-François, 46
Le Pen, Marine, 137, 222, 223
Lepper, Mark, 203
lesbians
  attitudes toward, 21, 51, 94–95, 108
  laws against, 37, 215
  loose states' social change and, 96, 97
Levine, Robert, 41, 42
Li, Chengguang, 141
libraries, noise pollution in, 41
life expectancies, 197, 198, 213
Lindh, John Walker, 220–21
Lithwick, Dahlia, 165
littering, 3, 7, 22, 36, 38, 39, 40, 71, 144
loose mind-set
  default setting for, 170
  description of, 166
  example of, 167
  noticing social norms in, 171–72
  questions for determining, 170
love lives, choices in, 204–5

lower class
  perceived threat in, 119
  poverty and economic uncertainty in, 116–17
  rule breaking and, 119–20
  safety and health threats in, 117–18
  school mismatches with, 132–36
  tightness of, 118–19
  uniformity in, 126–27
Lubrano, Alfred, 124

Malaysia, 50, 51, 53, 65, 68, 198
Manhattan, as a loose city, 23
marijuana use, 37, 81, 89, 177, 233
Marines, 150–51
marital status, 51–52
Markus, Hazel, 126
marriage
  Copper Inuit people and, 32–33
  loose versus tight cultures on, 51–52
  Nahua culture and, 31–32
  same-sex, in New Zealand, 21
  Singapore's unit for, 21
  tight-loose conflict in, 183–84
Matsumoto, David, 180
Mauritius, 14
Max, norm-violating puppet, 121–22
McHaney, Thomas L., 106
McKinsey & Company, 137, 152
media environment, 53–54, 136
medicine, Goldilocks Principle on, 195–96
meditation, brain impact of, 190
Medved, Jon, 142–43
Mercury Interactive, 156
mergers
  culture and performance of, 141–42
  DaimlerChrysler's cultural mismatch in, 139–40, 147
Mexico, 31, 95, 190
Microsoft, 155–56
middle class, language use in, 125
military, 150–51, 160
Mill, Janice, 171–72

368